MAINTENANCE

Jasper L. Coetzee

www.maintenancepublishers.com
In cooperation with
Trafford Publishing
www.trafford.com

Maintenance Publishers (Pty) Ltd
Web: www.maintenancepublishers.com

Published 1997
Reprinted 1998, 1999, 2000, 2001, 2002, 2003, 2004
North American Revised Edition 2004

Cover design by Pieter Els
Typesetting by the author
Printed, bound and distributed by:
Trafford Publishing, Victoria, BC, Canada
Web: www.trafford.com

Other publications by the same author:
What does being a True Christian imply?

Note for Librarians: a cataloguing record for this book that includes Dewey Classification and US Library of Congress numbers is available from the National Library of Canada. The complete cataloguing record can be obtained from the National Library's online database at: www.nlc-bnc.ca/amicus/index-e.html

ISBN 1-4122-0056-3

TRAFFORD

This book was published on-demand in cooperation with Trafford Publishing.
On-demand publishing is a unique process and service of making a book available for retail sale to the public taking advantage of on-demand manufacturing and Internet marketing. On-demand publishing includes promotions, retail sales, manufacturing, order fulfilment, accounting and collecting royalties on behalf of the author.

Suite 6E, 2333 Government St., Victoria, B.C. V8T 4P4, CANADA
Phone 250-383-6864 Toll-free 1-888-232-4444 (Canada & US)
Fax 250-383-6804 E-mail sales@trafford.com
Web site www.trafford.com TRAFFORD PUBLISHING IS A DIVISION OF TRAFFORD HOLDINGS LTD.
Trafford Catalogue #04-0190 www.trafford.com/robots/04-0190.html
10 9 8 7 6 5 4 3 2 1

For Louise

About the author

Dr. Jasper L. Coetzee, Pr.Eng., Ph.D., has been actively involved in maintenance practice in industry for the last 30 years. He started his working life as a Millwright apprentice. This was followed by studies in Mechanical Engineering at the University of Pretoria. Following a short training period as pupil engineer, he was appointed as Assistant Resident Engineer at a major iron mine in late 1974. While in this position he had, during subsequent periods, the responsibility for the maintenance of all the various areas of the mine.

He left the mine in late 1979 to join a major petrochemical group as Resident Engineer of one of their major collieries. During this time, he was responsible for all maintenance activities, the supply of services, surface operations as well as all project engineering. From late 1982 to the middle of 1985, he was responsible for all mechanical maintenance of one of the major petrochemical plants of the same group. This was followed by a period of 2 years during which he headed the project team that designed and chose a maintenance information system for the various plants/mines of the group.

He left in 1987 to set up a consultancy in the maintenance field. The main interest of his consulting work lies in the fields of Reliability Centered Maintenance, maintenance strategic management, failure analysis, and maintenance systems. He joined the University of Pretoria in 1993 as Senior Lecturer in Maintenance Engineering. In this (last) role, he was responsible for the administration and co-ordination of all courses in Maintenance Engineering presented by the University of Pretoria up to February 2000. He is presently responsible for a Masters degree in Maintenance Engineering presented at the University of Johannesburg.

Dr Coetzee is managing director of M-Tech Consulting Engineers (Pty) Ltd, an organization involved in maintenance knowledge development and transfer, maintenance consulting and maintenance analysis software manufacture and distribution. He is also a member of IFRIM (International Foundation for Research in Maintenance).

Apart from this book, Dr Coetzee is the author of numerous articles and the RCM and Failure Analysis software package, M-Analyst.

Preface

Maintenance Engineering encompasses the systematic study of the theory of the maintenance of systems and components as well as the management systems needed for the correct application of the theory.

Failure is one of the unfortunate facts of life. Whenever man produces equipment or tools to increase his own productivity, he also has to deal with this unwanted side effect. And, although much effort is expended to improve the reliability of machinery, the ever increasing sophistication and complexity of the modern technological wonders give rise to maintenance being one of the fastest growing industries in the world.

The subject of maintenance is surely one of the oldest known to man. Until relatively recently the subject was thought of as a very basic action for which only the most basic knowledge is needed. To have a maintenance organization at all was deemed to be a necessary but costly luxury. This view of the maintenance function totally ignores the fact that a properly managed maintenance function creates and maintains high levels of availability, reliability and operability of plant. These high levels translate directly into production capacity, productive output and thus company profit.

In line with the relatively low importance attached to the maintenance function in most industrial organizations, the only educational requirements attached to the posts of maintenance engineers and managers was a degree or diploma in mechanical or electrical engineering. This is of course completely inadequate, as these leaders in one of the most cost intensive industries in the world need to be able to manage the process of failure properly. There is presently a very commendable world wide drive to improve the education of maintenance personnel. This process is being led by a handful of maintenance academics from all parts of the world. Most of them (including the author) are members of the International Foundation for Research in Maintenance (IFRIM).

As a consequence of this new found importance regarding the education of Maintenance Engineers, the theory of maintenance need to be formalized such that it can be presented in well-structured maintenance courses. The objective of this book is thus to provide a proper theoretical and practical foundation for the practice of maintenance in the typical industrial organization of our day.

The author aims to build further at this work if he is allowed that by the Triune God, to whom he owes all the honor for his ability to render this contribution to the maintenance world.

Jasper Coetzee
23 July 1997

Soli Deo Gloria

Table of Contents

About the author 4

Preface 5

Contents 7

Introduction 19

Chapter 1 - *Introduction - why Maintenance?* 21

The need for maintenance 22

The objectives of maintenance 23

Profit impact of maintenance 24

Maintenance models 29

Chapter 2: *Historical Roots* 31

Introduction 31

Terotechnology 33

The EUT-model 33

References 35

Chapter 3: *The Maintenance Cycle* 37

The maintenance cycle model 37

The EUT-model revisited 43

References 44

Table of Contents

Continued

Maintenance Plan Design 45

Chapter 4: A framework of Maintenance Strategies 47

Maintenance Strategies 47
Design-out Maintenance 48
Preventive Maintenance 49
Use Based Maintenance 49
Predictive Maintenance 50
Corrective Maintenance 51
Pro-active Maintenance 51
References 51

Chapter 5: Failure characteristics and the Nature of Failure 53

Introduction 53
The definition of failure 54
The failure process 56
Quantitative description of failure 59
The Bath Tub Curve 62
The Bath Tub Curve concept 62
Problems with the Bath Tub Curve 64
Different shapes of the Bath Tub Curve 66
Causes of Failure 69
Failure pictures 75
References 76

Table of Contents

Continued

Chapter 6: A stepwise approach to the design of a Maintenance Plan: Introduction 79

Chapter 7: A stepwise approach to the design of a Maintenance Plan: Selecting failure modes as basis for the plan 83

Prioritization of plant items 84

Plant item break down 85

Prioritization of Maintenance Significant Items 87

Determine the Function(s) of each Maintenance Significant Item in the present operating context 87

Determine the Functional Failure(s) for each Function 88

Determine the Failure Mode(s) for each Functional Failure 89

References 92

Chapter 8: A stepwise approach to the design of a Maintenance Plan: Determining the Consequence of each Failure Mode 95

Operational Consequences 96

Non-operational Consequences 96

Safety or Environmental Consequences 97

Hidden Failure Consequences 97

Determining which failure consequences apply 98

References 99

Table of Contents

Continued

Chapter 9: *A stepwise approach to the design of a Maintenance Plan: Selecting suitable Maintenance Tasks* 101

The basis of Reliability Centered Maintenance 101

The preventive task selection process 102

Technical Feasibility vs. Economical Feasibility 104

Technical Feasibility 104

Scheduled On-Condition Tasks 105

Scheduled Reconditioning Tasks 106

Scheduled Replacement Tasks 106

Economical Feasibility 107

Basic Renewal Theory 108

Failure Density 108

Cumulative Failure Distribution 110

Survival Function 111

Hazard Function 112

The Weibull Distribution 113

Optimizing Use Based Maintenance 116

The Cost of Failure vs. the Cost of Prevention 116

Use Based Optimization 117

Optimizing Condition Based Maintenance 119

Basic Repairable Systems Theory 121

Non-Homogeneous Poisson Process Models 122

Cost Modeling for NHPP models 122

Integrated Failure Data analysis 123

The difference between data with and without a trend 124

References 126

Table of Contents

Continued

Maintenance Management 127

Chapter 10: The Annual Planning Process 129

Introduction 129

Maintenance Policy and Strategies 129

Setting up and maintaining a Maintenance Policy 131

Maintenance procedures as a part of the Maintenance Policy 137

The objectives of maintenance 138

Maintenance goal setting 139

Setting up an Annual Plan 140

References 144

Chapter 11: Maintenance Performance Measurement 147

The need for Maintenance Performance Measurement 147

Typical Maintenance Performance indices 147

Parameters to be measured 148

Maintenance Performance indices 159

Implementation of the measurement process 173

The use of indices in the control process 181

References 184

Table of Contents

Continued

Chapter 12: Maintenance Auditing 185
- Introduction 185
- The need for auditing 185
- The two audits: Physical audit and systems audit 187
- The components of the auditing process 188
  - The main categories 188
  - Audit components by category 189
    - Administration (Planning) effectiveness 189
    - Expertise and competence of personnel 195
    - Facilities (Maintenance Equipment and Workshops) 199
    - Management Processes 207
    - Maintenance Policy Setting 210
    - Organizational Climate and Culture 212
    - Safety and Housekeeping 215
    - Systems 215
- Implementation of the auditing process 225
  - Design of the auditing process 225
  - Organization of the auditing process 229
  - Performing the audit 230
  - Evaluating the results of the audit 232
- References 233

Chapter 13: Achieving Maintenance Management Excellence 235
- Introduction 235
- Implementation issues 235
- References 239

Table of Contents

Continued

Chapter 14: *Analysis of Maintenance Results* 241

Pareto charts 241

Cause and Effect diagrams 244

Control charts 245

Curve smoothing 251

Cusum charts 253

Forecasting 256

References 268

Chapter 15: *Use of Queuing Theory in Maintenance Capacity Decision Making* 269

Theoretical Background 269

Machine service modeling 272

Optimum service rate 275

Optimum number of service facilities 277

References 280

Maintenance systems 281

Chapter 16: *The relevance of Maintenance Systems* 283

The maintenance operational process 283

Control of maintenance actions 284

Maintenance history and maintenance policies 286

Managing maintenance 287

System Core Values 288

Modes of System use 289

Table of Contents

Continued

Chapter 17: Maintenance System Design 291

The components of a Maintenance System 291

Detailed Design 299

Equipment Data Base 299

Maintenance Scheduling 306

Maintenance Work Order Systems 312

Maintenance History 316

Responsibility Structure 317

Equipment Performance Monitoring 319

Cost Management 322

Work Management 325

Materials Management 329

Maintenance Optimization 336

The bigger systems picture 336

Chapter 18: The Systems Implementation Process 339

Project Team 339

Definition of Requirements 339

Buy or build? 340

System selection 344

Functional adaptation 345

User training 346

System testing and set-up 347

Final conversion 348

A macro view of the systems installation process 348

Table of Contents

Continued

Chapter 19: Management support 351

The importance of management support 351

The management champion 351

Involvement of managers in the implementation process 352

Chapter 20: Factors influencing Systems Success 355

Maintenance Cycle Definition 355

The maintenance plan 355

Set-up of the data base 356

Job card flow 356

Accuracy of feedback 356

Systems audits 358

Maintenance logistics 361

Chapter 21: Maintenance Scheduling 363

Scheduling Techniques 363

Critical Path Method Scheduling 363

Time Slot Scheduling 371

Intermittent Scheduling 376

Work Prioritization 381

Maintenance Scheduling 382

References 384

Chapter 22: Inventory Management 385

Economic Order Quantity 386

ABC analysis 389

Table of Contents

Continued

Minimum-maximum control 390

Inventory control model 391

Maintenance perspective 395

Purchasing 396

References 398

Appendices 399

Appendix A: Renewal Theory 401

Definitions 401

Probability Density Function 401

Failure Distribution Function 401

Survival (or Reliability) Function 402

Hazard Function 403

Expected life 405

Weibull Distribution 409

Parameter Estimation 411

Mathematical Modeling 412

Optimal preventive replacement age of equipment - optimization of profit/cost 412

Optimal preventive replacement age of equipment taking replacement times into account - optimization of profit/cost 414

Optimal preventive replacement age of equipment - optimization of availability 415

Block replacement 416

Table of Contents

Continued

Optimal frequency of inspections (or Condition Monitoring) of components (and equipment) - optimization of profit/ cost 416

Optimal frequency of inspections (or Condition Monitoring) of components (and equipment) - optimization of availability 417

References 418

Appendix B: Repairable Systems 421

Non-Homogeneous Poisson Process models 421

Parameter estimation for the NHPP models 422

Cost modeling for the NHPP models 423

General mathematical models 424

References 424

Appendix C: Integrated Failure Data Analysis 427

Data Trends 427

A word of caution 429

Laplace Trend Test 430

References 431

Appendix D: Selected Failure Data Analysis Examples 433

Renewal Theory 433

Repairable Systems 440

Appendix E: Example Maintenance Policy 445

Index 455

This page was left blank on purpose

Use it for notes

Introduction

This page was left blank on purpose

Use it for notes

Chapter 1 : Introduction - why Maintenance?

The subject of maintenance is surely one of the oldest known to man. Until relatively recently the subject was thought of as a very basic action for which only the most basic knowledge is needed. To have a maintenance organization at all was deemed to be a necessary but costly luxury. This view of the maintenance function totally ignores the fact that a properly managed maintenance function creates and maintains high levels of availability, reliability and operability of plant. These high levels translate directly into production capacity, productive output and thus company profit.

To maintain a high level of contribution to company profit, the maintenance organization must practice a high level of preparedness in the following areas:

1. Mechanisms (**processes**) must exist within the maintenance organization **to assist** management **in the management of the maintenance function**. These include proper management planning processes, processes for the measurement of the performance of the maintenance department and processes for doing regular (annual) audits.
2. As the primary task of the maintenance function is to manage failure in the organization, the organization should have a formal **process for setting up** (and regularly updating) **a maintenance plan** for the organization. It is impossible to reach the goal of a high contribution to company profit without such mechanism.
3. The results of the maintenance organization is dependent upon the proper execution of the maintenance plan and the general performance (quality, timeliness and efficiency) of the workforce. This necessitates the implementation of a proper **maintenance operational system** (typically a Computerized Maintenance Management System (CMMS).
4. The correct level of **maintenance technology** should be maintained to support the maintenance plan. This includes facilities (workshops, stores, handling equipment, cleaning equipment, ma-

chining facilities, etc.), tools and condition monitoring facilities (vibration measurement and analysis equipment, oil analysis facilities, thermography equipment, etc.).

5. Expertise regarding the specific **technical systems** that must be maintained. This **expertise** should have sufficient depth (a sufficient level of expertise should exist at each of the various management and operational levels of the organization). This ought to include the ability to diagnose faults and to analyze failures to establish root causes of failure (expert systems and fault trees may form an important part of this expertise).
6. A properly designed maintenance environment. The facilities and organization should be designed round properly thought through **maintenance logistics**. This includes the geographical lay-out, the internal lay-out of maintenance workshops, optimized personnel flows, material flows, information flows, etc.
7. A high level of **development of maintenance personnel**. Even with the best possibly designed maintenance system, one cannot hope to attain the correct results without the corresponding level of personnel development. Such development comprises formal training (as engineer, artisan, etc), management and supervision training, specific technology training and (of course) training in maintenance technology.

The objective of this book is to provide a proper theoretical and practical foundation for the practice of maintenance in the typical industrial organization of our day. As stated in the preface, the present text does not completely fulfill this requirement. It covers the area fairly well in subject areas 1, 2, 3 and 7 above, while it only has elements of the subject areas listed under 4, 5 and 6 above. This deficiency will, as stated in the preface, be addressed in subsequent editions of the book. In the meantime, the maintenance function in the organization and, more important, maintenance people can benefit from the application of the wealth of information contained in this book.

The need for maintenance

As all equipment is prone to breakdown, there must exist some function to replace or repair such defective unit(s) so that the production process can be restored. This function is called maintenance. It is one of the fastest growing disciplines in the industrial world. The reasons for this are manifold:

1. **Increased sophistication of production equipment** - the industrial revolution has started a secondary industry that is geared to the maintenance of machines and equipment. Following the second world war and the invention of the transistor, a new revolution, the information revolution, has started an avalanche of ever-increasing technological complexity.
2. **The need for a high return on investment** - one of the side effects of the information revolution is that there is an ever increasing pressure for higher productivity. This leads to more mechanization and an increase in the size of machines. The investment in production equipment is thus increasing as time passes. Because of the profit motive, this leads to an increase in the levels of availability that are required by manufacturing companies.
3. **The high cost of maintenance** - the cost of maintenance as a percentage of the cost of production is escalating at an alarming pace as a result of the increased mechanization and the sophistication of equipment. Depending on the industry, from 15 to 50 percent of the total (variable) cost of production is spent on the maintenance of equipment.
4. **The complexity of the maintenance function** - no other function in industry spans as wide a range of disciplines as that of maintenance. The management of maintenance abounds with problems of materials control, purchasing, personnel, quality control, finances, scheduling, design, project work as well as the management of the failure process.

The above-mentioned phenomena lead to the management and technology of maintenance being theorized and formalized at an ever increasing pace.

The objectives of maintenance (also see p 138)

The previous paragraph has shown that maintenance is an indispensable discipline and is growing in importance. As the maintenance function is an extremely complex one, it requires a proper understanding of the underlying (fundamental) maintenance objectives. The objective of maintenance can be formulated as follows:

It is the task of the maintenance function to ***support the production process*** *with* ***adequate levels*** *of* ***availability***, ***reliability*** *and* ***operability*** *at an* ***acceptable cost.***

This objective consists of four sub-objectives. These are:

1. *Availability* - availability is defined as the proportion of time that a technical system or machine is operative - in the non-failed state. The maintenance function must provide at least an acceptable level of availability to production (that level which adequately supports the production plan). To maximize maintenance's contribution to company profit, it should be the objective of maintenance management to provide maximum economically viable levels of availability.
2. *Reliability* - reliability is a measure of the number of times that the technical system or machine experiences problems. As such it provides an indication of the continuity of the production process. A technical system or machine can have high availabilities without being reliable. While high availabilities are important to ensure sufficient operating capacity, a low level of reliability will lead to a high proportion of nuisance stoppages, with a corresponding loss due to plant stop-start effects. Thus both high availabilities and high reliabilities are necessary to ensure that the maintenance function contributes significantly to company success.
3. *Operability* - operability is defined as the technical system's or machine's ability to sustain adequate (limited by the design) production rates. While high availability and reliability of equipment are of prime importance, it cannot produce the required result without being supported by adequate levels of operability.
4. *Cost* - any maintenance action should only be carried out if its cost implications are acceptable. Thus all maintenance policies, strategies, objectives and plans should have as a basis the optimization of cost (with the emphasis on long term costs).

Profit impact of maintenance

Maintenance is traditionally viewed as a cost center. It is essentially true that maintenance is a support function, which operates at a certain, not too easily manipulated, cost. Something which is often not appreciated is that it is also (and equally true) a fact that maintenance has a significant impact on the profit of the company through the availability, reliability and operability of equipment. This second fact is, generally speaking, the more important of the two. It inevitably leads to a complete shift in the maintenance management approach if this is understood properly. To illustrate this, we will discuss the following set of graphs:

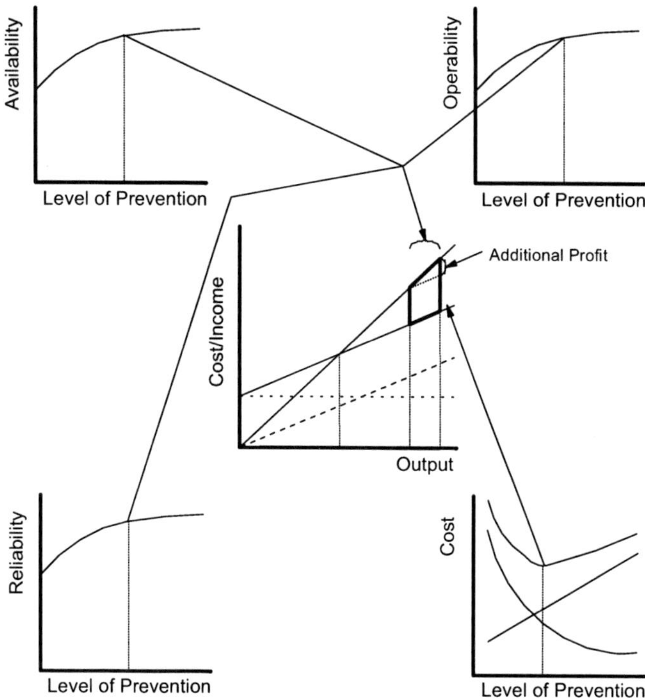

Figure 1.1 : The profit impact of maintenance

The above set consists of five graphs that will be discussed individually:

a. *Availability graph* - this graph depicts the increase of availability as the level of prevention increases. Machine downtime decreases considerably after implementing basic levels of prevention. The rate of availability increase gradually drops as the level of prevention increases.

b. *Operability graph* - the same trend as displayed in the availability graph is evident, although the gain is less marked.

c. *Reliability graph* - the same trend is again displayed - the level of reliability increases with an increase in the level of prevention.

d. *Maintenance cost graph* - this graph, shown below, depicts the cost of maintenance with increasing levels of prevention. As the level of prevention increases, the cost of breakdowns decreases in a hyperbolic fashion. At the same time the cost of prevention increases with increased level of prevention. The total cost graph, which is the sum of the cost of breakdowns and the cost of prevention, show a very marked minimum. This is the level of prevention that should be attained if maintenance is managed as a cost center.

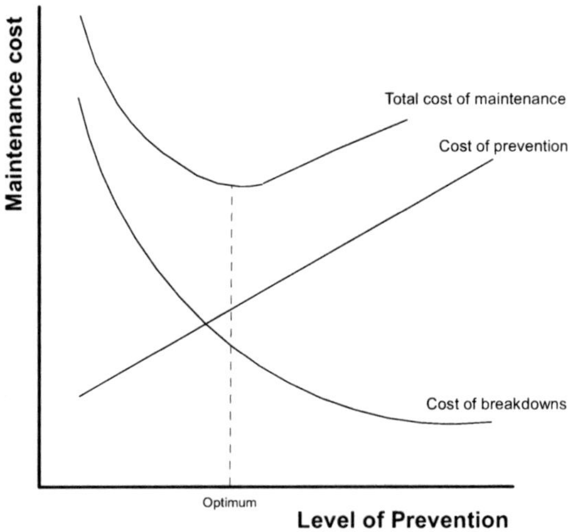

Figure 1.2 : Maintenance cost graph

e. *Classical company profit model* - this model, shown in figure 1.3, consists of a production cost graph, which is made up of a fixed cost and a variable cost component, and a sales income graph. The profit at a certain level of production is calculated as the difference between the income and the cost graphs. To the left of the break-even point a loss is being made, whilst on its right a profit is made. The effect of maintenance on the profit is that, by increasing the level of prevention, the increased availability, operability and reliability results in added production capacity. If this added production output can be sold, the additional capacity should be provided, even past the optimum maintenance cost, as the resultant increase in profit will more than offset the penalty in cost.

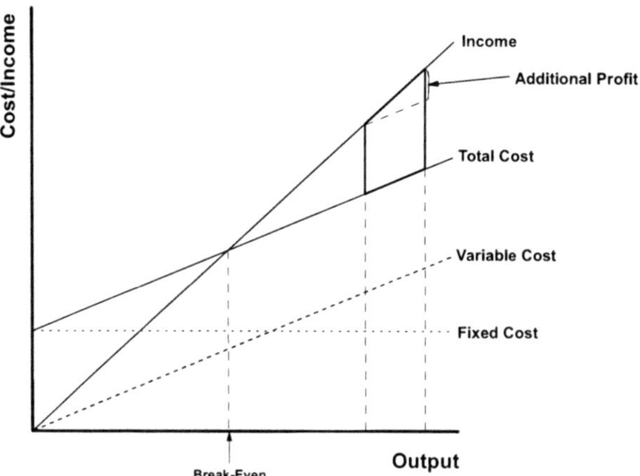

Figure 1.3 : Classical company profit model

It should thus be the objective of maintenance management to maximize the level of prevention if all production can be sold (as shown in the classical profit model discussion). Sometimes, however, a company operates in a captive market (it can only sell a certain level of production). In such a case, maintenance should supply the necessary levels of availability, operability and reliability while optimizing the cost of maintenance.

This page was left blank on purpose

Use it for notes

Maintenance Models

This page was left blank on purpose

Use it for notes

Chapter 2 : Historical Roots

Introduction

Maintenance started from very humble beginnings indeed. Maintenance was never even a function that was envisaged by the first builders of equipment. But, as failure is a fact of life, equipment needed repair. First it was not necessary to appoint special personnel to repair and maintain the equipment as the production man did his own (very basic) maintenance. Later, however, when equipment became more complex, the production man could no longer handle the maintenance himself and a man was needed to fulfill the role of maintainer. Later, as the maintenance function grew, managers had to be appointed to oversee and control the maintenance function. Today this function has grown to be one of the largest (if not the largest) functions in the typical industrial concern. This trend will continue as production machinery gets larger and more technologically advanced. And, even with the present trend of outsourcing of maintenance, this has the effect *firstly* that the maintenance man needs more expertise and *secondly* that the development of a proper theory of maintenance (and research in maintenance) is of paramount importance.

One should, right from the start, understand the relationship of maintenance to the production function and the manufacturer of equipment. This relationship is shown schematically in the diagram in figure 2.1. As can be seen from the diagram, there is a triangular relationship between the machine designer, the production function's use of the machine and the maintenance of the machine. In the *first place* the designer/manufacturer designs and builds into the equipment properties such as its failure behavior, reliability and maintainability, which directly influences the maintenance load. He also directly influences the production characteristics and profitability of the equipment through properties such as its operability, ergonomics and design life span. *Secondly*, the production function affects the machine's maintenance load through the function for which it is used and through the way it is applied (which, in turn, is determined by the training of the operator, the organizational culture, management style and the organizational structure itself). In the *third place*, the machine's continued effective production performance is determined by the effectiveness of the maintenance applied to it. This is dependent upon the maintenance plan implemented for the equipment, the level of expertise in the maintenance department, the maintenance technology and facilities employed as well as the quality of maintenance management.

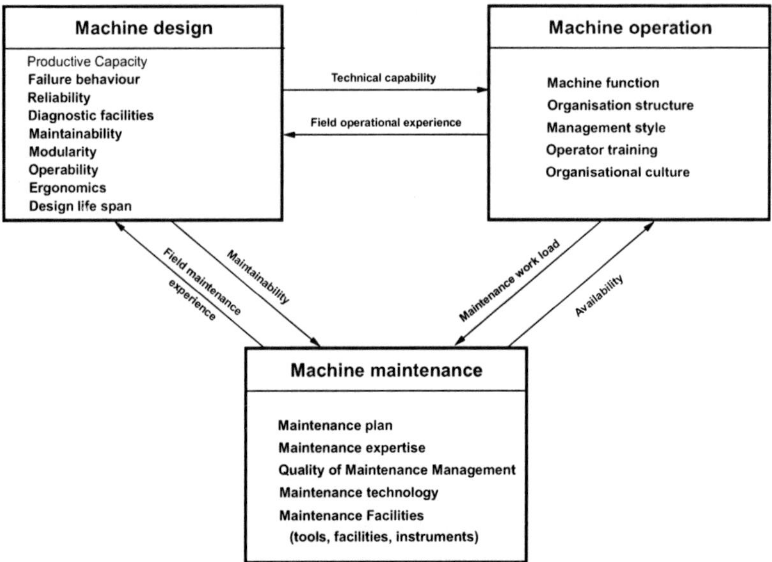

Figure 2.1 : The maintenance problem - a framework

The machine designer/manufacturer thus provides technical capability (see the arrows) to the production function and maintainability to the maintenance function in the organizations. In their turn the production and maintenance functions provide field operational and maintenance experience to the designer/manufacturer. The main function of maintenance is to provide availability of equipment to the production function, as well as to maintain the inherent reliability and operability of the equipment. The production function, in turn, directly influences the maintenance work load through their operating practices.

As the maintenance function is a complex one (chapter 1) it is necessary in both the practice and teaching of maintenance engineering and management to have a model of the function as a fundamental reference in all decision making, research and development of the theory of maintenance. Historically, this modeling process started in the late sixties with the survey which led to the development of the *Terotechnology* concept.

Terotechnology

Until the late sixties no serious thought was given to the conceptualization of the maintenance function in the organizations. Maintenance was still regarded as being a greasy and messy business without any notable substance. One would surely not go as far as spend unnecessary effort in attempting to systematize a simple business function? But the practice of maintenance provided different facts. Maintenance costs were on the rise and the service availability of the systems being maintained was unacceptably low. Slowly but surely the maintenance function grew in importance in boardrooms and the minds of decision makers.

One of the consequences of this opinion shift was the large scale survey commissioned in the late 1960's by the British Ministry of Technology. The findings of this report [1] was that firstly, maintenance was costing the United Kingdom some £ 3000 million per annum and secondly, production savings of around £ 200 million to £ 300 million could be effected through very basic improvements in maintenance. They proposed that the maintenance of a technical system should be seen in its larger context, which is its life cycle starting at conceptualization / specification / design and ending in the disposal of the system. They named their proposed wider approach "terotechnology". This approach is illustrated in figure 2.2 at the top of the next page.

The EUT-model

The Terotechnology model was lacking in many areas. One of the major problems was that it intended to widen the scope of the maintenance practitioner so much that it totally neglected the processes inside the maintenance organization itself. The Eindhoven University of Technology saw this limitation and concentrated more on the inner processes of the maintenance organization in devising what has become known as the EUT-maintenance model [2]. This model, while not dis-

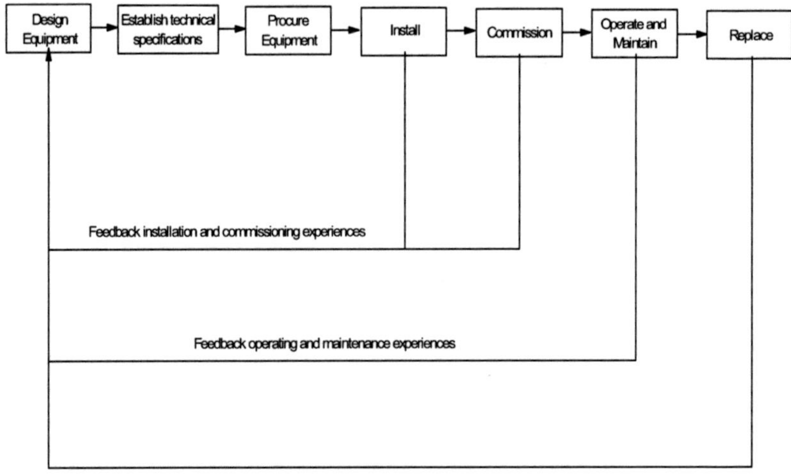

Figure 2.2 : Terotechnology model

regarding the process components defined in the terotechnology model, concentrates more in the area of the maintenance process itself. Specifically it emphasizes that the maintenance needs of technical systems present the maintenance organization with a certain maintenance demand, which must be met to be successfully. This demand should be met by utilizing different sources of maintenance capacity (operators, internal maintenance capacity, external capacity and O.E.M. product support). A simplified presentation of the EUT-model is presented in figure 2.3. Refer to [2] for a detailed representation.

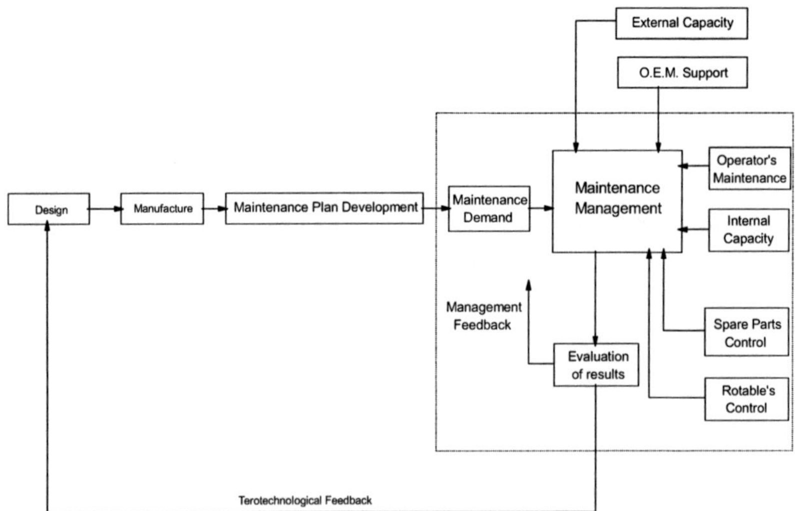

Figure 2.3 : EUT maintenance model

Whilst the EUT-model is a marked improvement on the Terotechnology model, it still does not explain the processes inside the maintenance organization well enough. What is necessary is a model to explain the processes inside the block named "Maintenance Management" in figure 2.3.

References

1. Ministry of Technology, A study of Engineering Maintenance in Manufacturing Industry, London 1969.
2. Geraerds, W.M.J., The EUT-maintenance model, IFRIM-report 90/01, Eindhoven 1990.
3. Husband, T.M., Maintenance Management and Terotechnology, London 1976.

This page was left blank on purpose

Use it for notes

Chapter 3 : The Maintenance Cycle

As was said in the final paragraph of chapter 2, the EUT-model is a marked improvement on the Terotechnology model. Although this is the case, it still does not explain the processes inside the maintenance organization well enough. It is thus necessary to develop a model to explain the processes inside the block named "Maintenance Management" in the EUT maintenance model figure in chapter 2 (figure 2.3). This 'inner model' of the maintenance organization is named **'the maintenance cycle'** and will now be described in some detail.

The maintenance cycle model

The maintenance cycle, which is shown in figure 3.1, consists of two superimposed cycles. The outer cycle represents the managerial processes in the maintenance organization, while the inner cycle represents the technical and operational processes. The first of these are shown in figure 3.2 at the top of the next page. It is important to

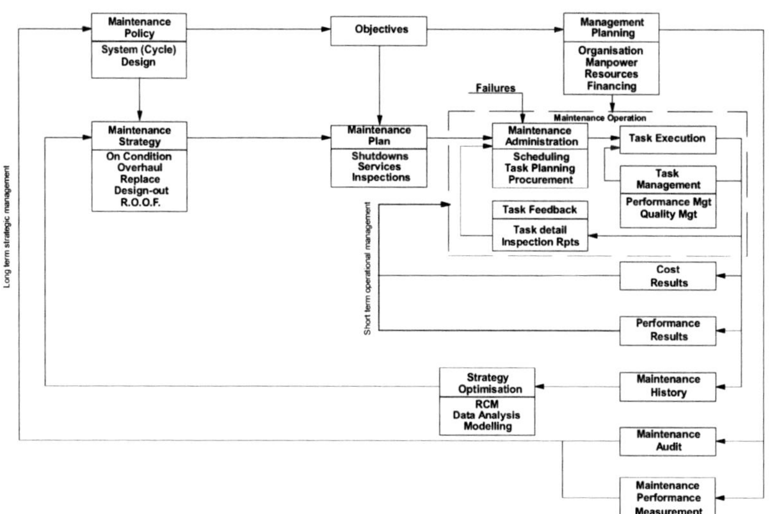

Figure 3.1 : The Maintenance Cycle

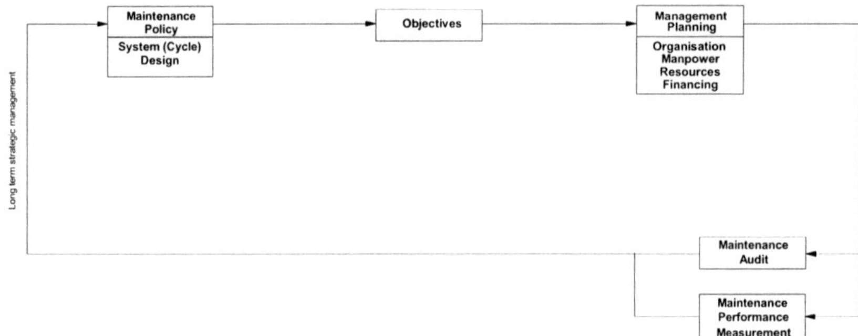

Figure 3.2 : The Managerial Sub-cycle

note that the outer and inner cycles do not represent different levels of management and/or operational staff, as the same persons will often operate both in the outer and the inner cycles. A second important point to note is that, as is the case with the EUT-model, the model is descriptive and not prescriptive. It thus seeks to describe the processes in the maintenance department of the typical industrial concern, without prescribing to a certain concern that their business should work exactly in this way.

The (managerial) sub-cycle has five embedded processes, which are described in much more detail in chapters 9 to 11:

- *Maintenance policy* - each maintenance department should have as driving force a document that states what the department wants to achieve. The Maintenance Policy describes, in broad terms, the direction in which the Maintenance Management Team wants to steer the maintenance organization. And, as the maintenance organization's functioning is described by the Maintenance Cycle, it follows that the policy document should, in a sense, 'design' the own Maintenance Cycle. It should thus address every block (element) on the Maintenance Cycle Diagram. It must thus state the company's stand on each of these (fundamental) issues. The policy document is typically drawn up and subsequently annually revised by the maintenance management team, using the Maintenance Cycle as guideline. At this point, the annual maintenance audit results should be available to guide the team through the process.
- *Objectives* - the maintenance management team should, on at least an annual basis, maintain and update the department's objectives. These should be based on, and should be in line with the framework as defined in the maintenance policy. The objectives should be de-

veloped by first doing an analysis of how well the maintenance organization is already performing in terms of the management team's direction as set out in the policy document. The results of the maintenance audit, that was done earlier, should also be reviewed again at this time. After this, it should be no more than a formality to set the objectives for the year ahead. Of course, in line with good management practice, the objectives should be very specific in terms of both the end results that must be achieved and the dates for achieving such results.

- *Management planning* - based on the policy document and the maintenance objectives, the maintenance management team plans the functioning of the maintenance organization. This planning process is typically started at the end of the objectives setting exercise. This is normally done by the maintenance chief asking his people to, with the new (updated) policy and objectives in mind, start the annual planning and budgeting process. The specific responsibility of maintenance management in this regard at all levels includes:

⇒ The maintenance organization - what type of organizational structure is used and why. How and when this is changed.

⇒ Manpower - strengths and types. Whether to use own labor or labor resources from outside the company.

⇒ Resources - what and how much (tools, materials, etc.).

⇒ Facility improvement plans.

⇒ How maintenance will be financed (running budget, special classes of accounts, standard tariffs, etc.).

⇒ The budget itself, with all its different categories.

- *Maintenance audit* - a formal audit of the department should be done on at least an annual basis. This includes both hard and soft audits. The hard audit consists of a proper inspection of the plant, using a well-defined check list and scoring mechanism. The soft audit, on the other hand, audits the department's management and technical systems' ability to ensure the long term achievement/ retention of the results required by the policy and objectives.

  The maintenance audit forms the annual measurement process that completes the maintenance management cycle's control loop. And, as is the case in any control system, measurement is really the key to success, in the sense that it tells you what improvements are necessary to enable you to reach your goals. Now, auditing is nothing more than that: it compares the state of affairs in the maintenance organization with a set of pre-defined standards to establish whether improvement is necessary or not. And, because maintenance is a complex function of the business, this process of measurement cannot be anything other than a fairly complex process itself. That is why there is a need for a properly structured formal maintenance audit once every year.

If the maintenance function in the organization achieves its goals in achieving a high level of maintenance performance, that will help assure high levels of plant profitability. If, on the other hand, the performance of the maintenance function is poor, the effect on plant profitability can be devastating (due to high levels of downtime and high maintenance costs). And, if one does not start by measuring (through a proper audit) the performance of the maintenance function, performance improvements cannot be realized. For, it is only through the knowledge of present performance levels afforded by the auditing process, that insight can be developed regarding the future direction(s) for improvement.

- *Maintenance performance measurement* - a combination of various performance measures into one single measure that gives an indication of the success with which the maintenance policies are being pursued. Maintenance management has to find subtle balances if the optimal level of maintenance is to be practiced. To be able to do this, maintenance managers need information that will enable them to find the relevant balance points. Measurement is a crucial part of any managerial process. Without measurement you cannot "close the loop" (that is the control loop). We thus have to find practical parameters that we can measure and use to help us optimize the maintenance process. The need for the measurement of maintenance performance stems from the need to contribute maximally to the company's profit. This can be achieved through high maintenance productivity in the absolute sense. In general, the maintenance function needs to optimize the level of prevention that it practices to optimize the available production capacity and thus its contribution to company profit.

The maintenance management cycle is a closed loop cycle and the process shown in figure 3.2 is repeated at a fixed frequency (normally annually).

The second sub-cycle (the inner cycle) is, as was stated previously, concerned with the technical planning and operational part of the maintenance department's business. The following figure depicts this sub-cycle.

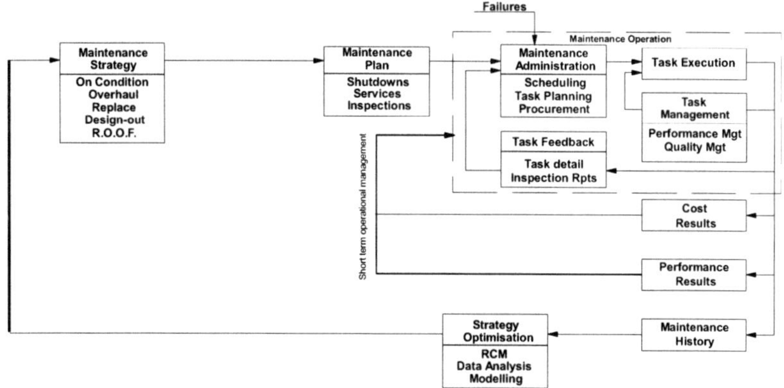

Figure 3.3 : The Operational Sub-Cycle

The inner cycle consists of two main processes:

- *Maintenance planning* - this includes the three blocks Maintenance Strategy, Maintenance Plan and Strategy Optimization.

  ⇒ **Maintenance strategy** - in this process a decision is taken as to the maintenance strategy selected for each maintenance significant component of each machine. Here, a decision must be taken as to whether firstly prevention, run to failure or design out strategies are selected. If prevention is practiced, a choice must secondly be made between condition based and use based strategies. And, in either of these cases, a choice has to be made regarding the specific strategy employed.

  Strategies are typically developed per facility or machine to be maintained. The methodology mostly used for this purpose is that of Reliability Centered Maintenance, combined with statistical failure analysis to understand the failure modes involved well enough to be able to develop strategies that will lead to a high positive impact on the profit of the company.

  ⇒ **Maintenance plan** - for each machine a maintenance plan is drawn up by combining the various component strategies into logical work units with specified scheduling frequencies. The resultant maintenance plan for a specific equipment type could, for example, consist of the following documents, neatly bound into a book that are available for reference purposes:

* A copy of the complete RCM analysis.
* Maintenance tasks that should be scheduled for performance at predefined intervals. These should list all action steps that should be performed, together with proper guidelines, lists of probable materials needed, any special equipment/tools needed and precautionary measures that should be taken.
* A forecast of the manpower needed in the different trades for the execution of the plan."

⇒ **Strategy optimization** - the selected strategies can be optimized at a regular (normally annual) frequency based on the aggregated machine history. Techniques such as Reliability Centered Maintenance (RCM), maintenance data analysis and mathematical modeling are employed in this process.

- *Maintenance operation* - this process, contained within a dotted square, consists of the blocks Maintenance Administration, Task Execution and Task Management.

⇒ **Maintenance administration** - this is the function traditionally known as maintenance planning and involves all aspects of task scheduling, task planning, procurement, issue of task documentation and feedback of task data.

⇒ **Task execution** - this is the process during which the maintenance worker performs the task as was specified in his/her task documents.

⇒ **Task management** - the supervisory process, where the task is controlled. This includes task areas such as quality control, expert advice to workers, task follow-up, requisitioning, prioritizing, backlog management, work efficiency management, budget control, safety and housekeeping and facility management.

The inner cycle is again a closed loop. Its feedback loops consist of the following managerial operational management and supervisory processes:

- The use of work feedback to initiate additional tasks.
- Failures in the plant initiate corrective maintenance tasks. This is not a closed cycle feedback item in the strict sense, except if we consider the plant as another process block in the inner cycle.

- Cost and performance results assist the department in achieving optimal operational excellence and control.
- Strategy optimization (discussed above) analyses maintenance history to optimize maintenance strategies.

A last comment is necessary - as is shown in the diagram of the full cycle, there is interaction taking place between the outer and inner cycles. They can, of course, not exist in isolation. The managerial processes define the scope within which the inner cycle processes can take place. Furthermore, the results of the inner cycle processes are really the measure of the success in applying the maintenance policy. They thus in their turn affect the content of the maintenance policy, objectives and the management planning process in the outer cycle.

The EUT-model revisited

In some respects the maintenance cycle duplicates the functions of the EUT-model. It is more complete and to the point in its description of the inner processes of the maintenance function. But it does not address the outer relationships of the maintenance organization at all, relationships which are described very well in the EUT-model. Thus, a combination of the two models would seem to be the solution at hand. Figure 3.4 is an attempt at the marriage of these two models in a logi-

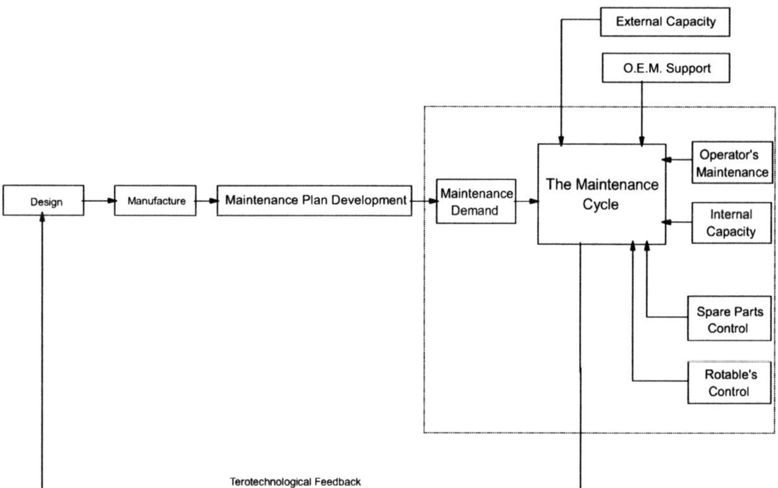

Figure 3.4 : The combined model

cal way. This now contains the best of three worlds, namely terotechnology, EUT-model and the maintenance cycle. This gives an adequate description of the functionality inherent in the maintenance function in and around the typical industrial concern.

References

1. Coetzee, J.L., Introduction to Maintenance Engineering, Annual short course, 1994.
2. Coetzee, J.L., Towards a General Maintenance Model, IFRIM-workshop, Hong Kong, 1997.

Maintenance Plan Design

Important Note

In the design of a maintenance plan one has to make use of a stepwise approach. Due to the inherent complexity of the decisions that have to be taken in the process of doing such design, there are a number of standard methodologies (or approaches) to the problem. It is the author's opinion that the Reliability Centered Maintenance (R.C.M.) approach is the best one presently available. It is the furthest developed due to the number of people using it in the field. But that does not say that the approach is perfect or that there is no negativity connected to it. There are a number of 'fly by night' so-called 'consultants' who decided that a lot of money could be made from training and 'helping' people in the application of the approach, without making very certain that the approach to R.C.M. that they advocate is a sound one. Nonetheless, while writing this text, the author was confronted with the decision of whether or not to use R.C.M. (or a number of other options), or to re-invent the wheel. Well, the idea of using R.C.M. for choosing the correct maintenance strategy is so well entrenched that it would be utterly silly not to use it as basis, especially so while it provides a sound basis for such purpose. This part of the text thus uses the R.C.M. structure as basis, without specifically being a text on R.C.M. itself (it goes much further than the normal text on R.C.M. in explaining failure, setting maintenance strategy and the development of a maintenance plan for the organization).

Chapter 4 : A framework of Maintenance Strategies

Failure is detrimental to the objectives of the organization. Each time failure occurs money is lost, either on the cost of repairing the failure (or the cost of an accident in the case of safety related failures) or due to production loss incurred or due to both the cost and the production loss. This is the primary reason for the existence of us, the maintenance people, in the organization. The process of failure has to be managed properly. And one of the most important aspects of such managed process is that of maintenance strategy setting - deciding what maintenance to do, when and how often. This is what Reliability Centered Maintenance (R.C.M.), which we will encounter in chapter 6, is about. RCM provides the maintenance strategist with a road map, which enables him to find the most suitable maintenance strategy/task for each situation. But, before we can start looking at R.C.M., we have to know which strategies are available and what the effect of each such strategy is.

Maintenance Strategies

Each time failure occurs, it affects the organization negatively. The negative effects can be anything from losing output, quality, timeliness to higher costs and threats to the safety of people or the environment. Sometimes the effect of the failure is not evident immediately (as in the case of the failure of non-fail safe safety devices), but can be the cause of a catastrophic multiple failure later. The organization has to make a conscious decision regarding the prevention or not of each important failure mode. If a failure is not prevented, money will have to be spent on repairing breakdowns at a later stage. Thus a trade-off exists between the cost of prevention on the one hand and the cost of failure on the other (and such costs do not only include monetary costs). Depending on the severity of the failure in terms of production lost, the cost of failure, the life of people or the effect on the environment the organization has to decide whether to prevent the failure from occurring (and to what lengths one is willing to go to do so) or whether the failure can be left to be handled when it occurs.

The end result of the RCM process is a maintenance plan for the organization. This consists of combining various maintenance strategies into logical work packets to be scheduled for execution by maintenance people. At the core of this are the selected strategies. While the strategies are the end result, it is best to start by understanding what the various strategies entail and what their place are in the total maintenance plan. To put the various maintenance strategies into perspective it is best to understand the strategy structure of maintenance as shown in the following diagram.

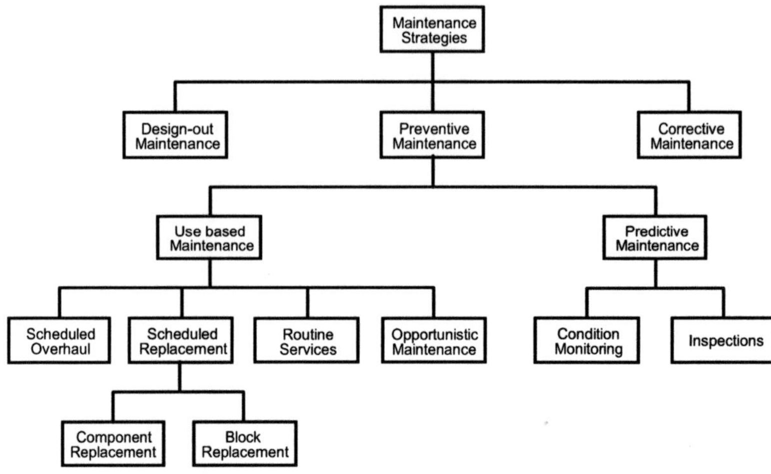

Figure 4.1 : Maintenance Strategies

The top of the structure is broken down into the design-out of failure modes, the prevention of them or the correction of failures. One thus has three options: leave the failure to occur and then correct it; or prevent it from occurring; or redesign the system/component to remove the failure mode.

Design-out Maintenance

This is not really a pure maintenance strategy, but is listed as such because it is used extensively by maintenance engineers. The objective is to redesign the particular system or component to decrease the need for maintenance by removing unwanted failure modes.

Preventive Maintenance

Preventive Maintenance can either be of the use based or the condition based variety. All maintenance strategies aimed at preventing failure from occurring are of the class Preventive Maintenance.

Use Based Maintenance

The traditional way of preventing failure from occurring is by replacing or reconditioning the item (sub-system or component) before failure occurs. The intuitive argument is that timely planned maintenance should lead to the prevention of unnecessary production delays. This technique is (wrongly) known to most people as Preventive Maintenance (P.M.) - as we said above, it is surely one of the class Preventive Maintenance, but not the only one. But, contrary to the intuitive belief, it is not universally applicable. We shall see later that this type of maintenance is only applicable (except in the case of use based routine services) to those cases where the risk to fail (hazard rate) increases with age.

Use based maintenance can in its turn be subdivided into:

1. *Age based maintenance* - maintenance actions are undertaken regularly based on the age of the equipment. Examples are scheduled maintenance work based on machine running hours, tonnage handled, production throughput and kilometers traveled.
2. *Calendar based maintenance* - maintenance actions are undertaken regularly based on expired calendar time, irrespective of production intensity. Examples are annual, bi-annual shutdowns to perform statutory work.

Use based maintenance tasks can be classified into of the following broad classes:

1. *Scheduled overhaul* - the machine or component is completely stripped and reconditioned to as near as the good-as-new condition as is possible.
2. *Scheduled replacement* - the item (sub-assembly or component) is discarded and replaced by a new unit.
3. *Routine services* - the plant/machine receives a service during which routine checks are made, oils and filters changed, greasing done and adjustments made.

Special categories of use based maintenance are:

1. *Block replacement* (or *group replacement*) - block replacement is based on the thought that similar components should have similar failure frequencies. Where the cost of lost production plus the labor cost in replacing a component is high in comparison to the cost of the component, it might be worthwhile to consider block replacement. There are two main classes of block replacement. In the first all similar components are replaced as a group (block) if one of them fails. Alternatively, all similar items can be replaced in a group (block) on a scheduled basis.
2. *Opportunistic maintenance* - sometimes important scheduled work is identified as work that will only be carried out if the plant is down for some reason (e.g., breakdown). This is typical in cases where the continuous operation of the plant is critical and/or the loss incurred during plant downtime is severe. The task(s) is (are) scheduled for execution but is (are) only carried out when the opportunity arises.

Predictive (Condition Based) Maintenance

This type of strategy is applicable to any failure mode where it is found to be technically feasible and worth doing - it has a special place in the cases where the risk of failure (hazard rate) does not increase with age as Use Based Preventive Maintenance cannot be used in those cases. The condition of the equipment/component is measured at predetermined intervals, so to determine when the component will fail. Only then will a replacement/overhaul be scheduled. Two main types of condition based maintenance can be identified:

1. Inspection - use is made of the five senses of a person (engineer, foreman, artisan) to determine the condition of the equipment or component. This can include the use of instruments that enhances the use of the senses through amplification or benchmarking.
2. Condition monitoring - some parameter is monitored to detect signs of imminent failure. Examples of these are:
   a. Vibration
   b. Shock Pulse
   c. Oil condition
   d. Acoustic emissions
   e. Equipment Performance
   f. Thermography

Corrective (Failure) Maintenance

This is a strategy of 'do nothing' or 'wait for failure'. It entails not trying to determine when the component will fail (condition monitoring or inspection) or doing anything to prevent the failure from occurring (use based). This is used when no other strategy can be applied with better end results. Corrective maintenance can be further classified into the following three classes:

- Replacement - this will be the strategy if the decision was to totally replace the component or unit upon failure.
- Repair - this will be the strategy if the decision was to repair the component or unit upon failure.
- Delayed decision - this will be the strategy if the decision was to either totally replace the component or unit upon failure or to repair it, based on a *in loco* inspection following failure.

Pro-active Maintenance

Pro-active maintenance is a philosophy that spans the whole of the maintenance strategy structure as shown above. Instead of using information gained from monitoring (or other means) to predict when a failure will occur, the same information is used to eradicate failure completely. Pro-active action is taken to completely remove the root cause of failure. To implement such a method, the correct instrumentation must be available to facilitate the necessary measurements being taken. Design-out plays a major role in Pro-active Maintenance.

References

1. Coetzee, J.L., Die struktuur van Instandhouding, paper presented at an Akademie vir Wetenskap en Kuns meeting, Sasolburg, 1988.
2. Coetzee, J.L., Introduction to Maintenance Engineering, Annual short course, 1994.
3. Gits, C.W., On the maintenance concept for a technical system - a framework for design, doctoral thesis, Eindhoven University of Technology, 1984.

This page was left blank on purpose

Use it for notes

Chapter 5 : Failure Characteristics and the Nature of Failure

Introduction

Failure is one of the unfortunate facts of life. It goes hand in hand with phenomena like fatigue, wear, erosion, corrosion, embrittlement, voltage and current peaks and the like. These should be limited as far as is possible through good design, good operating practices and proper care for the system. But, even so, failure will still occur. The maintenance man has to, by putting the correct maintenance strategies in place, manage the failure process such that the business experiences the minimum possible negative effects. Luckily, being maintenance workers (whether a manager, supervisor or artisan), failure is both the phenomenon that creates jobs for us and that has to be overcome as far as is possible. Thus, while fighting the phenomenon as far as is possible, one never gets discouraged by it. But the prerequisite for this attitude is to understand both the process of failure and the means to manage and counter it properly. Otherwise it can become a real nightmare. And, unfortunately, there are relatively few maintenance people that really have the necessary knowledge and understanding of the process of failure. This chapter is aimed at providing a basic knowledge of this very important subject area.

The components of any machine or system are subject to the effects of use. These can include ageing effects, effects derived from the design configuration, effects of the environment and the abuse of the system. These eventually lead to failure. The role of the maintenance function is to prevent failures as far as is possible, identify areas of redesign where that makes sense and do corrective maintenance where prevention or redesign will not produce technically and economically viable answers.

Traditionally there was the notion that all equipment wears out and inevitably becomes less reliable with increasing operating age. This led to the (wrong) conclusion that the overall rate of failure of the system will always be reduced by a limit on the age of critical components. We now know that this is not true in all cases. Some component failures can best be handled by measuring certain technical and operational parameters associated with them, so as to determine when they are on the verge of failure, thus being able to take preventive action before the failure occurs. Other failures (especially of critical or expensive components) are best eliminated by redesign, while others can be managed by age-related strategies.

Whatever else we do to manage the maintenance function, it is of critical importance that we understand the failure process well, both from a physical and a statistical angle. This chapter will concentrate on understanding the (physical) nature of failure, while the next chapter will address the statistical side.

The definition of failure

Our intuitive idea of failure is that of the system not being able to function. We do not normally include instances of reduced ability to perform the desired function as being failures. But they affect the productive process negatively and thus should form part of our definition of failure. Furthermore, even the possibility of a failure could be regarded in certain circumstances to constitute a failure. The definition that was penned by Nowlan and Heap, the authors of Reliability Centered Maintenance, is a very simple one that includes all these possibilities:

A failure is an unsatisfactory condition

This implies that a failure is any unwanted deviation from the original (design) condition of the system. And this, of course, is very user specific. It depends on the requirements of the particular user, more than on some airy fairy notion of the designer of the system specifying when failure has taken place. The designer's input is invaluable in the process of deciding when the system is performing according to requirements, but the fact is that this must be augmented by the specific requirements of the user(s) and on the consequences of failure in the particular operating context. Thus the definition of an unsatisfactory condition, for the same system, will differ considerably from organization to organization.

Failure can be classified into two types: *functional failure* and *potential failure*. The reason for this classification is that an unsatisfactory condition can either be a real inability to perform a necessary function or a judgment, based on physical evidence, that it will soon be unable to perform such function. These are discussed in more detail:

- **Functional Failure** - *a functional failure is the inability of an item (or the system/sub-system in which it is installed) to meet a specified performance standard.* This includes the total inability of the item to perform a specific function, as well as a situation where the item performs the function at a lower than required level.

  The same item can of course have more than one function. To properly understand the process of failure one has to identify all the possible functions of such item. A car's automatic transmission, for instance has the primary function of providing the correct gear ratios for accelerating the car and for differing operating conditions encountered while driving. But it also has at least one secondary function, that of the smooth transition from one gear ratio to the next. And while the transmission may still be performing its primary function, it may be regarded as having failed by the car's owner due to jumpy gear changes.

- **Potential Failure** - *a potential failure is an identifiable physical condition which indicates that a functional failure is imminent.* A potential failure is thus one which is related to a specific function in the sense that there is evidence pointing to the fact that the item will, within a short time period, develop a functional failure. In our example of an automatic transmission it may be that the owner, following noisy operation of the unit, replaced the transmission's oil and thus discovered a high level of wear debris in the old oil. Following discussion with an expert in the maintenance of such units he is convinced that the transmission is going to fail functionally within a relatively short time. The unit thus has developed a potential failure. If nothing is done to rectify the situation, it will fail shortly, with all the possible consequences of consequential damage (and cost) and unplanned (as well as inconvenient) downtime.

  The definition of potential failures as a specific class of failures is one of the greatest contributions RCM made to the theory of maintenance. This led to the concept of Condition Based Maintenance being accepted as one of the best ways of preventing failure. This, in turn, led to a completely new industry, providing instruments for the measurement of machine condition, being developed.

The failure process

Every machine/component encounters operational stress. During the design of the machine/component the designers made certain assumptions regarding the expected levels of these stresses. The unit was thus designed with a fundamental ability to resist stress. This ability is the strength of the machine/component to resist failure given the design operating stress assumptions. As long as the operating stress is lower than the unit's inherent strength it will not fail. Typical stress patterns are shown in the following figure:

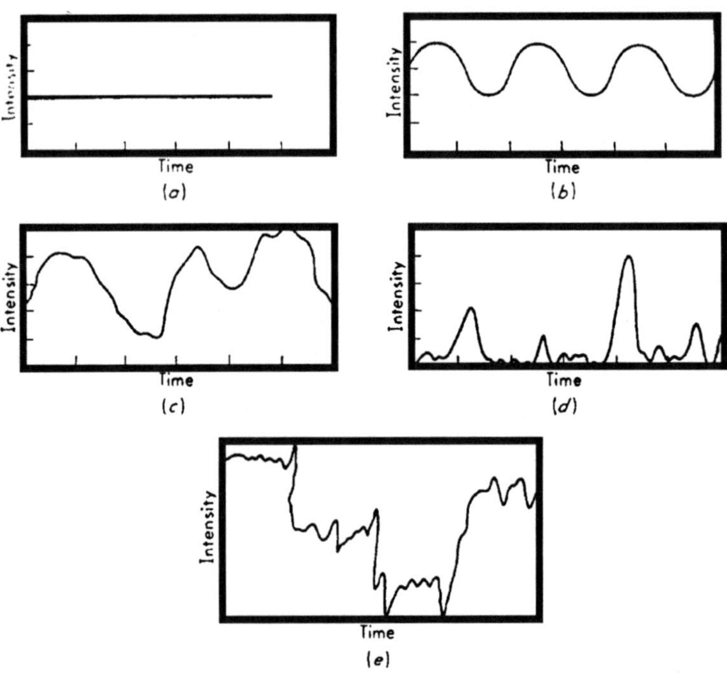

Figure 5.1 :
Patterns of stress variation with time: a) Constant; b) Cyclic; c) Strong persistence: d) Irregular value; e) Stepped value

When the stress that the unit encounters, for some or other reason, increases above the unit's resistance to stress, the unit fails.

This can take place in many ways. Some of these are listed and illustrated below:

- The stress that the unit encounters causes its inherent resistance to failure to deteriorate with use, eventually dropping below the stress value, thus giving rise to failure occurring.
- During operation (a) stress peak(s) occur(s), decreasing the unit's resistance to failure, which will eventually lead to failure.
- The stress applied on the unit is increased due to abuse until it rises above the resistance to failure, thus causing failure.

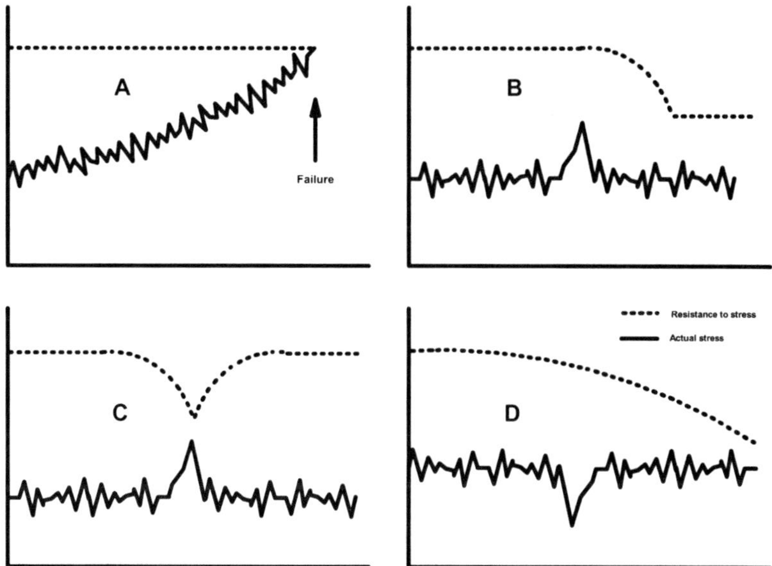

Figure 5.2 : Typical failure mechanisms

In each of these cases, the top line depicts the resistance to failure and the bottom one the stress encountered by the unit. Graph A shows the situation where the resistance to stress remains constant but the stress increases with use to a point where failure occurs. In graph B the resistance to stress is decreased permanently by the damage caused by a single stress peak. Graph C shows the same situation for a unit with a built in resilience in its stress resisting ability. The last case shows a unit where the resistance to stress decreases with use (a situation often encountered in practical situations).

It may sound as if the failure mechanisms described here are primarily found in mechanical systems. Although they are certainly applicable to mechanical component failures, they just as much describe failure in electronic and other systems. An electronic component just as much has an inherent design capability (its 'strength' or 'resistance to failure'), whether that be specified in Volts, Amperes or some other unit. When during the operation of a system incorporating such component, stresses higher than 'designed for' levels (or peaks) are encountered the component either fails or is weakened leading to later failure.

The following figure shows the resistance to failure and the stress for two identical components over time. Because of manufacturing drift no two items made will have exactly the same initial resistance to stress. The rate at which this resistance declines with age also varies. Furthermore, the actual stress encountered differs from case to case, resulting in a difference in life to failure. Even when these variations are small, they can have a large effect on the age at which the component fails.

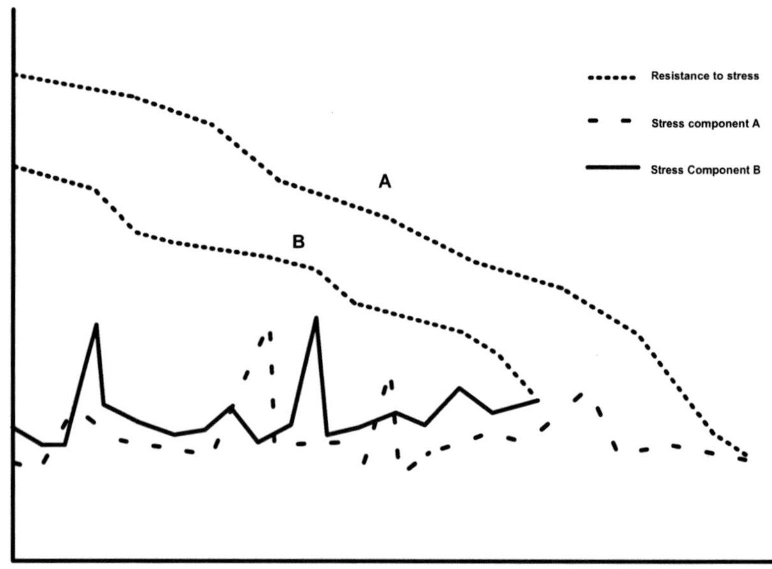

Figure 5.3 : Identical component life differences

It is important to note that the above figures are conceptual and are not exact theoretical representations. They serve only to illustrate the process by which failure take place. Later in this book we will encounter the hazard rate graph which shows the real relationship between a component's life and its risk to fail.

Quantitative descriptions of failure

The Reliability Centered Maintenance technique is a tool for the development of suitable maintenance strategies for the machinery being maintained. In the process of doing so it is often necessary to refer to failure statistics from the past to be able to take the appropriate decision regarding the strategy for managing a specific failure mode. There are a few commonly used quantitative descriptions of such failure statistics which are very useful for this purpose. These include the failure rate, mean time between failures, failure density, cumulative failure distribution, survival function and hazard function. Each of these is discussed in some detail later in the book, but a short description of them will assist us in fully understanding the work in the following paragraphs.

Failure Rate

The failure rate is an indication of how fast failures are following one another. It is calculated by dividing the number of failures by some quantitative measure of the cumulative use of the system or component to accumulate all these failures. The divisor often consists of the cumulative number of operating hours, but could just as well be the number of shifts, days, weeks, months, years or some measure of production delivered such as tons, cubic meters, units produced. The failure rate is a very useful measure in determining whether the reliability of a system or sub-system is busy improving (failure rate decreasing), constant or decreasing (failure rate increasing) over time. We will also use the failure rate for determining the economic life of a system.

Mean Time To Failure (MTTF)

The Mean Time To Failure (MTTF) is the reciprocal of the failure rate. Thus where the failure rate represents the number of failures per time (or other measuring) unit, the MTTF gives an indication of the average life between successive failures in operating hours (or other measuring unit). It thus serves the same purpose as the failure rate, and is sometimes preferred by maintenance people. As is the case with a decreasing failure rate, an increasing MTTF will be an indication that the system's reliability is improving, while a decreasing MTTF (like an increasing failure rate) will indicate reliability degradation.

Failure Density

The failure density gives a picture of the probability of failure of a *component* over its own life. It thus gives, at any particular point in the life of the component, the probability of failure at exactly that point. It is customary in the maintenance world to use the Weibull distribution to describe a component's failure behavior. A typical Weibull failure density function is shown in the following figure.

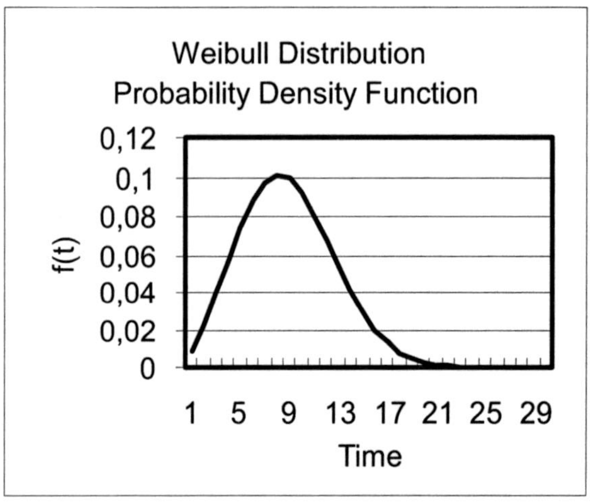

Figure 5.4 : Typical Weibull Failure Density

Cumulative Failure Distribution

By cumulative summation of the probabilities of failure as depicted in the failure density above, the Cumulative Failure Distribution results. It thus gives the probability that the component will have failed before or at any point in time (or other measuring unit) of a component's life. The Cumulative Failure Distribution always starts at a probability of zero, which is equivalent to stating that a new component will not be in the failed state. It will always eventually have a value of one (or one hundred percent), indicating that the component will eventually fail with one hundred percent certainty. The Cumulative Failure Distribution for the Failure Density of figure 5.4 is shown in figure 5.5.

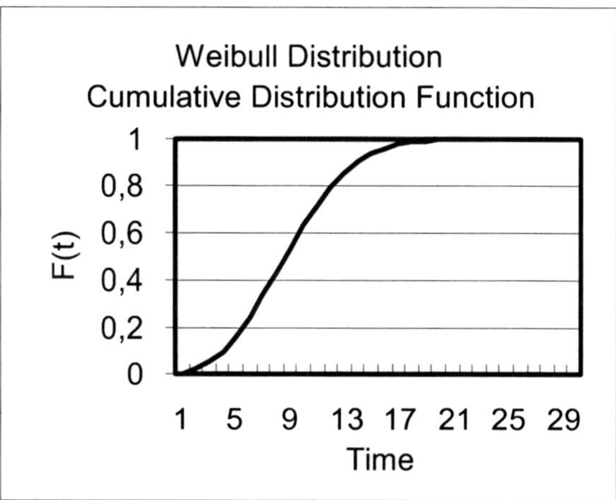

Figure 5.5 : Cumulative Failure Distribution

Survival Function

The Cumulative Failure Distribution gives the probability of failure before or at a certain age. The difference between that and a level of one hundred percent (in other words, the space above the curve of figure 5.5) gives the probability that the component will survive up to that point. This is a very useful measure, as it gives the percentage of units that will survive up to that age. The following figure (figure 5.6) depicts the Survival Function which is the complement of the Cumulative Distribution Function of figure 5.5.

Hazard Function

The most useful of the last four quantitative measures (also called the four reliability functions) is the Hazard Function. It is also called the conditional probability of failure or the momentary probability of failure. It gives the probability that the component will fail at a certain life, given that it has survived up to that age. It is calculated by dividing the value of the Failure Density at that age by the value of the Survival Function at that age. It is a measure of the risk of failure of the component at that specific age. If the Hazard Function is decreasing with age or constant, there will be no incentive towards Use Based Preventive Maintenance as the risk after such maintenance action will not be lower than before it. In such a case the only preventive strategy

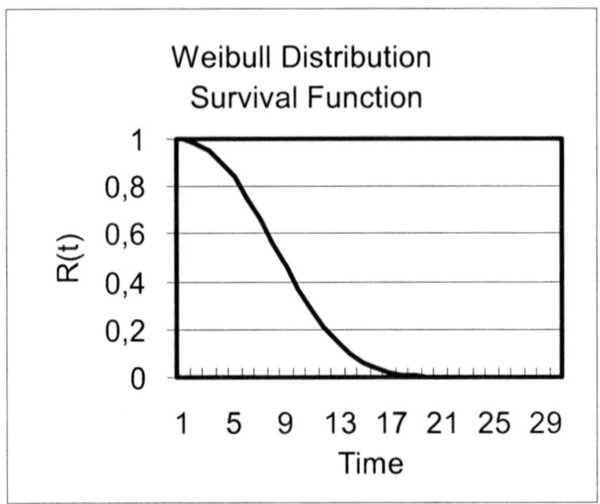

Figure 5.6 : Typical Survival Function

available will be that of Condition Based Preventive Maintenance. But, in the case of an increasing Hazard Function (a situation often encountered in components), Use Based Preventive Maintenance will certainly be an option, as that will lower the risk of failure. Whether or not one uses Use Based Preventive Maintenance in such circumstances will depend on the economics of such action and whether Condition Based Preventive Maintenance does not afford a better option. The Hazard Function for the failure situation of figures 5.4 to 5.6 is shown in figure 5.7, while the principle of lowering the risk of failure through use based replacement is illustrated in figure 5.8 for the case of an increasing hazard.

The Bath Tub Curve

The Bath Tub Curve concept

Most maintenance people are at least aware of the so called "bath tub curve." This curve is a special case of the Hazard Function and depicts the risk of failure of a typical component or system. Figure 5.9 shows the bath tub curve with its three failure regions:

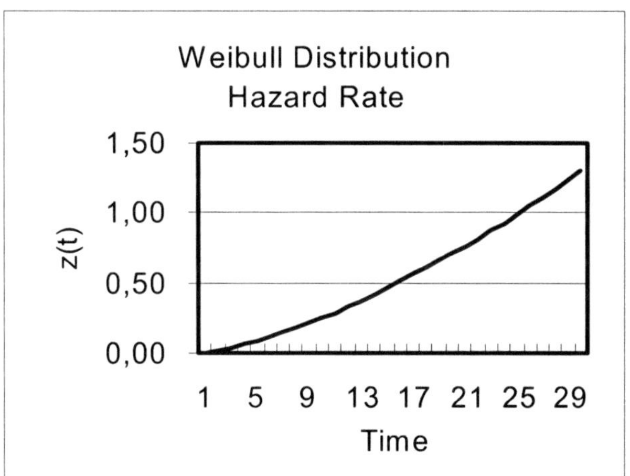

Figure 5.7 : Typical component Hazard Function

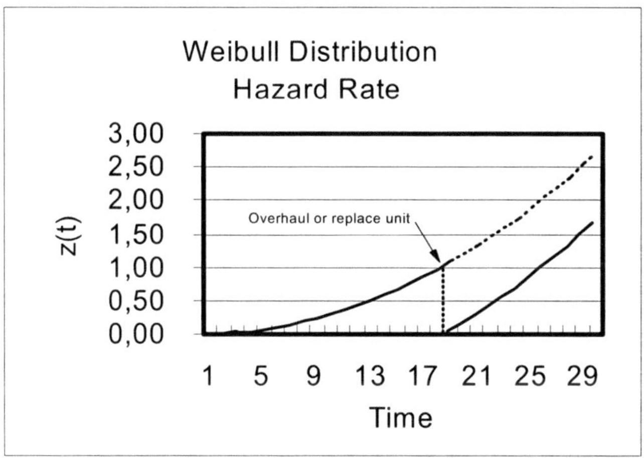

Figure 5.8 : The effect of Use Based Prevention

The *early failure* or *infant mortality* region is a fairly short period during the life of the component or system during which a relatively high risk of failure is experienced. This is mainly due to quality problems in manufacture and assembly. The *second region* is very long

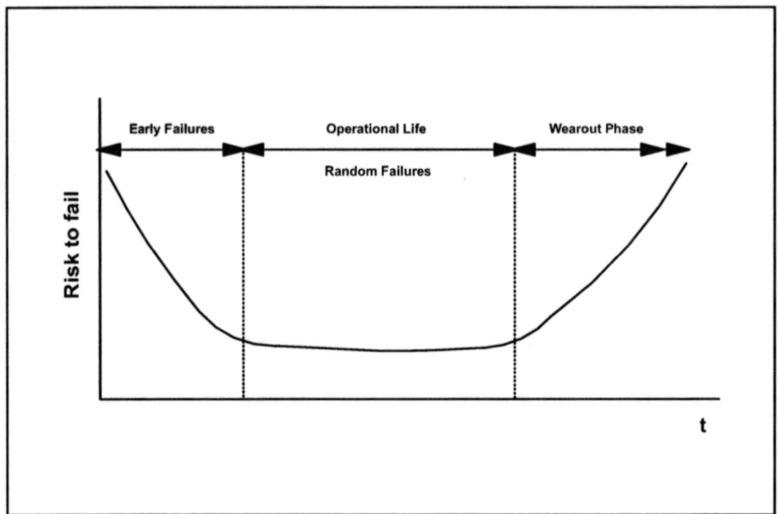

Figure 5.9: The bath tub curve concept

compared to the other two regions and spans the *working life* of the component or system. During this period a constant and fairly low risk of failure is experienced. The *third region (wearout)* sets in when the structural changes to the component or system during operational life due to wear and tear starts a process of relatively speedy degradation. The risk of failure thus increases fairly rapidly in this region.

Problems with the Bath Tub Curve

Conventional wisdom would have it that the Bath Tub Curve applies to all components and systems. It then explains the various failure phenomena from this premise and uses this concept in setting up maintenance strategies. We will show that this is not only an inadequate way of handling the failure process, but that it could lead to totally deficient maintenance strategies.

The *first* problem with the general bath tub concept is that not all components and systems have the early failure and wear out regions. Some have none of these two regions, while others have only one of them. The *second* problem with the bath tub curve is that not all components or systems have a constant risk to fail over its operating life. Some have a decreasing risk to fail, while others have an increasing risk to fail, as was stated above. This will become clearer as the book progresses. A *further* problem in the general application of the bath tub curve is the fact that the bath tub curve for components differ from that of systems. For a component the bath tub curve gives the risk to fail of the single component over its own life span (the Hazard Function z(t)). For a system the bath tub curve gives the failure rate of the system, comprising many components, over time. This is depicted in figures 5.10 and 5.11.

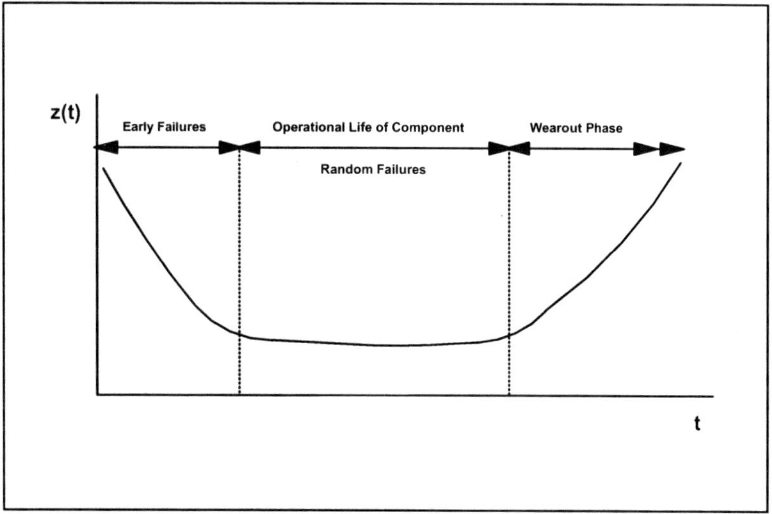

Figure 5.10: The Hazard Function Bath Tub Curve

A *last* problem regarding the bath tub curve for systems is Drenick's[1] (1960) limit theorem. This theorem stated that a constant failure rate will be resulting in a system consisting of many components. This is apparently inconsistent with the wear out phase of the failure rate bath tub curve. This is not necessarily so, as is illustrated in figure 5.12, which was proposed by Ascher and Feingold (1984)[2]. The system experiences an increase in the failure rate due to several components that fails for the first time (the conventional wear out region). After all components have failed at least once, the system's failure rate stabilizes at a steady state rate higher than that during its early life.

[1] Drenick, R.F. (1960). The failure law of complex equipment. J. Soc. Indust. Appl. Math., 8, 680-690.

[2] Ascher, H. , Feingold, H. (1984). Repairable Systems Reliability. Marcel Dekker.

This has important consequences for system replacement policies. In South Africa, where sanctions for many years forced policies of maintaining old capital equipment, this concept has been proven repeatedly.

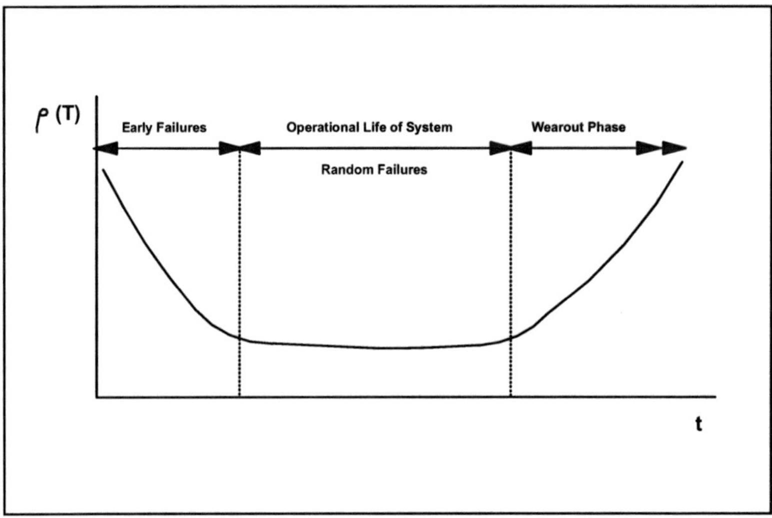

Figure 5.11: The Failure Rate Bath Tub Curve

Different shapes of the Bath Tub curve and its significance

When United Airlines started developing RCM, one of the first steps in the process was that they contracted actuaries to do life time studies on the various components and sub-systems of an aircraft. The results of these were used to start developing generalized procedures for the development of maintenance strategies for new equipment. The resultant failure patterns (really special cases of the Hazard Function Bath Tub Curve) was published in the original work by F. Stanley Nowlan and Howard F. Heap: Reliability Centered Maintenance. These graphs are shown in figure 5.13.

It is clear that most of these graphs are made up of one or more of the components (early failures, operational life and wearout zones) of the Bath Tub Curve concept. From experience with maintenance failure data, it is evident that most of these graphs were the results of studies of sub-systems (not components). This follows from Drenick's theorem, which states that systems/sub-systems tend to display a constant hazard over its operational life[3]. Of these graphs only graphs A and B displays wearout characteristics, whereas graph C displays a

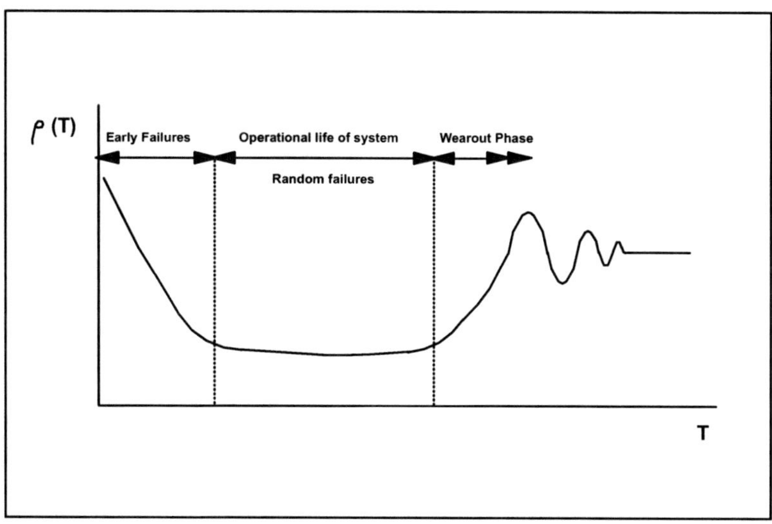

Figure 5.12 : Integration of the Bath Tub Curve concept with Drenick's limit theorem

gradual increase in hazard over the unit's operational life. Thus one can conclude that, at a systems level, in aircraft of that day and time, use based maintenance could only be used in 11% of the sub-systems studied. This percentage will probably be higher if the studies were pitched at a lower level, but the results of the study nevertheless shows that:

- In a high proportion of cases (89% in the study) use based preventive maintenance will not be effective (due to the hazard not increasing with time). In these cases the only strategies available are Condition Based Preventive Maintenance or Corrective Maintenance (apart from the possibility of redesign).
- A significant proportion of components (11% in the study) will benefit from use based maintenance. In these cases all possible maintenance strategies can be employed (use based, condition based and corrective maintenance), depending on the detailed char-

[3] In many cases the analyses leading to these results were probably wrong as will become clear later when we discuss the difference between the analysis techniques for component (Renewal Theory) and systems (Repairable Systems). It is clear that the actuaries used Renewal techniques for analysis, where-as in the case of many systems and sub-systems that was probably not correct (see Ascher, H. , Feingold, H. (1984). Repairable Systems Reliability. Marcel Dekker).

acteristics of the hazard curve, the economics involved and the effectiveness of the different categories of tasks.

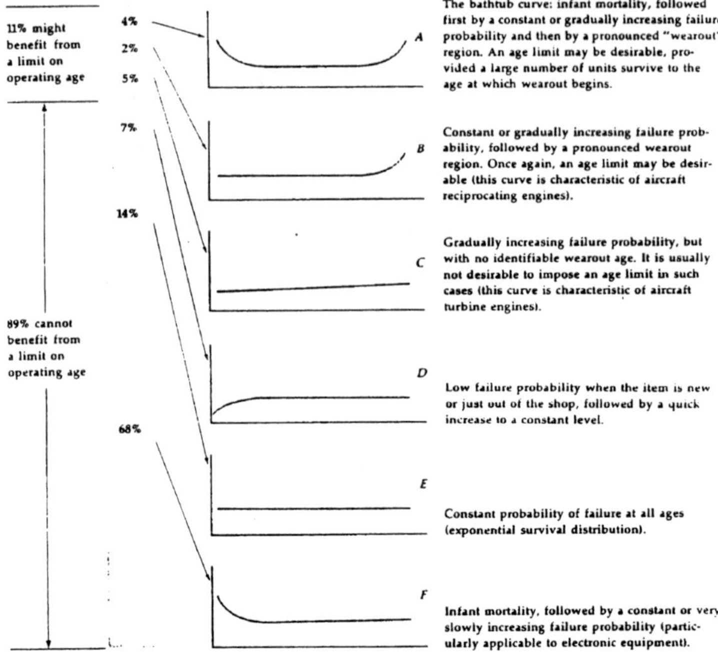

11% might benefit from a limit on operating age
89% cannot benefit from a limit on operating age
4%
2%
5%
7%
14%
68%
A
B
C
D
E
F
The bathtub curve: infant mortality, followed first by a constant or gradually increasing failure probability and then by a pronounced "wearout" region. An age limit may be desirable, provided a large number of units survive to the age at which wearout begins.
Constant or gradually increasing failure probability, followed by a pronounced wearout region. Once again, an age limit may be desirable (this curve is characteristic of aircraft reciprocating engines).
Gradually increasing failure probability, but with no identifiable wearout age. It is usually not desirable to impose an age limit in such cases (this curve is characteristic of aircraft turbine engines).
Low failure probability when the item is new or just out of the shop, followed by a quick increase to a constant level.
Constant probability of failure at all ages (exponential survival distribution).
Infant mortality, followed by a constant or very slowly increasing failure probability (particularly applicable to electronic equipment).

Figure 5.13 : Typical failure patterns (Nowlan and Heap)

- In 72% of the cases an infant mortality zone, which is characterized by a decreasing hazard, is present. This is typical of electronic equipment according to Nowlan and Heap (figure 5.13 comments adjacent to graph F). In only a few cases (4% - graph A) an infant mortality zone can be attributed to mechanical equipment (although the authors do not state specifically that graph A was for mechanical equipment, the full bath tub gives one that idea).
- In 7% of cases (graph D), the hazard increases fairly quickly as the sub-system starts its operating life and then stabilizes at a constant level.

These conclusions seem to show that the Bath Tub concept, despite its limitations and problem areas as stated above is very valuable in the process of maintenance strategy setting. But, one should keep the following points in mind:

1. Remember footnote 3 earlier on in the chapter, which is repeated here for convenience sake: In many cases the analyses leading to these results (those of Nowlan and Heap) were probably wrong as will become clear later when we discuss the difference between the analysis techniques for components (Renewal Theory) and systems (Repairable Systems). It is clear that the actuaries used Renewal techniques for analysis, where-as in the case of many systems and sub-systems that was probably not correct (see Ascher, H. , Feingold, H. (1984). Repairable Systems Reliability. Marcel Dekker).
2. Be aware of the fact that not all components of the Bath Tub concept are necessarily present in a specific failure study.
3. Furthermore, this study showed that in only 11% of cases an increasing hazard function is present while practical experience at the component level seems to indicate a much higher occurrence of cases with an increasing hazard.

The most important conclusion of all is that you can never know which failure pattern is present for a certain unit (sub-system or component) without analyzing the unit's failure data. Only after doing such analysis can one dare to set a maintenance strategy for the unit (unless, of course, one is willing to accept sub-optimum strategies with all the negative implications that will have on profit/cost). Thus, a very important part of strategy setting using the R.C.M. technique necessitates the analysis of the relevant failure data.

Causes of failure

To give a comprehensive description of all causes of failure would be impossible. One would have to look at all the Engineering disciplines one by one, and within each of them area by area to try and discern and describe all the possible failure causes. And in certain disciplines (such as electronics) the causes are often of a shock nature (such as a voltage spike), which requires no description of the failure cause. Thus we will limit ourselves to a few of the common failure causes in metals that are the common causes of failure in industrial equipment.

Fracture

There are two mechanisms of fracture in materials, *ductile fracture* and *brittle fracture.* Ductile fracture develops when the material is loaded (typically stretched) beyond its limits. Plastic deformation is carried to its extreme, causing a 100% reduction in area of the component, thus causing failure. Brittle fracture, on the other hand, takes place in situations where adjacent parts of the material are separated by stresses normal to the fracture surface. A schematic contrast between brittle fracture and ductile fracture is shown in figure 5.14. In case a) failure occurs in a ductile fashion before the level of fracture stress is reached. In case c) fracture occurs before deformation can occur by shear, e.g. glass, mica and cast iron. In case b) there is an overlap which is typical of many metals. Plastic deformation starts, but strain-hardening increases the tolerable stress until the fracture strength is exceeded. Thus, it is not uncommon to find metals undergoing some reduction in area before final brittle fracture.

Creep

Strength and strain characteristics of materials are time dependent, as is shown in figure 5.15. When a metal is stressed, it undergoes immediate elastic elongation, and in the first short period of time makes additional plastic adjustments at points of stress along grain boundaries and at flaws. After these initial adjustments, a slow, nearly steady state of stress, called creep, sets in and continues until sufficient strain has occurred so that a necking down and reduction of cross-sectional area occurs. After this and until rapture, the rate of elongation increases because there is less area to support the load. The creep

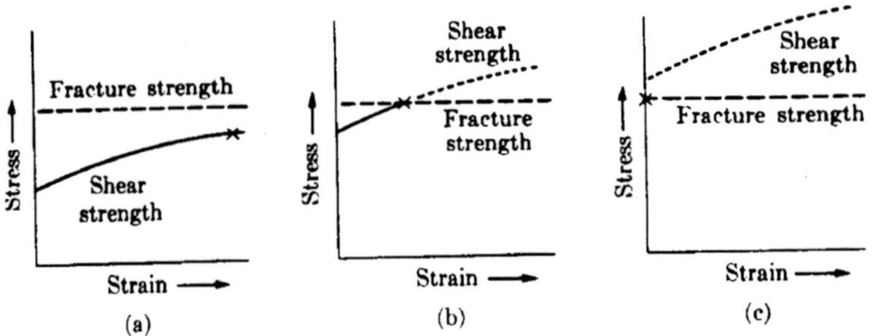

Figure 5.14: Fracture - the cross indicates the point of failure

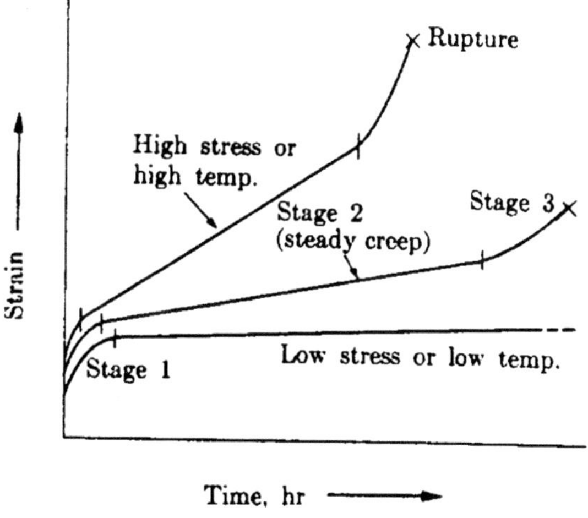

Figure 5.15: Creep

rate is equal to the slope of the steady creep part of the curves in the figure. The following is evident:

⇒ The creep rate increases with temperature

⇒ The creep rate increases with stress

⇒ The total strain (i.e. elongation) increases when either the applied stress or the temperature increases

⇒ The time before failure by rupture is decreased as the stress or temperature is increased.

Fatigue

Fatigue failure takes place under situations of repeated loading. This is a type of loading where the load is repeatedly applied and removed, or the magnitude (and frequently the direction) of the load is changed, many thousands of times during the life of the component. The physical effect of a repeated load on a material is different from that of a static load, the failure always being a brittle fracture, regardless of whether the material is brittle or ductile. Under repeated loading a crack forms in a region of high localized stress. This crack then propagates under further repeated loading cycles until a fairly small area carries the total load. When this area gets small enough brittle fracture takes place. Figure 5.16 shows the number of stress cycles be-

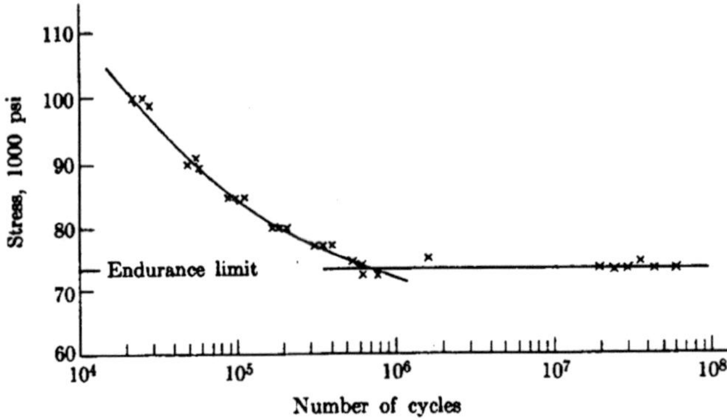

Figure 3.15: S-N curve for 4340 steel, hot-worked bar stock

fore failure in a steel which has been repeatedly loaded. These curves, which are available for most materials, is commonly called S-N curves (for Stress-Number of cycles). To increase the number of cycles before failure, the repeated stress placed on the component must be reduced. The level of maximum stress represented by the horizontal part of the curve is called the endurance limit.

Sliding wear

When two solid surfaces slide over each other, with or without lubrication, sliding wear takes place. This type of wear excludes the case where there are contamination between the two surfaces, which is called abrasive wear and which is discussed in the following paragraph. There are a few mechanisms of sliding wear which we will subsequently discuss:

1. *Plasticity dominated wear* - many different mechanisms have been proposed for the severe wear of metals. All involve plastic deformation, but differ in the detailed processes by which material is removed. By critical examination of the worn surfaces and the wear debris one can attempt to determine the specific mechanism involved. It is not always easy to determine the mechanism without a doubt, but such an inspection always provides useful information. One will often find plate-like debris particles in sliding wear of this kind.

2. *Oxidative wear* - flash temperatures of several hundred degrees can readily be generated in sliding. The magnitude of these temperatures depends strongly on velocity. Only moderate sliding speeds are needed with most metals before these hot-spot temperatures become high enough to cause significant surface oxidation. As example 700°C is reached at a sliding speed of 1m/s for steels.
3. *Fretting wear* - fretting consists of small oscillatory movements between two solid surfaces in contact. Fretting normally occurs as the consequence of a deliberate movement of the surfaces, but in some cases fretting occurs between two surfaces which are meant to be static in relation to one another. This is often the case where vibration is present. Fretting causes fatigue cracks in the damaged surface which, if the component is a cyclically loaded component, will cause a large reduction in the fatigue strength of the component.
4. *Abrasive wear* - abrasive wear takes place if solid particles find their way into the space between two surfaces sliding on one another. Abrasive wear can occur in two ways: plastic flow and brittle fracture. Both often occur together, but plastic flow can occur on its own under certain circumstances. In the case of plastic flow the solid grit particles that find their way between the surfaces causes the surfaces to deform plastically (actually to flow in response to the grit particles cutting trough the surfaces). In the case of brittle fracture the grit particles cause the brittle material of the surfaces to crack due to surface pressure. These cracks leads readily to material removal by impact from the grit particles. One can envisage more plastic flow occurring in soft surfaces and more brittle fracture in hard surfaces.
5. *Erosion - as* in the case of abrasion, erosion can involve both plastic deformation and brittle fracture. Erosion occurs when solid particles strike against a surface. The particle exerts an impact force on the surface when it decelerates from its native velocity to standstill or gets deflected with a negative velocity. This impact force causes damage to the surface, which can be plastic or brittle in nature. Just as in the abrasion case the exact mechanism depends on the softness or otherwise of the materials involved.

Table of failure causes

The following table was compiled from the results extracted from two American Society for Metals (A.S.M.) case history manuals for failure analysis. The results are listed in a grid format, showing the typical causes of failures they encountered from two angles. The top row gives the cause class, while the left column gives the inherent failure mode.

Table 5.1 : Table of failure causes

	Design/ Manufacture	Service Related	Materials	Environment
Fatigue			x	x
Corrosion	x	x	x	x
Microstructure			x	x
Stress			x	x
Heat		x	x	x
Forging				x
Casting				x
Welding				x
Heat Treating		x		x
Other Manufacturing				x
Materials selection				x
Friction/ Lubrication			x	
Materials Defects		x		
Mixed materials		x		
Ageing		x		
Fracture		x		
Hydrogen Embrittlement	x			

Failure pictures

This part of the book will not be complete without a proper reference to the techniques of physical failure analysis. As was stated in the preface, this is one of the areas where the present book lacks depth. It is thus the intention of the author, as was stated in the preface, to add a full chapter (or section) on failure analysis. In the meantime, the following framework provides a basis from which the maintenance engineer can investigate the possible causes of failure. The framework will help the investigator to pinpoint the exact cause of failure by working through the following questions in their chronological order. The root cause of failure or failure mode should be evident if this process is followed methodically. The questions are classified into five categories:

1. *The failure condition*
   * what do we see if we look at the failed component?
   * is there any damage evident?
   * what must be done to repair the damage / how long will it take?
2. *The failure width*
   * how localized is the damage?
   * what secondary damage is evident?
   * is the failure evident at the systems level?
   * is there a threat to safety or the environment and in what way?
3. *The failure situation*
   * what was the operating situation when the failure occurred?
   * was there evidence of any potential failure before the failure occurred?
   * what was the plant's operating performance like just before the failure?
4. *The failure originator*
   * where and when did it occur?
   * is there any evidence that points to the root cause of the failure?
5. *The failure mode*
   * what initiated the failure?
   * can the root cause be establish with a fair degree of certainty through synthesis based on the facts gathered using the question logic above?

Table 5.2 : Typical failure analysis category answers

Failure Condition	Failure Width	Failure Originator	Failure Situation	Failure Mode
Deformity	Primary damage	Commissioning damage	Normal operation	Wear
Tear	Secondary damage	Operational damage	Overuse	Corrosion
Fracture		Transportation damage	Environmental effects	Fatigue
Collapse		Storage damage		Ageing
Corrosion		Maintenance damage		Overloading
Wear		Bad design		Lack of lubrication
Leak		Deviation from OEM specification		Previous damage
Production				

The answer to the last category's questions is of course the failure cause that we want to discover. But to get to the root cause (the failure mode) we have to go through the process of building a failure picture which consists of the answers to the five categories of questions above, answered one by one (from the first to the fifth , in that order).

Some typical answers to each of the five categories are listed in table 5.2 above.

References

1. Nowlan, F.S. and Heap, H., Reliability Centered Maintenance. National Technical Information Service, US Department of Commerce, 1978.

2. Ascher, H. and Feingold, H., Repairable Systems Reliability. Marcel Dekker, 1984.

This page was left blank on purpose

Use it for notes

Chapter 6

A stepwise approach to the design of a Maintenance Plan

Introduction

The application of the R.C.M. technique to design a maintenance plan for the organization too often leads to either a design task which becomes so large that it is abandoned; or the end result presents the organization with such a high preventive work load that the R.C.M. technique is discredited. Not one of these scenarios should prevail. The problem is that R.C.M. is often applied as is to all the equipment of the organization. Now, that is exactly what the R.C.M. technique prescribes. You take all the equipment of your business, break each of them down into the tiniest parts and then proceed to analyze the possible failures of each of these (millions) of tiny parts, so to ensure that you maintain in such a way that the reliability of your total plant is preserved at the highest possible level. This approach is fine when developing a maintenance plan for a large aircraft of which thousands will be sold, and for which the highest possible reliability retention is absolutely crucial. The same may be true for significant portions of a nuclear power plant. But this is not true for the average industrial concern. For them the R.C.M. approach is too cumbersome and proposes a maintenance plan that is not practical.

The way in which the R.C.M. approach is to be implemented should thus differ substantially in two areas: it must *firstly* not be as heavy on resources to develop the plan and, *secondly*, the resultant maintenance plan should effectively decrease the total maintenance workload (preventive time plus corrective time). The *first* of these objectives can be reached by prioritizing the plant items for which a full R.C.M. analysis will be done. This prioritizing approach will be fully described in the next and following sections. Through doing that and by limiting the number of items for which formal maintenance strategies should be developed, the total workload for the design of the plan can be limited. The *second* problem is much more serious in that the R.C.M. technique easily lends itself to abuse. People that are trained in the application of the technique easily becomes so motivated that they tend to be over enthusiastic in finding preventive tasks for every possible failure mode that could present itself during the life of the equipment. The only way to curtail this enthusiasm is through the application of strict discipline. The rules that should be adhered to, to ensure that a lean but effective maintenance plan results (for the items selected through prioritization), include the following:

1. The organization should have at least one *well trained R.C.M. facilitator* (in the absence of such a person a trained facilitator can be hired from a R.C.M. consultant). This person should be a well trained and experienced maintenance engineer (typically a bright university graduate), with a very good knowledge of maintenance theory (with the accent on failure theory - physical and statistical). He must be able to assess and analyze failure situations accurately through the collection of information from operating and maintenance staff, as well as from failure data. He must also be an expert in the application of the R.C.M. technique. This man should be used to lead all the R.C.M. sessions as facilitator. In these sessions it is his task to get as much as possible information about the failure behavior of the specific equipment on the table. He is not to participate in contributing technical knowledge regarding the specific situation. His role is rather to ensure that the R.C.M. technique is applied maximally to the available information, so to develop the best possible maintenance plan (having a lean but effective content), using as few man-hours as is possible in the design process. It is clearly not easy to find such a man, as he will probably be promoted to a management post before contributing much towards the development of a maintenance plan. But that depends on the seriousness with which the individual organization regard the maintenance plan. After all, this plan **is** pivotal in determining whether they will be successful in their maintenance approach. And it is of course always possible to use an external facilitator.
2. *The team for the design of a maintenance plan* for a specific type of equipment should typically consist of four persons (apart from the facilitator). There should be a supervisor and artisan from the maintenance side and a supervisor and operator from the production side. They should be the most knowledgeable people on the operation and maintenance of the equipment that the organization has. As is the case with any design work, the quality of the forthcoming maintenance plan is directly proportional to the quality of the people used in designing the plan.

3. *The maintenance manager for whom the plan is developed should be actively involved in the process.* This does not mean that he has to sit in on the sessions, but he must 'run the show'. He will thus be the driving force requesting the maintenance plan's development. He is also the person bringing the team together and arranging for the services of a facilitator. But, still more important, he is also the person who works through the resultant R.C.M. analysis, approving the maintenance plan and arranging for its (successful) implementation. He has to 'foot the bill' at the end of day, whether that be a bill reflecting maintenance success or one reflecting maintenance failure. He must thus be convinced that by making use of R.C.M. he will increase his chances of success. It makes no sense to use the technique just to 'be in', without commitment to make the end result worthwhile.
4. *In R.C.M. as applied in industrial situations, there are no "may be's"* - in other words, you never specify a maintenance task for a failure mode that may exist, but which has never shown itself to exist. In the standard R.C.M. approach, because it wants to ensure the maximum possible reliability of an airplane, **all** possible failure modes have to be investigated. But, in the average industrial organization that is not important at all. We want to achieve the highest possible effective availability of the plant, whilst at the same time retaining a high proportion of the built in reliability and operability. We will thus only investigate the **proven** failure modes for the plant items which we have selected, through prioritization, for R.C.M. analysis.

This page was left blank on purpose

Use it for notes

Chapter 7

A stepwise approach to the design of a Maintenance Plan

Step 1 : Selecting failure modes as basis for the plan

A maintenance plan consists of an array of maintenance tasks, of a preventive nature, with their accompanying prescribed task frequencies. Such a plan is based, not on the equipment itself or even the parts of the equipment, but on the failure modes of the equipment. Thus, to design a maintenance plan, we have to find all the relevant failure modes. Only then can we design a meaningful maintenance plan.

As can be imagined, it involves quite a process to identify all the failure modes that will be used as a basis for the plan. This process will be broken down into six separate steps. These steps are the following:

⇒ Prioritization of **plant items**

⇒ Plant item **breakdown**

⇒ Prioritization of **Maintenance Significant Items**

⇒ Determine the **Function(s)** of each Maintenance Significant Item in the present operating context

⇒ Determine the **Functional Failure(s)** of each Function

⇒ Determine the **Failure Mode(s)** for each Functional Failure

By working through the above mentioned six steps, the bottom line will consist of a list of failure modes for which suitable maintenance strategies should be found. These strategies, taken together, then make up the maintenance plan. But, before getting to the processes of strategy setting, we will discuss the six steps listed above in more detail.

Prioritization of plant items

In the later chapter on the Analysis of Maintenance Results the use of Pareto Charts to limit the scope of managerial action is discussed in some detail. The same technique can be utilized to effectively limit the scope of the R.C.M. analysis, so that it only includes the more critical plant items in terms of benefit achieved from the implementation of a formal maintenance plan. It was stated earlier that the major reason for the R.C.M. technique not being used more widely, is the perception that it 'costs an arm and a leg' to design a maintenance plan using the technique. This objection can be largely eliminated through the use of Pareto Charts.

The easiest way to limit the scope through the use of Pareto Charts is to make a list of all groups of plant items, together with the contribution of each of these items to the profit of the organization. It is not so important what method(s) is (are) used to calculate the individual groups of plant items' contribution to profit, as is the need for consistency in these calculations over the different plant item groups. Often the organization's financial department can assist in these calculations. These values can then be used to establish which plant items are the most important in terms of contribution to profit, using the Pareto technique as described later. The logical step will then be to do a full R.C.M. analysis for these (high priority) items only. This will produce a good result in terms of company profit. If needed, the scope can later be increased through the inclusion of less important plant items for R. C.M. analysis. But care should be taken that the scope is never increased to such an extent that the benefit that could be reaped from an improved maintenance plan is outweighed by the cost of the additional R.C.M. analyses and the added cost of prevention.

The end result of the prioritization will thus be a list of the groups of plant items for which the availability, reliability and operability are of prime importance in the pursuit of maximal profit. This list will typically include around 20% (although the specific cut-off point is

---

[1] Care should be taken not to disregard those plant items that do not contribute directly to profit, but which are of cardinal importance in ensuring long term profit. A good example of such items is the equipment used to remove the overburden in a strip mining situation. Although it does not contribute to profit directly, the mining operation will come to a standstill if they are not available for production. In such a situation they should share with the primary production machinery (loading, transport and beneficiation equipment in the example) in the contribution to profit.

prescribed by the characteristics of the plant items themselves) of the total of plant item groups.

Plant item break down

For each of the plant item groups in the list developed above a plant item break down should now be carried out. This is a step by step break down of the item into first large sub-systems, then smaller sub-assemblies, then sub-sub-assemblies and lastly parts. This is shown schematically in figure 7.1.

In most industrial situations it is again too cumbersome to break the equipment down to the last little part, so to find the maintenance strategies for every possible failure mode. Thus, when working with industrial plant, we each time before breaking an item down further use the logic shown in figure 7.2 to determine whether we need to break the item down further.

The *first* question when deciding whether or not to break an item down another level is: "Will a functional failure on the lower level have an impact on the equipment?" Our objective is to find the lowest level of **Maintenance Significant Items** - those items for which to set maintenance strategy. Those are the items which do not contain items, which in themselves have significant failure modes, which could affect the items on the higher level. If the answer is 'no', no further break

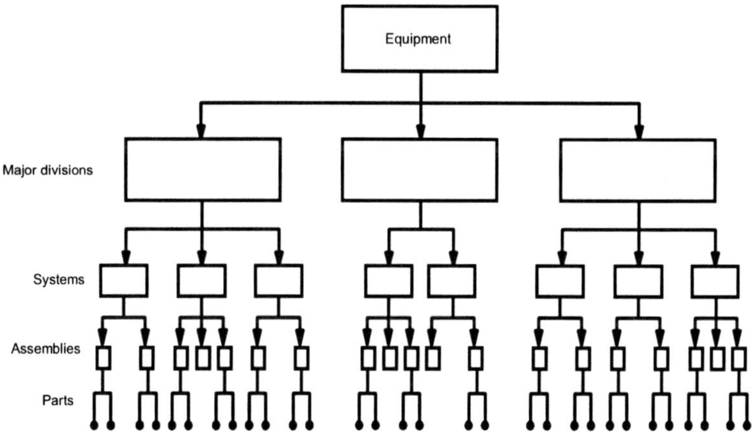

Figure 7.1 : Equipment breakdown structure

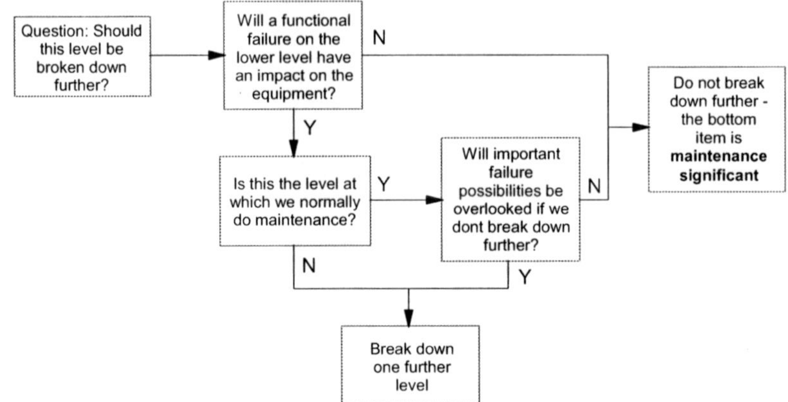

Figure 7.2 : Item breakdown decision diagram

down is required, because those items on the lower level is not maintenance significant. If the answer is 'yes', the *second* question is : "Is this the level at which we normally do maintenance?" If we normally do maintenance to items on a lower level, then it would make no sense to stop breaking down at this level. Only if the answer to this question is 'yes', will one contemplate stopping the break down process at this level. But one first has to ask the *third* question: "Will important failure possibilities be overlooked if we don't break down further?" If there are no such possibilities, no further break down is required, because those items on the lower level is not maintenance significant (that is, the present item is maintenance significant). Otherwise the break down process has to continue.

By repeatedly going through this decision process, level by level, item by item, one can identify all those items that are Maintenance Significant. Those are the bottom-most items in the break down tree (figure 6.1). Some of these items will still be sub-assemblies, or even sub-systems, while other will be parts (single cell items). What matters, though, is that it is only for these bottom-most items that maintenance strategies are devised. By setting proper strategies for them, the items higher up in the hierarchy will be properly maintained, as they (the higher up items) are made up of lower level (maintenance significant) items. Thus, in essence, the end result of this plant item break down process is a list of Maintenance Significant Items.

Prioritization of Maintenance Significant Items

We now, after completing the plant break down process, have a list of Maintenance Significant Items. To further limit the size of the R.C.M. task, we should prioritize the Maintenance Significant Items, such that we need only devise maintenance strategies for the more important ones. We can again make use of Pareto Charts (as we did above in the prioritization of plant items). To do this, we would list next to each Maintenance Significant Item its contribution to the equipment's downtime in percentage. The objective with the use of the Pareto Chart will then be to identify those items that contribute most to the downtime of this (important) equipment (as identified as being important through the prioritization of plant items). The end result of this process will thus be a (much smaller) list of important Maintenance Significant Items. It is for the items in this list that we will now devise maintenance strategies.

Determine the Function(s) of each Maintenance Significant Item in the present operating context

For each of the Maintenance Significant Items in our list we will now list its functions. In some cases an item has only one function, but often such item has more than one function. An example is our automotive automatic transmission. We said that the primary function of such unit is to provide the correct gear ratios, but that a secondary function would be that it should provide smooth gear changes. These functions could also differ from application to application. That is why our heading states specifically: 'in the present operating context'. The functions of an automatic transmission in a racing situation will surely differ from that in a normal family sedan! So, we list all the functions of each Maintenance Significant Item, taking into account the operating context.

Something which is as important as the functions themselves as we progress through the analysis, is the identification of what we regard as full functional performance. Before we attempt the next step, which is the listing of functional failures for each function, we have to know what will constitute such a failure. For our primary function of the automatic transmission, we have to state that it has to provide the correct gear ratios, which are four forward ratios and one reverse ratio - we could also specify when it should change over from one gear to the next, etc. Through having such standards, which constitute full functional performance, it is now easy to identify functional failures.

A second example that we will use throughout our text, is that of an electronic house alarm system. The primary function of such unit is to provide warning of intrusion. This function can be further specified by stating that the warning should be supplied through an audible alarm that is unmistakably discerned by neighbors 50 meters away and which notifies a central control room through a telephone line within 30 seconds of the alarm being set off. Such a unit has a myriad of secondary functions, of which we will only use two in our example. One of these secondary functions is the possibility to bypass certain alarm zones to facilitate inhabitants moving around while the alarm is activated. One can specify further that it should be possible to activate and de-activate such function at will. A second secondary function is the provision of an entry delay to allow inhabitants to de-activate the alarm. It can be further specified that such delay should be 30 seconds, or whatever the case may be.

Determine the Functional Failure(s) for each Function

For each of the functions identified, we now have to identify the functional failures that will constitute a loss of function. Often there are more than one functional failures for each function that was identified. But before we can do that, we have to remember what a failure is. In chapter 5 we defined the term failure as being an *unsatisfactory condition.* We also discerned between *functional failures* (the inability of an item to meet a specified performance standard) and *potential failures (an identifiable physical condition which indicates that a functional failure is imminent).* In this section we wish to identify all functional failures (and thus not potential failures). This can be best communicated through examples.

Before we look at the specific examples, the reader is reminded of an important prerequisite for using the R.C.M. methodology profitably, which was stated earlier in this chapter. We said in the introduction that one of the prerequisites was that *"in R.C.M. as applied in industrial situations, there are no 'may be's'* - in other words, you never specify a maintenance task for a failure mode that may exist, but which has never shown itself to exist." Thus, when identifying functional failures, we just list those that have occurred in the past (in your own or related businesses).

For our example of the automatic transmission's first function: "provide the correct gear ratios", functional failures may be (1) transmission does not provide ratios at all; (2) one ratio defect; and for its second function: "smooth transition between ratios", the functional failure (3) change over is rough.

For our second example, that of the electronic home alarm system, the functional failures for the first function: "provide warning of intrusion" may be (1) does not provide warning at all; (2) does not provide audible warning; (3) audible warning too soft (cannot reach 50 meters); (4) does not notify central control room. Take note of the effect that the standards that were set for the function has on the identification of functional failures. Without proper standards some of these failures might have been completely overlooked. For our second function: "bypass alarm zones" our functional failures will be (5) not possible to bypass alarm zones; and (6) not possible to un-bypass alarm zones. For our third function: "entry delay", the functional failures are: (7) does not allow entry delay; (8) too short entry delay; (9) too long entry delay.

The best way of handling the analysis detail is to put it into a table as is shown in tables 7.1 and 7.2 on the following page.

Determine the Failure Mode(s) for each Functional Failure

Each of the functional failures listed in tables 7.1 and 7.2 can now be analyzed with the intent to find the underlying failure modes. These are the base of the maintenance strategies and the maintenance plan that will be developed. They are the **root causes** for the functional failures occurring. Each functional failure can have one or more failure modes (root causes of failure). We will identify these for all the functional failures identified, but only for the first group of each example.

For the automatic transmission's functional failure "Transmission does not provide ratios at all", the failure modes (remember that there are no may-be's) might be: (1) control system failure; (2) hydraulic pump failure; (3) torque converter failure. For the alarm system's functional failure "Does not provide warning at all", the failure modes are: (1) power pack failure and (2) main board failure, while for the functional failure " Does not provide audible warning", the failure modes are: (3) siren failure and (4) siren circuit failure. The re-

Table 7.1 : Automatic Transmission

Function	Functional Failure
Provide the correct gear ratios - four forward ratios and one reverse ratio	Transmission does not provide ratios at all
	One ratio defect
Smooth transition between ratios	Change over is rough

Table 7.2 : Electronic home alarm system

Function	Functional Failure
Provide warning of intrusion - warning should be supplied through an audible alarm that is unmistakably dis-cerned by neighbors 50 meters away and which notifies a central control room through a telephone line within 30 seconds of the alarm being set off	Does not provide warning at all
	Does not provide audible warning
	Audible warning too soft (cannot reach 50 meters)
	Does not notify central control room
Bypass alarm zones - it should be possible to activate and de-activate such function at will	Not possible to bypass alarm zones
	Not possible to un-bypass alarm zones
Entry delay - delay should be 30 seconds	Does not allow entry delay
	Too short entry delay
	Too long entry delay

Table 7.3 : Automatic Transmission

Function	Functional Failure	Failure Mode
Provide the correct gear ratios - four forward ratios and one reverse ratio	Transmission does not provide ratios at all	Control System failure
		Hydraulic pump failure
		Torque Convertor failure

Table 7.4 : Electronic home alarm system

Function	Functional Failure	Failure Mode
Provide warning of intrusion - warning should be supplied through an audible alarm that is unmistakably discerned by neighbors 50 meters away and which notifies a central control room through a telephone line within 30 seconds of the alarm being set off	Does not provide warning at all	Power Pack failure
		Main board failure
	Does not provide audible warning	Siren failure
		Siren circuit failure
	Audible warning too soft (cannot reach 50 meters)	Siren failure
	Does not notify central control room	Main board failure
		Telephone interface failure
		Telephone line failure

mainder of the analyses are listed in tables 7.3 and 7.4 (for the first group of each example).

The importance of finding the correct failure modes cannot be stressed enough. Remember that we started with a list of significant items, which was selected as being those where the maximum effect of proper maintenance strategies can be had. If we, in other words, identify the correct failure modes for these items, we will eventually develop a maintenance plan that will have a significant impact on the bottom line of the organization.

At the end of this step, we sit with a list of the most important failure modes in relation to their negative effect on company profit. We now have to find maintenance tasks that will reduce the negative effect on profit maximally.

Before moving on and using the failure modes to choose the correct maintenance strategies, it is important that the failure modes should be fully documented. The *first* reason for this is that, although the persons involved in the identification of the failure modes might have understood them properly at the time, this may not be the case after some time has expired. A *second* reason is that other people working with the end result (the maintenance plan) may not understand the rationale behind some parts of it properly and might want to refer back to the original documentation. A *third* reason is that the maintenance plan has to be updated periodically - if it was documented properly in the first instance, the process of updating will be relatively fast.

The failure modes are documented by explaining the mechanism of the failure mode fully. This includes describing the failure using the questions listed under the paragraph heading "Failure pictures" at the end of chapter 5. The objective is to make clear to the person(s) setting up the maintenance strategies exactly what effects should be countered through the strategy, if at all possible.

References

1. Coetzee, J.L., Introduction to Maintenance Engineering, Annual short course, 1994.
2. Nowlan, F.S. and Heap, H., Reliability Centered Maintenance. National Technical Information Service, US Department of Commerce, 1978.

3. Moubray, John, Reliability Centered Maintenance. Butterworth Heinemann. 1991.

This page was left blank on purpose

Use it for notes

Chapter 8

A stepwise approach to the design of a Maintenance Plan

Step 2 : Determining the Consequence of each Failure Mode

We now have a list of all the failure modes, together with a full description of the failure mechanism. It should now be possible to select a maintenance task for the particular failure mode. But, as will become clear later, the task is also dependent on the consequences of the failure. These consequences can be any of the following four categories:

⇒ Operational Consequences

⇒ Non-operational Consequences

⇒ Safety or Environmental Consequences

⇒ Hidden Failure Consequences

Each of these categories has its own, very specific, impact on the choice of applicable maintenance tasks. Thus, before we can get to the step of task selection, we need to decide for each failure mode which category of failure consequences apply. To understand the difference between the above mentioned four categories, we will look at each of them shortly.

As background to our study of the four categories of failure consequences, let us refer back to the strategy tree of chapter 4. Remember that we basically have three choices of strategies: prevention, correction or redesign. This is the choice that we have to make for each failure mode in designing our maintenance plan. And, because we want to save money, we always try to apply prevention and, if that is not the correct option, then apply one of the other two. To decide whether prevention is a viable option we make use of two criteria: *technical feasibility* and *economical feasibility*. We will discuss these in much more depth in the next chapter, but in principle a preventive task is technically feasible if it is successful in decreasing the failure rate. Furthermore, it is economically feasible if the cost of implementing the task is less than the saving it will bring about. With this as background we can now discuss each of the four categories of failure consequences, with a view to understanding the reason for making a distinction between them.

Operational Consequences

This and the next category (non-operational consequences) are the most obvious categories of failure consequences. They are the two categories for which the consequences are primarily of an economic nature.

For a failure mode to have operational consequences, it must affect the production output of the business negatively. It thus causes a production loss, with an accompanying loss in sales and thus profit. Each time that a failure thus occurs, money is lost due to production being lost, as well as due to the cost of repairing the failure.

For a preventive task to be an acceptable strategy it must firstly be technically feasible in preventing a failure mode with operational consequences. That is, it must reduce the risk of failure to a low enough level so that the benefits of the preventive action (less production lost and lower breakdown costs) is worth the cost of implementing it. Secondly, it must also be economically feasible. The added cost due to the implementation of the task must be lower than the benefit in terms of reduction of lost production and cost of failure. We will see in the next chapter that this is a bit of an oversimplification, but it is good enough for now.

If a preventive task is not found that is both technically and economically feasible, the default strategy is to repair the failure mode only after failure (corrective maintenance) with redesign as an option.

Non-Operational Consequences

This category is very similar to the previous one (operational consequences) in that its consequences are also primarily of an economic nature. Its difference lies in the fact that it does not affect the production output of the business negatively. Its negative economic effect is thus limited to the cost incurred in repairing the failure each time that such failure occurs.

For a preventive task to be an acceptable strategy, it must firstly be technically feasible in preventing the failure mode. That is, it must reduce the risk of failure to a low enough level so that the benefits of the preventive action (lower breakdown costs) is worth the cost of implementing it. It must, secondly, be economically feasible - the added cost due to the implementation of the task must be lower than the benefit in terms of reduction of the cost of failure.

If a preventive task is not found that is both technically and economically feasible, the default strategy is to repair the failure mode only after failure (corrective maintenance) with redesign as an option.

Safety or Environmental Consequences

This and the next category (hidden failure consequences) differs completely from the previous two. In both these cases safety and the environment is involved in some or other form - in the case of safety and environmental consequences directly and in the case of hidden failure consequences indirectly. These are the two categories for which economics play a lesser role due to the possible loss of life and permanent environmental damage.

Definition : A failure mode that has safety or environmental consequences has the potential to affect the safety of people or the environment negatively.

For a preventive task to be the acceptable strategy in this category it must reduce the risk of failure totally or to a very (acceptably) low level. If a preventive task is not found that reduces the risk to a low enough level, the default strategy is to redesign, as a compromise in this category is not acceptable.

Hidden Failure Consequences

This is the one category where its name says nothing of the real consequences of failure. The real problem in a failure mode that remains hidden after failure, is not that it is hidden, but that it may cause a multiple failure due to the function not being available. This is especially so in the case of non fail safe safety devices. The safety device may fail without any direct adverse consequences - nobody even knows about the failure, because it is hidden. But when circumstances arise where the safety device should save the day and it is non-operative, then the adverse consequence, that of a so-called multiple failure, arises.

Definition : A failure mode that has hidden consequences has the potential to affect the safety of people or the environment negatively through the occurrence of a multiple (very often catastrophic) failure.

For a preventive task to be the acceptable strategy in this category it must reduce the risk of a multiple failure to an acceptably low level. If a preventive task is not found that reduces the risk to a low enough level, the default strategy is to specify a failure finding task or, if that is not effective, to redesign if a multiple failure can negatively affect safety or the environment.

Determining which failure consequences apply

In the foregoing paragraphs a description was given regarding the effects of the specific failure consequence on the decision concerning the correct maintenance strategy. This, in a certain sense, is to hatch the chick before the egg was produced. But it was done specifically to show where we are heading.

If we have a certain failure mode, we now have to decide under which category of failure consequences will its strategy selection be carried out. Only if we understand the consequence of failure properly can we make the correct choice of maintenance strategy, as we saw above.

The diagram in figure 8.1 is used to select the correct failure consequence for the specific failure mode. It comprises a simple choice diagram based on three questions. The logic is as follows:

⇒ Question 1 : *Is the loss of function due to the occurrence of this failure mode evident to the operations personnel?* In other words, if the item failed according to this specific failure mode, will the failure effects be visible to the operating personnel? They may not know that the function is in a failed state because they are not in a position to sense (see, feel, hear, smell) it, or it may have no external visible signs. If no, then the failure mode has hidden consequences.

⇒ Question 2 : *Does the failure mode cause a loss of function or secondary damage that could have a direct adverse effect on operating safety or the environment?* Is there any possibility that the loss of function could kill or hurt someone or cause damage to the environment or be contrary to some law? If yes, then the failure mode has safety and environmental consequences.

⇒ Question 3 : *Does the failure mode have a direct adverse effect on operational capability?* Will the normal business (production,

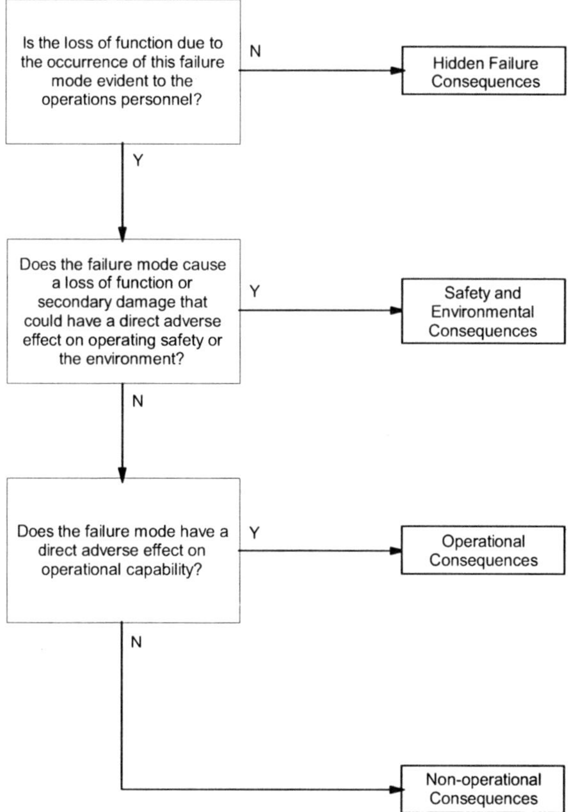

Figure 8.1 : Failure Consequences Decision Diagram

quality, customer service) be affected when a failure occurs according to this failure mode? If yes, then the failure mode has operational consequences. Otherwise (if the answer is no), the failure mode has non-operational consequences.

References

1. Coetzee, J.L., Introduction to Maintenance Engineering, Annual short course, 1994.
2. Nowlan, F.S. and Heap, H., Reliability Centered Maintenance. National Technical Information Service, US Department of Commerce, 1978.
3. Moubray, John, Reliability Centered Maintenance. Butterworth Heinemann. 1991.

This page was left blank on purpose

Use it for notes

Chapter 9

A stepwise approach to the design of a Maintenance Plan

Step 3 : Selecting suitable maintenance tasks

This is where we were heading all the time. We want to know which maintenance tasks can we implement which will increase the availability of equipment such that it causes an effective rise in profit. The analysis up to now was aimed at identifying those failure modes that, if we could eliminate them or reduce their occurrence significantly, will have a marked effect on the bottom line of the organization.

But before we take any decisions regarding the maintenance tasks themselves, we must first have a look at R.C.M.'s standard decision tree for the choice of preventive tasks. This is really the heart of the R.C.M. methodology.

The basis of Reliability Centered Maintenance

The Reliability Centered Maintenance technique is built around the fact that, in most instances, we do not know the failure characteristics of a certain system or component. It thus proposes a basic framework for the evaluation of maintenance tasks that take this fact into account. This framework is shown in figure 9.1. The tasks are evaluated and selected in the order *on-condition* (condition based) task, *scheduled reconditioning* (overhaul) task, *scheduled replacement* task. Thus if any one of the three basic tasks is selected the remainder of the selection process is truncated - if one of these are not selected the answer of the task selection process is *corrective maintenance* (or *no scheduled maintenance* or *replace only on failure* (r.o.o.f.)) - if this is not acceptable *design-out maintenance* is the only alternative left.

The basic premise of the RCM technique is thus to propose a condition based task as the first strategy option. Only if this is not viable will the technique propose either a scheduled reconditioning or

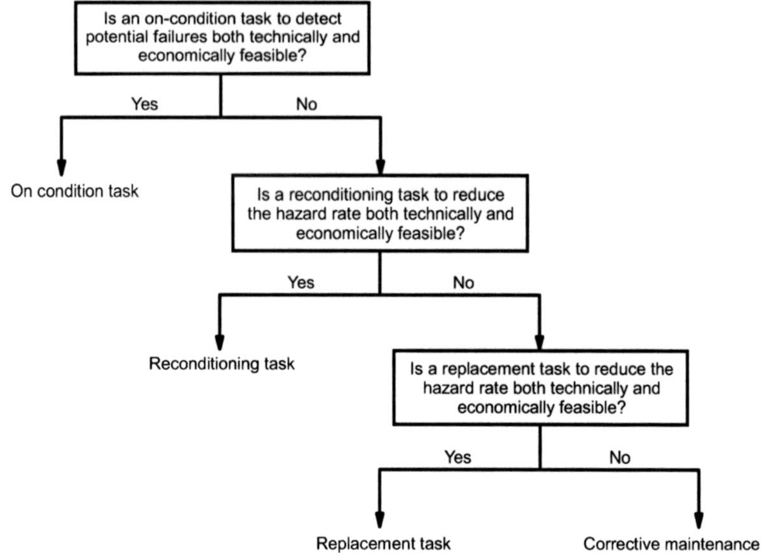

Figure 9.1 : Basic RCM logic

scheduled replacement task. The selection of maintenance task always takes place in the order shown in figure 9.1. It thus ensures that the task with the least risk of doing unnecessary (costly) work is selected in each case.

The preventive task selection process

The preventive task selection phase of RCM analysis involves a systematic study of each failure mode to determine whether one of the maintenance tasks pictured in figure 9.1 will satisfy both the criteria for technical and economical feasibility.

- The first task to be considered for each anticipated failure mode is an on-condition inspection:

  "Is an on-condition task to detect potential failures both technically and economically feasible?"

  If the answers to both aspects (technical and economical feasibility) of this question is yes, an on-condition task is put into the maintenance program for that failure mode. The technical feasibility of an on-condition task frequently requires the expertise of engineering

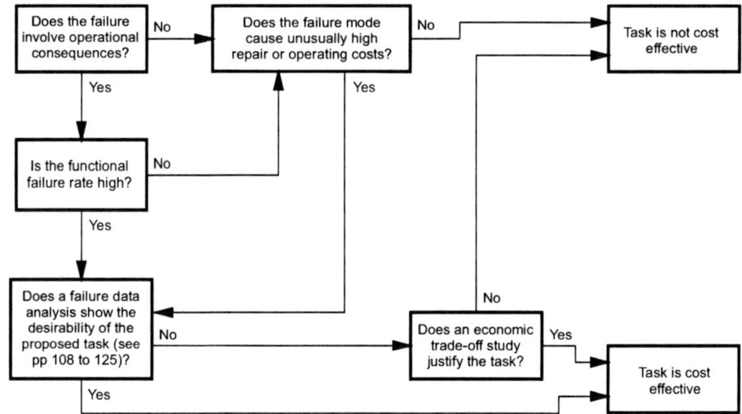

Figure 9.2 : Cost effectiveness Decision Diagram

specialists. The economic feasibility of any task (on-condition and the others that follow) can be analyzed using figure 9.2 (this figure is not used in the case of hidden, safety or environmental consequences).

- If an on-condition task is not applicable, the next choice is a scheduled reconditioning task:

  "*Is a reconditioning task to reduce the hazard rate both technically and economically feasible?*"

  In this case the question of technical as well as economical feasibility requires an analysis of operating data. Thus, unless the age-reliability characteristics of the item are known from prior experience with a similar item exposed to a similar operating environment, the assumption in an initial program is that the item will not benefit from scheduled reconditioning. In the absence of information, the answer to this question is no, and we wait for the necessary information to become available after the equipment goes into service.

- A no answer to the reconditioning task brings us to the question of a scheduled replacement task:

  "*Is a replacement task to avoid failures or reduce the hazard rate both technically and economically feasible?*"

  In an initial maintenance program the only items scheduled for replacement will be those for which the manufacturer has specified safe-life limits.

Technical Feasibility versus Economical Feasibility

Each of the three basic tasks are selected through a question that stipulates that the task must be both technically and economically feasible before selecting it. Technical feasibility refers to the ability of the task to prevent the failure from occurring, while economic feasibility refers to whether the benefit of doing the task is such that it makes it worthwhile to spend the money involved in implementing the task.

Technical feasibility

Technical feasibility depends on the technical characteristics of both the failure mode and the task. The task must be able to prevent the failure mode to some specified level of certainty. This specification differs for the various failure consequences:

- *Hidden failure consequence*: the task must reduce the risk of a multiple failure to an acceptable level. Remember that in the case of a hidden failure the failure itself does not have the negative effect, but if it is not found and repaired it will eventually lead to a multiple failure which may or may not be worth preventing depending on the risk involved. If the hidden failure can lead to a costly or unsafe multiple failure, the risk is high. On the other hand, if the hidden failure will not lead to a multiple failure or the resulting multiple failure is of no consequence then the risk involved is negligible (this is to say that the equipment has been over designed in this area and the specific function can in actual fact be removed). If a suitable task that reduces the risk to an acceptable level is not found then the initial default action is a scheduled failure finding task.
- *Safety or Environmental failure consequence*: the task should reduce the risk of the failure either totally or to a (very low) acceptable level. Where safety or environmental issues are at stake one cannot compromise. If a preventive task that reduces the risk of failure to a low enough level is not found, redesign is compulsory (the default action).
- *Operational and non-operational consequences*: the task should reduce the risk of failure to a low enough level so that the benefits of the preventive action is worth the cost of implementing it. If no suitable preventive task is found, the initial default action is corrective maintenance (no scheduled maintenance).

Scheduled On-condition Tasks

In many cases, the failure effects are so serious that we ideally want to prevent failure from occurring. As use based preventive maintenance is often not technically feasible, we then need to identify failure before it occurs. We call this type of task an *On-condition Preventive Task* (or a *Condition-based Preventive Task*) because the preventive action follows identification of near failure by some Condition Monitoring technique, such as Vibration Analysis or Oil Monitoring. We react to the presence of a known near-failure condition (a Potential Failure). The effectiveness (and thus the technical feasibility) of an On-condition task to prevent failure from occurring depends very much on the following:

- It must be possible to unequivocally identify the potential failure through the condition monitoring or inspection method that was chosen. There should be no doubt in the minds of the condition monitoring expert and the maintenance manager involved that this level of the parameter being monitored constitutes a potential failure.
- Normally when the condition of a component starts deteriorating it first deteriorates fairly slowly. This is true up to a point where the rate of deterioration starts accelerating. When we monitor such a deterioration process, it is important that the lag time between the point where our monitoring establishes that a potential failure exists and the point of actual functional failure is fairly consistent and more than enough to take preventive action (that is to prevent the failure completely or to limit the consequences of failure sufficiently). It is important to note that, unless the monitoring frequency is disproportionately high, the potential failure is sometimes identified a considerable time after the initial point where the potential failure could first be identified.
- The condition monitoring or inspection frequency envisaged must be practically achievable. The time between inspections (condition monitoring) must be sufficiently less than the time interval between the point at which the potential failure becomes evident and the point of functional failure to ensure that the potential failure will be identified in time. If the time between monitoring points is set less than half the lead time to failure (the time interval between the first identifiable indication of the potential failure and the functional failure) one could be fairly sure that the potential failure will certainly be identified in time for preventive action to be taken. In practice it might sometimes be necessary to start monitoring at a

higher frequency once the potential failure has been identified, to accurately predict when functional failure will occur. This is especially so in the case where the lead time to failure spans a long time (sometimes weeks or even months).

Scheduled Reconditioning Tasks

Scheduled Reconditioning (or overhaul) Tasks are of the class Use Based Preventive Maintenance. There are two prerequisites for the technical feasibility of a scheduled reconditioning task:

- It must be possible to restore the sub-system or component to a fairly good condition through reconditioning. The ideal is to the good-as-new condition, but that is not always attainable.
- The hazard function (risk to fail) of the item must increase with age. Only when the hazard increases with age will reconditioning produce an item (sub-system or component) that is less prone to fail. This is illustrated in figure 9.3.

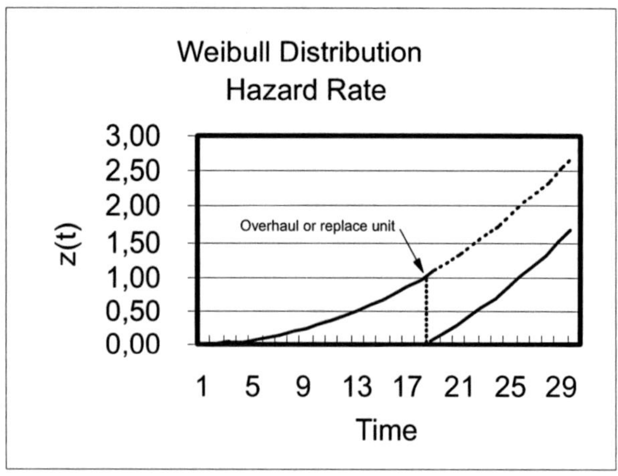

Figure 9.3 : Effect of Use Based Prevention

Scheduled Replacement Tasks

As in the case of scheduled reconditioning tasks, Scheduled Preventive Replacement Tasks are of the class Use Based Preventive Maintenance. As in the previous case such a task will be technically feasible if:

- It is possible to restore the function to a fairly good condition through replacing the sub-system or component . The ideal is to the good-as-new condition, but that is not always attainable.
- The hazard function (risk to fail) of the item is increasing with age. Only when the hazard increases with age will replacement produce an item (sub-system or component) that is less prone to fail. This is illustrated in figure 9.3.

Economical Feasibility

In a certain sense, it is fairly easy to determine whether a certain preventive task is technical viable. Engineers understand the technical side much easier than to decide on the cost effectiveness of the proposed method. Figure 9.2 was given to assist in this process. But life is not always as easy as to simply use a decision diagram such as figure 9.2. In general one can say that for the various failure consequences the following guidelines apply to decide whether a task is economically feasible:

- *Hidden, safety and environmental consequences*: Here technical feasibility plays a much greater role than economical feasibility. The reason for this is that the consequence of failure in this area is in most cases detrimental to the health and life of persons and/or plant. Thus one normally has to find a preventive task that works. But one cannot disregard the cost of the proposed action altogether. In some or other way one has to establish whether the proposed action is the only or least expensive way to solve the problem. This can entail comparing the cost of alternative preventive actions against one another or against the possibility of redesign to solve the problem.
- *Operational consequences*: In the case of operational consequences the standard answer to the problem of whether a preventive task is economically feasible is: If the cost of the preventive task is less than the cost of the operational consequences (in other words the value of production lost) plus the cost of repairing the failure, then the task is economically feasible. As we will see in subsequent paragraphs, this is an overly simplistic view. A more balanced view is that the task is economically feasible if the total cost (cost of downtime plus cost of failures incurred plus cost of prevention) is at a minimum - this will become clear in the following paragraphs.

- *Non-operational consequences*: In this case the answer to the question of economic feasibility is the same as for operational consequences, except that the cost of lost production does not feature (the failure does not affect the operation).

The heading of the present section suggests that there is a play-off between technical feasibility and economical feasibility. This is not really the case. But in many practical situations one has to take a decision based more on the one than on the other. As was previously stated, in the case of hidden, safety and environmental failure modes the technical feasibility often plays a larger role than whether the task is economically feasible. On the other hand, in the case of operational and non-operational consequences, the question of whether the task is economically feasible is of paramount importance. In the end the bottom line is always money related.

Basic Renewal Theory

Traditionally it was assumed that both scheduled reconditioning and scheduled replacement leaves the item in the *good-as-new* condition after the preventive action. A theory called 'Renewal Theory' developed around this premise. In other words, the Renewal Theory is the theory that explains failure situations where use based preventive actions lead to complete restoration. This theory can be approached from different angles using different mathematical theory bases. Often it is approached from the side of statistical distributions. It is generally accepted that failures (where the renewal assumption hold) take place according to some or other distribution. The one that is used most often in maintenance work is the Weibull distribution, named after the author of the distribution. It is a very versatile distribution that can simulate most failure situations found in maintenance practice.

The four reliability functions were defined in chapter 5. They were the Density Function, the Cumulative Distribution Function, the Survival Function and the Hazard Function. More formal definitions are given in section A.1 of appendix A. The descriptions of these functions, as given in chapter 5, with some additional clarifying comments are repeated here.

Failure Density

The failure density gives a picture of the probability of failure of a component over its own life. It thus gives, at any particular point in the life of the component, the probability of failure at exactly that point. It is customary in the maintenance world to use the Weibull distribution to describe a component's failure behavior. A typical Weibull failure density function is shown in figure 9.4.

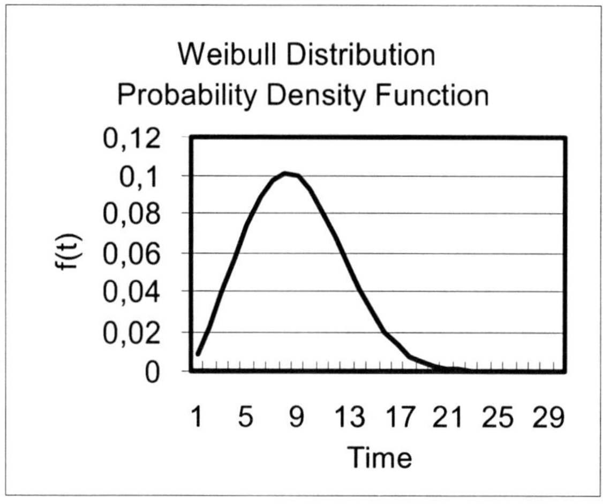

Figure 9.4 : Typical Weibull Failure Density

The use of the density function f(t) is described using the following example: figure 9.4 states that the probability of failure (of the component to which the density function in figure 9.4 applies), at the exact age of 5 time units is in the order of 0,06 or 6 %. The sum of all such probabilities is given by the area under the curve of figure 9.4, which is 1 (or 100%). This is equivalent to stating that the component must eventually fail (in the example above before 23 time units) with 100% certainty. The cumulative probability of failure at say 5 time units is given by the total area under the curve to the left of 5 time units. This (cumulative) quantity is known as the Cumulative Failure Distribution F(t). The density function can be estimated directly from failure data using the discrete definition in appendix A (equation A.1). The use of these discrete definitions to estimate the four reliability functions directly from the underlying failure data is illustrated in the examples given in appendix A.

Cumulative Failure Distribution

By cumulative summation of the probabilities of failure as depicted in the failure density, the Cumulative Failure Distribution results. It thus gives at any point in time of a component's life the probability that the component will have failed before or at that specific age. The Cumulative Failure Distribution always starts at a probability of zero, which is equivalent to stating that a new component will not be in the failed state. It will always eventually have a value of one (or one hundred percent), indicating that the component will eventually fail with one hundred percent certainty. The Cumulative Failure Distribution for the Failure Density derived from figure 9.4 is shown in figure 9.5.

In the same way as we did with the Density Function above, we can read the cumulative probability of failure off the graph in figure

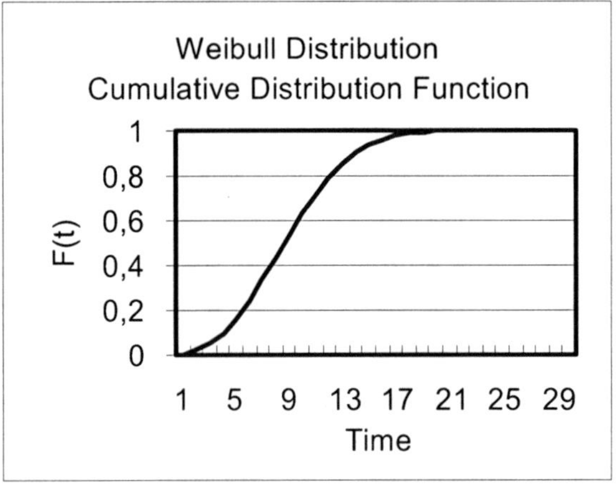

Figure 9.5 : Cumulative Failure Distribution

9.5. We can thus for example say that the probability that the component will fail before or at 9 time units is 0,5 or 50%. The Cumulative Failure Distribution is an extremely handy function to understand the failure characteristics of the component at hand. A very important property of the Cumulative Distribution Function is that 63% of all components fail at or before the expected life of the component (that is the typical life). The Weibull name for the expected life is the characteristic life, which is given by the Weibull scale parameter η. The value of η for the above example is 10. Thus at a life of 10 time units the value of $F(t)$ is 0,63 (or 63%). Thus, in the case of renewal, 63% of components always fail before or at the characteristic life. That is not to say that the component should be replaced or reconditioned before that time, because 37% of components have lives longer than the characteristic life (some of them as high as 21 time units or twice the characteristic life in the above example). The decision regarding when to replace normally involves both the specific failure characteristics (as represented in the graph above) and the economics involved in the situation, as we shall shortly see.

The Cumulative Distribution Function can again be estimated directly from the failure data using the discrete definition of appendix A (equation A.3), as is illustrated in the two examples in that chapter. The complementary function to the Cumulative Distribution Function is known as the Survival Function (or Reliability Function).

Survival Function

The Cumulative Failure Distribution gives the probability of failure before or at a certain age. The difference between that and a value of one hundred percent (in other words, the space above the curve of figure 9.5) gives the probability that the component will survive up to that point. This is a very useful measure, as it gives the percentage of units that will survive up to a specific age. The following figure depicts the Survival Function which is the complement of the Cumulative Distribution Function of figure 9.5.

As was the case with the Cumulative Distribution Function above, we can again read the cumulative probability of survival off the

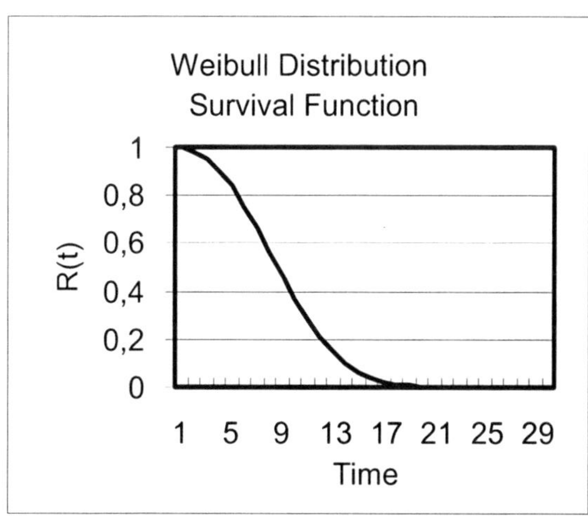

Figure 9.6 : Typical Survival Function

graph in figure 9.6. We can thus say that the probability that the component will survive up to a life of 9 time units is 0,5 or 50%. As with the Cumulative Failure Distribution, the Survival Function is an extremely handy function to understand the failure characteristics of the component at hand. In the case of the Survival Function it will always show that 37% of components survive up the expected life of the component (that is the typical life). Thus at a life of 10 time units the value of R(t) is 0,37 (or 37%). Thus, in the case of renewal, 37% of components survive up to the characteristic life.

The Survival Function can again be estimated directly from the failure data using the discrete definition of appendix A (equation A.5), which method is illustrated in the examples of that chapter. The last reliability function that we will discuss here is known as the Hazard Function and is a combination of the Density Function and the Survival Function as is shown in appendix A.

Hazard Function

The most useful of these four quantitative measures (also called the four reliability functions) is the Hazard Function. It is also called the *conditional probability of failure* or the *momentary probability of failure*. It gives the probability that the component will fail at a certain life, given that it has survived up to that age. It is calculated by dividing the value of the Failure Density at that age by the value of the Survival Function at that age. It is a measure of the risk of failure of the component at that specific age. If the Hazard Function is decreasing with age or constant, there will be no incentive towards Use Based Preventive Maintenance as the risk after such maintenance action will not be lower than before it. In such a case the only preventive strategy available will be that of Condition Based Preventive Maintenance. But, in the case of an increasing Hazard Function (a situation often encountered in components), Use Based Preventive Maintenance will certainly be an option, as that will lower the risk of failure. Whether or not one uses Use Based Preventive Maintenance in such circumstances will depend on the economics of such action and whether Condition Based Preventive Maintenance does not afford a better option. The Hazard Function for the failure situation of figures 9.4 to 9.6 is shown in figure 9.7.

As was stated above, this is certainly the most useful of the four reliability functions. One can read the real hazard (risk) of failure di-

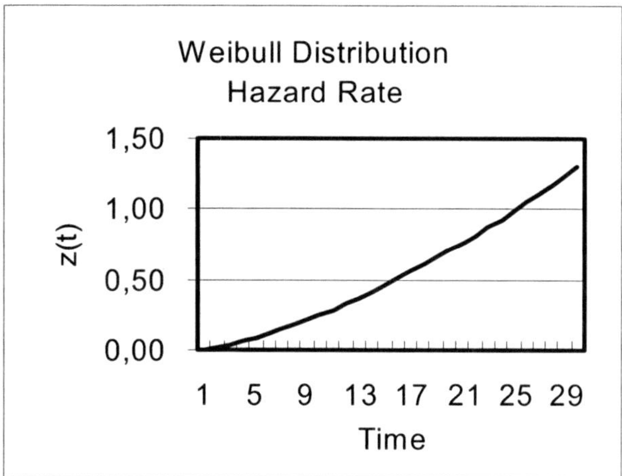

Figure 9.7 : Typical component Hazard Function

rectly from the Hazard Function graph. Thus, in the case depicted in figure 9.7, one can say that, if the component has survived up to age 15 time units, the probability of it failing the next instant is 0,5 or 50%. Likewise the probability of failure of a component that survived up to 25 time units is 1,0 or 100%.

The shape of the Hazard Function is of paramount importance in deciding on the proper maintenance strategy. An increasing hazard function affords the possibility of Use Based Preventive Maintenance, while a decreasing or constant Hazard Function does not.

The Weibull Distribution

The Weibull distribution was the result when Weibull in 1951 suggested an empirical formula that could handle most real life failure data. Most important for our purpose is the fact that it can handle all the more frequently encountered shapes of the hazard function, including those of the Exponential and the Normal distributions. This leads to the possibility of using only this one distribution for most practical failure analysis applications. There are two forms of the Weibull distribution, a two parameter version and a three parameter version. The two parameter Weibull distribution is fully described in appendix A.

The use of the Weibull Distribution is by estimating values for its parameters, such that the distribution closely resemble the distribution of time to failure found in the observed data. This process of parameter estimation is described in section A.4 (equations A.14 and A.15). The two Weibull parameters (two parameter version) is β and η - β is the shape parameter and η the scale parameter. Thus the shape is dependent on β - see figures 9.8 to 9.11 - and the time scale depends on η. η is also called the characteristic life, which is the same as the expected life of the component. Thus the typical life that one would expect from an component like that, based on past history, is η time units. Another important feature of the value η is that 63% of all components of that type will fail before η time units and 37% after that. As we saw in figure 9.3, it is only for values of β larger than 1 (hazard increasing) that we would expect Use Based Preventive Maintenance to be worthwhile. Thus the first important function of failure data analysis is that, only when we know that our data's hazard function is increasing with time, will Use Based Preventive Maintenance be effective. But that still does not say that Use Based Preventive Maintenance will be worth the expenditure. And we also do not know how often should we do the Use Based Preventive Maintenance. These questions will be answered in the next section.

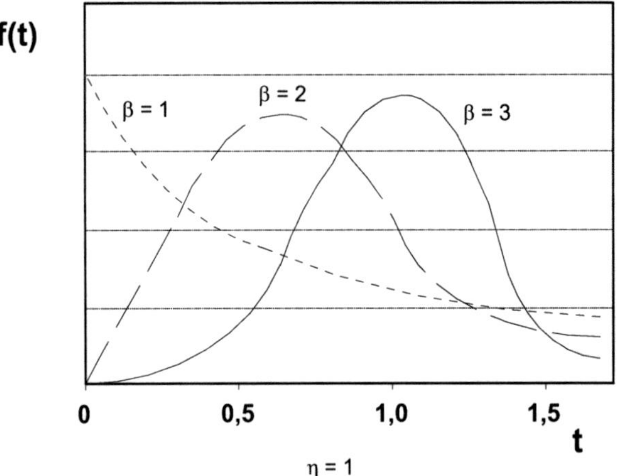

Figure 9.8 : Shapes of the Weibull Density Function

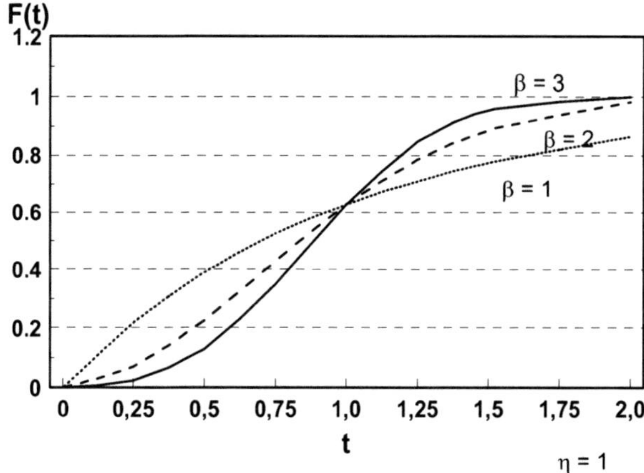

Figure 9.9 : Shapes of the Weibull Cumulative Distribution Function

A note on the three parameter Weibull Distribution is in order here. It has a third parameter γ, which is the minimum life of the component. In some cases a component never fails at a age less than a certain life. This life is the minimum life of the component. The task of the third parameter is to shift the whole distribution to the right by γ time units.

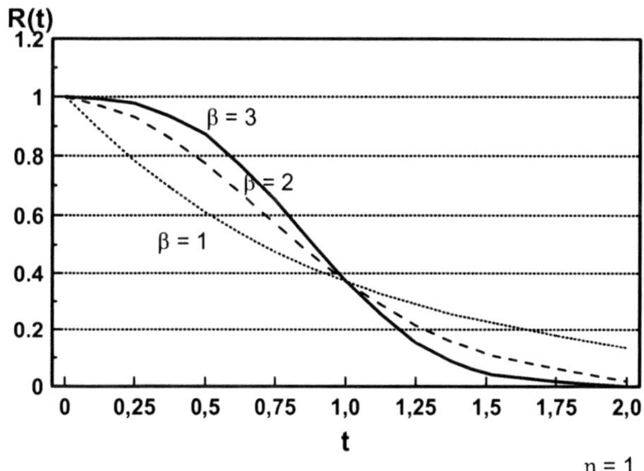

Figure 9.10 : Shapes of the Weibull Survival Function

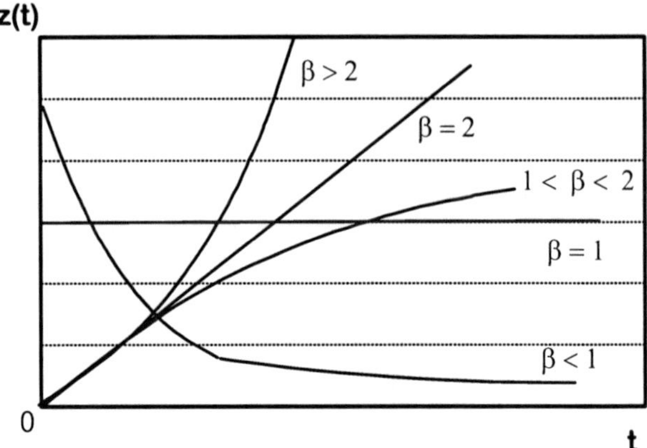

Figure 9.11 : Shapes of the Weibull Hazard Function

Optimizing Use Based Maintenance

As was stated at the end of the previous section, after we successfully fitted a Weibull distribution to our failure data, we are able to decide whether Use Based Preventive Maintenance is an option at all (we can decide on the effectiveness of such a strategy, using figure 9.3 as basis). But we still do not know whether the use of such strategy is worthwhile. First of all, for it to be worthwhile, the cost of failure repair must be higher than that of preventive action.

The Cost of Failure versus the Cost of Prevention

Earlier in this chapter we saw that technical feasibility plays a much greater role than economy when dealing with failure modes that are hidden or have safety or environmental consequences. But in the case of failures with operational or non-operational consequences the economy plays a major role. When deciding whether to make use of Use Based Prevention as well as for the optimizing algorithms of this section, we will make use of the cost of prevention, which is denoted C_p and the cost of repair after failure C_f.

Non-operational Consequences

When we deal with failure modes with non-operational consequences, we are not interested in losses suffered due to downtime (the downtime has no operational consequences). Thus we will define our two cost quantities by:

C_f = Cost of spare part(s) for failure repair + Cost of labor for failure repair

C_p = Cost of spare part(s) for preventive action + Cost of labor for preventive action

Operational Consequences

If the failure of the component affects the output of the unit (operational consequence) then the money value of lost production must be taken into account. The two cost quantities will then become:

C_f = Cost of spare part(s) for failure repair + Cost of labor for failure repair + Value of lost production while doing failure repair

C_p = Cost of spare part(s) for preventive action + Cost of labor for preventive action + Value of lost production while taking preventive action

In many cases the preventive action is taken during an existing maintenance shift, in which case no production will be lost due to the preventive action.

Use Based Optimization

The mathematical models on pages 412 and 414 are profit/cost based optimization models for optimizing Use Based Preventive Maintenance. These models are utilized in the case of operational and non-operational consequences. They make use of the two quantities C_p and C_f to find the value of t_p (the time between instances of Use Based Prevention) which gives the lowest cost per time unit. The difference between these two models is that the first do not take into account the time taken for respectively the failure and preventive actions, while the second model takes that into account. In most cases the two models do not give significantly different answers, but in cases where the time taken for failure repair differs significantly from that of preventive action or where the time taken for repair is a significant proportion of the Mean Time Between Failures the second model will always give better answers. The typical output from these models is a graph of the cost per unit time against the time between preventive actions. Such a graph is shown in figure 9.12.

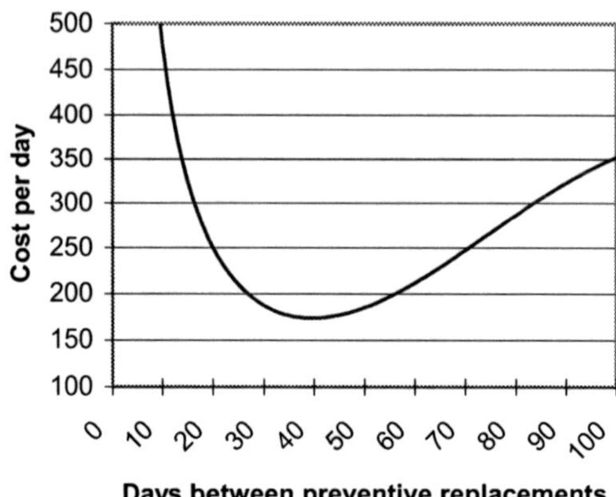

Figure 9.12 : Typical cost curve

From the above curve it can be seen that the optimum level of cost occurs at 40 days at a cost of R 173,58 per day. But, apart from the model giving us the optimum frequency at which prevention should take place, the graph supplies us with the following additional information:

- The slope of the cost graph on both sides of the optimum determines whether we will stick to the optimum value rigorously. In the example above, if we keep our preventive frequency between 32 days and 48 days we will not have a cost increase of more than 5 % above the optimum. In this specific case there already exists a weekly maintenance shift which will be utilized for the preventive replacement of the bearing. This has the effect that the time between replacements should be either 35 or 42 days. The cost at 35 days is R 176,34 per day and that at 42 days R 174,26 per day. Thus 42 days will be the preferred frequency, but if necessary replacement can be advanced to 35 days without breaching the 5% added cost barrier.

- The value of the cost graph on the furthest right hand extreme gives the cost per time unit when no preventive replacements take place (repair only on failure). In our example case this value is R 391,61 at 200 days (which is not shown on the graph). This is 126% above the optimum cost. Thus in this case we can see that it is of paramount importance that we do preventive replacements. But there are cases where the sensitivity of the graph to the right is so low that we will decide on a corrective maintenance strategy.

The third model (page 415) is a model that optimizes availability of the component by minimizing the downtime per unit time. This gives a similar graph to figure 9.12, but in availability terms. This model is used in the case of hidden failure modes and safety and environmental consequences where cost or profit is not the driving motive, but rather the availability of the function. Figure 9.13 shows an example of the result of using this model. As in the case of the cost model, the sensitivity of the graph plays a large role in deciding how strictly one will keep to the optimum preventive frequency, if at all.

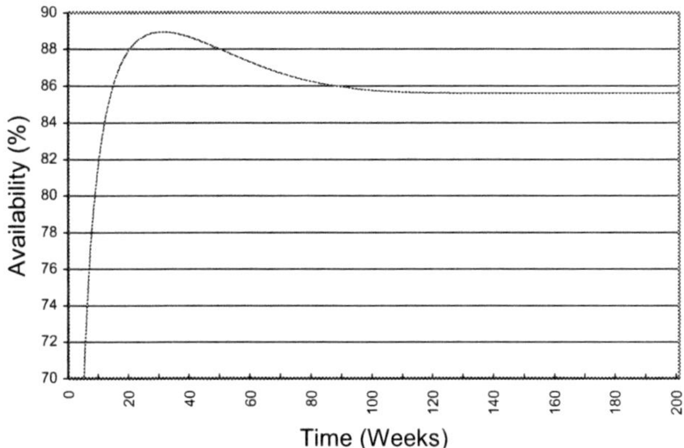

Figure 9.13 : Sample availability graph

The fourth Use Based Preventive Maintenance model is used in the case of block replacement. It is described fully on page 416. The specific block replacement strategy is used where a machine or system has more than one of the same component, working in similar circumstances. The strategy is to replace any one of the components when it fails, but to replace the total block of components at a fixed frequency, regardless of any failure replacements between block replacements. A simplifying assumption is made in developing the block strategy, namely that very few failures will take place between block replacements. A sample cost graph for block replacement is shown in figure 9.14. The low tail to the right has to be disregarded as the simplifying assumption is not valid in that area.

Optimizing Condition Based Maintenance

The second model on page 416 and the one on page 417 describe inspection models. These are used for optimizing Condition

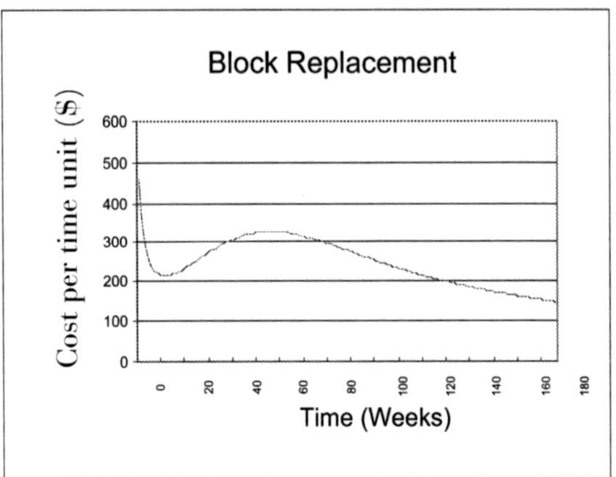

Figure 9.14 : Block Replacement cost graph

Based Preventive Maintenance frequencies in much the same way that Use Based Preventive Maintenance frequencies are optimized by the first 4 models. The only difference is that, instead of using the survival function based on failure history to estimate the division between preventive replacements and failure replacements, the efficiency of the inspections to 'catch' failures before they happen is used. This efficiency η_c is expressed as a function of the time between inspections. Again there are two models - one optimizing cost and the other availability, with outputs similar to that of figures 9.12 and 9.13.

The catch in using inspection models is that the relationship between the effectiveness of inspections and the time between inspections must be known. This is obtained in the following way: Calculate your effectiveness of inspection based on your historically used inspection frequency. Then modify the frequency based on your feel for the situation. After another year you will (by again calculating the effectiveness of inspection for that year) have a second point on the graph of effectiveness of inspection against time between inspections. By regression you can now fit a straight line through these two points. The resulting function can then be used in the inspection models to produce an optimized solution. After another year another point can be added to the graph and a new function (probably not a straight line) fitted through the three points. This new line will produce a still better optimized (probably fairly good by this time) inspection frequency. In this way you can produce an optimized inspection frequency in a few year's time.

We saw earlier in this chapter how use can be made of failure data at the component level to make and optimize maintenance strategy using **Renewal Theory**. In the process of using that theory, we were assuming that repair led to the ***as-good-as-new*** condition. But, as we know, things are not always as easy as using the same theory for all cases. On the systems (total machine) level we often sit with *reliability degradation* over time. We normally do not renew a system to the as-good-as-new condition when we repair it. We rather do ***minimal repair***, which says that we just replace or repair the component(s) that failed. That is, we repair it to the ***bad-as-old*** condition (the same condition it was in before the breakdown. For this case we have another theory which we can use to get more understanding of the systems situation. This theory is called **Repairable Systems Theory**. We can even use this theory to take decisions regarding the optimal replacement times of whole systems.

Basic Repairable Systems Theory

In **Repairable Systems Theory** we make use of regression to model the long term life trend of a system. A system is made up of many components, each with its own failure characteristics which can be modeled using **Renewal Theory**. But the system itself (that is, if it degenerates over time) must be modeled using regression techniques. If the system do not degenerate over time we can of course make use of **Renewal Theory** to model the failures of the system. Such stable systems are indeed rare and thus we need another theory to cope with systems. We can model two quantities over the long term life of a system: the times between failures and the failure rate. It is customary to use the failure rate in the modeling of systems failure trends. One of the classes of models that have emerged for this purpose is the **Non-Homogeneous Poisson Process (N.H.P.P.)** models. Two formats of the *NHPP* models are presented in appendix B, together with general mathematical regression models, which can be utilized to model the life trend, with the purpose of forecasting the average life between breakdowns for the system.

The time in systems modeling are denoted by T, the long term arrival times to failure, whereas we used short term time t, the inter-arrival times, in the Renewal Theory. The failure rate is denoted by $\rho(T)$.

Non-Homogeneous Poisson Process Models

Two formats of the NHPP models are described in appendix B: the shape $\rho_1(T)$, which is upwards concave, and the shape $\rho_2(T)$ which is convex. Both of them have well developed theory for the expected number of failures in a certain interval, the probability of survival over an interval and the mean time between failures. Both models have two parameters, which can be estimated fairly easily using the techniques of section B.2.

Cost modeling for NHPP models

As is the case with renewal, we have cost modeling tools in Repairable Systems theory as well. In this case the objective is to determine the economical life of the system, working from the failure trend (NHPP model) of the system, the average cost of minimal repair C_f (based on past history) and the cost of total systems replacement C_p. The theory of such cost models is shown in section B.3. An example of such a cost graph is shown in figure 9.15.

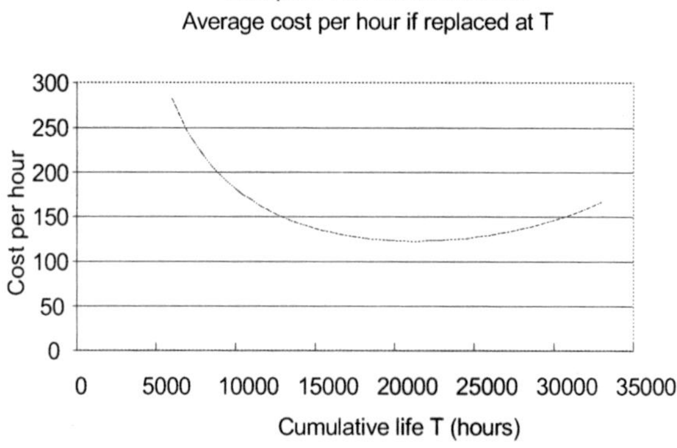

Figure 9.15 : Example system replacement cost graph

According to figure 9.15 the best age for system replacement is at 21293 hours of operation. At this age the minimum average life operating cost of 123,00 Australian Dollar/hour (this exercise was done for a paper delivered in Australia) is achieved. To evaluate this replacement age properly, we again have to study the graph to assess the importance of replacing the system at exactly that age (in other words, we have to evaluate the sensitivity of the graph).

Other benefits of the repairable systems models are that they can accurately model the expected number of failures in a given (future) interval, the expected reliability in such interval, as well as the expected future life between failures of systems.

General Mathematical Models

Chapter 14 (page 256 to 267) gives the procedure for fitting any of five general mathematical models to a set of data points). These can also be used to model a system's life trend:

⇒ Linear Curve

⇒ Quadratic Curve

⇒ Hyperbolic Curve

⇒ Exponential Curve

⇒ Geometric Curve

A test (the r-test) for determining the goodness of fit of such curves is also included. These curves (as well as the NHPP curves) can be used to model the long term trend and to forecast the expected Mean Time Between Failures over the next few failure cycles. Table 14.8 also gives a 95% confidence interval for the forecasting process, which is the statistical width of the distribution within which the individual times to failure over the next few failure cycles will lie, but with their average at the forecast value.

Integrated Failure Data Analysis

We have now covered both the **Renewal Theory** and the **Repairable Systems Theory** in some detail. We now have to find out when to use which theory. This is described fully in appendix C. We will give a short description of the process here, without trying to repeat the detailed work of appendix C.

In **Renewal Theory** we studied the case where the assumption was made that repair (or overhaul) resulted in the **as-good-as-new** situation. In **Repairable Systems Theory**, on the other hand, we studied the case where reliability degradation takes place over time and repair is not to the as good as new situation. This is called the as **bad-**

as-old or **minimal repair** situation. In the first case (renewal) the component (or system) was repaired (or overhauled) to the as-good-as-new condition. In the second case (repairable systems) the system (or component) is minimally repaired (or overhauled) at failure to the as-bad-as-old condition. In this last case repair (or overhaul) results in bringing the system (or component) back to the condition it was in just before failure. This does not imply that it will immediately fail again, but that it was not restored to the original (new) condition.

Each of these theories, on its own, presents a viable alternative for maintenance failure data analysis. The problem now is to decide which one of these theories to use when. Of course, one could decide (assume) that one or the other theory is the most viable one, but this will not necessarily lead to a valid solution. The better way is to use the data itself to lead one in the analysis process. This will now be discussed in some detail in the following paragraphs.

The difference between data with or without a trend

So what is the difference between data with and without a long term trend? Think of your own salary: if your salary has been increasing yearly (including inflation correction), you cannot make any detailed analysis of your income situation over a few years without at least making some corrections for inflation, etc. Why is that? The reason is that you cannot compare apples with pears. You have to compare apples and apples. There was a trend over the years which you cannot ignore when doing your analysis. The same holds for failure data. If the system (or component), for which you are doing the analysis, is experiencing reliability growth (lives between failures are getting longer) or reliability degradation (lives are getting shorter), then the individual lives cannot be thrown into the same hat (distribution) for analysis. That is, we cannot use *renewal theory* in such case; we are then forced to make use of *repairable systems theory*.

But how do we know when we have such a trend? We know it through the use of a trend test. The trend test proposed on page 430 is the Laplace (1773) trend test, which have over and over been proven to be one of the best tests for trend in failure work. The Laplace quantity, when calculated for a failure data set without trend, will produce a value with an average of 0 and a standard deviation of 1. That is, we will conservatively conclude that:

⇒ If the value of L lies between -1 and +1, the data set has no inherent trend and the renewal theory can be used for analysis.

⇒ If the value is smaller than -2, the data set shows a definite inclination towards reliability growth and the repairable systems modeling can be used for trend analysis (although our cost model for system replacement only holds for the reliability degradation case).

⇒ If the value is larger than +2, the data set shows a definite inclination towards reliability degradation and the repairable systems theory can be used for analysis.

⇒ If the value is between -1 and -2 or between +1 and +2, we are in a gray area where, statistically speaking, both the renewal theory and the repairable systems theory can be used.

The decision process (Asher & Feingold) for deciding which theory to use is shown in figure 9.16.

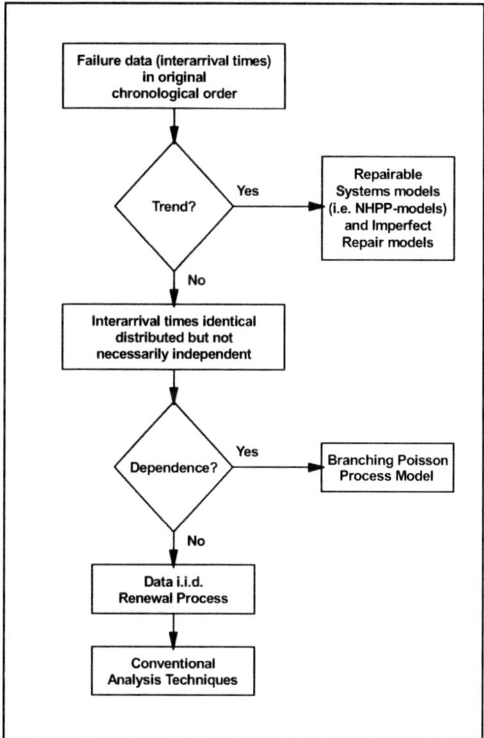

Figure 9.16 : Data Analysis Framework

References

1. Ascher, H. and Feingold, H., Repairable Systems Reliability. Marcel Dekker, 1984.
2. Coetzee, J.L., Introduction to Maintenance Engineering. Annual short course, 1994.
3. Coetzee, J.L., The analysis of failure data with a long term trend. Masters Thesis, University of Pretoria. 1995.
4. Coetzee, J.L., Reliability Degradation and the Equipment Replacement Problem. ICOMS-96, Melbourne, Australia, 1996.
5. Coetzee, J.L., Maintenance Strategy Setting - a dangerous affair. Maintenance in Mining Conference, Johannesburg, 1996.
6. Coetzee, J.L., The role of NHPP models in the practical analysis of maintenance failure data. Reliability Engineering and System Safety **56**, 1997.
7. Jardine, A.K.S., Maintenance, Replacement and Reliability. Pitman, 1979.
8. Nowlan, F.S. and Heap, H., Reliability Centered Maintenance. National Technical Information Service, US Department of Commerce, 1978.
9. Moubray, John, Reliability Centered Maintenance. Butterworth Heinemann. 1991.

Maintenance Management

This page was left blank on purpose

Use it for notes

Chapter 10

The Annual Planning Process

Introduction

We have introduced the Maintenance Cycle, as a means to understanding the business of maintenance, in the first chapter. We have also shown that the maintenance cycle consists of a managerial sub-cycle (outer cycle) and an operational sub-cycle (inner cycle). Our aim is now to develop the outer cycle over this and the next two chapters. This chapter will concentrate on the three blocks *Maintenance Policy*, *Objective Setting* and *Management Planning*. Chapter 11 will then look at *Maintenance Performance Measurement*, while Chapter 12 will develop the concept of *Maintenance Auditing*.

The first three blocks of the outer (managerial) sub-cycle of the Maintenance Cycle can together be named *The Annual Planning Process*, which is the heading of this chapter. We will now develop this process in some detail. We will *first* look at the question of **Maintenance Policy** making from three different angles. *Thereafter* we will look at **Maintenance Objectives** and *lastly* will investigate the "planning" aspects of the Annual Planning Process, under the heading *Setting up an Annual Plan*.

Maintenance Policy and Strategies

One of the problems often encountered when using the terms *Maintenance Policy* and *Maintenance Strategies*, is that these terms are understood wrongly. In general management theory, the term Strategy is often used for the wide and somewhat general business "philosophy" being followed by the organization. Policies would then be those more specific ways of conducting the business within the wider scope of the business strategy. In the technical world of *Maintenance Engineering* (which is to a large extent inherited from the worlds of Reliability Engineering and Statistics), these terms have come to be used differently.

In the maintenance world, the term *Policy* is the one that describes the maintenance department's wider "management philosophies" regarding the way in which the maintenance business is conducted within the organization. As such, the *Maintenance Policy* will, in wide terms describe the direction of the maintenance department within the organization, so as to fulfill its role as good as is possible under its own circumstances. On the other hand, the maintenance department should set up a maintenance *strategy* for every important facility or machine that should be maintained. Such a strategy will often entail that major parts (the critical few that, if maintained correctly, will contribute most to the success of the maintenance action) of the facility or machine be identified and a strategy set up for each part. The strategy for the total machine will then be the sum of the strategies of its constituent parts. This then results in a maintenance plan for the facility or machine, which is then given through to the Maintenance Administration function to be scheduled for execution by the maintenance work force. This is typically done using a technique, such as Reliability Centered Maintenance, which is based on both the reliability characteristics of the unit and the financial realities involved. But, all this (maintenance strategy setting) takes place in the inner (operational) sub-cycle of the Maintenance Cycle. We will thus not be addressing the whole question of strategy-forming at all, but it was mentioned to get the difference between the *Maintenance Policy* for the organization and the various *Strategies* for the facilities/machines being maintained clear.

The Oxford Dictionary of Current English describes the word "policy" as having the meaning of (a) "course of action adopted by a government, business, individual, etc." On the other hand, the description given opposite the word "strategy" is "long term plan or policy", while the word could also imply (the) "art of war" or (the) "art of moving troops, ships, aircraft, etc. into favorable positions". We can thus see that both uses of the terms can be allowed under these definitions, although the author believes that the terms are used more correctly in the maintenance world.

And of course, no one of these different uses of the terms are inherently the "correct" ones - what should be correct is our ways of interpreting the words, so that when we encounter them in a certain context, we understand the message correctly.

Setting up and maintaining a Maintenance Policy

In the previous paragraph we, hopefully, came to the conclusion that the Maintenance Policy describes, in broad terms, the direction in which the Maintenance Management Team wants to steer the maintenance organization. And, as the maintenance organization's functioning is described by the Maintenance Cycle, it follows that the policy document should, in a sense, 'design' the own Maintenance Cycle. It should thus address every block (element) on the Maintenance Cycle Diagram and state the company's stand on these issues.

The policy document is typically drawn up, or more typically, annually revised by the maintenance management team, using the Maintenance Cycle as guideline. At this point, the annual maintenance audit results should be available to guide the team through the process. It might be worthwhile to make use of a facilitator of this process, but the accent must be on ownership of the eventual end product. If such a person is thus used, it should just be as a catalyst to get the best possible end result, but not with the idea of shunning the responsibility for hard and fundamental thinking regarding the own business.

The typical issues that should be addressed in the maintenance policy document will now be addressed one by one. In each case reference will be made to the example policy document in appendix E.

General Philosophy

The general philosophy ought to be written as introduction to make clear why the company take the specific stand on the various issues. This could include statements on the key objective of the maintenance function in the company, the vision and mission of the maintenance team, as well as statements regarding the relationships of the maintenance organization with other functions in the business. The introduction part of the example policy document in appendix E addresses this issue:

> *"The effective use and maintenance of a company's assets has a significant effect on the general level of productivity. The cost of maintenance at XYZ constitutes a large portion of the total operational cost. It is thus necessary to formulate a purposeful maintenance policy to direct the Maintenance Department towards optimal results. In this venture the XYZ Mission, and the quality principles are thoroughly taken into account."*

Key Objective

The key (or main) objective of any organization is defined as the all-absorbing goal that the organization wants to achieve under all circumstances. The features of the key objective is the following:

- There can only be one key objective for the maintenance organization
- The key objective will never change, will never be opposed and will apply under all circumstances.
- The success or failure of the maintenance organization will be based on the achievement or not of this objective.
- This objective will be the same under different managements (though it might be worded differently) and thus serves as the spine of continuity of the maintenance organization.

This objective will probably be related well to the generalized objective of maintenance, as defined in chapter 1: *"The objective of the maintenance function is to support the production process with adequate levels of availability, reliability, operability and safety at acceptable levels of cost."*

In the example policy document included as appendix E, the key objective was set in the "vision" and "mission" parts of the document. A mission statement is really nothing else than the key objective as defined above, but in some circles it sounds nicer to call your key objective a "mission statement". The vision of an organization is some statement of where they would like to be some time in the future. The implication is that they are not there yet. In this sense, the vision is subordinate to the key objective (or mission). If you do not achieve your key objective, you are "dead". But if you do not achieve your vision, you may not be as well off as you would have liked to be, but you will not be "dead". The key objective stated in the "mission" statement of the example of appendix E reads:

> *"The mission of the maintenance team is to ensure optimum levels of availability, reliability and operability of equipment through effective maintenance practices, continuous improvement and a safe working environment, so as to meet the demands of our clients."*

This is then qualified further by the following aims:

⇒ *To support our production and other colleagues in an efficient and professional manner in the achievement of their objectives.*

⇒ *To ensure that all assets operate at the required performance and availability levels for their planned economic lives.*

⇒ *To act to increase the reliability and performance of assets through a program of continuous improvement.*

⇒ *To manage human resources in such a way that it maximizes added value to both the individual and XYZ.*

⇒ *To create and maintain safe work practices and a safe work environment and to preserve our environment.*

Procedure for the development of specific objectives

The policy document on its own, without any planning to achieve the broad policy outlines, will just be a nice, but very dead, document. After the policy document has been developed, it is necessary to go through an objective setting process as is depicted by the "objectives setting" block of the Maintenance Cycle. The exact way in which this objectives setting process should take place, should be spelt out in the policy document. This ought to include the setting of the meeting(s) during which the overall objectives setting process will take place, the timing of these meetings and the way in which objectives will be developed.

Management Planning

The next process that must be defined in the policy document is that of management planning. This process is typically started at the end of the objectives setting exercise. This is normally done by the maintenance chief asking his people to, with the new (updated) policy and objectives in mind, start the annual planning and budgeting process. The specific responsibility of maintenance management in this regard at all levels includes:

- The maintenance organization - what type of organizational structure is used and why. How and when this is changed.
- Manpower - strengths and types.
- Resources - what and how many (tools, materials, etc.).
- Facility improvement plans.
- How maintenance will be financed (running budget, special classes of accounts, standard tariffs, etc.).
- The budget itself, with all its different categories.

Maintenance audits

The policy document should describe in some detail what auditing strategy is to be followed, who should do such audits and when the audits will be done. Refer to chapter 12 on detailed information regarding audits. Specific issues that should be addressed include:

- How frequently should audits be performed.
- What audit approach will be followed.
- What should the content of such audits be. A specific issue that should be addressed regards the question of whether only a hard audit (inspection of the plant) will be done or a soft audit (the inspection of the maintenance system(s)) as well. Refer to chapter 12 for more detail.

Maintenance performance measurement

The whole issue of regular (monthly) performance measurement should be addressed as well. See the approach of the sample policy document in appendix E for one way of approaching this. More detail can be found by studying chapter 11, which develops the whole area of performance measurement in great detail. In principle, the following issues need to be addressed:

- What should be measured?
- How is it to be interpreted?
- How are the various measures combined in a single meaningful measure?
- What is the management impact of the results of such measurement going to be?

Maintenance strategy development

As was mentioned earlier, strategies are developed per facility or machine to be maintained. The typical methodology used for this purpose is that of Reliability Centered Maintenance, combined with statistical failure analysis to understand the failure modes involved well enough to be able to develop strategies that will lead to a high positive impact on the profit of the company. This part of the policy should clearly state which approach should be taken in developing a maintenance plan, as well as when, by whom and by what method(s), such a plan will be updated.

An example of such a policy description is given in the sample policy document in appendix E:

"Formal maintenance plans should be developed for all primary production equipment. The responsible engineer is the driver of the development process. Each such responsible engineer must compile an action plan for all his/her primary production equipment with goal dates for completing the maintenance plans. Following approval of this plan at the monthly Engineering Management Meeting, the responsible engineer will report back on a monthly basis regarding the status of the development of maintenance plans.

The basis for the development of maintenance plans is the Reliability Centered Maintenance (RCM) technique. The plans are developed by a team consisting of a facilitator (typically the Planning Engineer can be used for this by arrangement), chief foreman or foreman, production chief foreman or foreman, an artisan and an operator. The main requirement for the people used in this team is that they should be the most knowledgeable and experienced people regarding the operation and maintenance of the specific machine. The document attached as Appendix A gives an overview of the maintenance strategies typically used by XYZ for use in this process. Where possible the strategies developed will be the result of a proper failure data analysis using the available failure history. The resulting RCM study and maintenance plans must be audited and approved by the responsible engineer.

The resultant maintenance plan for a specific equipment type will consist of the following documents, neatly bound into a book that are available for reference purposes:

A copy of the complete RCM analysis.

Maintenance tasks that should be scheduled for performance at predefined intervals. These should list all action steps that should be performed, together with proper guidelines, lists of probable materials needed, any special equipment/tools needed and precautionary measures that should be taken.

A forecast of the manpower needed in the different trades for the execution of the plan."

The maintenance operations modus operandi

The maintenance operational function is of course, in a certain sense, the heart of the maintenance action. You could have the best possible policies, plans and strategies, but can still fail due to misapplication of the manpower of the department. This is also one of the areas where a lot of the good ideas concerning maintenance fall flat. It is thus very important that a well thought through policy regarding the operational part of the maintenance cycle be added to the policy document. The audit instrument in chapter 12 can be used as a checklist for setting up this part of the policy document. Typical issues that should be addressed in this part of the policy document includes:

- Training of personnel
- The administration task (see the sample policy document in appendix E for an example).
- Supervisory standards
- Facility standards
- Safety standards

Maintenance Systems

No maintenance organization of our day can succeed without proper and successful application of computerized maintenance operational and management information systems. Because this is so, the policy document should be very specific regarding the thoughts of the management team for the successful application of maintenance systems. The systems audit category in chapter 12 can be used for this purpose.

Use of management information

The maintenance managers of our generation has access to a wealth of management information. The problem is that most of it is not used properly due to one or both of the following two reason. *Firstly* there is a laisez faire maintenance management climate in most of our industrial organizations. This has taken on distressing dimensions. *Secondly*, a large proportion of maintenance managers are not properly trained to really use the information to the benefit of the organization. This issue must surely be addressed in the policy document with the view to rid the organization of gross incompetence. The management processes and organizational climate categories of the audit instrument presented in chapter 12 can be used as a checklist for this purpose.

General issues

Being a policy document, one can expect that quite a number of general issues, which are of importance at any specific point in time, can and should also be addressed. Examples of such issues include, without being exhaustive, items such as the training of personnel, modification of plant, technological improvement, equipment replacement and statutory requirements.

Maintenance procedures as a part of the maintenance policy

The maintenance policy is a necessary and worthwhile document in a few ways. *Firstly*, the process that the maintenance management team must go through to decide on the policies for the various areas covered in such a document forces them to think fundamentally about the difficulties in making a success of their maintenance responsibility. They have to find solutions for these difficulties to make a success of their charge. *Secondly*, if handled correctly by the maintenance chief, the documentation of their discussions forces the team to commit themselves to the end result. In a certain sense, the process of developing the policy then serves as a team building exercise, which should promote group cohesion and team work. *Thirdly*, it communicates to the maintenance organization the thoughts of the management team, thus forming a type of backbone in the execution of the maintenance task.

But, as could be expected, the policy document is not everything. It cannot be, because it is a limited document with a limited scope. Its purpose is to guide and to clarify, not to prescribe in detail. Thus something added is needed to provide in the need for exact direction in the execution of the different tasks which need to be coordinated to achieve success. This 'something' is provided through detailed procedures (documents spelling out in detail how a specific task area should be done). Therefore, it is good to keep note of the different areas that will need detailed procedures, while in the process of producing the policy document. These procedures can be developed by dividing the task of writing the different procedures between the members of the management team.

These procedures really form a part of the wider 'maintenance policy'. They are not 'policy' as far as that term having the meaning of a broad guiding principle. But they are policy in the sense that they really complete the process of ensuring that the job is done in such a way that the vision of the maintenance management team in creating the policy will prevail. And it is in this sense that we can regard them as being a part of the maintenance policy. It would for example be possible (and it will make sense) to bind the policy, together with all the procedures flowing from it, into one document named 'the maintenance policy', which then in total contains all policy guidelines towards achieving success.

The objectives of maintenance (also see p 23)

Before looking at the process of maintenance objectives setting, one should be familiar with the general objectives of the maintenance function in the typical organization. The overall objective of the maintenance function can be formulated as follows:

> *"The objective of the maintenance function is to support the production process with adequate levels of availability, reliability, operability and safety at an acceptable cost."*

This objective consists of five sub-objectives. These are:

1. Availability of equipment - it is the task of maintenance to provide at least an acceptable level of availability to production (sufficient to support the production plan). It should be the objective of maintenance management to provide maximum economically viable levels of availability.
2. Reliability of equipment - high availability without the accompanying level of reliability (i.e. long continuous production runs) will not produce the required result. Repeated short production disturbances has just as detrimental an effect as low availability levels.
3. Operability of equipment - while high availability and reliability of equipment are of prime importance, it must be supported by adequate levels of operability. Operability is defined as the machine's ability to sustain adequate (design) production rates.
4. Safety of equipment - the lives of people cannot be measured in terms of money. It has always been one of the more important objectives of the maintenance function to ensure that equipment are safe. And, as unsafe conditions lead to catastrophic failures and severe damage, this can directly impact on the availability of plant

as well, leading to direct losses being incurred.

5. Cost - any maintenance action should only be carried out if its cost implications are acceptable. Thus all maintenance policies, strategies, objectives and plans should have as a basis the optimization of cost (with the accent on long term costs).

Maintenance goal setting

The meetings for objective setting can, to a large extent, coincide with those for developing (or revising) the policy document itself. Thus one will not need additional meetings of the top management team, but the two processes can smoothly merge, but with two very distinct end results. The policy document should very specifically be complete before progressing into the process of the development of objectives.

A good way of handling the timing of the whole of the annual process, is to develop an annual planning wheel, as was done in the example presented in appendix A. This will very likely ensure that the annual process will be scheduled correctly in future, especially if this is handed over routinely to the administrative staff doing the scheduling of the annual calendar.

The objectives should be developed by first doing an analysis of how well the maintenance organization is already performing in terms of the management team's direction as set out in the policy document. A good way of doing this is to, while the team's minds are still fresh regarding the content of the policy document (in other words, just after the annual review of the policy), do a SWOT (Strengths, Weaknesses, Opportunities and Threats) analysis. By doing this, all the organization's strong and weak points with regard to their future vision, as well as the opportunities and threats in their environment will be laid bare. The results of the maintenance audit, that was done earlier, should also be reviewed again at this time. After this, it should be no more than a formality to set the objectives for the year ahead. Of course, in line with good management practice, the objectives should be very specific in terms of both the end results that must be achieved and the dates for achieving such results.

Setting up an Annual Plan

The process of setting up an annual plan is typically started at the end of the objectives setting exercise. This is normally done by the maintenance chief asking his people to, with the new (updated) policy and objectives in mind, start the annual planning and budgeting process. The specific responsibility of maintenance management in this regard at all levels includes:

- The maintenance organization - what type of organizational structure is used and why. How and when this is changed.
- Manpower - strengths and types.
- Resources - what and how many (tools, materials, etc.).
- Facility improvement plans.
- How maintenance will be financed (running budget, special classes of accounts, standard tariffs, etc.).
- The budget itself, with all its different categories.

Organizational requirements

When one plan the organization of the maintenance function, there are two main issues on which fundamental decisions should be taken before progressing into the detail of organizational design. These are:

- What ground level organizational design is going to be adopted. There are at least three popular options:
  - ⇒ Organization by craft - in this type of organization a supervisor will have a number of the same craft in his team. He and his team thus specializes in one specific craft. Whenever a task should be done that needs a craftsman with this specific craft, that man will come from this specific team. The benefit of this type of organization is that such a group really tend to specialize - they really know their job. This leads to a high quality and efficiency of workmanship. The disadvantage of this type of organization is that tasks can be delayed due to different plant priorities being weighed against one another in situations of competing requests for service.
  - ⇒ Organization by area - an area organization has a geographical orientation to maintenance. A supervisor is responsible for all the maintenance of a particular area and has all the necessary crafts reporting to him. This group of people normally do all day to day

maintenance work (including preventive tasks and breakdowns). They might from time to time need more people when a task is very large. In such a situation people might be hired or retrieved from a central pool of artisans. The advantages of this type of organization are that response times are fast and there is a pronounced loyalty of the work team towards their plant area. The disadvantage is a lack of specialization, which may lead to poor quality of workmanship.

⇒ Multi-skilling - this is really a variant of the previous one, where not only the supervisor supervises multi-disciplinary tasks, but the artisans are trained in more than one trade, thus being able to do a full multi-disciplinary task without the help of other tradesmen. Another possibility of multi-skilling occurs where a production worker (i.e. an operator) is trained to do maintenance work as well. The advantages of this organizational type includes those for area organization. This also leads to higher efficiency and flexibility in the workforce. The disadvantage of area organization is again there, but is more pronounced. Quality of workmanship really becomes an issue with multi-skilling.

Which one of these three options to choose depends on the situation at hand. One has to evaluate the various options for a certain situation, taking the advantages and disadvantages listed above into account. Another important point is that one rarely finds only one or the other organizational type present in a maintenance organization. It is often a mixture which will work best.

- What higher level organization is going to be adopted.

⇒ Firstly, there can again be organized by skill or by area. Again the same advantages/disadvantages apply. Again one rarely finds only the one or the other. Mostly there is a mixture of these two basic organizational types, so to try to get most benefit from the advantages of both types without having too much of the disadvantages.

⇒ Secondly, there is the question of centralization versus decentralization. Some maintenance chiefs prefer to work with centralized organizations, while others prefer decentralization. In the maintenance organization itself, the most pronounced example of this is to be found in the Maintenance Administration (Planning) function. If this function is centralized there will be strong functional leadership leading to excellence in the administration work. But centralization tends to lead to some maintenance areas not getting the attention they deserve. If the function is decentralized, areas will often be very satisfied with the level of attention. But, typically, the quality of administration work will take a serious nosedive.

Again, it is mostly a mixture of centralization and/or decentralization that will work best.

It is important that the organization structure be, at least in principle, rethought in the process of the annual maintenance management planning. One must be sure that the structure will achieve what should be achieved in terms of the policy document and the procedures and specific objectives flowing from it.

Typically, the basic principles might be set by the management team following the objective setting exercise. Then the detail will be filled in during the detailed individual planning process, later to be combined into one whole after approval by the engineering chief. Of course, during this same exercise, the numbers of people in the different categories should also be rethought. It is here where more benefits of the craft organization type and centralization come to the fore. Because of the more concentrated effort one often finds that these can make use of less people than their counterparts.

Resources

Apart from money and people, the main resources that the maintenance function need are facilities (workshops, handling equipment, manufacturing equipment and tools) and bought-in services. During the planning process each of these should be thought through in a fair amount of detail to ensure that facilities will not be a stumbling block in achieving what the management team set out to achieve.

One of the major activities in resources planning is the annual budgeting process. Here, after finalizing the policy and objectives for that year, each area will prepare a maintenance budget for the next period, based on proven parts and materials usage from the past, escalated if necessary to allow for inflation and known deterioration trends. These area budgets will, after approval by the maintenance chief, be merged into one budget for the maintenance function, being combined with the budget for personnel, derived from the organizational planning phase above.

A very important facet of the annual planning phase comprises the facilities plan. Just because the facilities may have been sufficient for the present period, does not necessarily imply that it will also be sufficient for the next period. And, more often than not, the present state of facilities are far behind what is needed in most maintenance organizations. Again this should be done per area and then later, after approval, consolidated into one facilities plan. Although one should be critical of the requests to avoid unnecessary expenditure, valid requests should not be turned down if you are serious about achieving success in attaining the goals set in the policy and specific objectives.

Another part of the resources plan involves the services that are bought in. Some of them are directly in competition with the organization/personnel plan, in the sense that bought-in services can substitute for own personnel. One of the typical applications for bought-in services are in very specialized areas where it does not pay the company to have own (and probably under-utilized) specialized personnel. Another application of bought-in services is to provide manpower for peak workloads.

Annual Plan

Maintenance is a very important part of the business. It plays a crucial part in the profitability of the business. To ensure that its contribution to the business is maximized, a business plan for the next financial year, including a five-year forecast, should be prepared annually. This business plan is thus used as driver of and control over the actions of the maintenance function.

Although most maintenance organizations have a formal budget, very few have a formal annual plan. An annual plan serves to formalize the planning process' various outputs into one document, which is used throughout the year as a reference document. Such document can take on a variety of formats and the one presented here should thus be regarded as an example of the possible formats. What is important in the format is that it properly documents the planning process into a single document for reference and control purposes. The following format has been found to be extremely helpful in the management of complex maintenance situations by the author:

- Each division (or section) of the maintenance department should prepare its own mini-annual plan. The Engineering Manager will then prepare an overall plan, that is a summary of the divisions' (or sections') plans plus any central issues not addressed by those. These individual plans should then be bound together under one cover, the book then being known as the annual plan for the maintenance department.

- Each of these plans should address all the salient features of the planning process. Thus, a typical plan should include:
  - ⇒ A description of the situation in the specific division/ section/ department which explains why the plan has its specific features.
  - ⇒ Specific objectives for achieving the policy requirements in the particular part of the organization - these objectives should be 'SMART' (Specific, Measurable, Achievable, Reward-able, and with a definite Time constraint).
  - ⇒ An organization structure and approved personnel plan. This should reflect the result of the organizational planning process.
  - ⇒ Resources - what and how many (tools, materials, etc.).
  - ⇒ A summary of the approved maintenance budget for the division/ section/ department. This summary must be such that it has the maximum use for the reader of the plan and for control purposes. All classes of budget should be represented separately to maximize the usability of this portion of the plan. Specific detail attention should be given to special expense classes such as capital plans, provision accounts and extraordinary expenditure. This budget is based on proven parts and materials usage from the past, escalated if necessary to allow for inflation and known deterioration trends.
  - ⇒ Complete approved facilities plan. This is again used mainly to ensure that the plan is carried out as planned. It makes no sense to prepare a good facilities plan, only to repeat it during the next year's planning phase. One of the objects of a facilities plan is to assure that the organization's facilities are such that the maintenance policy is achievable. The fact that maintenance facilities have been sufficient in the past, does not necessarily imply that it will remain sufficient - changing maintenance requirements may necessitate facility improvements.
  - ⇒ Capital budget.

The plan for a specific division/ section/ department can be used during monthly personal discussions with the relevant personnel for control purposes to ensure that the organization achieves what it set out to do. After all, that is the purpose of the whole management cycle of the Maintenance Cycle.

Process of compilation

During the start of the budget cycle, the Engineering Manager will typically convene a meeting of all Maintenance Engineers, Senior

Planners, Production Superintendents, their managers and all related interested parties. During this meeting, the following will take place:

- Production present their short and medium range plans, with emphasis on the following:
  - ⇒ The production hours needed from all primary production equipment.
  - ⇒ Production limitations: a listing of production limitations that will effect the maintenance plan significantly.
  - ⇒ The production schedule.
  - ⇒ Problem areas.

  The two parties (maintenance and production) then negotiates on areas where maintenance does not feel comfortable in meeting any of the above. This negotiation process can continue throughout the budgeting period to find mutually acceptable solutions, which would serve to meet the company's profit targets.
- Perform a SWOT (Strengths, Weaknesses, Opportunities and Threats) analysis to identify the strengths and weaknesses of the maintenance organization, as well as the opportunities and threats from the maintenance external environment.
- Use the results of the audit (chapter 12), performance measurement (chapter 11) and the SWOT analysis above to work through the maintenance policy, revising and updating it if necessary.
- Draw up overall maintenance objectives that will ensure that:
  - ⇒ The year's outcome will conform to the Maintenance Policy.
  - ⇒ The Strengths and Opportunities are utilized optimally.
  - ⇒ Weaknesses and Threats are being addressed to eliminate or reduce their effects. The accent will be to turn them into opportunities or eliminate them. If this is not possible, the approach will be to minimize their negative effects.

Individual Planning

The next step in the management planning process is to develop detailed plans and budgets within the constraints set by the Planning initiation meeting. This is done using the following steps:

- Each lower management level (down to lowest supervisor level) develops their own objectives and KPI's that fully supports those of the immediate superior level. Those of the top-level maintenance managers support the objectives set by the Planning initiation meeting. Thus, the objectives of the various levels and KPI's cascade downward from top to bottom, thus ensuring attainment of the objectives set by the Planning initiation meeting. The immediate superior level approves its subordinates' objectives, and KPI's to ensure that the superior's objectives and KPI's are fully supported.

- Engineers are typically responsible for their own mini-planning processes (through their planning and supervisory personnel) that will result in budgets for their own division. This is done as follows:

⇒ Obtain long term projections of all scheduled work to the end of the next financial year from the maintenance system (CMIS).

⇒ Obtain condition-monitoring reports, where available, for all equipment for which he/she is responsible.

⇒ Obtain inspection reports of the physical condition of equipment from supervisors.

⇒ Consolidate the above information (taking his/her own objectives and KPI's into account) into a maintenance plan and budget for the following year. This plan includes the following:

* All maintenance work to be done on equipment in his/her responsibility area.
* Any necessary changes to his/her organization structure.
* Changes in personnel strength requested with a proper motivation.
* Facilities/resources needed (other than personnel).
* Training of personnel.
* Finances needed (operational budget).
* Capital budget.

⇒ Update capital plan (equipment replacement and development projects) based on own objectives and KPI's.

References

1. Coetzee, J.L., The Systems Approach to Maintenance Profitability. Annual short course, 1997.

Chapter 11

Maintenance Performance Measurement

The need for Maintenance Performance Measurement

We have seen in chapter 1 that maintenance management has to find subtle balances if the optimal level of maintenance is to be practiced. To be able to do this, maintenance managers need information that will enable them to find the relevant balance points. Measurement is a crucial part of any managerial process. Without measurement you cannot "close the loop" (that is the control loop). We thus have to find practical parameters that we can measure and use to help us optimize the maintenance process.

The real need for the measurement of maintenance performance, as in anything else, stems from the need to contribute maximally to the company's profit. This can be achieved through high maintenance productivity in the absolute sense. As was seen in chapter 1, the maintenance function needs to optimize the level of prevention to optimize its contribution to company profit. The result of such optimizing action will be maximal profit if the company can sell all the units that it can produce (at fixed prices). Otherwise (the company operates in a captive market) the result will be minimized cost.

Typical maintenance performance indices

As was said in the previous paragraph, we need parameters that we can measure, which will tell us how we are doing regarding our maintenance task. The main aim of this is to help us optimize our contribution to company profit. As single parameters do not carry as much information as we need, we often rather make use of indices, which are combinations of two or more parameters in some relationship to each other. We will thus concentrate on the use of such indices, but before we do that, we need to first define the parameters that will make up the various indices.

Parameters to be measured

The objective of maintenance is to *optimize the availability* and *reliability* of production equipment and *maintain its operability* at an *acceptable cost* level (to achieve maximum profit). Thus, the parameters to be measured are the following:

- Machine efficiency
  - ⇒ Availability
  - ⇒ Reliability
  - ⇒ Production rate efficiency
- Cost efficiency
  - ⇒ Task efficiency
  - ⇒ Organizational efficiency

The maintenance cycle is used as a basis for developing the detailed parameters to be measured. This will be done using four categories:

- Machine/Facility maintenance efficiency
- Task efficiency
- Organizational efficiency
- Profit/Cost efficiency

Note: All measurements are for the last period. This is sometimes referred to as 'the period' and sometimes 'the current period' in our subsequent discussion.

Machine/Facility maintenance efficiency

Figure 11.1 at the top of the following page shows the maintenance cycle with the areas, which represents the parameters to be measured in this category, highlighted.

Maintenance management has defined the mission (as set forth in the maintenance *policy*) and the *objectives* of the department. The primary objective in this category (Machine/Facility maintenance efficiency) is to assess the effectiveness of the maintenance *strategic planning* and the maintenance *operation* functions in attaining these. Our aim is to determine the effect of these functional areas on the equipment itself, bearing in mind that we are interested in the availability and operability of the equipment. There are four parameters to be measured in this category:

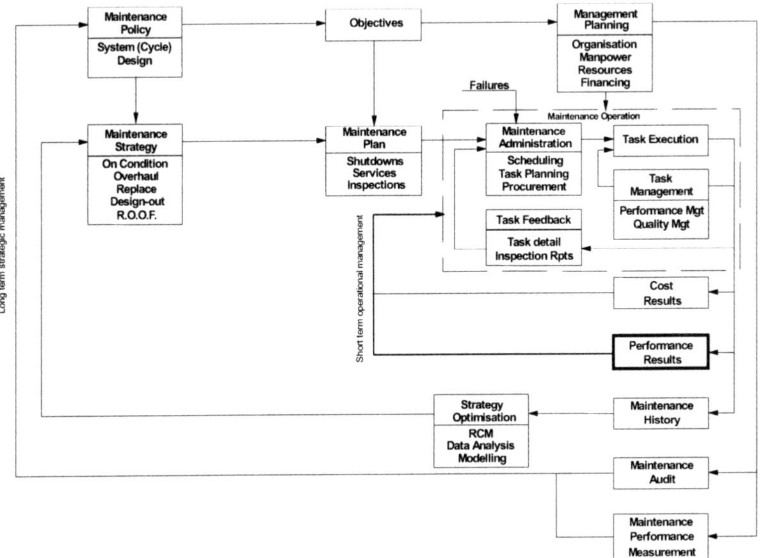

Figure 11.1 : Machine/Facility maintenance efficiency measurement area

- Total production time
- Downtime
- Number of breakdowns
- Production

Note: The last paragraph in this section will discuss the width of application of these measurements. We do not want to confuse ourselves at this (early) stage by repeatedly thinking of that issue. The approach here is thus to limit ourselves to the measurement of these quantities for one machine only.

1. Total production time

This quantity, denoted T_{tot}, represents the total time that our machine could be operated, if there was no maintenance downtime involved. This is not the theoretical time that "the machine could be used if all three shifts were operated seven days per week". It rather represents the total time that production people are present with the objective of using the machine for production. T_{tot} does not, however, exclude the time that the machine is not utilized. Diagrammatically this can be illustrated as follows:

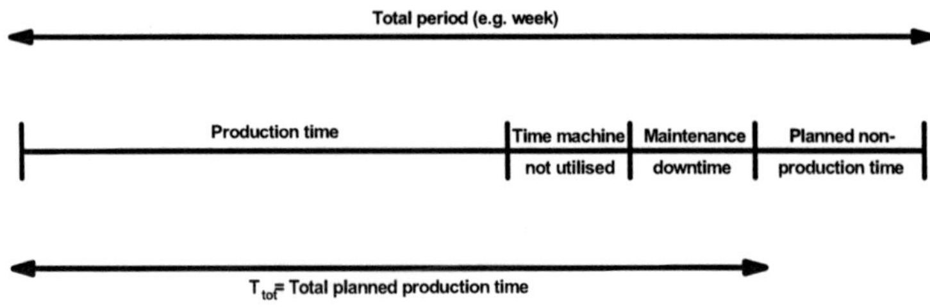

Figure 11.2 : T_{tot} in relation to full production period

T_{tot} thus includes the full period except for those times for which the production schedule does not allow.

2. **Downtime**

Downtime will be denoted D and represents those times during which the machine is inoperative for maintenance purposes. This includes all scheduled daily, weekly or other services, inspections, condition monitoring, preventive maintenance as well as breakdowns. It also includes any delay time during such occurrences. Examples of these are waiting for spares, waiting for transport, waiting for crane, waiting for artisan, etc. All these occurrences are thus deemed to be the responsibility of the maintenance department to manage. This can again be illustrated by using our total period diagram:

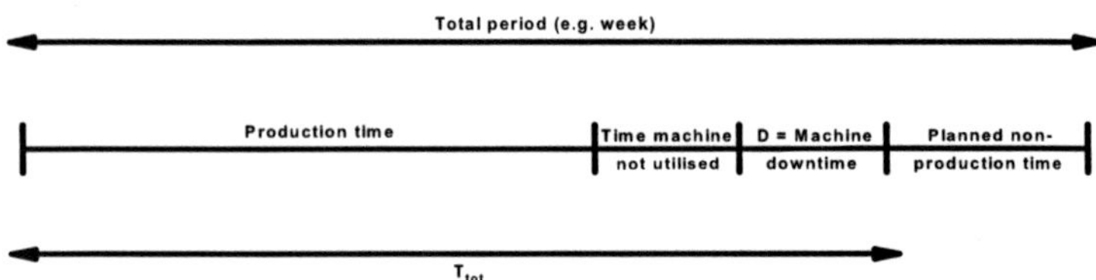

Figure 11.3 : D in relation to total production time

To summarize, D includes all those times either directly or indirectly attributable to maintenance.

3. **Number of breakdowns**

The number of breakdowns, N, is the number of times the machine had to receive unplanned maintenance attention during the period.

This does not include any daily, weekly or other services, inspections, condition monitoring or preventive maintenance. If, however, the machine has to receive repeated attention for the same problem, each of these incidents is counted as a breakdown. We are thus interested in the number of times that the production process was interrupted for non-planned maintenance work. The downtime D, as defined above, gives an indication of the total size of all disturbances to the production process. Contrary to this, the number of breakdowns N, gives an indication of the nuisance that unplanned incidents caused to the production process.

4. Production

The total machine production for the period, P, is the value as reported to the production system. This is the figure that will be reported on all management documents and which will be compared to the budgeted figure.

The scope of measurement

As mentioned previously, a single machine was used in this section to simplify the discussion of the various measurement parameters. In principle all these measurements could, and should, be done on a machine by machine basis to evaluate the result of maintenance actions on each machine. Our concern is more with the effectiveness of the total maintenance organization (or a part thereof). We would thus prefer to apply these principles on wider front. To enable the maintenance manager to do this he/she will have to decide what he/she regards as the primary production machine(s) of the organization. The values T_{tot}, D, N and P will then be averaged values over all of these machines for the period.

Task efficiency

We will again make use of the maintenance cycle to demarcate the areas for which we have to define measurement variables (parameters). See figure 11.4 at the top of the next page.

In this category (Task efficiency) we want to assess the efficiency with which tasks are being carried out. We thus want to measure the effectiveness of *task execution* and *task management*. This directly reflects back to the effectiveness of the *management planning* process. It is important to note that this is a secondary category. We wish to maintain equipment, the effectiveness of which was measured in the

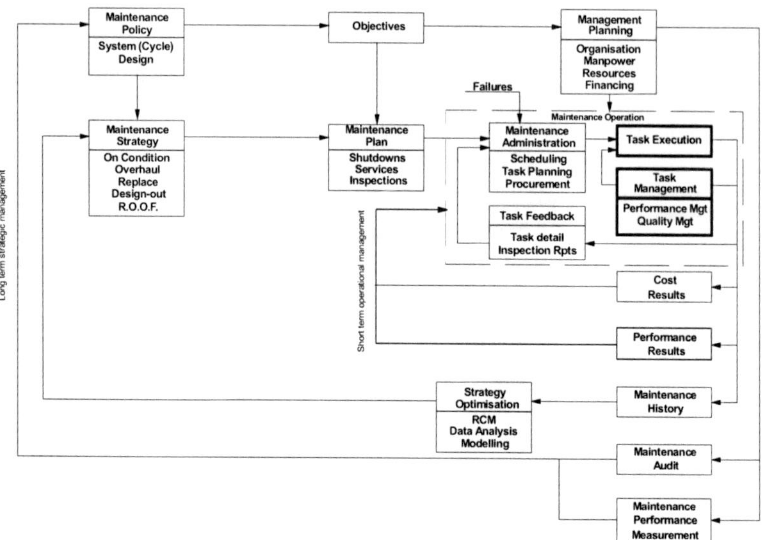

Figure 11.4 : Task efficiency measurement area

first category, and tasks are just a vehicle to get there. This (secondary) category is very important, though, as the effectiveness of task execution and management will reflect directly in our primary categories (machine results and profit/cost).

There are six measurement parameters in this category:

- Number of tasks completed
- Number of tasks received
- Number of tasks overdue
- Clocked time
- Time allowed on tasks
- Time spent on tasks

1. Number of tasks completed

The number of tasks completed for the period, N_C, represents all the tasks completed for the department/section. These include tasks carried over from previous periods, whether they have not yet been started or are in a semi-complete state at that time. Thus N_C is a measure of all those tasks having a completion date that falls in the present period. The exact definition of what a task is, is not so important as long as it is applied consistently. In some maintenance organizations a task will represent all actions carried out by a number of people to complete a job. In other (organizations) a task will be defined as the work assigned to a single person as his/her part in completing the job. As was said, consistency in the application of this definition is important to be able to compare tasks completed with tasks received and tasks outstanding.

2. **Number of tasks received**

   This quantity, denoted N_R, represents the number of tasks that was received during the period. Thus N_R is a count of all tasks for which the date of receiving falls within the specified period. It is again of prime importance to note that the definition of what a task is must be applied consistently. See the previous paragraph (number of tasks completed) for a discussion of this.

3. **Number of tasks overdue**

   The number of overdue tasks, N_O, is a count of all tasks that have been received, but have not been completed at the agreed upon completion date. This includes tasks received during the present and previous periods that are overdue. It thus includes all tasks that were in non-complete or semi-complete state at the end of the present period and which are overdue. It excludes all non-complete or semi-complete tasks that are not overdue. The definition of what a task is, must again be applied consistently, as described in the paragraph on the number of tasks completed. Some organizations would like to discern between current overdue tasks and tasks overdue for longer periods. This is a valid distinction but tends to complicate the measurement of maintenance performance. It will thus not be included in this discussion.

4. **Clocked time**

   This measure represents the total worker time that was available to the organization for maintenance purposes during the period and is denoted T_C. It includes the time clocked by all maintenance workers to whom tasks are allocated for completion. Thus, if a certain category of worker's time is not reported separately (e.g. artisan helpers), their clocked time should not be included in T_C. It must be stressed, however, that, if optimum efficiency is to be attained, all workers should receive own task documentation (including allowed time). In such case they should report actual times and their clocked times should also be included in T_C. Clocked time includes all time that maintenance workers are present on the company premises. It thus includes all unproductive times, such as the time needed for putting on work clothing, tea times, lunch breaks, meeting times and washing after work. There could of course be an agreement between the company and workers that some of these activities are performed in the workers' own time. In such a case these times would not be included in the clocked times. The idea is to include all times for which the company pay, so that measures can be developed to show how effective the total clocked time is being utilized in the maintenance process. When one or more categories of unproductive times are being excluded, this immediately becomes areas for which no managerial action can be taken. After all, it does not help to wish away these times - they are there, some of them to stay that way, others to be improved upon. Fact is, they should be visible to maintenance management.

5. Time allowed on tasks

Time allowed on tasks, T_A, is the total of worker time allowed for during the detailed planning of maintenance tasks. If more than one worker works on the same task and their actual time worked on the task is reported separately, their times allowed on the task should be aggregated. This measure should include all the allowed times for all tasks that have completion dates that occurred during the period for which the measurement is made. It thus excludes the allowed times for tasks that are non-complete or semi-complete. It includes the times of tasks carried over from previous periods as non-complete or semi-complete, but which were completed during the present period.

6. Time spent on tasks

This parameter, T_W, is the total time spent for the period on all completed tasks. Similar to the time allowed on tasks, it includes the times spent by all workers for whom time worked is reported separately. It again includes all actual times spent on all tasks that have completion dates that occurred during the present period. It thus excludes actual times spent on tasks that are non-complete or semi-complete. It includes the times spent on tasks carried over from previous periods as non-complete or semi-complete (the full times spent), but which were completed during the present period.

Organizational efficiency

Figure 11.5 shows which areas of the maintenance cycle are involved in the measurement of organizational efficiency.

In this category the effectiveness of the maintenance organization (*planning, administration* and *task management*) to design and implement an adequate maintenance strategy is being measured. It is the task of the maintenance engineers to, with the aid of techniques such as RCM (Reliability Centered Maintenance) and maintenance data analysis, develop maintenance plans for the equipment to be maintained. These plans must then be put into effect by the maintenance administration function (traditionally called maintenance planning). The resultant tasks are then carried out by maintenance supervisors (task management) with the aid of their workers. This measurement category seeks to measure the effectiveness of this process. There are six parameters to be measured in this category:

- Time planned for scheduled tasks
- Time planned for overdue scheduled tasks
- Time spent on scheduled tasks
- Time spent on breakdowns
- Cost of breakdowns
- Total direct maintenance cost

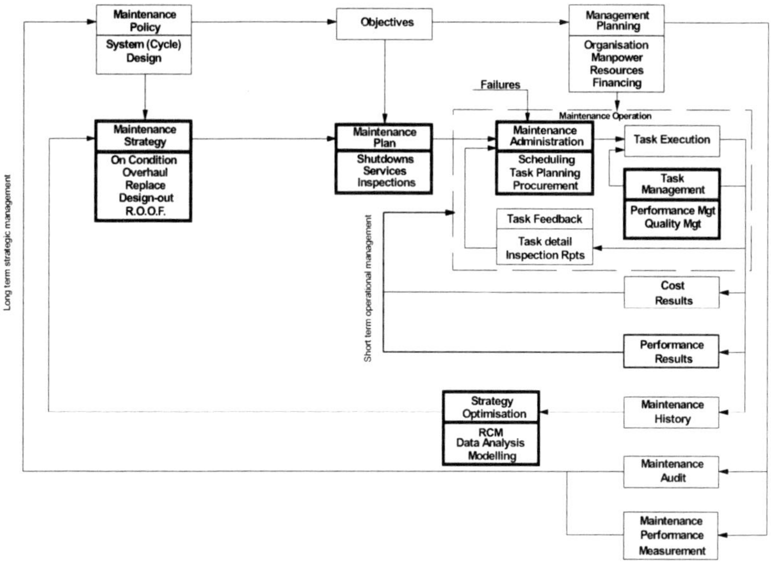

Figure 11.5 : Organizational efficiency measurement area

1. **Time planned for scheduled tasks**

   The time planned for scheduled tasks, T_{S_P},is the sum of all the allowed times for scheduled tasks scheduled for completion up to the end of the period. It thus includes all allowed times for scheduled maintenance tasks that should be complete at the end of the period. It excludes all scheduled tasks with scheduled completion dates after the end of the period and includes scheduled tasks that were non-complete or semi-complete at the start of the period.

2. **Time planned for overdue scheduled tasks**

   This measurement parameter, T_{S_O}, is the sum of all the allowed times for scheduled tasks that are overdue at the end of the period. All scheduled tasks with scheduled completion dates up to the end of the period, but which are either non-complete or semi-complete at the end of the period, are included in T_{S_O}. It also includes the allowed times of overdue scheduled maintenance tasks from previous periods.

3. **Time spent on scheduled tasks**

   This measure represents the total time spent on scheduled tasks during the period and is denoted T_{S_A}. It includes the times spent by all categories of workers on all scheduled tasks with completion dates before the end of the present period. It thus excludes times for scheduled tasks that are non-complete or semi-complete at the end of the period. It includes the full time for scheduled tasks carried over as non-complete or semi-complete from previous periods and completed during this period.

4. **Time spent on breakdowns**

   The time spent on breakdowns, T_B, is the total time spent during the period on breakdowns. It includes the times of all personnel working on breakdown tasks that were completed during the period. It thus excludes work on any non-complete or semi-complete breakdown tasks at the end of the period. It includes the work on breakdown tasks carried over as non-complete or semi-complete from previous periods and which were completed during the present period.

5. **Cost of breakdowns**

   This parameter, C_B, represents the cost of all breakdown work during the present period. For convenience it is taken as the total cost reported by the cost system for breakdown tasks during the present period.

6. Total direct maintenance cost

This is the (direct) maintenance cost reported by the cost system for all work. It is denoted C_D and excludes any non-maintenance work (hence the 'direct' in the title).

Profit/Cost efficiency

Use is made of the maintenance cycle again to demarcate the area of measurement in this category.

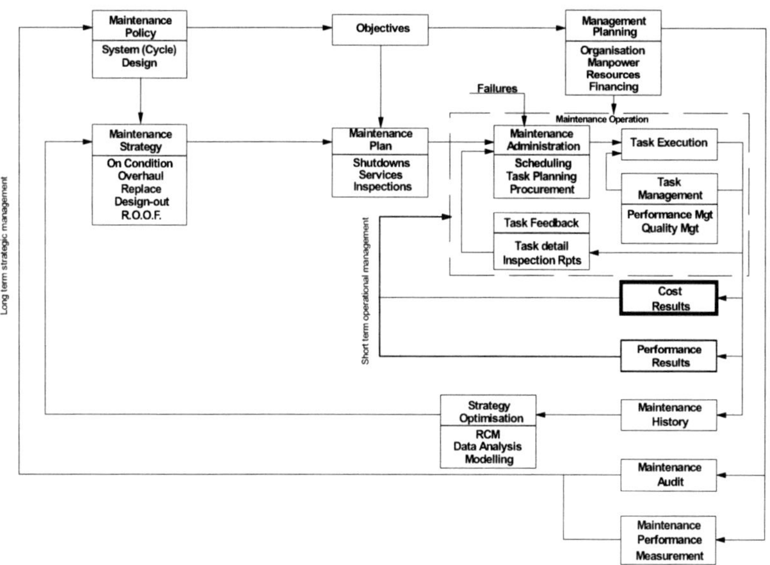

Figure 11.6 : Profit/Cost efficiency measurement area

As was the case with the first category (machine/facility maintenance efficiency), the objective in this category is to assess the effectiveness of the maintenance *strategy planning* process and the maintenance *operations* process in attaining the mission and objectives of the department. This is the measurement of the bottom line and thus also serves to indicate how well the maintenance *policy*, *objectives* and *management planning* served as drivers toward success. There are five parameters to be measured in this category:

- Total maintenance cost
- Cost of lost production
- Cost of maintenance materials from stock
- Value of stock at end of period
- Plant investment value (Replacement value)

1. **Total maintenance cost**

   This is the total cost figure as reported by the cost system for the maintenance department for the period. It is denoted C_T, and includes all cost incurred by the maintenance department, including non maintenance expenditure (project work, modifications, etc.).

2. **Cost of lost production**

   This parameter, denoted C_L, represents the value of all production lost during the period due to unplanned maintenance occurrences. It does not include 'losses' due to planned daily, weekly or other services, inspections, condition monitoring or preventive maintenance. We are interested in the value of the production that could have been produced, if the unplanned incidents did not occur.

3. **Cost of maintenance materials from stock**

   The cost of maintenance materials from stock, C_P, is the cost reported for the period by the cost system of all issues from stock to the maintenance department.

4. **Value of stock at end of period**

   The value of stock at the end of the period, C_S, is the value of the maintenance stock as reported by the stores' organization for the end of the period.

5. **Plant investment value (replacement value)**

   This measure, denoted I, represents the present (replacement) value of the plant being maintained. The original investment value of the plant must thus be escalated using the production price index or the plant must be valued on an annual basis to obtain the replacement value.

Maintenance performance indices

While the parameters defined in the previous section (21 of them) represent all the parameters needed to establish the effectiveness of the maintenance function, it is often more effective to compare two or more parameters to arrive at a performance ratio. Such performance ratios (or indices) serve to enhance our understanding of the message conveyed by the various measurement parameters discussed above. The use of performance indices is thus presented as a better way of presenting the measurement data. Some of the indices even give additional information not apparent in the original data. This section will divide the various indices into four groups:

- Maintenance results
- Maintenance productivity
- Maintenance operational purposefulness
- Maintenance cost justification

Maintenance results

The objective of the maintenance function is to provide production with adequate levels of availability, reliability and operability at an acceptable cost (refer to fig.11.1). This paragraph seeks to enumerate the success of the maintenance actions in attaining the first three (availability, reliability and operability). The cost of the maintenance actions will be enumerated in the last paragraph of this section. We are presenting five indices for evaluating maintenance results:

- Availability
- Mean time to failure
- Breakdown frequency
- Mean time to repair
- Production rate

1. **Availability**

   Availability is measured as the percentage of time (of the total production time) that the machine is available to be used for production purposes.

$$A_V = \frac{T_{tot} - D}{T_{tot}} \times 100 \quad (\%) \tag{11.1}$$

A_V = Availability
T_{tot} = Total production time for period (hours)
D = Downtime for period (hours)

Availability is a measure of the department's overall capability to keep the company's equipment in running order.

2. **Mean time to failure (MTTF)**

Although availability gives an indication of the average efficiency of the company's equipment maintenance, it does not provide a measure of the reliability of the (maintained) equipment. While availability measures the average percentage up-time, it does not measure the regularity with which maintenance is required to get to said level of availability. As it is important to the efficiency of the production process to have long average production runs, a measure of the reliability of the equipment must be provided. The average up-time is such a measure:

$$MTTF = \frac{T_{tot} - D - T_{nu}}{N} \tag{11.2}$$

MTTF = Mean Time To Failure (hours)
T_{tot} = Total production time for period (hours)
N = Number of breakdowns during interval $[0, T_{tot}]$
D = Downtime for period (hours)
T_{nu} = Time machine not utilised (hours)

This measure is also called the average up-time (the consistency with which a proper level of production can be sustained).

3. **Breakdown frequency**

This is an alternative measure of the system reliability as measured by the previous measure (average up-time):

$$B_D = \frac{N}{T_{tot} - D - T_{nu}} \tag{11.3}$$

B_D = Breakdown frequency (breakdowns/hour)
T_{tot} = Total production time for period (hours)
N = Number of breakdowns during interval $(0, T_{tot}]$
D = Downtime for period (hours)
T_{nu} = Time machine not utilised (hours)

4. Mean time to repair (MTTR)

The previous two measures provide an indication of system reliability or the average length of the "up" cycle. What is needed additionally is a measure of the average length of the "down" cycle. This is also called the maintainability of the equipment and measures the ease with which the equipment can be repaired.

$$MTTR = \frac{D}{N} \tag{11.4}$$

MTTR = Mean Time To Repair (hours)
N = Number of breakdowns during interval $(0, T_{tot}]$
D = Downtime for period (hours)

This measure is also called the breakdown severity (the effect that an average breakdown has on the production process).

5. Production rate

This is not a pure maintenance measure at all, but provides the means by which the effect of maintenance on operability can be assessed.

$$P_R = \frac{P}{T_{tot} - D - T_{nu}} \tag{11.5}$$

B y

P_R = Production Rate (production units/hour)
T_{tot} = Total production time for period (hours)
P = Production for period (production units)
D = Downtime for period (hours)
T_{nu} = Time machine not utilised (hours)

building a bona fide impression of maintenance results using the five indices above, the efficiency with which the equipment is maintained can be assessed. The parameters used in the calculation of these indices can be obtained as follows:

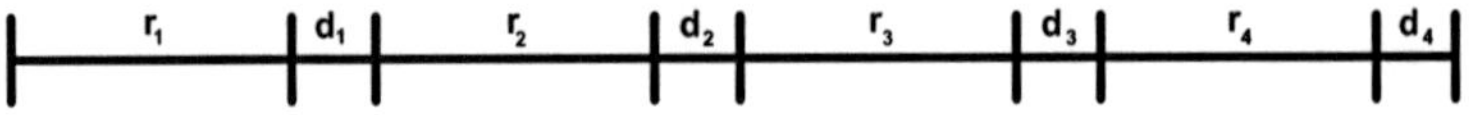

$$\vdash r_1 \dashv d_1 \vdash r_2 \dashv d_2 \vdash r_3 \dashv d_3 \vdash r_4 \dashv d_4 \vdash$$

$$T_{tot} = (r_1 + r_2 + r_3 + r_4) + (d_1 + d_2 + d_3 + d_4)$$

$$D = d_1 + d_2 + d_3 + d_4$$

$$N = 4$$

Another often used measure, the MTBF (Mean Time Between Failures) measures reliability and maintainability simultaneously:

$$MTBF = MTTF + MTTR \tag{11.6}$$

Due to the MTBF being a combined measure, its use is not recommended as it can lead to confusion.

Maintenance Productivity

The second group of maintenance performance indices (refer to figure 11.4) addresses three distinct productivity indices:

- Manpower utilization
- Manpower efficiency
- Maintenance cost component

1. **Manpower utilization**

   The manpower provided to the maintenance organization has a base capacity (the number of clocked hours). It is the task of maintenance supervision to make optimal use of this capacity.

$$M_U = \frac{T_W}{T_C} \times 100 \quad (\%) \tag{11.7}$$

M_U = Manpower Utilisation (%)
T_W = Time spent on tasks (hours)
T_C = Clocked time (hours)

Since most maintenance teams have spare capacity to be able to handle crisis situations, this figure is rarely high in a maintenance situation. Values of 65-75% are generally accepted. This figure measures the ability of the supervisor to keep his men at worthwhile tasks.

2. Manpower efficiency

As each maintenance task has a certain task content, a maintenance worker can be measured against his/her capability to handle such task(s).

$$M_E = \frac{T_A}{T_W} \times 100 \quad (\%) \tag{11.8}$$

M_E = Manpower Efficiency (%)
T_W = Time spent on tasks (hours)
T_A = Time allowed on tasks (hours)

If a maintenance worker handles his task workload in a time T_W, which is shorter than the allowed time, T_A, his efficiency will be higher than 100%. If, on the other hand, he takes longer than the allowed time, his efficiency will be below 100%.

An interesting feature of the last two measures is that they tend to check one another. Maintenance managers/supervisors mostly do not apply these two measures because "the people will 'jippo' them". If used properly, that will not happen. The first measure, M_U, is used to measure the effectiveness of the supervisor and the second, M_E, that of the workers. If the worker tries to superficially decrease T_W to achieve high efficiencies, his supervisor's effectiveness will drop (M_U), thus causing him to complain. He will then prompt his subordinate to increase the T_W values, which the worker will be reluctant to do past his achieved times. Another interesting point is that the total planned worker effectiveness:

$$M_T = \frac{T_A}{T_C} = M_U \times M_E \tag{11.9}$$

3. Maintenance cost component

This is a productivity index in the sense that it compares the cost of maintenance to that of production. The classical definition of productivity is:

$$\text{Productivity} = \frac{\text{Input}}{\text{Output}} \times 100 \quad (\%) \tag{11.10}$$

(in inverted form). Because maintenance is one of the inputs into the production process, a similar ratio can be developed for the maintenance discipline:

$$R_C = \frac{C_T}{PC} \times 100 \quad (\%) \qquad (11.11)$$

R_C = Maintenance cost component (%)

C_T = Total maintenance cost for period

PC = Total production cost for period

The higher this ratio becomes, the less productive the maintenance function is (in the sense that it contributes a very high proportion of the total production costs). It would thus be the objective of maintenance management to decrease this ratio over time.

Maintenance operational purposefulness

The previous two groups measured the efficiency of maintenance actions (maintenance productivity) and its effect on the equipment being maintained (maintenance results). The present group (refer to figure 11.5) seeks to enumerate the efficiency with which maintenance work is organized and controlled, using generally accepted maintenance practice guidelines. Maintenance operational purposefulness again consists of two sub-groups. The first of these measures the efficiency of the work planning process in the maintenance cycle and the second the efficiency of carrying out such maintenance plans. These two areas are called work planning efficiency and work completion efficiency respectively. Work planning efficiency has three indices:

- Scheduling intensity
- Breakdown intensity
- Breakdown severity

1. **Scheduling intensity**

   The intensity of scheduling gives an indication of the intensity with which the organization practices prevention in preference to corrective maintenance. In the first section we discussed the profit impact of maintenance. One of our concerns there was that it is difficult to know exactly where we are on those conceptual graphs. The scheduling intensity provides an indication of our level of prevention.

$$W_S = \frac{T_{S_A}}{T_C} \times 100 \quad (\%) \tag{11.12}$$

W_S = Scheduling intensity (%)

T_{S_A} = Time spent on scheduled tasks for period (hours)

T_C = Clocked time for period (hours)

If W_S is low, we are practicing a low level of prevention and can expect a high cost of breakdowns. Our potential to improve our maintenance results (especially availability) by increasing the level of prevention should also be high. A value of 30% for W_S seems to be a good level for most industries. This should only be used as a guideline, though, in the process of establishing own standards for W_S by experience.

2. **Breakdown intensity**

Breakdown intensity gives a measure of the percentage of time spent on corrective maintenance work. In a certain sense it is the opposite of the scheduling intensity, thus providing a clue as to the level of prevention being practiced. But, because of the fact that:

$$T_{S_A} + T_B << T_C$$

T_B = Time spent on breakdown tasks for period (hours)

T_{S_A} = Time spent on scheduled tasks for period (hours)

T_C = Clocked time for period (hours)

The breakdown intensity does not provide a good measure of the level of prevention. What it does, though, is to serve as a good macro index of the further potential to increase the level of prevention such that availability will benefit and costs decrease.

$$W_B = \frac{T_B}{T_C} \times 100 \quad (\%) \tag{11.13}$$

W_B = Breakdown intensity (%)

T_B = Time spent on breakdown tasks for period (hours)

T_C = Clocked time for period (hours)

3. **Breakdown severity**

   While breakdown intensity (the previous measure) provides a measure of the percentage of man hours spent on breakdown work, the present measure provides an indication of the cost effect of the present level of breakdown work.

$$R_B = \frac{C_B}{C_D} \times 100 \quad (\%) \qquad (11.14)$$

   R_B = Breakdown severity (%)

   C_B = Breakdown cost for period

   C_D = Total direct maintenance cost for period

   A high value of R_B serves as an indication that breakdown work is still a high part (in terms of value) of the total maintenance budget. Depending on the type of equipment involved, this might indicate that a substantial cost saving may be obtained by increasing the level of prevention.

The second area of measurement of maintenance operational purposefulness addresses the efficiency of work completion. There are three indices in this area:

- Work order turnover
- Size of backlog
- Scheduled maintenance work enforcement ratio

4. **Work order turnover**

   This measure gives an indication of the success of the maintenance organization in handling incoming tasks.

$$W_T = \frac{N_C}{N_R} \qquad (11.15)$$

   W_T = Work order turnover

   N_C = Number of tasks completed in period

   N_R = Number of tasks received in period

   A figure lower than one will indicate an increase in backlog, while a figure greater than one indicates a decrease in backlog. As it is most efficient for the maintenance team to operate with a stable one or two week's backlog, this figure should on most occasions have a static unitary value. Because maintenance is prone to developing occasional high backlog, the organization must be able to, at times, increase W_T to a value substantially higher than one.

5. **Size of backlog**

   While the previous measure indicates the ability of the maintenance function to handle the work load, it does not measure the size of the backlog. The present measure will do that.

$$W_O = \frac{N_O}{N_C} \qquad (11.16)$$

W_O = Size of backlog (periods)
N_C = Number of tasks completed in period
N_O = Number of tasks overdue at end of period

   This measure puts a value to the size of the backlog in time periods (weeks, months, years). As was said in the discussion of the previous measure, a stable backlog of one or two weeks is highly desirable. If this value is too low, the maintenance work force may at times be idle. If, on the other hand, this value is too high, the maintenance workforce may not be able to reduce it to an acceptable size without increasing W_T to a value considerably higher than one. This will probably involve the hiring of temporary staff.

6. **Scheduled maintenance work enforcement ratio**

   When maintenance organizations start moving towards prevention in preference to corrective maintenance, adequate scheduling mechanisms must be employed. In most cases this is done successfully. Most organizations, however, struggle to enforce these scheduled tasks. They either do not have the managerial discipline to do so, or have severe resistance to these tasks at the lower levels of the maintenance hierarchy. The present measure is meant to help maintenance management in establishing how well they (the organization) are doing in this area.

$$W_E = \left[1 - \frac{T_{S_O}}{T_{S_P}}\right] \times 100 \quad (\%) \qquad (11.17)$$

W_E = Scheduled maintenance work enforcement ratio (%)

T_{S_O} = Time planned for overdue scheduled tasks (hours)

T_{S_P} = Time planned for scheduled tasks (hours)

If all scheduled tasks are performed as planned, W_E will have the value 100%. If, however, no scheduled tasks are done, W_E will have the value 0%. The size of W_E thus serves as an index of how successful the maintenance organization is in enforcing scheduled work on the scale:

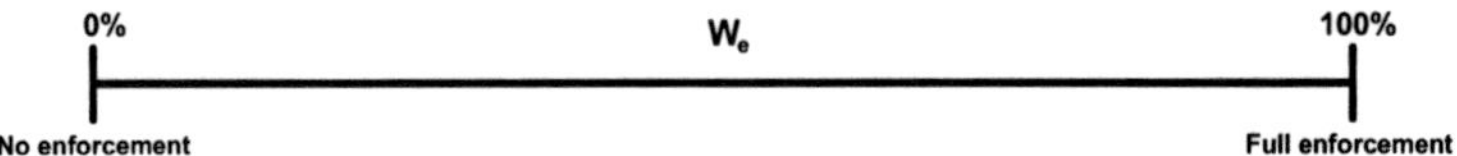

It must be noted that, due to their definitions, T_{S_O} and T_{S_P} are out of phase. This must be taken into account when evaluating the value of W_E.

Maintenance cost justification

The last group's purpose is to establish whether the maintenance plans and its execution can be justified in cost terms (refer to figure 11.6). Remember that the objective of maintenance is to make equipment *available* in an *reliable* and *operable* condition at an *acceptable cost.* Clearly this group is measuring, together with the first group (maintenance results), whether the maintenance organization is achieving its goal. As every organization's existence is ratified by its ability to make profit, this group of indices is of considerable importance. They help the organization (together with the previous group - operational purposefulness) to find the optimum balance for the level of prevention. The group consists of the following six indices:

- Maintenance cost intensity
- Sundry cost component
- Stock turnover
- Maintenance cost effectiveness
- Overall maintenance cost effectiveness
- Maintenance improvement justification

1. **Maintenance cost intensity**

   This is an index often used in industry. It is intended to give the maintenance organization an indication of the cost of maintenance when measured against the level of production achieved.

$$R_I = \frac{C_D}{P} \quad \text{(Cost/Production unit)} \tag{11.18}$$

   R_I = Maintenance cost intensity
   P = Production for period
   C_D = Total direct maintenance cost for period

   This index could also be calculated, using the total maintenance cost C_T:

$$R_I = \frac{C_T}{P} \text{(Cost/Production unit)} \tag{11.19}$$

   R_I = Maintenance cost intensity
   P = Production for period
   C_T = Total maintenance cost for period

   The interpretation of this index is that it should cost a fixed amount per production unit to maintain the plant. Of course this is a gross oversimplification, but this does not negate the value of this index in the control of the cost of the maintenance function. This index is thus used to ensure that maintenance costs do not increase out of proportion to the level of production achieved. As it is intended as a maintenance index, the first form of the formula given above is preferred.

2. **Sundry cost component**

   As the maintenance department is often (normally?) burdened with non-maintenance functions, it is important to be able to discern between maintenance and non-maintenance cost.

$$R_D = \left[1 - \frac{C_D}{C_T}\right] \times 100 \quad (\%) \tag{11.20}$$

R_D = Sundry cost component (%)

C_T = Total maintenance cost for period

C_D = Total direct maintenance cost for period

Ideally one would prefer this index to have a zero value ($C_D = C_T$) in which case maintenance management will be able to spend their total time in managing the maintenance function.

3. **Stock turnover**

This is an often forgotten part of the cost effectiveness of the maintenance function. As it is maintenance management that creates stock for maintenance purposes, it is also maintenance management's responsibility to ensure that stock levels are kept within reasonable limits. The level of stock has a notable impact on the profit of the company. The cost effect of maintenance stock keeping should thus be handled as an integral part of the cost of maintenance. This index helps the maintenance department in doing this.

$$R_S = \frac{C_P}{C_S} \quad \text{(number of times)} \qquad (11.21)$$

R_S = Stock turnover for period

C_P = Cost of maintenance materials issued during period

C_S = Value of maintenance stock at end of period

The objective is to keep R_S as high as possible without starving the maintenance department of much needed spares and materials. This index is mostly calculated for a year's results. This can be for a financial year or a moving average year.

4. **Maintenance cost effectiveness**

This is the only practical index that can be used to compare maintenance costs over company and industry boundaries. It compares the cost of maintenance to the present level of investment in equipment.

$$R_E = \frac{C_D}{I} \times 100 \quad (\%) \qquad (11.22)$$

R_E = Maintenance cost effectiveness (%)

C_D = Total direct maintenance cost for period

I = Investment value (replacement value)

This index is usually calculated on an annual basis, using the maintenance costs for the last financial year. Typical values for R_E could be anything from 1% to 20% per annum depending on the industry and the circumstances. Standards must be determined on an individual basis. A figure between 1 and 2% should be a reasonable estimate for most industries.

5. **Overall maintenance cost effectiveness**

The previous index compared the cost of maintenance to the investment in equipment. As maintenance has a secondary (negative) cost effect, namely the losses incurred during non-planned downtimes, there is a need for an additional index that includes this.

$$R_O = \frac{C_D + C_L}{I} \times 100 \quad (\%) \tag{11.23}$$

R_O = Overall Maintenance cost effectiveness (%)
C_D = Total direct maintenance cost for period
C_L = Cost of lost production due to breakdowns for period
I = Investment value (replacement value)

While this index helps one to establish whether your maintenance costs are busy improving against the investment value, it also has the added advantage that it includes the effect of maintenance decisions. It thus combines a pure maintenance cost justification index with a maintenance results index.

6. **Maintenance improvement justification**

The last index to be discussed is one that shows the maintenance department whether its improvement drives are bearing fruit. It is based on the principle that the cost of maintenance plus the cost of downtime production losses should have a decreasing trend under conditions of improvement. During improvement drives one typically expect the cost of maintenance to rise due to an increased level of prevention (if one assumes that it is past the optimum). In return one then expect a decrease in downtime losses if the improvement is worthwhile.

$$R_J = \frac{C_{D_{n-1}} + C_{L_{n-1}}}{C_{D_n} + C_{L_n}} \tag{11.24}$$

R_J = Maintenance improvement justification
C_{D_i} = Total direct maintenance cost for period i
C_{L_i} = Cost of production due to breakdowns for period i
n = Current period
n - 1 = Previous period

One expects R_J to have a value larger than one under improving circumstances and a value less than one under deteriorating circumstances. R_J can of course also be expressed as a percentage, if that is necessary for consistency with the other indices.

Performance indices and the profit impact of maintenance

Although this subject was dealt with while discussing the individual performance indices, it is necessary to show how a balanced use of some of these indices helps the maintenance manager to determine the best level of prevention for his/her particular circumstances. Refer to the graphs in figure 11.7.

The following indices are the ones that affect this balance in particular:

⇒ Availability (A_V)

⇒ Scheduling intensity (W_S)

⇒ Breakdown severity (R_B)

⇒ Maintenance cost intensity (R_I)

⇒ Maintenance improvement justification (R_J)

It is important to understand that these graphs are conceptual and that they cannot be drawn such that the optimal level of prevention could be determined with certainty. Maintenance management should use the five indices listed above (and some of the other indices) to establish whether they should increase or decrease the level of prevention. In this process W_S and R_B will serve as indications of the present level of prevention, R_I as a measure of the cost level achieved and A_V as measure of the (availability) results already achieved. These four indices should give the maintenance manager a fair indication of his position on the profit/cost/availability graphs shown below. The last measure, R_J, is the proof of the pudding. If used properly, while increasing (or decreasing) the level of prevention, R_J will show whether the right decision was taken. A word of caution is necessary here. In using

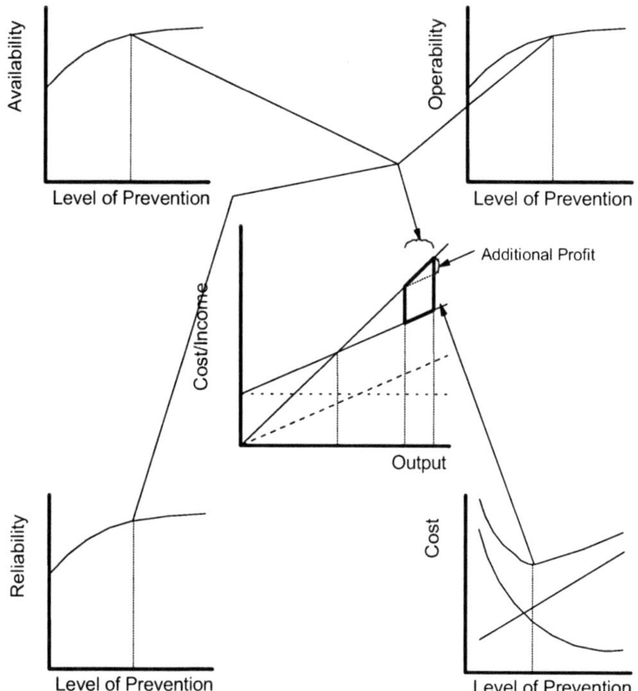

Figure 11.7 : The profit impact of maintenance

these indices for this (or any other) purpose, enough time must be allowed to pass before drawing any conclusions. Maintenance results can be very unpredictable over the short term due to large short term fluctuations in expenditure, as well as the (relative) slow process of finding a new balance for the availability of equipment.

Implementation of the measurement process

In the previous sections we have stepwise developed maintenance performance indices. While the individual performance indices are a great help in measuring various aspects of maintenance performance, we have to combine them in some way to give an indication of the performance of the maintenance function as a whole. The experience gained in the previous section will undoubtedly help us in the process. Furthermore, our grouping of the indices into four groups provides us with a good base for building an integrated multi-parameter measurement process. As any one process will not necessarily produce satisfactory results in all maintenance organizations, we will discuss ways of setting up your own measurement and control process. This will ensure that the maximum level of measurement efficiency is obtained.

Choosing the indices to use

Each company should set up its own, tailored, measurement process that addresses its needs best. The first step in this process is to identify the indices to use. This can take place in formal sessions between the maintenance chief and his direct subordinates. They can start by critically examining all the indices listed previously (and additional ones if necessary). Each of the indices listed above and its inherent parameters must be discussed with a view to include or exclude it in the final model for the organization. In this process the following should be taken into account:

- There must remain an adequate number of indices in each of the four groups above to ensure proper measurement of that facet.
- While working through the list of indices, the maintenance cycle and the profit impact of maintenance should always be kept in mind to ensure that all important facets are measured.
- It may not be possible to measure some of the listed measurement parameters due to system problems. By being creative, one can often get past this impasse by redefining indices to include different parameters than the ones used here.

The result of this process of defining the indices (and parameters) to be used will thus be a list of indices. This can now be used for the further definition of the measurement model.

Setting measurement standards

The indices defined above can now be used in the formulation of some measurement model. Such a model will only be of worth if a standard is set for each measure in the model. These standards are the values for the various indices that will indicate success. As such they represent the input values to the control process and are thus the numerical equivalent of the objectives of the department. The management team (of the department) should thus set up these standards by discussing the different indices and its effect on the attainment of the department's objectives. It is important to again stress the use of the maintenance profit impact model in determining the goal values for the various indices.

The main groupings of the list of indices will now be used to illustrate the process of setting up standards:

- ***Maintenance results*** - these indices are meant to show whether the organization's objectives in the availability and reliability, as well as the operability of equipment is being achieved. These parameters all have interrelationships with the level of prevention on the one hand and the quantity produced on the other hand. This can easily be seen by studying the graphs in the integrated profit impact model. Thus, if a high level of prevention is being practiced, high levels of availability, reliability and operability of equipment will be achieved, effectively increasing production capacity. This will result in higher profit under the following conditions:

  * The company must have the ability to sell all the units that it can produce.

  * The maintenance cost increase due to the high level of prevention must be less than the potential profit increase.

  If the above two conditions are not being met, the objective should be to opt for the lowest possible maintenance cost position. This can be done by carefully balancing the objectives in this group with those in the groups 'Maintenance operational purposefulness' and 'Maintenance cost justification'.

- ***Maintenance productivity*** - the indices in this group portray the work execution effectiveness as well as the overall effectiveness of the maintenance organization. As such, these measures play a role in determining whether the most efficient use of resources is being made. The higher the values of the manpower utilization and efficiency and the lower the value of the maintenance cost component, the better in productivity terms. This should reflect in the lowering of maintenance cost. The maintenance cost component will thus only achieve its lowest possible level if the optimum level of prevention is being practiced. It must be stressed, however, that this is not necessarily the position that the company would want to achieve. A higher profit may be achievable at the expense of a higher than optimum level of prevention.

- ***Maintenance operational purposefulness*** - this category of indices assesses whether the right maintenance strategies and management approach are being followed to achieve the maintenance organization's goals as set forth in the maintenance policy and maintenance objectives. They are thus indicative of whether the maintenance organization is 'making the grade'. Some of these indices, i.e. the work order turnover and size of backlog do exactly that. It must however be stressed that a high backlog and/or a low value of work order turnover will eventually result in high costs and low profits due to secondary effects such as important preventive tasks not being done. The other indices in this group, additional to its measurement of purposefulness, measure the level of prevention. The scheduling intensity measures the proportion of maintenance tasks that are scheduled. As most preventive tasks are also scheduled tasks, this is a valid indication of the level of prevention being practiced. The breakdown intensity, on the other hand, is a measure f the proportion of maintenance tasks handled on a corrective basis. The higher this figure, the lower the level of prevention. Breakdown severity also measures the proportion of maintenance done by waiting for breakdown, but does so in cost terms. As such it gives even a better indication of the extent to which prevention is not being practiced. The scheduled maintenance enforcement ratio shows whether schedules are adhered to.
- ***Maintenance cost justification*** - all of these indices measure the maintenance department's cost efficiency. As such all of these indices measure whether the department's cost is at an optimal level and/or the department's contribution to profit is maximal. The two indices, maintenance cost intensity and maintenance cost effectiveness, both measure the overall cost level. One does so against the level of production (thus indicating in absolute terms the cost efficiency relative to the production - or profit - made) and the other against the investment in the business (indicating whether maintenance is being overdone or not). Stock turnover shows the efficiency of the use of capital to carry stock and have a profit impact. Overall maintenance cost effectiveness also measures the cost impact of the company's level of prevention, as is evident by inspecting the maintenance cost balance. This index grouping has the effect of further accentuating the need for higher levels of prevention. Maintenance improvement justification does exactly that - it measures whether the organization is achieving results from cost increases or decreases, again based on the maintenance cost balance.

The last measure, sundry cost component, only serves to indicate the maintenance organization's ability to focus on maintenance alone.

Setting up a multi-parameter measurement process

Following the choice of measurement indices and the setting up of measurement standards, a formal measurement process must now be devised. This can, in its simplest form, consist of measuring and comparing each of the chosen indices with its standard in an individual graph with trend indications. By studying the literature on measurement systems, one tends to be convinced that there are better ways. This section thus aims at devising a multi-parameter measurement process to combine the individual measurements into one logical whole. This is of course not easily done and the specific combination(s) has the effect of obscuring the underlying detail. It is thus recommended that the individual indices be portrayed in trend graphs, together with trend graphs of the combined indices.

The method of combination that is recommended is one employing features from both the *Du Pont* and *Nippon Denso* methods. The Du Pont method's beauty lies in its effective graphical portrayal of the various indices. Its drawback is that it can only handle four indices per graph. The Nippon Denso method, on the other hand, does not give a graphical presentation, but its point weighting system of integration allows any number of indices to be combined. Using a point system (Nippon Denso) to combine our twenty indices first into four groups and then into one overall result (Du Pont) should give us the best of both worlds. If the results of each of these combination processes are portrayed over time using trend techniques, we have the best of three worlds.

The choice of weighting parameters of course presents a problem. We have to decide which indices have the most and which less effect on the combined index. This should again be done by the maintenance management team, taking into account the effect of the various measures in their environment. The choice of weighting parameters can, of course, not be an exact science and thus the choice is done heuristically. We, furthermore, would prefer to work in similar units, so that the same figures have the same meaning for different indices and combined measures. This implies that a normalization process should be used. The benefit of this is that our combined result will always have a value of 100% if we have reached our goals. Another matter is that some of our indices decrease for the same change that increases the other indices. We must, in such cases, measure the negative change as a positive contribution. The first group of indices, maintenance results, will be used as a case in point. The breakdown frequency could, for example, be left out, as it is an alternative for MTTF. Three of the four remaining indices (A_V, MTTF and P_R) have a positive effect on the maintenance results if they increase. The mean time to repair, however, has a negative effect if it increases. We thus want to measure negative changes in MTTR as improvements. The following table shows illustrative values, which a management team has chosen, for the measurement standards and weights respectively.

Table 11.1 : Measurement Standards and Weights

Measure	***Standard***	***Weight***
A_V	85 %	0,8
MTTF	1000 hr	0,1
MTTR	200 min	0,05
P_R	500 t/h	0,05
Total		1,00

The first step is now to change all weights, so that they include normalizing parameters for the individual standards (to a base of 100). These normalizing parameters are calculated as follows:

$$A_V : n_1 = \frac{100}{85} = 1,1765$$

$$MTTF : n_2 = \frac{100}{1000} = 0,1$$

$$MTTR : n_3 = \frac{100}{200} = 0,5$$

$$P_R : n_4 = \frac{100}{500} = 0,2$$

These are then multiplied with the weight in the table above to give an overall weight. When the original standard is multiplied by this, the normalized weighted standard is derived.

Table 11.2 : Calculation of the normalized weighted standard

Measure	Standard	Weight	Normalizing Factor	Overall Weight	Normalized Weighted Standard
A_V	85 %	0,8	1,1765	0,9412	80
MTTF	1000 hr	0,1	0,1	0,01	10
MTTR	200 min	0,05	0,5	0,025	5
P_R	500 t/h	0,05	0,2	0,01	5
Total					100

As can be seen, the new standard for the first group of indices will now add up to 100 if all the standards are achieved. By using the actual measurements for A_V, MTTF, MTTR, P_R, multiplying it with the respective overall weight parameters and totaling, an overall score out of 100 will be the result. We are thus enabled to score our performance for the group, maintenance results, out of 100. This brings the whole measurement process and its results within the grasp of virtually all maintenance personnel. We have one outstanding issue, however. The changes for MTTR must be measured negatively as previously discussed. Thus, for this one measure, the result of the measurement, after multiplying with the overall weight, will be subtracted from the normalized weighted standard instead of the latter being subtracted from the former as in all other cases. Thus table 11.3 was prepared for an illustrative set of values.

For these measurement values, we are thus achieving 96,34 out of 100, or 96%, of our original goal. This looks like a result that we can use! This result can now be graphed to get a long term trend. We can do the same for the other groups. The last step is then to calculate the overall maintenance performance result. For this purpose weights must again be set by the maintenance management team to weigh the

Table 11.3 : Calculation of Normalized Weighted Measurement

Measure	Standard	Normalized Weighted Standard	Measurement Value	Overall Weight	Deviation from Standard	Normalized Weighted Measurement
A_V	85 %	80	00	0,9412	-1,8824	78,1176
MTTF	1000 hr	10	891	0,01	-1,09	8,91
MTTR	200 min	5	233	0,025	-0,825	4,175*
P_R	500 t/h	5	514	0,01	0,14	5,14
Total		100	Total			96,3426

*Negative calculation

four groups' results. Table 11.4 presents such a tabular combination of the four groups' results, using sample data. Note that the result figure for *Maintenance Results* is the one calculated above.

Clearly this result is more meaningful than the original diverse performance indices. The point is that we now know that we are achieving 95% of what we set out to do. We also know that we have a further 5% to improve by. The value of the model really lies in its ability to handle complex relationships between various maintenance indices in such a way that a single meaningful result is produced. We

Table 11.4 : Overall Maintenance Performance Calculation

Group	Result	Weigh	Final Score
Maintenance Results	96,34	0,3	28,9
Maintenance Productivity	94,05	0,1	9,41
Operational Purposefulness	82,85	0,2	16,57
Cost Justification	101,18	0,4	40,47
Total		1,0	95,35

can now work backwards through the model to establish which areas to concentrate on. In our example case, it seems as though operational purposefulness (82,85%) should be our main target area. The other areas that have values lower than 100% are maintenance results (95,34%) and productivity (94,05%). Both of these scores are higher than that of operational purposefulness. Furthermore, maintenance results is the result of efficiency in the productivity and operational purposefulness areas, while the final weight attached to productivity is the lowest. We will thus be able to benefit most from improving our operational purposefulness. Analyzing the detailed table for operational purposefulness shows that we should in turn concentrate on the low level of scheduling and the enforcement of scheduled work as a first priority. This is tantamount to saying that we have to increase our level of prevention. We should thus concentrate most of our effort in this area.

This section has shown how an integrated model can be devised from a diverse set of individual maintenance performance indices. It has also illustrated the model's ability to pinpoint the area(s) on which should be concentrated to improve the overall result.

The use of indices in the control process

We have earlier introduced the idea of viewing maintenance management as a control process. In this paragraph the control process will be built out further into a full fledged maintenance control model. The basic control process is repeated here for reference purposes.

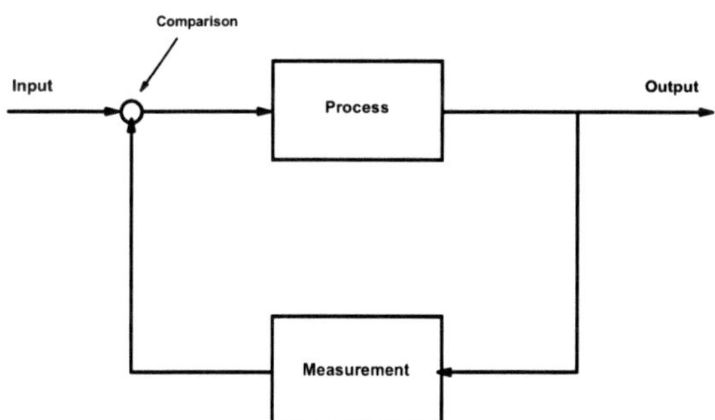

Figure 11.8 : Control Process

This basic model can now be used to devise a custom control process for maintenance. This process is shown in figure 11.9.

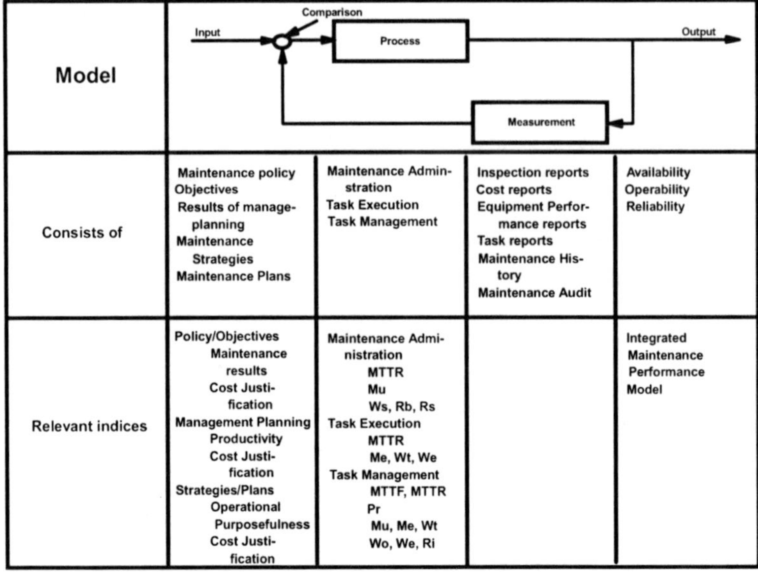

Model				
Consists of	Maintenance policy Objectives Results of manage-planning Maintenance Strategies Maintenance Plans	Maintenance Administration Task Execution Task Management	Inspection reports Cost reports Equipment Performance reports Task reports Maintenance History Maintenance Audit	Availability Operability Reliability
Relevant indices	Policy/Objectives Maintenance results Cost Justification Management Planning Productivity Cost Justification Strategies/Plans Operational Purposefulness Cost Justification	Maintenance Administration MTTR Mu Ws, Rb, Rs Task Execution MTTR Me, Wt, We Task Management MTTF, MTTR Pr Mu, Me, Wt Wo, We, Ri		Integrated Maintenance Performance Model

Figure 11.9 : The Maintenance Control Process

The above figure attempts to show the complex relationships between the various components of the maintenance cycle. It also specifies which of the twenty indices should be used to measure which parts of the maintenance cycle to effect proper control. It must be stressed, however, that there are no clear-cut boundaries - the above model is an attempt to improve the understanding of the measurement model. A few comments will clarify the figure:

a. The control cycle input consists of the following components:

* *Maintenance policy/Objectives* - the effects of these are best measured using the summary measure, maintenance results, as well as the measure cost justification.

* *Management planning* - the result of the management planning process can be measured using the summary measures productivity and cost justification.

* *Maintenance strategies/plans* - the correctness of the company's maintenance strategies/plans should be measured using the

summary measures operational purposefulness and cost justification.

b. The maintenance (operational) process, in its turn, has the following organizational parts:

  * *Maintenance administration* - the quality of the work done by the maintenance administration function (traditionally 'maintenance planning') can be assessed using the indices MTTR (job turnaround time), M_U (manpower utilization), W_S (Scheduling intensity), R_B (Breakdown severity) and R_S (Stock turnover).

  * *Task execution* - the contribution of the work force can best be assessed using the indices MTTR (job turnaround time), M_E (Manpower efficiency), W_T (Work order turnover) and W_E (Scheduled maintenance work enforcement ratio).

  * *Task management* - the role of the supervisory personnel is to ensure prompt and lasting results without too much expenditure. Whether this result is achieved, can be measured using the indices MTTF (Equipment reliability), MTTR (Job turnaround time), P_R (Production rate), M_U (Manpower utilization), M_E (Manpower efficiency), W_T (Work order turnover), W_O (Size of backlog), W_E (scheduled maintenance enforcement ratio) and R_I (Maintenance cost intensity).

c. As the measurement indices are an integral part of measurement, no one single index can be used to measure the efficiency of the measurement process itself.

d. The overall efficiency of maintenance, that is the output of the control cycle, is measured using the integrated performance model as developed above. The results are assessed using the four summary measures:

  * Maintenance results
  * Maintenance productivity
  * Operational purposefulness
  * Cost justification

  as well as the combined results in the Integrated maintenance performance measure.

References

1. Coetzee, J.L., The Measurement of Maintenance Performance. Annual short course, 1994.
2. Coetzee, J.L., Measuring Maintenance Performance. Annual Maintenance Convention, Johannesburg, 1996.
3. Hibi, S., How to measure Maintenance Performance. Asian Productivity Organization, 1977.
4. Luck, W.S., And now you can really measure Maintenance Performance. Factory Management and Maintenance, McGraw-Hill, volume 114 no 1, Jan 1956, p. 81-86.
5. Priel, V.Z., Twenty ways to track Maintenance Performance. Factory, McGraw-Hill, March 1962, p. 88-91.
6. Priel, V.Z., Systematic Maintenance Organisation. MacDonald and Evans, 1974.

Chapter 12

Maintenance Auditing

Introduction

One finds that the subject of maintenance auditing is emerging more and more in serious discussions of the management of maintenance. But, one also finds out very soon that no well structured methodology regarding the application of the idea of auditing in the maintenance field has been developed yet. There are organizations actively involved in the field of maintenance auditing and improvement, but the author has not, up to now, been convinced that they necessarily have the best approach. The material presented in this chapter has been derived from a combination of own experience, various sources as is listed in the list of references and a good deal of common sense. This, if properly utilized, will enable the individual organization to design and develop their own auditing system as one of the important components in a properly operative annual maintenance managerial cycle.

The need for auditing

We saw that the maintenance audit forms the annual measurement process that completes the maintenance management cycle's control loop. And, as is the case in any control system, measurement is really the key to success, in the sense that it tells you what improvements are necessary to enable you to reach your goals. Now, auditing is nothing more than that: it compares the state of affairs in the maintenance organization with a set of pre-defined standards to establish whether improvement is necessary or not. And, because maintenance is a complex function of the business, this process of measurement cannot be anything other than a fairly complex process itself. That is why there is a need for a properly structured formal maintenance audit once every year.

If the maintenance function in the organization achieves its goals in achieving a high level of maintenance performance, that will help assure high levels of plant profitability, as we saw in chapter 1. If, on the other hand, the performance of the maintenance function is poor, the effect on plant profitability can be devastating (due to high levels of downtime and high maintenance costs). And, if one does not start by measuring (through a proper audit) the performance of the maintenance function, performance improvements cannot be realized. For, it is only through the knowledge of present performance levels afforded by the auditing process, that insight can be developed regarding the future direction(s) for improvement.

As was seen in chapter 1, the level of prevention is the primary quantity that the maintenance manager can manipulate to determine the maintenance function's contribution to company profit. But, because of the complexity of the maintenance function, this is not an easy task. *Firstly*, his knowledge of the present level of the level of prevention is imperfect. This knowledge is based on his 'gut' feel of the present state of his maintenance strategy mix, taking into account the values of the monthly performance indices as discussed in chapter 11. *Secondly*, the specific prevention level may, due to circumstances outside his control, not always produce the results he predicted from his (imperfect) knowledge of the situation. *Thirdly*, his production counterparts may not fully utilize the production capacity that he provided through the chosen level of prevention, thus jeopardizing the level of profit contribution that he envisaged. And, *fourthly*, his own maintenance costs may produce unpredictable results, as is often the case in the maintenance world, again due to imperfect knowledge.

All this leads to the maintenance audit being, together with the maintenance performance measurement process, such an important instrument in the process of understanding the maintenance environment better. Only through this improved understanding of one's present situation can one, in a pro-active way, effect the necessary predisposition of the management team in the annual reworking of the maintenance policy, procedures, objectives, annual plan and maintenance strategies to ensure the long term success of the maintenance function. And that is, after all, the reason for the existence of the maintenance function in the first place. Only by a meaningful contribution to the profitability of the company can the maintenance function justify its own existence.

The two audits: Physical Audit and Systems Audit

There are two aspects that should be addressed in any maintenance audit: (1) the performance of the maintenance function as is evident in the results (both physical and in terms of figures) of the maintenance actions being undertaken, and (2) the extent to which proper systems have been put in place to ensure the attainment of such results. If only the first is done, success may never be had, as it is essentially the provision of a proper systems base that will ensure that plans can be transformed into commensurate results. On the other hand, if only the second is addressed, one will never be sure that the actions being prescribed by the systems are being converted into measurable results.

Both the physical audit and the systems audit is normally performed by an audit team using a checklist. Whether the checklist is divided into two parts, or are one integrated auditing instrument, the important principle is that both the physical and systems aspects should be addressed separately.

The Physical Audit

The physical audit should make provision for two quantities being measured. The first of these is an evaluation of the results achieved by the specific division of the maintenance function. This is normally measured in terms of the direct results achieved, i.e. the availability, reliability (normally measured in Mean Time To Failure - MTTF), operability (in terms of production rate being achieved) and cost of maintenance. These figures are compared to industry standards, if those are available, past performance and the goals set for the specific period. Secondly a number of physical parameters indicating whether acceptable results are being achieved are evaluated. This is done by organized plant visits during which the various members of the team visually (and through using the other senses, notably hearing) inspect the results gained through the maintenance actions being performed.

The Systems Audit

As was stated in the opening paragraph of this section, the physical audit should be augmented by a systems audit. The parameters being evaluated here, as well as the performance standards being measured against, are set up by the management team during the annual management planning sessions as described in chapter 10. The audit is done by the audit team in two steps. The *first* of these is done during the various sessions with the management team to evaluate their predisposition towards system driven management, to evaluate their actions towards this goal and to determine their perception of the systems situation on the floor. This is, *secondly*, augmented by visits to selected incumbents of supervisory and administration (planning) functions to establish how well systems have been deployed and how effective they are.

The components of the auditing process

There are certainly many ways in which one can design a maintenance audit instrument. The one presented here is one such possibility. The important issue is to have a comprehensive spectrum of audit questions and to combine them in as good a way as is possible, so as to achieve a high standard of maintenance practice.

The main categories

Certainly, mankind (and especially engineers) tend to think and analyze better if subject areas are classified in some or other way. It is thus good to start the topic of maintenance audit categories by deciding which main areas should be covered when developing an audit instrument (very much in the same fashion that we developed the performance measurement instrument). We can use our model, the Maintenance Cycle, to do this. The best way to do this is by using the outer cycle (management cycle) of the Maintenance Cycle to think through, from a managerial perspective, which main categories of audit components are essential. Of course, in the process one should keep in mind the inner cycle all the time as it represents the operational processes that have to be managed.

By doing this the following main categories are derived. They are firstly listed in alphabetical order, after which each category will be discussed one by one to describe the logic for having such a category and its connection to the maintenance cycle. The main categories are:

- Administration (Planning) effectiveness
- Expertise and Competence of personnel
- Facilities (Maintenance Equipment and Workshop facilities)

- Management Processes
- Maintenance Policy Setting
- Organizational Climate and Culture
- Safety and Housekeeping
- Systems

These eight main categories, which are proposed as the main framework of an audit process, will now be discussed one by one to provide a clear picture of its right of existence and its relationship to the Maintenance Cycle.

Audit components by category

Now that we have developed our framework, we can fill it in with the detailed audit components or questions. These are, of course, not all of the same importance and a weighting process will be discussed later to ensure that a balanced result is obtained. It must again be stressed that the individual firm using an audit instrument will probably want to reclassify some of these components under different headings than the ones presented here (in addition to adding more components or deleting some of those introduced here).

Administration (Planning) effectiveness

Administration (Planning) Personnel Training and Aptitude

⇒ Technical education of maintenance administrative (planning) personnel - technical education is an important ingredient to the long term effectiveness of the administrative (planning) function. A good mix of technical and administrative skills are important in this crucial support function. Typically one should look for at least a T3/T4 person to head this function, while the Administrative (Planning) Officers in individual offices should have no less than a N3/N4 qualification. All of these persons should preferably come from a suitable trade background and should have good administrative capabilities. Clerks should be persons with a definite inclination towards administration (not typists).

⇒ Technical techniques training of administrative (planning) personnel - as the administrative (planning) function is the primary support function of maintenance operations, it is imperative that these personnel be well versed in the techniques utilized for good maintenance planning and control. The level of training needed will differ from company to company, but they should at least get basic training in concepts such as the why and how of Preventive Maintenance Techniques, the why of Reliability Centered Maintenance, the rudiments of Condition Based Maintenance. They should also receive fairly advanced training in the procurement of spares and materials, as well as detailed task planning.

⇒ Systems training of administrative (planning) personnel - as administrative (planning) personnel operate and administer the bulk of the organization's maintenance systems, it is imperative that they be well trained at an advanced level in maintenance systems technology. That is, they should know why and how the systems work in the way they do. Clerks should at least know how to operate the systems.

⇒ Characteristics of administrative (planning) personnel - these personnel must all have a marked preference for systems work. They should think administratively in a very systematic way (they should tend to think in terms of flow charts). They should also have a strong administrative orientation, together with a feel for the planned maintenance requirements of the equipment they serve. Senior personnel should know what the critical success factors for their function are, and should have a clear view of the future development of their personnel and function.

Organization of the administrative (planning) function

⇒ Span of control - because the Administrative (Planning) Officers each have a responsibility for administrative work, his span of control cannot be to large. Supervisory work in this function is of an intensive and detailed level, thus necessitating a fairly narrow span of control. Typical maximum spans of control are: 5 senior Administrative (Planning) Officers reporting to the Administrative (Planning) Chief, 3 Administrative (Planning) Officers (in charge of individual offices) reporting to each senior Administrative (Planning) Officer, while Administrative (Planning) Officers should have no more than two clerks (typically one) reporting to him.

⇒ Clerical support - clerks should be appointed as support staff. They should do all system data capturing and routine administrative tasks to leave the Administrative (Planning) Officers free to devote themselves to task planning.

⇒ Organization structure - there are certain advantages and disadvantages inherent in both the centralization and decentralization of the administrative (planning) function. As such it is important that this issue has been thoroughly analyzed and debated. The organizational form should also be in line with the requirements of the maintenance policy.

⇒ Functional reporting - the whole administrative (planning) function is functionally responsible to the Chief Administrative (Planning) Officer, even when the administrative (planning) function is decentralized. This is important to retain a high level of functional expertise in the administration of the maintenance plan.

⇒ Level of reporting of the Chief Administrative (Planning) Officer - the importance of the administrative (planning) function is reflected in the level of reporting of its chief. The Chief Administrative (Planning) Officer should report directly to the company's maintenance chief.

⇒ Administrative (Planning) Officer workload - this workload should be regularly reviewed. The typical workload for any one Administrative (Planning) Officer (supported by one clerk) should be support for no more than 12 artisans.

⇒ Administrative (Planning) Officer relations with other personnel - as this is a support function that provides a service to foremen, artisans and indirectly to the production department, there is a high potential for destructive conflict. There should thus exist good work relations between Administrative (Planning) Officers and other personnel. This should be reflected in a relationship of mutual respect and dependence between Administrative (Planning) Officers and foremen, in such a way that there is a harmony in achieving the goals of the organization.

Work Planning

⇒ Work Order definition - as work orders form the basis of the orderly execution of the maintenance plan, it should be well structured and the work described in full detail. Each maintenance task should have at least a well defined work order. For larger tasks the task should be subdivided into more than one lower level child work orders, structured in a hierarchy under the parent work order. This should be done such that it facilitates the subdivision of work into logical compartments to facilitate work and cost control.

⇒ Resource Planning - this should include:

* Materials Planning - the maintenance administration (planning) function should plan the materials requirements of planned maintenance tasks in detail. This should include the procurement of all materials before a planned maintenance task is being issued.
* Manpower Planning - the maintenance administration (planning) function should plan the work content of each maintenance work order in detail. This includes the number of workers needed of the various skills. For each maintenance task various task methods are considered, the best one chosen and described as formal task description. This description should be such that it helps the artisan in completing the task successfully in the least possible time span. In addition to this a standard task time should be developed and set for each planned task - a standard method such as time study or analytical estimating can be used for this purpose. This standard task time should generally be fairly accurate and realistic.
* Maintenance Equipment Planning - the planning of a planned maintenance task should include the specification of any special tools and equipment that will be needed. Furthermore, the availability of such tools and equipment should be checked before issuing the task to be done.
* Logistical Planning - many maintenance tasks takes longer than it should, due to the logistics of the task not being thought through and properly planned. As such the planning process should include work flow planning, material flow planning and personnel flow planning. Furthermore, the procurement of resources and support documentation such as drawings and manuals should be regarded as an integral part of the logistical planning function.

⇒ Preventive planning - to avoid negative incidents from occurring, the planning task should include the following:

* Safety Planning - no task in industry can be deemed complete if safety has not been considered. As such, the planning of a planned maintenance task includes the specification of any spe-

cial precautions that must be taken and the safety equipment that will be needed. The availability of such special safety equipment should be checked before issuing the task to be done.

* Quality Requirements - where-as the safety of persons is a primary condition that should be met to be responsible towards staff, quality is likewise a primary condition to be met in terms of the responsibility towards the continuity of the productive process and thus the profit of the company. The planning of a planned maintenance task should thus include the specification of any special quality requirements that must be met.

* Opportunistic Maintenance - The concept of opportunistic maintenance is that some maintenance tasks, although being very important, should be delayed until the plant becomes available for maintenance work due to a production stoppage or a breakdown. The maintenance administration (planning) function should be adept at identifying these opportunities, with a view to slotting in opportunistic tasks.

⇒ Attributes of the planning task

* Level of Prevention - the level of prevention being practiced directly impacts on the production capacity and thus the profit of the company. The level of preventive work done should thus be fairly high and should be regarded as being optimal.

* Planning Coverage - to achieve a high level of prevention, the percentage of planned work in relation to the total maintenance workload should be fairly high. This should also be reflected in a relatively low breakdown workload. The higher the planning coverage, the higher the personnel utilization that will be reached as well. Specific objectives should be set to improve the relationship between planned and unplanned work, while the ratio of planned to unplanned work is continuously monitored.

* Planning lead time - it is important that Administrative (Planning) Officer have sufficient time available for the planning tasks, as the quality of planning is directly proportional to the time spent on it. As such, a standard and realistic lead time is allowed for every planning job that must be done and no pressure is exerted on planners to perform planning tasks in less than the standard lead time allowed.

* Planning Effectiveness - As planning effectiveness directly impacts on the effectiveness of the whole department, planning ef-

fectiveness should be fairly high when measured through ratios such as the percentage planned work and the percentage breakdown work.

Work Scheduling

⇒ Scheduling Techniques - because work scheduling is such an important part of the planning process (due to the effectiveness of breakdown prevention depending on it), the best possible scheduling techniques should be taught to, and used by all planners. This includes:

* Time slot scheduling to locate scheduled work on the maintenance calendar.
* Critical path scheduling to plan all complex work in an optimal way.
* Workshop flow processing algorithms to plan the work flow through jobbing workshops.
* Task priorities to sequence the work of all area maintenance (field) workshops.

⇒ Scheduling Utilities - because of the importance of scheduling, all the necessary scheduling utilities should be provided to and used by administrative (planning) personnel: project scheduling software using Critical Path Method or PERT and having proper facilities for resource leveling and Gantt chart production, as well as scheduling calendars and personnel availability schedules.

⇒ Scheduling Output - the following output should be produced from the scheduling process on a regular basis: A weekly (or other period as required) schedule per work group should be produced and supplied to the supervisor of the work group, together with the task documentation which should be placed in preferred order of execution on a work assignment board or equivalent.

Task Support

⇒ Task Documentation - the quality of task documentation provided to an artisan directly affects the quality and success of the work he delivers. He should thus at work execution time the worker be issued with a job card, a check list (if the task at hand involves regular scheduled work for which such check list exists), a work permit (if the work must be done in a hazardous area) and engineering drawings (if the work requires the worker having a drawing at hand). Check lists should be updated regularly and should generally list at least the 20% highly important checks identified by a 80/20 (Pareto) analysis.

⇒ Feedback of Job Data - complete and accurate feedback of job data is crucial as it provides the information that renders the maintenance systems effective. As such, job feedback from artisans should be punctual and accurate. In promoting this, foremen should be champions who actively promotes proper task feedback. The maintenance administration (planning) function should update the maintenance data bank promptly when receiving job data.

Expertise and Competence of personnel

Training and Development of Personnel

⇒ Basic Engineering Education: Engineers and Technicians - in today's competitive business world, maintenance personnel need to be a high caliber. Although not guaranteeing this, a sound education in engineering is a basic ingredient for success. Maintenance engineers should thus have a good basic engineering education (B. Eng., B.Tech. or equivalent) plus an applicable Government Certificate of Competency. Furthermore, maintenance technicians ought to have a good basic technical education (T3, N6 or equivalent).

⇒ Approved Engineering Training - additional to having a proper education in engineering, engineers should go through a period of a approved training during which time they gain practical experience. This training should be at least two years of a practical on the job training program as approved by ECSA as being an adequate prerequisite for registration in the respective category. The appointment of maintenance engineers in managerial positions should only take place after such practical training has been completed.

⇒ Career Growth Path: Engineers - a well-documented career growth path for maintenance engineers should exist to ensure that valuable expertise is being retained in the maintenance organization.

⇒ Coaching and Mentor System: Engineers - the period of practical training of engineers should be overseen by experienced engineers. To bring this into effect, a well thought out mentor system must exist to assist in the effective build up of expertise during the practical training of young engineers. This system should make effective use of the expertise and experience of older engineers. It should also ensure that the needs of the young engineers for career path development are being met, while ascertaining that each pupil receives training in all the relevant fields of expertise.

⇒ Technical or Academic School Education: Artisans and Artisan Helpers - the following educational standards are necessary for maintenance workers: artisans should generally have an educational level of at least standard 8 (grade 10) or N1, while preference should be given to artisans with an educational level of standard 10 (grade 12) or N3 or higher. Artisan helpers should have an educational level of at least standard 6 (grade 8).

⇒ Experience: Technicians and Artisans - the technicians and artisans employed should have a high level of applicable experience.

People Skills

⇒ Managerial Training - managerial training of engineers is of primary importance. Therefore, all maintenance engineers and managers ought to be trained in basic management theory (at least two weeks' full time or equivalent part time training). Furthermore, maintenance engineers should be encouraged to enroll for a management enrichment course such as the Management Development Program (UNISA), an MBA or equivalent.

⇒ Negotiation Skills - as maintenance managers are often in situations where they have to negotiate, they have to be trained in negotiation. This should include persuasive and decision making communication, as well as negotiation with labor unions, suppliers, customers and clients.

⇒ Problem solving and decision making skills - some of the most frequently used techniques in a maintenance department includes problem solving and decision analysis. All managers , supervisors and technicians thus ought to be trained to use problem solving skills (situation analysis, group problem solving techniques and contingency planning) effectively.

⇒ Time Management Skills - all managers should know how to utilize their time efficiently.

⇒ Supervisory Training - supervisors must receive formal training in supervision theory and financial management. This training must be of a high quality.

Technical Skills

⇒ Preventive Maintenance - Preventive Maintenance is one of the corner stones of good maintenance practice. The theory of preventive maintenance should thus be understood well by all maintenance engineers. All personnel must be aware of and believe in the benefits to be reaped from a proper preventive maintenance program.

⇒ Reliability Centered Maintenance - RCM is the only complete scientific approach available to decide on the maintenance policies applicable to each machine/component. All maintenance engineers should thus know and understand the concepts of Reliability Centered Maintenance. A specific individual (preferably an engineer with an academic inclination) (referred to as the Maintenance Expert or M.E.) should also be set apart to lead the RCM drive towards optimal preventive maintenance. This individual must be fully trained in the use of RCM.

⇒ Condition Monitoring - condition based maintenance is not any longer an option for the average maintenance department, but an absolute necessity. To apply condition monitoring effectively, a proper technical background of the underlying principles and of the various techniques is necessary. Maintenance managers and supervisors should thus understand the basic theory of condition monitoring, the reasons for monitoring and the positive results that can be achieved through monitoring. They must also be able to interpret the results of such monitoring meaningfully. The ME ought to be fully trained in the theory of condition monitoring and should thus be able to identify and select the right application areas for the various condition monitoring techniques.

⇒ Maintenance Data Analysis - maintenance failure data analysis is an important prerequisite for the proper application of RCM (and thus for policy formulation). Maintenance engineers should thus understand the principles and theory of maintenance data analysis (MDA) sufficiently to be able to interpret the results of such analyses and to communicate sensibly with the ME. The ME must be fully trained in the mathematical and statistical theory of MDA. He or she can thus assist the maintenance engineers by doing such analyses on request and producing reports stating the results of such analyses clearly. Software should be available to assist the ME in this task.

⇒ Maintenance Systems - as maintenance systems give structure to all maintenance actions, all managerial personnel should know the systems used and maintenance systems theory by heart. All senior maintenance personnel, as well as the ME, must thus be fully trained in the theory and application of maintenance systems. A period of training (at least three months) in the maintenance administration (planning) office should form an essential part of the practical training of young engineers and must also be a prerequisite for an appointment to a foreman post.

⇒ Maintenance Cost Control - as maintenance cost is the "bottom line", knowledge and experience of cost control measures are essential. All managers and supervisors must thus fully understand the techniques of maintenance cost control and must also be able to effectively draw up a maintenance budget.

⇒ Maintenance Control - all managers and supervisors should fully understand the techniques and functions of maintenance control. This includes amongst others how to control work backlog, personnel utilization and personnel efficiency effectively.

⇒ Fault Elimination - all maintenance engineers should be trained in the techniques of fault elimination.

⇒ Approved Apprenticeship - artisans form the front line of attack in the maintenance department. As such, apprentices should have an educational level of at least standard 8 (grade 10) or N1 (standard 10 (grade 12) or N3 preferred). Artisans ought to be trained using a training scheme that fully complies with the need that have to be met, while artisans that are appointed from outside the organization have qualifications that compare favorably with the artisans trained inside the organization.

⇒ Artisan Helper Training Scheme - artisan helpers should be trained using a training scheme that fully complies with the need that have to be met.

⇒ Fault Tracing - as equipment breakdowns lead to costly downtime, speedy tracing of faults is of paramount importance. All maintenance personnel should thus be trained to trace equipment faults fast and effectively. This includes training in the proper reading of logical diagrams and the use of fault trees. The effect of this must be that, when equipment faults occur, they are normally located and diagnosed speedily.

Facilities (Maintenance Equipment and Workshop facilities)

Workshops

⇒ Workshop Adequacy - Adequate workshop facilities are of primary importance in providing a proper maintenance service. To ensure this, the workshops that exist should generally *considered to be adequate* by the audit team. Secondly, the *layout of the workshops* must allow effective work flow. Thirdly, whenever a change in the tasks being performed or the age of the present workshops requires it, the workshop layout and size should be *updated through a capital project.*

⇒ Workshop Specialization - workshop specialization promotes in-depth-knowledge of the teams handling maintenance tasks and improves the quality and performance of maintenance work. In general, in-plant-maintenance should be handled by *area maintenance workshops* (decentralized to handle the day to day maintenance of the specific plant area). All specialized maintenance (tasks which require special knowledge and skills, such as those on technologically advanced equipment) should be handled by specially equipped "*specialized service*" *workshops.* A third type of workshop, which should exist, is *general service workshops*, equipped (both regarding the workshop equipment and trades specialization) to handle tasks such as large welding and boilermaking assignments. Furthermore, if the need for frequent manufacturing tasks (such as the manufacturing of a machine part) exist, these should be handled by *specialized manufacturing workshops.*

⇒ Work Reception (Input) Area - sufficient reception (input) area is necessary to promote smooth and efficient work flow. As such, each workshop ought to have a separate work reception area that is equipped with sufficient storage space and materials handling facilities to effectively receive new tasks.

⇒ Work Dispatch (Output) Area - sufficient dispatch (output) area is likewise necessary to promote smooth and efficient work flow. Each workshop should thus have a separate work dispatch area that is equipped with sufficient storage space and materials handling facilities to effectively dispatch completed tasks.

⇒ Equipment Washing Facilities - to provide a quality maintenance service, it is important to properly clean the equipment before and during maintenance work. For this reason, workshops handling the maintenance or overhauling of dirty equipment in the workshop ought to have washing bays equipped with apparatus for cleaning the equipment before and during the maintenance process.

⇒ Work in Process Storage - proper work flow and good housekeeping standards are promoted by having sufficient work in process storage space. Therefore, each workshop must have an adequate work in process storage area. This area is utilized to store the task and task related materials while waiting for materials and personnel to complete the task.

⇒ Sub Store Space - most maintenance work requires the immediate availability of frequently used materials (such as bolts and nuts, welding rods, steel plates, seals, bearings, etc.). This necessitates the use of sub-stores. Each workshop should thus have an adequate sub store area, which is used to store materials that are used so frequently that an own small stock has to be kept in the workshop.

⇒ Tool Store - larger and more expensive tools should not be duplicated and must be available to all personnel. To store these a tool store is needed in each workshop where such a need exists. This could range from a specially dedicated cabinet to a fully fledged tool store that allows specialized tools and equipment to be stored and retrieved effectively. If necessary, a dedicated or part-time store's should also be appointed to keep effective control over tool and equipment issues and returns.

Tools And Equipment

⇒ General Adequacy of Tools and Equipment - adequate tools and equipment are vital for maintenance efficiency. For this reason both the tools and equipment in the tool store, as well as those in the artisans' tool boxes, must be of *good quality*. Secondly, the tools and equipment used should be *updated* whenever a major change in technology (of either the equipment serviced or the tools themselves) requires such a change. The tools and equipment used to perform tasks ought to be *well sized and rated* for the task at hand.

⇒ Artisan Tool Lists - tool lists and their enforcement are a absolute necessity in providing a good maintenance service. There should, firstly, exist a *standard tool list* for every type of artisan. It should, secondly, be a requirement that every new *artisan must have or acquire the tools on the standard tool list* for his trade before work commences. Thirdly, *regular tool inspections* ought to be performed to ensure that every artisan's tool box is fully stocked and that the tools are in satisfactory condition. Lastly, whenever a *tool is destroyed* through use in service of the company and no abuse is suspected, the company should replace the tool for the artisan at company cost. If the artisan is at fault, the company should assist the artisan in purchasing the tool through company buying channels.

⇒ General Availability of Tools and Equipment - maintenance tasks cannot be performed well if the right tools and equipment are not available. The audit should thus ensure that the *tools and equipment that are needed to complete the majority of the jobs* that the specific workshop handles are normally available. It must also ascertain that, *whenever tools and equipment that are not available are needed,* management make plans to acquire, hire, loan or manufacture them after making sure that the task cannot be performed without them.

⇒ Materials Handling Facilities (For Example Cranes) - workshop work flow efficiency to a large extent hinges on the availability of proper materials handling facilities. Each workshop and maintenance working place should thus be equipped with materials handling facilities that allow effectual completion of the task(s) at hand.

⇒ Machining Facilities - maintenance tasks cannot be executed fast and with the right quality if the necessary machining facilities are not available. Therefore, each workshop should be equipped with *sufficient machining facilities* to handle the normal machining work that has to be carried out in the specific workshop. Furthermore, *specialized machining workshops* ought to be equipped with machining centers that are of sufficient new design to ensure efficient and accurate workmanship.

⇒ Welding Facilities - maintenance tasks cannot be executed properly if the necessary welding facilities are not available. Each workshop should thus be equipped with *sufficient welding facilities* to handle the normal welding work that has to be carried out in the specific workshop. Further to this, specialized boiler-making and welding workshops are equipped with *welding centers* that are of sufficient new design to ensure efficient and accurate workmanship.

⇒ Equipment Servicing Facilities - servicing tasks can only be handled if the right servicing facilities are available. It must thus be ensured that each workshop is equipped with sufficient equipment servicing facilities to handle the servicing work that has to be handled in the specific workshop. These include test equipment, handling equipment, inspection and condition monitoring equipment, access facilities and lubricating equipment.

⇒ Testing Facilities - equipment fault finding and quality overhaul on repair work is dependent on the availability of the right test equipment. Workshops that have to repair equipment or equipment sub-assemblies should thus be equipped with test facilities for *tracing equipment defects* efficiently. Secondly, workshops that have to overhaul equipment sub-assemblies must be equipped with test facilities to *test the performance of the completed unit(s)* over a suitable burn-in period before returning it to its user.

⇒ Work Benches - work benches are the primary "furniture" that should be supplied for the use of each artisan. The audit must thus, firstly, ensure that a *work bench is supplied for each artisan* that has to have access to such a facility. Secondly, the work benches ought to be *designed* and built or purchased with the task of the specific artisan in mind. Work benches should also, in general, form *efficient work centers* at which or from which the artisan performs a quality job.

⇒ Tool Boxes - proper tooling of each artisan can only be expected if he/she is provided with good and functional tool boxes. Thus, a tool box *should be supplied* for each artisan and must be *designed* and built or purchased with the tool storage requirements of the specific artisan in mind.

⇒ Services Adequacy - every workshop and office should be designed and built with adequate electricity, water, steam and air services. The audit team should thus make sure that: Workshops and offices have *adequate electricity supplies*, enough *electricity outlet points* of the right types, *adequate water supplies*, enough *water points* of the right types, adequate *air supplies* (where necessary), adequate *air supply points* of the right types, adequate *steam supplies* (where necessary) and enough *steam supply points* of the right type.

Office Facilities

⇒ General Adequacy of Office Facilities - the audit team must firstly ensure that the office facilities supplied are *generally adequate* for the functions that they service. Secondly, offices should be functional and finished and furnished in such a way that they promote the *general productivity* of office workers. The *sizing of offices* must thirdly be such that they support the work that has to be carried out in them effectively.

⇒ Clerical support - a *sufficient level of clerical support*, that will effectively support the maintenance tasks at hand, should exist at all times. Furthermore, clerks must only be appointed after *a thorough screening process* to ensure that they will psychologically be able to handle the task and that they have the appropriate level of qualifications and experience.

⇒ Filing Facilities - proper filing ensures efficient administration and information retrieval. All offices must thus have filing facilities that are commensurate with the tasks being performed in them.

⇒ Typing Facilities - sufficient typing facilities and typists must be provided by the company to support the maintenance function.

⇒ Computer Facilities - no maintenance department can presently perform its maintenance tasks effectively without computer support. Computer facilities thus ought to be provided to *support the maintenance function* are both adequate and effective. Secondly, each maintenance manager and supervisor should to have effective *access to computer terminals* to support their managerial role with good up to date information. Thirdly, maintenance administration (planning), scheduling and work execution should be efficiently supported by the computer system(s).

⇒ Printing Facilities - sufficient printing facilities must exist to supply in the need for the *expedient printing of maintenance operational documents*. Furthermore, a quality printing service should be available for the production of maintenance manuals and forms.

Personnel Facilities

⇒ Toilet Facilities - toilet facilities should, firstly, be available to all personnel in *locations* that are relatively near to all personnel working places. The number and size of toilet facilities should, secondly, in general, be considered adequate by all personnel. Thirdly, toilet facilities ought to be maintained well and must normally be clean and hygienic.

⇒ Worker Dining Facilities - each workshop or workshop group should have a *proper worker dining room* with enough tables and chairs for the number of workers that have to dine there. These dining facilities should, secondly, be *kept neat.* It also ought to have a kitchen type *wash up basin.*

⇒ Change Room Facilities - each workshop or workshop group must have change room facilities that are *adequate for the number of workers* that have to wash and change clothes there. It must also be kept neat at all times and must, thirdly, be equipped with *an adequate number of showers and wash basins* with an adequate supply of hot and cold running water.

Work Environment

⇒ Lighting Adequacy - the lighting in all *offices* should be such that it places the minimum strain on incumbents' *eyes* while doing administrative tasks. Furthermore, the lighting in all *workshops* should be such that it allows workers to do accurate work without excessive strain on their eyes.

⇒ Heating and Cooling Adequacy - all *offices* should be equipped with sufficient heating and cooling devices (natural or otherwise) to allow personnel to work at their optimum efficiency. *Workshops* should be equipped with roof insulation and natural draft ventilation for summer and heating for winter conditions. These must be such that they ensure a level of comfort favorable to high productivity of the workers.

⇒ Facility Maintenance - the maintenance of all facilities must be of a high standard and ensures that the facilities remain in the optimum condition for effective operation.

⇒ Facility Improvement - facilities ought to be continuously improved as new and improved ways of supporting the maintenance of the firm's equipment becomes available.

⇒ Tool Store Control - the control of tool stores is important as specialized tools and equipment must be kept available and in good condition. For this reason the audit must evaluate whether there exists an *asset register for the tools and equipment* in the tool store, that *regular stocktaking* takes place to ensure that all tools and equipment are in good condition and complete, that every workshop tool store is under the control of a full time or part time *store's clerk*, that no tools are *issued* by anyone else than the store's clerk, that *tool issue requisitions* are used to control the issue and return of tools and that *tool losses* occur very rarely.

⇒ Sub Store Control - the control of sub stores is critical as sub stores can easily get out of control, leading to high inventories and wastage. The audit team must thus ascertain that every workshop sub store is under the control of a *full time or part time store's clerk*, that no parts or materials are *issued* by anyone else than the store's clerk, that *issue requisitions* are used to control the issue of spares and materials, that only spares and materials that are *very frequently used* are kept in workshop sub stores and that sub stores are *audited on a regular basis* (i.e. three monthly) by a senior supervisor.

⇒ Green Areas - green areas are a fairly recent development to accommodate and promote group interaction. It was found that healthy group interaction leads to a lower level of formal management and an improvement in work performance. The organization should thus, firstly, *provide green areas* in positions easily reached by personnel to support group discussion. Work teams should, secondly, use green areas daily for the *early morning or beginning of shift planning* as well as for problem solving sessions. Thirdly, green areas must give a fair degree of *privacy and have a low noise level*. Basic facilities such as *a white board and board markers* should, fourthly, be supplied in all green areas. Lastly, graphs showing the *group's performance* in previously identified critical success areas ought to be displayed prominently.

Work Support

⇒ Maintenance Manuals - no maintenance worker can produce the right results without access to proper maintenance manuals. As such, each workshop must have a *bookshelf* where at least one maintenance manual for each type of machine maintained by that workshop is kept. Secondly, new machine purchases should specify *that proper maintenance manuals* should be supplied with the machine when delivered. A delivery must not deemed to be complete without the simultaneous delivery of the agreed upon number of maintenance manuals. Thirdly, maintenance manuals must be kept in a *good condition* and are replaced whenever their condition warrants it, or when machine updates requires it.

⇒ Parts Manuals - as is the case with maintenance manuals, support of the maintenance work through the availability of proper parts manuals are essential. Each workshop should thus have a *bookshelf* where at least one parts' manual for each type of machine maintained by that workshop is kept. Secondly, new machine purchases should specify that *proper parts' manuals* should be supplied with the machine when delivered. A delivery is not deemed to be complete without the simultaneous delivery of the agreed upon number of parts' manuals. Parts' manuals must, thirdly, be kept in a *good condition* and must be replaced whenever their condition warrants it, or when machine updates requires it.

⇒ Stock Catalogues - Each workshop should have a *bookshelf* where at least one set of stock catalogues are kept (if stock catalogues are not computerized). Stock catalogues must, secondly, be kept in *a good condition* and are replaced whenever their condition warrants it. Thirdly, pressure must be exerted on the stores' organization to *update stock catalogues* when machine updates requires it.

⇒ Engineering Drawings - a maintenance department cannot function properly without access to engineering drawings. For this reason, an *engineering drawing office* or outside drawing office service must exist which keeps engineering drawings for all plant items updated. New machine purchases should, secondly, specify that *proper engineering drawings* should be supplied with the machine when delivered. A delivery should not be deemed to be complete without the simultaneous delivery of the agreed upon number of sets of engineering drawings. Thirdly, each workshop should have a *storage facility* where the most often used engineering drawings are kept. Engineering drawings must, fourthly, be kept in a *good condition* and replaced whenever their condition warrants it. Fifthly, pressure must be exerted on the drawing office to update drawings when machine updates require it.

⇒ Register of Manuals - a register ought to be maintained of all manuals and drawings kept in the workshop. All issues must be recorded for control purposes.

Management Processes

⇒ Vision and Mission of the Organization - no maintenance department can exist on its own or be effective if its role in the organization is not clear. It is thus of paramount importance that the vision and the mission of the organization are documented. The maintenance department should also take specific actions to ensure that all employees in the department are committed to the vision and mission of the organization.

⇒ Vision and Mission of the Maintenance Department - to ensure that the maintenance department contribute towards the attainment of the vision and mission of the organization the maintenance department should have its own vision and mission, which supports the vision and mission of the organization. All maintenance employees must be fully familiar with, and committed to, the vision and mission of the maintenance department. This must be visible in their practicing of the vision and mission in their daily work.

⇒ Core Values - there should be clarity on the norms and values that employees should display in performing their day to day work. There should be visible commitment to these values.

⇒ Medium and Long Term Plans - the maintenance department, like any other, should have medium and long term plans aimed at meeting the needs of the department in a fast changing environment. Maintenance management must ensure that these plans filter through to the people in the various sections responsible for implementing the strategies. They should also have the means to control the implementation of these medium and long term plans.

⇒ Goals and Objectives for All Levels - work groups at all levels in the maintenance department ought to set measurable objectives and standards.

⇒ Budgeting - all maintenance managers should be trained in a standard process for compiling annual budgets. This should lead to realistic and attainable budgets and must be the basis for strictly controlling the actual spending.

⇒ Measuring Performance - work performance and outputs should be formally measured and assessed against set objectives, standards and medium and long term plans. These should be displayed such that all employees are aware of the position. All employees must receive frequent feedback on their individual performance, while the department's outputs should regularly be compared to industry norms.

⇒ Methods and procedures - purposeful action should be taken to ensure that work methods and procedures for all critical tasks are documented and adhered to by all personnel. These work methods and procedures should be continuously reviewed and upgraded to ensure that tasks are done in the best possible ways.

⇒ Cost Efficiency - there should be a plan to identify the major causes of high costs. This ought to be augmented by up to date cost reduction objectives and goals for each work group.

⇒ Recognition - the department should have a recognition process catering for both formal and informal recognition. This must ensure that good work performance is recognized consistently.

⇒ Remuneration - it must be ensured that work outputs of employees have a direct impact on their pay. The department should take a firm stand on the fair and equitable remuneration of the maintenance department's employees.

⇒ Training - there should be clarity on the knowledge and skills requirements for all positions in the maintenance department, as well as which key competencies will enhance long term success in the department. It must be ensured that the training people receive addresses these requirements in a systematic, orderly and cost effective way.

⇒ Personnel and Management Policies - employees must be consistently informed on new and revised personnel and management policies. These policies should be evaluated from time to time by the department, so as to make recommendations to management on necessary changes.

⇒ Performance Appraisal - the department's managers should have formal appraisal sessions with all employees at regular intervals. These should result in individual training and development plans for all employees. If done correctly, employees will experience the performance appraisal as something positive and helpful.

⇒ Problem Solving - there must be a formal generic problem-solving process used throughout the maintenance department. This should include a way of dealing with problems which cannot be solved because of a lack of authority. The bottom line must be that the department succeeds in eliminating the root causes of problems.

⇒ Communication - the department must have a formal process for communication in all directions. This includes that all supervisory personnel communicate effectively with employees and that people feel that communication in the maintenance department is sound.

⇒ Selection - departmental managers and supervisors must be skilled in a standard selection process to ensure that the best people will be selected for vacancies in the maintenance department. This should lead to a general happiness with the quality of people appointed from outside, while the best people are generally promoted to senior positions.

⇒ Client Needs - the maintenance department must know who the clients of the maintenance department are and what their needs are. It should take conscious and continuous action to meet client needs, leading to clients that are satisfied with the standard of service rendered to them.

⇒ Approval Authority - there should be clearly defined formal cost and other approval authority for management and supervisors in the department. People should generally be satisfied with, and accept the responsibility going with, the approval authority delegated to them.

⇒ Organization Charts - there must exist formal up to date organization charts relevant to the needs and demands of the organization and the maintenance department. This should be such that departmental structures are aligned with the maintenance philosophy and strategies. The organization charts must also conform to general principles for organizing an organization.

⇒ Disciplinary Process - the department ought to have a formal process for managing discipline. These disciplinary procedures must be known, accepted and used by all managers and supervisors in the maintenance department. Supervisors should be satisfied with the authority they are allowed to exercise in respect of discipline, while all employees perceive the application of discipline in the maintenance department as fair.

Maintenance Policy Setting

⇒ General Maintenance Policy - a well thought through maintenance policy forms the corner stone of effective maintenance practice. Therefore, a document must exist that gives the general approach (philosophy) towards maintenance followed by the company. This document should be in line with the Maintenance Cycle concept and with the organization's goals and the prevailing economic climate. All responsible personnel ought to be thoroughly aware of the contents of this document and understand its relevance to their maintenance tasks. They should also be fully committed to carry into effect the stipulations of this document.

⇒ Maintenance Procedures - to give effect to the general and specific maintenance policies, it is important that procedures exist that document standardized methods for doing maintenance administration and planning. Written and formal maintenance procedures must thus exist that regulate the actions of maintenance personnel. These should be derived directly from the maintenance policy.

⇒ Application of the policy and procedures - the maintenance policy and procedures will only be effective if they are properly applied. Managers and supervisors should thus use the policy as guideline when taking decisions. They should also keep their subordinates informed of the maintenance policies and see to it that they do their work accordingly. To ensure this they issue rules and regulations for their own department/section which ensures adherence to the policies.

⇒ Reliability Centered Maintenance - RCM is the only complete scientific approach available to decide on the maintenance strategies applicable to each machine/component. As such, it is used as the primary means to determine equipment-specific maintenance strategies. Secondly, all personnel that play a leading role in RCM work ought to be fully trained in the use of the technique. Thirdly, no person that does not have a good academic foundation in the mechanisms of failure and the mathematics of failure, should be used to lead RCM sessions or do RCM analyses - ideally all analyses should be led by the ME.

⇒ Maintenance Data Analysis - Maintenance data analysis is an important prerequisite for the proper application of RCM (and thus for strategy formulation). Maintenance engineers should thus understand the principles and theory of maintenance data analysis (MDA) sufficiently to be able to interpret the results of such analyses and to communicate sensibly with the ME. Secondly, the ME should be fully trained in the mathematical and statistical theory of MDA. He or she ought thus to be able to assist the maintenance engineers by doing such analyses on request and producing reports stating the results of such analyses clearly. Software should be available that assist the ME in this task.

⇒ Maintenance Data Analysis Techniques - it is of extreme importance that the maintenance data is first classified before being analyzed. Maintenance data analysis (MDA) as practiced by the company should differentiate between data with and without a long term trend to decide whether to apply Repairable Systems Analysis Techniques or Renewal Techniques.

⇒ Maintenance Optimization Models - maintenance optimization models should be used to decide on the frequency of maintenance tasks. All engineers and especially the ME has access to specialized software for maintenance strategy optimization.

⇒ Profit Impact Awareness - all maintenance managers and supervisors should be aware of the profit impact of maintenance (being the main driver of the maintenance strategy mix), as well as the effect of the level of prevention on company profit. They should also know and understand the composition of the maintenance strategy tree and use it to develop a maintenance strategy mix that are conducive to high company profit.

⇒ Maintenance Analyst - not all maintenance managers/engineers have the knowledge, time or inclination to do the maintenance failure data analysis necessary for the development of maintenance strategies. Therefore, a specific engineer should be set apart as ME (Maintenance Expert) on a full or part time basis, depending on the size of the department. This individual must be fully trained in maintenance engineering technology and failure data analysis. He/she should also have access to specialized software to assist him/her in the task.

⇒ Policy Update - the maintenance policy and procedures should be updated regularly (annually) to cope with changing demands.

⇒ Reliability Policy - when new equipment is purchased or existing equipment modified the reliability impact of each alternative design on equipment availability should be evaluated by using cost effective standard reliability engineering techniques.

⇒ Preventive Maintenance Policy - maximum availability through a high level of preventive maintenance should be pursued to maximize maintenance's contribution to company profits (unless the company is operating in a captive market).

⇒ Condition Monitoring Policy - the company's condition monitoring policy should includes that use is being made of a specialized service (internal or external) to do monitoring (for example vibration monitoring, oil analysis) on a regular scheduled basis. If an internal service for condition monitoring exists, the personnel manning this service must be adequately trained and experienced to be able to deliver a professional analysis service that produces accurate pre-failure warnings.

⇒ Repair Policy - breakdowns ought to be analyzed to determine whether a benefit in terms of less break-stops can be obtained by replacing spares other than the one that failed during the off time of the machine.

⇒ Overhaul Policy - all critical production machines should be overhauled from time to time to lengthen their life and to maintain a high level of reliability and operability.

⇒ Replacement Policy - the company should have a formal equipment replacement policy, which includes that a production machine or one of its critical parts is replaced when, after a proper techno-economical study, it is found that the new unit will make a higher contribution to long term profit than the present one. This assessment is made based on a sound economical criterion such as the net present value, internal rate of return or pay back period.

Organizational Climate and Culture

⇒ Teamwork - the members of maintenance work groups should work together as a close team - this is characterized by clear signs of group cohesion and the positive manner in which team members support one another.

⇒ Attitude - employees in the maintenance department ought to display a positive attitude towards the organization, the department, managers, supervisors and co-workers. This should be complemented by a loyalty towards the department - this is characterized by the way in which they defend the department, its managers, supervisors and other employees.

⇒ Productivity - employees in the maintenance department ought to be productivity conscious. Outputs of the department and divisions /sections should be continuously measured and utilized as a basis for improvement.

⇒ Creativity - employees in the maintenance department should always be discovering better and smarter ways to do the work (employees show initiative in solving work problems). The climate in the department should be innovative (new ideas are encouraged and promoted).

⇒ Responsiveness to Change - the management of the maintenance department ought to see the introduction of new methods and technology as an opportunity to improve the operation of the department and simultaneously build an innovative climate. The personnel of the department should be willing and eager to apply new methods and technology (low resistance to change).

⇒ Recognition - a climate should exist where management/ supervisors of the maintenance department deliberately look for opportunities to "catch people doing things right". The recognition process of the department should be accepted by all.

⇒ Response to Technological Developments - the maintenance department ought to, at all times, be aware of developments in the technological field applying directly or indirectly to its situation. It should also immediately take steps to investigate the effects of the technology on bottom line results.

⇒ Motivation - employees should feel that their needs are addressed within the department - they should display enthusiasm and a capacity for action. This is characterized by all members of the maintenance department doing more than is expected (they walk the "extra mile").

⇒ Relations in the department - a trust relationship should exist between all people in the department. The different race and cultural groups in the department ought to work together in harmony (without destructive friction).

⇒ Relations with other departments - the different departments ought to trust one another. Employees should be aware that different departments need one another.

- ⇒ Relations with the Top Management - a trust relationship should exist between the maintenance department and top management. Top management should be kept informed on both the positive and negative in the department.
- ⇒ Supervision - supervisors in the maintenance department ought to show a balance in managing people and work output. They should also maintain a fine balance between administration (office work) and on site supervision. Thirdly, they should be respected for their competence in both their managerial and technical functions. They should also, fourthly, treat employees fairly.
- ⇒ Training - employees in the maintenance department should be satisfied with their training (on the job training, formal training, management and supervisory training). Supervisors should know what the training and development needs of their subordinates are.
- ⇒ Philosophy on mistakes - mistakes should be seen by all as a learning experience, though employees display discontentment with repetitive mistakes (the root causes of problems are detected and eliminated - problems do not repeat themselves).
- ⇒ Trust - a trust relationship ought to exist between management / supervisors and workers. Additional to this, people should be able to fully rely on one another (people do what they commit themselves to do).
- ⇒ Client Focus - clients ought to be completely satisfied with the service they get. The real needs of all internal and external clients of the department should be known and are systematically addressed.
- ⇒ Ethics - the personnel of the maintenance department should act responsible in their contact with other people and also in the way they do their work. They ought to respect generally accepted values and norms.
- ⇒ Work attendance - absence without permission ought not to be a problem in the maintenance department.
- ⇒ Sick Leave - people should not abuse sick leave in the maintenance department - when someone is off sick one should know that he/she is really ill.
- ⇒ Grievances - there should be very few grievances in the department. All grievances ought to be solved completely. Employees should be clear on the grievance procedure of the organization.

⇒ Waste and Rework - an attitude of doing things right the first time should exist. Employees should be aware of the costs and other negative effects of waste and rework. This should lead to the result that waste and rework in the department are reduced to the bare minimum.

⇒ Completed Work - personnel should render completed work and should have an attitude of not letting unsatisfactory work slip by undetected. All work that has been started in the maintenance department ought to be followed through to satisfactory completion.

⇒ Quality - quality ought to be a way of life in the department.

⇒ Labor Relations - labor relation policies and procedures should be known by and adhered to by management and supervisors in the maintenance department. Steadfast relationships should be established with representatives of labor organizations.

⇒ Working Conditions - employees ought to be satisfied with what management is doing to ensure safe and acceptable physical working conditions in the maintenance department.

Safety and Housekeeping

⇒ Use a validated and standardized industrial safety audit.

Systems

Equipment Register

⇒ Equipment register System Adequacy - the equipment register contains all fixed equipment data and serves as basis for the maintenance systems. It should be ascertained by the audit whether the equipment register system used should *generally be regarded as being adequate* for the company's use.

⇒ Equipment Numbering (Physical) - the physical numbering of equipment is an important facet of systems implementation. The audit should firstly determine whether *plant numbers are chosen* for their simplicity and their ability to make the various machines and locations easily identifiable to the people working with them. Secondly, all plant items should be *codified and numbered before being used*. There must, thirdly, exist an effective and workable standard for *fixing location and equipment numbers* to plant structures, machines and sub-assemblies. Lastly, all locations and equipment must be *numbered according to the standard* mentioned above.

⇒ Equipment Classification - to assist in meaningful reporting and comparison, equipment (and rotables) must be classified, depending on the numbering system used, into equipment groups and equipment types. (Equipment group is a wide classification including all equipment with a similar production function (for example all dump trucks), while equipment type is a narrower classification of all identical machines or sub-assemblies).

⇒ Equipment Structure - the equipment structure keeps record of the relationship between a machine and the sub-assemblies fitted to it. The machines should be hierarchically decomposed into functional sub-components (Rotables), each with its own classification. This allows the collection of history for each individual rotable.

⇒ Equipment Location - the equipment location (position) is an important parameter for reporting and comparisons. The physical location of each piece of equipment should be registered in the equipment data base.

⇒ Equipment Dependencies - equipment dependencies are used by the system to decide when to schedule certain maintenance tasks as well as in preparing certain reports. The *dependencies between the various production machines* (the effect of the downtime of one machine on (an) other machine(s)) should, firstly, be registered in the equipment data base. Secondly, the dependencies between various machines ought to be used to *increase the effectiveness of maintenance scheduling* and to *facilitate the policy of opportunistic maintenance.*

⇒ Equipment Spare Parts - the system must be able to produce parts lists for equipment and must also carry failure history for every spare part. To do this, all *equipment spare parts* that are maintenance significant should, firstly, be *registered* in the maintenance information system. Secondly, the maintenance system should allow for and require the use of hierarchical decomposition of the lowest level of functional sub-components that were classified as a piece of equipment into a *hierarchy of spare parts.*

⇒ Equipment Usage - equipment usage entails keeping record of the "mileage" of the machine. This is done using a hour meter reading or a cumulative time or production figure. Each machine should *be equipped with a physical or logical meter* recording the time or production usage of the machine. Secondly, the *meter readings* from this meter must be used as basis for maintenance scheduling and the component life history being kept.

Work Order Management

⇒ Work Order Management System Adequacy - just as the equipment register holds all fixed equipment data, the Work Order Management system holds all data concerning the jobs that have to be done on equipment. The work order management system used should generally be regarded as being adequate for the company's use.

⇒ Work Order And Task Definition - maintenance tasks must be defined well to ensure good work from the artisan. Work orders are a means of grouping tasks together (task organization) which assists in task control and cost accumulation. As such, each *major grouping of tasks* should, firstly, be grouped together and defined as a maintenance work order. Further to this, each task (which will result in a job card being issued) must be *registered* as being part of one of the lowest level work orders. Thirdly, *different level work orders* should be defined to allow the grouping of work in logical compartments to facilitate the control of maintenance work.

⇒ Work-Order Structure - work-orders should be available on different levels. There can thus exist a master work order for a total plant shutdown and several work-orders for certain major jobs during the shutdown. The work in the master work order will then consist of all the work in the other (subsidiary) work orders. It should be possible (and it should be used as such) to structure work-orders in a multilevel hierarchy allowing large maintenance work to be broken down to facilitate task control.

⇒ Work-order as cost collection basis - the maintenance work order should form the basis for maintenance cost collection.

⇒ Tasks and Job Cards - each lowest level work order should *be broken down into the tasks* that must be completed to complete the work order. A task must be registered for each such maintenance job that constitutes a *self contained work package* involving one worker. At work execution time a job card should be issued for each task that was registered in the system. Fourthly, each task should have a standard execution time.

⇒ Task Documentation - a maintenance task can only be performed properly by the artisan if the right documentation/information is supplied at task issue time. The audit should thus ascertain that at work execution time the *worker is issued* with a job card, a check list (if the task at hand involved regular scheduled work for which such check list exists), a work permit (if the work must be done in a hazardous area) and engineering drawings (if the work requires the worker having a drawing at hand). It should, secondly, be determined whether check lists are updated regularly and generally list at least the 20% highly important checks identified by a 80/20 (Pareto) analysis. Thirdly, engineering drawings must be available and must be complete and up to date.

⇒ Feedback Of Job Data - maintenance systems are only as good as the quality/completeness of the data fed back to it. It should thus be determined whether workers *feed job data back punctually and accurately* to maintenance administration (planning). Secondly, maintenance administration (planning) should promptly and accurately update the maintenance data bank when receiving job data.

Scheduling

⇒ Scheduling System Adequacy - the scheduling system schedules the maintenance jobs kept in the Work Order Management system. As such it must generally be regarded as being adequate for the company's use.

⇒ Scheduling Techniques - the efficiency of maintenance systems is at its best when a combination of scheduling techniques are used. *Time slot scheduling* should firstly be used to locate scheduled work on the maintenance calendar. Secondly, *Critical Path Scheduling* should be used to plan all complex work in an optimal way. *Workshop flow processing algorithms* should, thirdly, be used to plan the work through jobbing workshops, while, fourthly, *task priorities* should be used to sequence the work of all area maintenance (field) workshops.

⇒ Scheduling Facilities - just as a combination of scheduling techniques are optimal, a variety of scheduling facilities should be used. The scheduling system should thus include *facilities for network processing, resource level and production of Gantt charts*. It should, furthermore, use *scheduling calendars and personnel availability schedules* as basis for the scheduling being performed.

⇒ Time and Attendance - the maintenance scheduling system should keep track of the times at which workers are available at the work for scheduling purposes.

Stock Control

⇒ Stock Control System Adequacy - the stock control system controls the spares inventory and all issues/returns from it. As such, the stock control system used should generally be regarded as being adequate for the company's use.

⇒ Stock Issues and Returns - the maintenance system must include facilities for stock withdrawal and returns, which are well interfaced with the stock control system.

⇒ Determination of which items to keep in stock - maintenance users should create stock items after careful consideration of the stock investment implications.

⇒ Determination of General Stock Levels - as stock levels impact the efficiency of maintenance as well as the profitability of the organization, the right system must exist and be used effectively. Maintenance users should, firstly, determine general stock levels of maintenance stock items. This is done after analysis of the economic implications of out-of-stock occurrences versus the stock investment implications. Secondly, stock levels should be monitored continuously by stores' management, advising maintenance users when anomalies occur.

⇒ Annual Stock Review - the continued keeping of stock items that do not move within the span of one calendar year should be reviewed annually by maintenance users.

⇒ Monitor Commodity Turnover - commodity turnover must be monitored on a monthly basis by both stores' management and maintenance users.

⇒ Monitor Out-of-Stock Frequencies - Out-of-Stock frequencies ought to be monitored on a monthly basis by both stores' management and maintenance users.

Work Management

⇒ Work Management System Adequacy - the work management system assists the user in managing all tasks that are in progress (scheduled and non-scheduled). As such, the work management system used should generally be regarded as being adequate for the company's use.

⇒ Backlog Management - the amount of work outstanding (the backlog) at any moment in time is a very good indicator of whether the maintenance department is coping with the maintenance task. Available work backlog history should thus, firstly, be used to arrive at *an acceptable level of backlog* that can be used as a standard for comparison purposes. Secondly, work backlog must be *reported monthly* and immediate and effective steps taken if it increases above the accepted standard level. *Backlog control* should, thirdly, be effective and result in relatively low and stable levels of backlog. Furthermore, the backlog control system ought to ensure that *missed scheduled work* is brought under the attention of the appropriate manager.

⇒ Personnel Utilization and Efficiency Control - personnel utilization is an indicator of how well maintenance supervision makes use of the people assigned to it. Personnel efficiency, on the other hand, is an indicator of the level of training and competence of the artisan. The system should, firstly, supply management with *effective reports* for the control of personnel utilization and efficiency. Secondly, maintenance management ought to *use the personnel utilization and efficiency reports extensively* to improve the utilization and efficiency of personnel. The work force's *personnel utilization and efficiency* should, fourthly, be *high* as a result of these actions.

⇒ Modification Control - there should exist a written procedure to control the modification process. This should include a formal application form that must be submitted to senior management for approval before a modification may be made to a machine. It should also allow for the monitoring of the performance of such modifications.

⇒ Guarantee Control - guarantee management is an area which directly affect the level of maintenance costs. The maintenance system should thus, firstly, allow *multiple guarantees* to be registered for a single piece of equipment. Secondly, the system's operation must be such that a *check is made whether a guarantee applies* before the issue of task documentation. Thirdly, valid guarantee claims must be *actively pursued* to ensure that losses are limited to the absolute minimum.

⇒ Efficient Responsibility Structure - it is important to be able to ascertain who was responsible for a certain action or expenditure. Therefore, every official that has stock withdrawal or purchasing approval rights must be allocated a *responsibility code* (or alternative) that allows him to be identified as being responsible for a specific acquisition. Secondly, the maintenance system should have a facility for defining the maintenance *responsibility structure*, thus facilitating multilevel reporting.

Cost Control

⇒ Cost Control System Adequacy - the cost control system handles all budgeting and cost control activities. As such, the cost control system used should, generally, be regarded as being adequate for the company's use.

⇒ Budgeting System - the budgeting system allows the user to create a budget based on maintenance history. Firstly, the cost control system should *incorporate an efficient budgeting system*. Secondly, the budgeting system ought to use as basis a *quantity budget* that it creates from maintenance history by using forecasting techniques. Thirdly, the final budget should be compiled by *merging the quantity information with price information* stored by the system.

⇒ Cost Allocation - to be able to control costs effectively, certain control structure must exist: Cost should, firstly, be allocated *through cost allocation codes* and by making use of *task cost* as far as is practically viable. Secondly, the cost system structure ought to be such that cost can be *reported by responsibility, by area (geographical), by equipment and by task*.

⇒ Cost System Facilities - the cost system must present information in formats that will assist the user in deciding whether corrective action is necessary. *Actual costs* must thus, firstly, be accumulated against cost accounts and presented in reports against the respective budgets. Secondly, costs must be evaluated by *comparison against budget* and through the *use of cost indicators, graphs and trend techniques*.

⇒ Low Maintenance Costs - the maintenance costs of the firm should be in control and reflect a consistent low level of expenditure.

Equipment Condition and Performance Monitoring

⇒ Equipment Condition and Performance Monitoring System Adequacy - the equipment condition and performance monitoring system assists the user in monitoring his equipment. As such, the equipment condition and performance monitoring system used should generally be regarded as being adequate for the company's use.

⇒ Condition Monitoring and Inspection - condition monitoring/ inspection is one of the maintenance policies suitable to the majority of machines/components. The system should thus, firstly, *allow multiple condition monitoring and inspection occasions* to be registered and scheduled per single piece of equipment. Secondly, condition monitoring and inspection ought to *be regarded as one of the primary means of preventive maintenance*. Thirdly, condition monitoring and inspection should be *performed on a regular basis* and the results are recorded in the system. Fourthly, *diagnosis must regularly be performed* on the condition monitoring and inspection history to identify any significant trends. Lastly, *prompt action* should be *taken* when trend analysis indicates an impending failure.

⇒ Equipment Performance Monitoring - performance monitoring provides the maintenance manager with management information regarding the success of maintenance actions and the health of equipment. *Equipment performance* should thus be monitored continuously. Furthermore, the *primary parameters that are monitored* should include equipment availability, equipment utilization, equipment production rates, equipment production losses and equipment costs. Thirdly, *the secondary parameters* that are being monitored ought to include component failure rates, condition monitoring results and machine running parameters monitoring results. Fourthly, *diagnosis must regularly be performed* on the equipment performance monitoring history to identify any significant trends. Lastly, *prompt action* should be taken when trend analysis indicates any deterioration.

⇒ Equipment Performance Monitoring Results - the results of performance monitoring is an indicator of the success achieved by the maintenance department. Therefore consistent *high equipment availability levels* should be maintained. Further to this, consistent *high equipment production rates* are being maintained.

⇒ Reliability Centered Maintenance Implementation - RCM is the only complete scientific approach available to decide on the maintenance policies applicable to each machine/component. The reliability centered maintenance technique should thus be used to determine the maintenance policies of the organization.

⇒ Equipment Failure Data Analysis - equipment failure data analysis is an important prerequisite for proper application of RCM. Equipment failure data should, therefore, firstly be *analyzed on an ongoing basis* to establish any significant trends and develop valid failure distributions. Secondly, *prompt action* must be taken when trend analysis indicates any deterioration. Thirdly, the company ought to have acquired suitable software for equipment failure data analysis.

⇒ Fault Elimination - for a maintenance department to be successful it is important to eliminate faults of a recurring nature. A *formal fault elimination procedure* should thus exist which specifies the process of identifying unacceptable recurring faults, allocating responsibilities for fault elimination actions and controlling that results are being achieved. Secondly, most *recurring faults* ought to be *dealt with fast and effectively*.

Equipment History

⇒ Equipment History System Adequacy - the equipment history system keeps all data regarding failures, work done and equipment monitoring for future analysis. As such, the equipment history system used should generally be *regarded as being adequate* for the company's use. Secondly, the history records of equipment part failures should *support the failure data analysis function* well. Thirdly, the history records of equipment cost should *support the equipment performance monitoring function* well. Lastly, the equipment history system must also support the *other equipment performance monitoring parameters* (availability, utilization, production rates, production losses, condition monitoring and machine running parameters monitoring) well.

General

⇒ Reporting Adequacy - reports are the major means by which the maintenance system(s) communicate to the managers/users. The reports that are generated and distributed should thus generally regarded as *being adequate* for the company's use. The *reporting frequency* used should also generally be regarded as being adequate for the company's use. Thirdly, *reports must be received timely* by the relevant line personnel. The reporting function should, fourthly, supply each level of maintenance management *with summary reports reflecting the performance of the next lower level. Detail* should, lastly, *not be included in reports* (as far as is possible), but must be available on request.

⇒ System Security - system security ensures data integrity and that valuable data is not lost. The system must thus, firstly, have an *effective security system* that limits entry to the system, use of another person's data and entry into editing functions by password. Secondly, the *sign-off process when leaving a terminal is strictly enforced. System audit runs and total system backups* should, furthermore, made on a daily basis to prevent data being lost.

⇒ System Implementation Base - it is important that the system is implemented on a platform suitable to the specific maintenance situation. The maintenance information system should, at the present time, be implemented on a *computerized platform.* Secondly, the system should make use of *computer technology that will produce optimum results* (such as 486, 586, Pentium, networking, etc.). The opinion of computer experts should be sought if any doubt exists. Thirdly, the *data base* should be situated in an *optimal position* (centralized or decentralized). Fourthly, the *number of artisans supported per work station* must not be to high.

⇒ System Operation - the split between on line and batch processing should be optimal. Normal data base updates and retrievals are done in on line mode during office hours. Time consuming system maintenance runs (such as data base optimization for fast retrieval and longer report runs) are done during night time in batch mode.

⇒ Implementation Width - the system should be fully implemented for the total organization.

⇒ Maintenance Management Support of Systems Drive - maintenance managers of all levels ought to lead the systems implementation drive with vigor. They must actively support and seek systems driven management.

⇒ Maintenance Technology Training - the maintenance systems can only be effective if the users have the necessary knowledge and attitudes. All *maintenance managers* must thus be *fully trained* in maintenance engineering technology. Furthermore, all maintenance managers and supervisors should be *fully trained in maintenance systems technology.* Lastly, all *artisans* should be trained *in basic maintenance systems technology.*

Implementation of the auditing process

In the previous section we listed various components under the different categories. One can use this as the auditing instrument in exactly that format. But it may be that you would like to first customize it for your own organization. This process will be described in some detail in the following paragraphs. Even if you use the instrument as is, it will still entail some work regarding the way of the combination of the results (weighting) and deciding on the values of performance standards. We will also have to look into the way in which one organizes the auditing process, the audit process itself and the evaluation of the audit results.

The design of the auditing process

Choice of components and categories

As is the case with the measurement process, it pays to spend some time in the design of the auditing process. The best way to do this is for the management team to set time aside to work through the above list of components category by category. This process is best accomplished during a few days away from the bustle of the business. It will be good when starting with this whole process of developing an integrated management cycle to spend one or two long weekends away from the office to think these processes through in detail and to internalize the concepts involved.

The process of choosing the components of the audit can be done in a few steps. First of all it is wise to critically work through the instrument in its present format component by component and make modifications to the components as required. During this critical evaluation some of the components may be eliminated, while some new components may be defined. This is a long and cumbersome process, but is important to ensure that the audit instrument presents a good fit to the goal that the management team would like to accomplish. The second step is then to categorize the different components under headings that make sense to the management team. The important thing is that we should be able to eventually give a score to, lets say, our 'systems performance', etc. The third step is to prioritize the components in each category and then give a weighting factor to each component. The prioritization can be done by giving a 10 to the most important component and a 1 to the least important component. The priorities for the other components can then be filled in by comparing them to the one with the highest score, the one with the lowest score and relative to each other. These priority factors may be used as is to achieve a weighting of the various components. Lets say, during the actual audit, we score individual components on a scale of 1 to 10. By adding together all the weights for a certain category and multiplying the total with 10, we will then get the value of the weighted total that represents a 100% score for the category. If a certain component gets a score of say 6 and our weighting factor for the component is 8, our weighted score for the component will be calculated as follows:

$$\text{Weighted Component Score} = 6 \times 8 = 48\%$$

in percent, where-as the non-weighted score was 6/10=60%. The general expression for this is:

$$\text{Weighted Component Score} = (\text{Component Score} \times \text{Weighting Factor})$$

By adding the weighted component scores for the individual components in a category and using the following formula, a total percentage score for the category will result.

$$\text{Category Score} = \left(\frac{\text{Sum Weighted Scores}}{\text{Sum Weights} \times \text{Maximum Score per Component}} \right) \times 100\%$$

One can of course use schemes other than the one used as an example. One possibility is to prioritize on a 5 to 10 point scale instead of a 1 to 10 point scale. That will ensure that all components have a definite contribution to the final audit score for the category. On the 1 to 10 point weighting scale, those components with low (1 or 2) weighting factors will practically be eliminated from the audit, which is probably not what the management team would want. Lastly, one should prioritize the different categories in the same way to obtain weighting factors for combining the scores of the individual categories into one percentage score for the total audit. Again using lets say a 5 to 10 point scale for the prioritization, the total score for complete audit will be calculated as follows:

$$\text{Total Audit Score} = \left(\frac{\sum(\text{Category Score} \times \text{Weighting Factor})}{\sum \text{Weights}} \right)$$

Choice of operating units

The maintenance audit can be done for the plant as a total unit, if its only purpose is to precede the next annual management planning cycle. But there are many advantages to segmenting the maintenance organization into its logical operating units and doing the audit per operating unit. One of the advantages is that the audit for a specific operating unit can then be used to precede the annual management planning cycle for that specific operating unit, while the combined results can still be used for the organization as a whole. A second advantage is that the audit results can be used as a management tool to identify the operating units with problems that should be addressed to ensure success.

Performance standards

For each of the chosen components a level should be defined which, if it is reached, will constitute a 100% attainment of success in that specific component. This can be done at the same time as the process of component selection. Thus, while working through the components one by one and critically evaluating each one in turn, time is also given to the development of a performance standard for that specific component.

Audit checklist design

The audit checklist should be designed after choosing the various components and categorizing them. A good checklist design would be to have a separate list per category, with one summary list combining the results of the various categories. Each of these lists will then have columns for (1) component number, (2) component name, (3) component weight, as discussed above, (4) component score and (5) weighted score. Instead of the component name alone, one could of course include the full component description as well, but that will lengthen the checklist considerably and would make it unwieldy. The audit team should rather have a separate document with the full component descriptions, like the one we had above. An added feature of such a checklist should be a heading listing the person/team doing the audit, the date of the audit, the name of the organization/operating unit, etc. An example of such a document is shown below:

Person/Team:	Team 1	Organization:	XYZ Soap
Audit Category:	Maint. Admin	Oper. Unit:	Soap Cutter
Approved:	Joe Soap	Date :	19/4/97

Component Number	**Component Name**	**Weight (/10)**	**Score (/10)**	**Weighted Score (%)**
1-1	Technical education	8	7	56
1-2	Management training	6	6	36
1-3	Systems training	10	8	80
1-4	Planner aptitude	9	9	81
2-1	Span of Control	7	8	56
2-2	Clerical Support	8	4	32
2-3	Organization	7	7	49
etc.	etc.	etc.	etc.	etc.
Totals		55		70,9%

Combination of results

One of the best ways of combining the results, apart from the tabular presentation and calculations presented above, is to make use of spine diagrams. An example for the figures in the above table is shown in figure 12.1.

The organization of the auditing process

Scheduling the audit(s)

The audit(s) must be scheduled well in advance of the detail annual planning (budgeting) process, so that there will be enough time for the relatively long processes of updating the maintenance policy, objectives setting and so on. It should be kept in mind that the typical

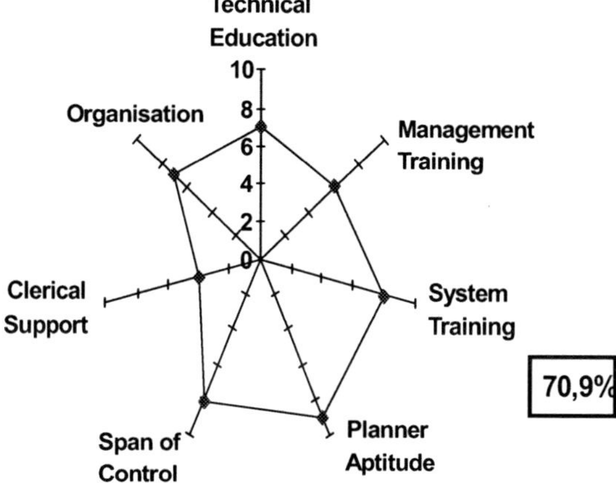

Figure 12.1 : Spine diagram representation of data

person that would be used in the audit team is fairly busy, so special care must be taken to plan the audit at least 3 months in advance. Remember that this is one of the most important events on the annual calendar! Enough time should be allowed for the audit itself (typically a full day or more - the specific length of time will depend on whether the personnel of the plant has prepared themselves well in advance for the questions that may be asked), and for the processing of the figures and drafting of the report afterwards. Depending on the support that the team has for this purpose and the width of the audit (the number of individual operating units audited), this could take anything from 2 days to a full week. The exact time has to be determined through experience.

Composition of the audit team(s)

One could compose (an) audit team(s) in a few ways. Firstly, you could use people solely from your own plant. Secondly, you could mix people from inside your own concern with people from other plants in the group (if it is an organization of that size) or from competitor's plants or from organizations specializing in doing audits. Thirdly, one could have the total audit done by an outside concern. There are of course advantages and disadvantages to all the approaches. People from inside the organization know the organization well, but tend to be blind regarding the faults of the organization and to have tunnel vision regarding the possibilities for improvement. People from competing plants know the technological area well, but may be trying to prove that they are better by being overly critical. People from outside concerns (consultants and the like) should have fairly open minds and should be able to have a wide angle vision, but they may not know the technological area that well. Of course, one of the most important principles is that the specific operating unit's own staff must not be members of the audit team auditing their specific operating unit.

Regarding the types of persons and the numbers that should be involved, the following rules should apply: Firstly, the audit team members should be fairly senior maintenance managers with a high level of insight and experience in the field. Secondly, an audit team should typically consist of more than one, but less than four people (thus 2 to 3 people) to keep the balance between low cost and quality of the audit.

Performing the audit

The audit can be done in a variety of ways. The method presented here is just one of the possibilities, but should produce good results in most circumstances. After going through a few audit cycles, the organization will be clear in their own minds regarding the specific methods that they regard as being the best.

The first step in the audit process is that the audit team should prepare itself. For this purpose they should firstly acquire and individually review the audit instrument, audit results of previous audits at the specific organization, as well as the maintenance policy, objectives and maintenance management plan (if such documents exist). Thereafter they should get together and discuss their strategy for the audit. This could include that they decide to concentrate on certain problem areas (if these has been highlighted by previous audits), or on areas where the maintenance policy and objectives has placed particular emphasis or they may decide to divide the various audit categories between the individual members of the team.

We will assume that the audit for the whole plant will be performed in one uninterrupted interval of time. The audit team will then start by having a meeting with the maintenance management team, prior to the operating unit visits. The objectives of this meeting are, firstly, to meet the top managers, secondly to get an overall impression of the quality of the organization's maintenance management inclination and thirdly to start gathering information regarding the success of maintenance actions. This meeting should not take longer than one hour.

After the visit with the management team, the operating units will be visited one by one. The modus operandi for each of these visits will be the same. First, a meeting is held with the operating unit's maintenance managers/supervisors to gain firsthand knowledge concerning their views and practices and to ask certain general questions. Thereafter, a visit to the administrative (planning) office(s) to ascertain how well the operating systems are deployed on the ground. The third step is a visit to the individual workshops of the unit. The accent during this visit is on housekeeping and general organization of the workshops (see the facilities category of audit components above). This is followed by a visit (walk trough) of the plant itself, to judge upon the quality of the maintenance work performed in the plant. During these visits to the administrative (planning) office(s), workshops and plant, a person from the specific plant area should guide the audit team. This person does not contribute anything towards the audit itself. His only role is to act as guide. Lastly, a second visit is paid to the operating unit's managers/supervisors. At this time document proof of the maintenance operating results (availability, reliability and operability of machines, cost results, safety results, maintenance performance measurement results) of the operating unit should be presented to the audit team. The audit team can now ask last questions regarding the maintenance of the specific operating unit. Particular emphasis should be placed, at this time, on the use of management information to assist in the management of the maintenance function.

After the visits to the various operating units have been completed, the audit team will visit the plant's maintenance management team for a second time. They should now be presented (after seeing the results) with any additional information that the plant maintenance management would like to bring under their attention. They should also be afforded a further chance to ask clarifying questions at this time, after which they will typically thank the management for their support and leave. They should particularly refrain from giving any opinions or verdicts regarding the audit - this should be left until the final report.

It is important that the audit team gather all the relevant information during the audit visit itself. They should not have any clarifying contact with the organization following the audit and before the presentation of the audit report. Such contacts could lead to the results of the audit being infested by subjective opinions and information that has not been proven.

Evaluating the results of the audit

The evaluation of the audit results is a fairly complex affair. Firstly the various audit components must be scored for the individual operating units. Each of these scores contains elements of the physical condition of the plant, housekeeping, the information regarding maintenance parameters and the evaluation of the systems that are in place. The scores for the individual components must then be combined, using the weighting process described above, into a percentage score per audit category per operating unit. The individual categories' results per operating unit should then be combined, again using the weighting process described above, into one integrated score for the operating unit. The overall results for the company can simply be calculated by averaging the results of the category scores and overall scores of the various operating units.

The scores from the calculations above should be evaluated by the audit team, together with any impressions, comments which they may have jotted down during the audit and the main areas of concern listed. This should be augmented by areas where the organization has done exceptionally well. This is an very important facet of the audit. This normally takes place a few days after the audit and the team can easily miss certain important points that should be mentioned in the final report. Care should thus be taken to ensure completeness of the evaluation.

The final report can certainly be presented in more than one format. It is, however, important that the report at least address the following:

- Executive summary
- Overall scores summary
- Listing of areas where the company did exceptionally well, with specific reference to the operating units that contributed most to these successes.
- Listing of areas where the company need to improve considerably, again with reference to the operating units where the most attention will have to be concentrated.
- Addenda with the detailed audit results.

In addition to producing a neat, well appointed report, the impact of the audit can also be improved by the personal presentation of the final report to the company's maintenance management team by the audit team. To further improve the impact of the report, a summarized executive presentation can be delivered using overhead projection slides or something equivalent. After this, it is up to the organization's maintenance management to properly take the audit facts into account when executing their management planning cycle.

References

1. Coetzee, J.L., The Systems Approach to Maintenance Profitability. Annual short course, 1997.

This page was left blank on purpose

Use it for notes

Chapter 13

Achieving Maintenance Management Excellence

Introduction

In the previous chapters (chapters 10-12) we have stepwise developed the outer (managerial) sub-cycle of the Maintenance Cycle. This sub-cycle is crucial to the success of the organization. *Firstly*, it describes the process of developing a maintenance policy, a document aimed at providing structure and co-ordination of all actions of the maintenance department. *Secondly*, it ensures that the policy is translated into action through the development of specific objectives. This is *then* used as the primary input to the annual management planning process. The *loop is closed* through the two measurement processes, the first (Maintenance Performance Measurement) which provides measurement on a fairly continuous basis, allowing control over the operational sub-cycle. The second of these (Maintenance Audit) measurement processes affords feedback of the success achieved in implementing the maintenance policy.

While the individual processes, as described, are a great help in executing the various aspects of the business of maintenance, we have to combine them in an integrated fashion to really reap the full measure of benefits that are possible with such instruments.

Implementation issues

The previous chapters each addressed the implementation of that specific instrument on its own. There are, however, certain implementation issues that are common to all three areas - these will be discussed in this short chapter. The most important of these concerns the commitment of the management to use such a systematic approach consistently. The company will gain little by implementing these techniques in a haphazard way. Before fully integrated implementation of these outer cycle processes, the following should be true of the company:

- Maintenance *management must be sure that they want to implement a formal system* of annual management planning, performance measurement and auditing and are committed to seeing the resultant change process through. One must be heedful that maintenance managers do not only pay lip service regarding such a commitment. The prospective results may lure them into wanting the benefit of such systematic approach without realizing the effort to be spent in making it work. There are a few points that are important in this regard:
    * All managers should have adequate knowledge of the principles behind implementing such processes.
    * Success will not come by measuring, but by using the measurement results to take managerial action. This will take much hard work over a period of a few years. It can also place short term strain on relationships within the department. The result should of course be more than worthwhile, but it is important to realize that it will come at a price.
    * The most important requirement is that maintenance managers must display the will to improve. In this regard it will be of great benefit if a champion for the process could be found within management. The maintenance chief will of course be the best person to take on this role, if he/she is so inclined.
- It is of the utmost importance for the process to succeed that there be a *proper maintenance policy*, which the whole maintenance department is committed to. This should be augmented by a proper set of maintenance objectives, maintenance plans and maintenance procedures. These should be properly communicated to all personnel and positive steps should be taken to ensure that they change their work ways accordingly. It is important to remember that, while this change in the department is planned and designed by managers operating in the outer cycle, it is directed in its effect towards the inner cycle. The objective of this integrated approach to maintenance management is to achieve excellence through changes effected in the inner cycle. This is done by:
    * Implementing an appropriate planned process of setting up and regularly updating a maintenance plan for the organization.
    * Properly executing the maintenance plan in the maintenance operational cycle (see area within dotted lines on the maintenance

cycle). Issues such as good administration of the maintenance plan, good supervision, the training of personnel and the general attitude of the workforce are specific target areas.

* Ensuring correct managerial action in the inner cycle based on task quality, task feedback, cost feedback and performance feedback (both the performance of personnel and of machines being maintained).

- Every person in the department should be *committed to react positively* when management instigates changes based on the measurement results. This implies that the annual maintenance management planning process must be 'sold' to the whole department's people. A process of culture change may thus be required it the measurement process is not to be only a temporary fad. One must get the department's people as far as to eagerly await the latest results.
- All persons involved, but especially management must bring themselves *not to overreact to every little change in the results*. Remember that the management process in the maintenance department, as any other, can be viewed as a control process. As such, it has all the usual components of a control process:

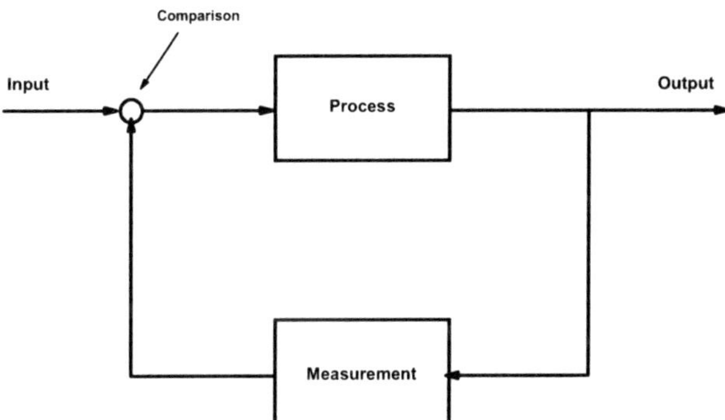

Figure 13.1 : The control process

The input to the control process consists of the policies, objectives and plans devised by the managerial and planning process. The output, in its turn, consists of the actual results achieved (availability, cost, etc.). The process is the whole maintenance operational cycle. Our aim is to devise the best possible annual maintenance management planning process to enable us to improve our input after comparison of the output results with the input standards. As all such control processes have certain dynamic response characteristics, we must be wary of any unnecessary big changes in the input standards and/or the process. Control theory teaches us that each such control system has a certain level of damping built into it - the trick lies in finding the correct level of damping for the specific control system, such that the response of the control system will be predictable and controllable. In a 'people system' the damping depends on many factors, of which the main ones are a happy and stable workforce, good relationships, a positive attitude towards the work and a stable management approach. Taking note of this, the following points are important:

  * The management team should understand the necessity of building a stable workforce, fostering good relations and so forth (the audit lists on *Management Processes* and *Organizational Climate and Culture* can be consulted in this regard)
  * There must be an inherent stability in the way which the maintenance management team as a whole, as well as the individual functionaries react to unfavorable results - if they overreact the inherent damping of the system may not be enough to prevent the system from getting out of control. The reaction to unfavorable audit and measurement results (if any) must be in small, controlled steps rather than large changes that could lead to instability.

- The *measurement figures* must be reliable and trustworthy. This implies that good systems must be available for supplying these measurements. Of course, in many cases we do not have such reliable systems in place and want to implement a measurement process to help us improve our systems. When this is the case, we have to try to, manually if that is necessary, ensure that we use the best figures available at any moment. The fact that this is the situation found in most practical maintenance situations, again stresses the need for slow, controlled change.
- The person managing the *annual maintenance management planning process* must be someone who understands maintenance, its profit impact and the measurement/change process well. This could in principle be anybody (even the maintenance chief), but he/

she must have enough time to spend a day or two per month in verifying the measurement figures, interpreting the results and drawing up recommendations to the maintenance management team.

- There must *be clear agreement of what the result of the process should be.* All persons involved must thus have the same ultimate goals - they should strive towards the same result.

References

1. Coetzee, J.L., The Systems Approach to Maintenance Profitability. Annual short course, 1997.

This page was left blank on purpose

Use it for notes

Chapter 14

Analysis of Maintenance Results

To be able to manage the maintenance function well, the maintenance manager must be able to analyze a wide range of maintenance data. This includes availability of equipment, mean time between failures, production rates, cost figures, task times, component life history, condition monitoring and many more. In any one of these the typical analysis means that are required are:

- *Data selection techniques* - these are used to select certain specified occurrences from a data set. Examples are the selection of all high cost areas and the selection of the components that are the main contributors to these high costs. The technique that will be used for this purpose is the Pareto chart.
- The *isolation of the cause* of a certain failure or problem. The cause and effect, or fishbone diagram, will be used for this purpose.
- Determining whether a *process* performs within certain predetermined *limits*. Examples of this could be cost, availability, MTBF (mean time between failure) and vibration levels. The techniques that could be used for this purpose include control charts, cusum charts and curve smoothing.
- Determining whether there is an *underlying trend* in data. This is used to choose the necessary actions to either amplify or counteract the trend. Techniques used for this purpose are curve smoothing and cusum charts.
- Forecasting techniques - these are used to project the historical trends into the future. Especially during the budgeting process extensive use are made of these techniques.

Pareto charts

The Pareto chart is based on a phenomenon known as the Pareto principle. The principle states that there are usually a few contributors (the vital few) that are responsible for the major portion of the problem being investigated. The other contributors (the trivial many) are typically responsible for a relatively small part of the problem. This is very often stated by a rule of thumb, the 80/20 rule, which says that 80% of the problem under investigation is caused by only 20% of the contributors.

A Pareto chart is constructed in four steps:

- Determine which are the contributors to the problem being investigated.
- Determine the level of contribution of each contributor to the problem. This can include things such as counting the number of occurrences of a certain event or adding the costs for a certain type of occurrence ((depending on the problem). Convert these figures into percentages of the total.
- Draw a bar chart of these results. The bars are ordered from left to right in descending order based on their heights. It is customary, if there are a number of very small contributors to combine them under the title 'others' and to draw this bar on the very right hand side of the chart. Display the names of the various contributors to the problem on the x-axis. Use one Y-axis (on the right hand side of the chart) for the number of occurrences (or the cost contribution). A second Y-axis (on the left hand side of the chart) is used for a percentage scale (0 - 100). The reason for using two Y-scales is the following: The percentage scale is better suited to data interpretation, while the count (or cost) scale is better suited for making comparisons between charts. A Pareto chart drawn to reflect the situation after an improvement plan was implemented is often compared to the one on which the improvement plan was based. On these two charts the percentages for the different contributors may be very similar, while the number of occurrences may have fallen drastically. Thus a percentage scale is not suited to making comparisons between charts.
- Add a line showing the cumulative percentage achieved by the addition of each additional contributor. The Pareto principle is confirmed by a break in the slope of this line. The contributors to the left of and including the break are the vital few. These should be considered first when taking action to eliminate the problem.

Example 1

A certain civil engineering contracting organization has identified one model of their bulldozer fleet as being a major contributor towards their very high maintenance costs. They have analyzed the maintenance material costs for these machines for a full financial year with the results as shown in table 14.1 (using the method as described above). The content of table 14.1 is shown in the form of a Pareto chart in figure 14.1. Clearly the cumulative percentage line has a break at 84,7%. The Pareto analysis thus shows that maintenance strategy improvement analyses should be concentrated on the track group, the hydraulic system and the final drives. Further analyses (using the same technique) can now be used to pinpoint the specific component(s) in each of these three groups that are causing the high costs (if the data is available).

Table 14.1 : Maintenance materials costs - Example 1

Contributors	Cost $ m	% of total	Cumulative %
Track group	20,416	45,8	45,8
Hydraulics	10,563	23,7	69,5
Final drives	6,768	15,2	84,7
Blade	2,105	4,7	89,4
Engine	2,013	4,5	93,9
Transmission	1,216	2,7	96,6
Electrical	0,734	1,6	98,2
Ancillaries	0,514	1,1	99,3
Frame	0,236	0,5	99,8
Totals	44,565	99,8	

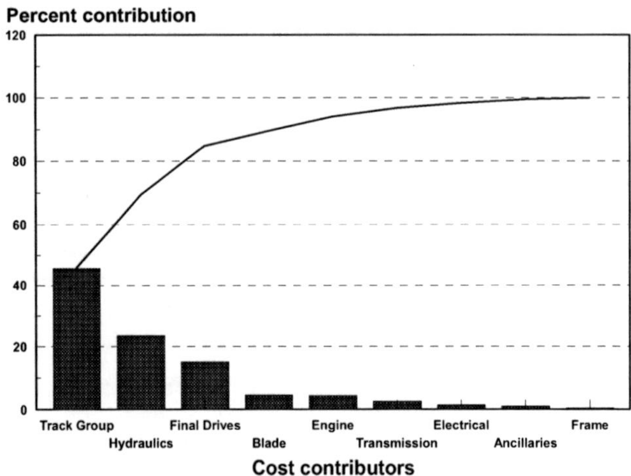

Figure 14.1 : Pareto Chart - Example 1

Cause and Effect diagrams

The types of problems that arise in industrial settings are very diverse. Cause and effect, or fishbone, diagrams can be used to determine what the cause(s) of a specific problem (the effect) is. The diagram looks, as its alternative name suggests, like a fishbone with the arrow towards the right pointing to the effect. The branches each represent a category of possible causes that are analyzed further into a list of possible causes in each category. The cause and effect diagram helps one to organize information about causes of a problem in a logical way that can be used in the process of solving problems. The technique is used effectively in quality circle groups for this purpose.

There is no one right way of constructing cause and effect diagrams. We will describe a method known as the 5M cause and effect diagram. The '5M' depicts five of the six diagram labels that start with an 'M'. These are: Men, Materials, Machines, Methods, Measurements. The best way to perform such an analysis is to make use of a group of people from maintenance and production that are considered to be the experts on the use and maintenance of the equipment at hand (if the problem is equipment related).

The steps to construct a cause and effect diagram is:

- Define the problem. Use a clear problem definition statement, along with a quantification of its severity. Place the problem on the right in the diagram.
- Draw six major branches. Label them with the category names: men, machines, materials, methods, measurement, environment.
- For each major branch, list the possible causes in that category that could result in the stated problem.
- For each branch, prioritize the list of potential causes. Place only the most important causes on the diagram.

Example 2

The Pareto analysis done for the bulldozers in example 1 shows beyond any doubt that the track group is the major source of high cost. The possible causes for this problem are now analyzed using the 5M cause and effect diagram. This is shown in figure 14.2.

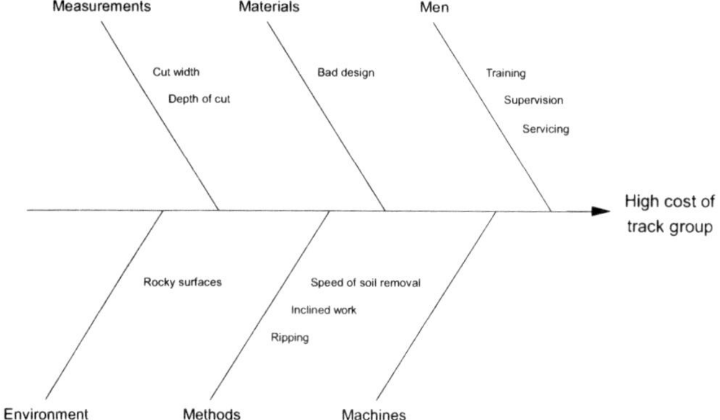

Figure 14.2 : Cause and Effect Diagram - Example 2

From this can now be selected the most probable cause (or combination of causes) to be solved. Until the problem is solved this diagram can serve as road map for the problem solving process.

Control charts

Control charts help one to ascertain whether a process that you are monitoring is performing within certain pre-set limits. It makes use of two principles:

- Most real life process measurements have a normal distribution, with a characteristic average μ and standard deviation σ. If the process is busy changing, the average μ and/or standard deviation σ will change over time.
- The distribution of new measurements will be the same as that of historical measurements, if there is no change in the process. In other words μ (the average of the data) and σ (the standard deviation) will remain the same for a stationary process. The Normal or Gaussian distribution is a symmetrical bell shaped distribution. Its highest probability is situated at the expected value of a single data point, μ. The width of the bell shape is dependent upon the variability in the data, depicted by the standard deviation, σ. The probability of occurrence tends toward zero in the two extremities of the X-axis, $\pm\infty$. The Normal distribution is shown in figure 14.3.

The average μ and standard deviation σ of a sample of data points are given by:

$$\mu = \frac{\sum_{i=1}^{n} x_i}{n}$$

$$\sigma = \left[\frac{\sum_{i=1}^{n}(x_i - \mu)^2}{n-1}\right]^{\frac{1}{2}} \qquad (14.1)$$

μ = Average

σ = Standard deviation

x_i = The i_{th} observatio n

n = Number of observatio ns

The normal distribution has the property that 68,27% of all data points with that distribution will fall within the bounds $\mu\pm\sigma$. This can be extended to 95,45% of all data points that fall within the limits $\mu \pm 2\sigma$ and 99,73% that fall within $\mu\pm 3\sigma$. These properties can now be used to determine whether new data points are from the same distribution or not. These properties are illustrated in figure 14.4. It

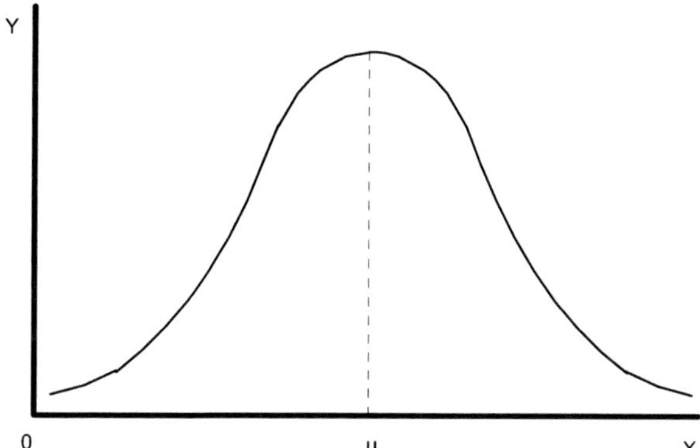

Figure 14.3 : The Normal Distribution

has become customary to use the $\mu \pm 3\sigma$ limits for control purposes. With these limits any data point belonging to the same distribution with a probability of 99,73% fall within the limits $\mu \pm 3\sigma$. We could thus say that any data point falling outside these bounds is (with high probability) not from the same distribution.

A control chart is constructed by drawing horizontal lines at the three values $\mu - 3\sigma$, μ and $\mu + 3\sigma$. The first and the last of these are the control boundaries, while the middle one is the average or expected value. This chart is now used to plot fresh data values on. Any data point falling within the control boundaries with high probability belongs to the same distribution from which μ and σ were calculated. Any data point falling outside these boundaries with high probability does not belong to this distribution. The probability of a value from the present distribution falling outside the $\mu \pm 3\sigma$ boundaries is only 0,27%. Likewise it can be shown that the probability of two out of three items in a row falling outside the boundaries $\mu \pm 2\sigma$ is only 0,24%. On the basis of these, the following rules can be used to determine when measurement data comes from a different distribution, indicating a long term process parameter value shift. The process distribution (μ and/or σ) is busy changing if:

- ⇒ A new data point is outside the $\mu \pm 3\sigma$ limits.
- ⇒ Nine data points in a row fall to one side of the average μ.
- ⇒ Six data points in a row have a steadily increasing or decreasing trend.

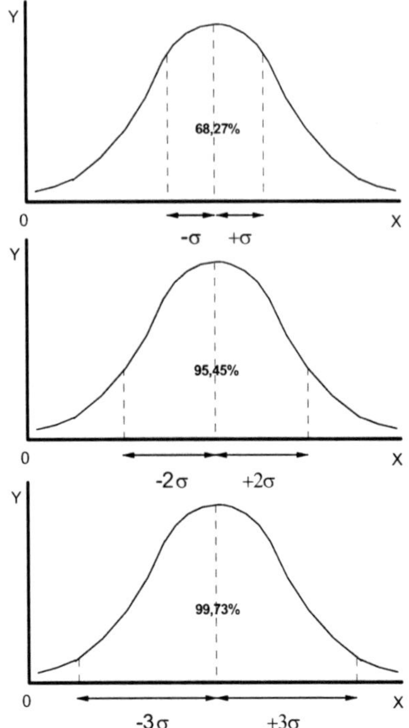

Figure 14.4 : Bounded Probability of Occurrence

⇒ Fourteen data points in a row have values that alternate up and down.

⇒ Two out of three data points in a row fall outside the $\mu \pm 2\sigma$ limits.

⇒ Four out of five data points in a row fall more than σ away from the expected value of μ, on one side of μ.

⇒ Fifteen data points in a row fall inside the $\mu \pm \sigma$ limits.

⇒ Eight data points in a row fall outside the $\mu \pm \sigma$ limits.

Example 3

The historical availability data for a large, expensive industrial machine has an average of 84% and a standard deviation of 2% ((figures rounded for ease of computation). The following monthly availabilities are now available for the last fifteen months (these were not used in computing the historical figures):

Table 14.2 : Availability data - Example 3

Month	*Availability %*
1	84
2	83
3	86
4	81
5	85
6	86
7	85
8	86
9	89
10	87
11	85
12	88
13	84
14	87
15	82

There is a general feeling under the company's managers that the machine's availability is showing and upward trend. We will use the technique of control boundaries to either confirm or reject this notion. Figure 14.5 shows the above availability data superimposed on the historical control boundaries.

We can now apply the eight rules above to determine whether the company has a change in their availability distribution.

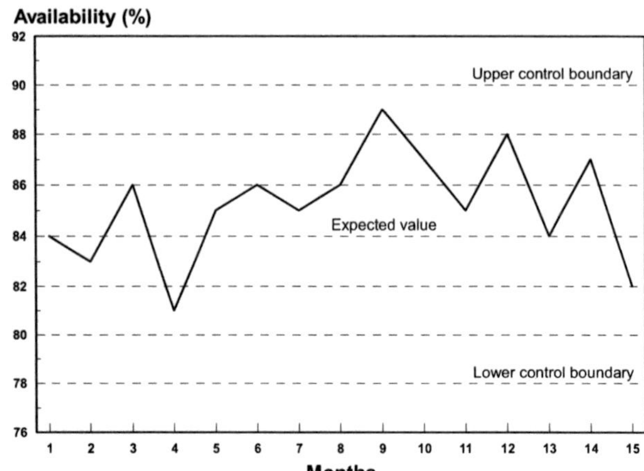

Figure 14.5 : Control Graph - Example 3

Rule 1 - there are no data points outside the $\mu\pm3\sigma$ limits.

Rule 2 - the maximum number of data points to one side of the average is 8 - one less that required for significant change.

Rule 3 - no short term sustaining trends.

Rule 4 - no alternating data points.

Rule 5 - only one data point outside the $\mu\pm2\sigma$ limits.

Rule 6 - maximum two data points to one side outside the $\mu\pm\sigma$ limits.

Rule 7 - maximum two data points inside the $\mu\pm\sigma$ limits.

Rule 8 - maximum two data points outside the $\mu\pm\sigma$ limits.

There is thus no statistical evidence of any change in the availability distributions. It seems, though, that there was a tendency towards improved availability (rule 2) from month 5 to month 12, but this tendency has subsequently been reversed.

Control charts are used:

⇒ To determine whether a process is running between predetermined limits.

⇒ To determine whether improvement or deterioration is taking place.

Typical applications include availability, utilization and production rate data as well as cost and any other single quantity that has to be monitored and/or controlled over time.

Curve smoothing

When plotting raw measurement data, one can often not discern any trend. The reason for this lies in the high level of fluctuation in the data. One way of dealing with this situation is by smoothing the original data so that the underlying trend becomes apparent. This is done by utilizing a smoothing technique where the amount of smoothing is controlled through the choice of the value of a smoothing parameter. While an unsmoothed data graph often has a too high level of fluctuation, smoothing too much can lead to a graph devoid of any meaning. There are two simple smoothing techniques that can be applied to most maintenance data without undue difficulty in calculation. These are the **moving average technique** and the **exponential smoothing technique**.

Moving average

If the successive data values are labeled x_i (with i denoting the i_{th} data value), then the n-period moving average is calculated for each data point as:

$$a_i = \frac{\sum_{j=i-n+1}^{i} x_j}{n} \qquad (14.2)$$

The smoothing effect can be controlled by varying the length of the smoothing period. A long smoothing period will result in a very smooth graph whereas a short smoothing period will result in very little smoothing.

Exponential smoothing

A second relatively uncomplicated method of smoothing is the exponential smoothing technique. In this technique each new smoothed data point is calculated from the previous smoothed data point and the present unsmoothed data point. This is done by introducing a smoothing constant, which is a figure between zero and unity. The new smoothed value is calculated by:

$$s_i = \alpha x_i + (1-\alpha)s_{i-1} \tag{14.3}$$

$s_i = i_{th}$ smoothed value
α = Smoothing constant

The benefits of the technique of exponential smoothing over moving averages are:

- Less cumbersome calculations. If 6-period moving average has to be calculated, 6 values must be averaged each time. For an equivalent exponential smoothing calculation α times the newest data value is added to (1–α) times the previous smoothed value.
- Less history needs to be kept. For a 6-period moving average, the 6 latest data points must always be available. In contrast to this, only the newest data value and the previous smoothed value must be available for an exponential smoothing calculation.
- In exponential smoothing the value of α determines how much weight is attached to new data, compared to historical figures. Low values of α (below 0,5) results in more emphasis of historical results while high values of α favors the new data. Low values of α will thus result in more smoothing than higher values.

The value of α that will simulate an n-period moving average can be calculated from:

$$\alpha = \frac{2}{n+1} \tag{14.4}$$

Lastly, it must be mentioned that both these smoothing techniques can be combined with the concept of control boundaries to good effect.

Example 4

Using the availability data of example 3, we can now produce smoothed graphs to attempt to detect trends. We compute a five month moving average for the availability data and compare that with exponential smoothing using $\alpha = 0{,}4$. This result is shown in tabular format in table 14.3 and graphically in figure 14.6. Both these smoothed lines confirm our verdict that there was a positive trend in availabilities up to month 12, but that it was followed by a negative trend during the last 3 months.

Table 14.3 : Smoothed Availability Data - Example 4

Month	Availability %	5 month moving average %	Exponentially smoothed (α=0,4) %
1	84		84,0
2	83		83,6
3	86		84,6
4	81		83,2
5	85	83,8	83,9
6	86	84,2	84,7
7	85	84,6	84,8
8	86	84,6	85,3
9	89	86,2	86,8
10	87	86,6	86,9
11	85	86,4	86,1
12	88	87,0	86,9
13	84	86,6	85,7
14	87	86,2	86,2
15	82	85,2	84,5

Cusum charts

Another method of determining whether data has an underlying trend is by using Cusum charts. It is a very handy technique due to its amplification of the underlying trend (if there is such in the data). The Cusum method will clearly show trends in situations where

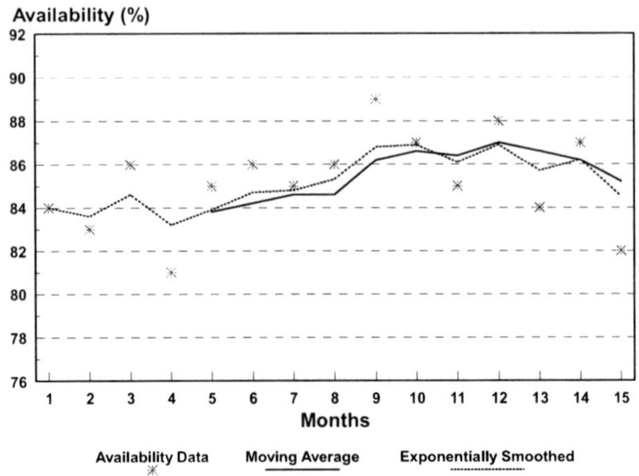

Figure 14.6 : Smoothed Availability Data - Example 4

curve smoothing will leave the user wondering. The cumulative sum (cusum) chart is simply a graph of the cumulative total of a series of data, or a graph of the cumulative difference between each of the individual data points and a constant (target) value. On the other hand, cusum charts have more limitations than curve smoothing techniques. It can only show trend effectively over a relatively short time span.

The first cusum method (the cumulative total of a series of data against time) will indicate increased rate if it curves downward over time. No trend will be shown by a constant upwards cusum slope. The second cusum method (cumulative difference between the data points and a constant value) will show an increasing trend (curve upwards) if the average of the data points is higher than the reference value. On the other hand, the curve will curve downwards if the average of the data point is lower than the reference value.

Example 5

We now use the cusum technique to help us determine whether we have a positive trend in the availability data of examples 3 and 4. We firstly use the cumulative total to examine the trend in the data.

The results in table 14.4 are graphically portrayed in figure 14.7. Clearly the cumulative cusum technique shows no positive or negative trend (the graph does not concave up or down). The second cusum

Table 14.4 : Cumulative Total of Availability data - Example 5

Month	*Availability %*	*Cumulative Total*
1	84	84
2	83	167
3	86	253
4	81	334
5	85	419
6	86	505
7	85	590
8	86	676
9	89	765
10	87	852
11	85	937
12	88	1025
13	84	1109
14	87	1196
15	82	1278

technique (the cumulative difference) gives the results shown in table 14.5 when compared to the average of 84% in the historical data.

These results are graphically displayed in figure 14.8. This technique, which amplifies any trend significantly, shows that, compared to the historical average of 84% there is a significant increasing trend. The question now is: why did the cumulative cusum chart not show a

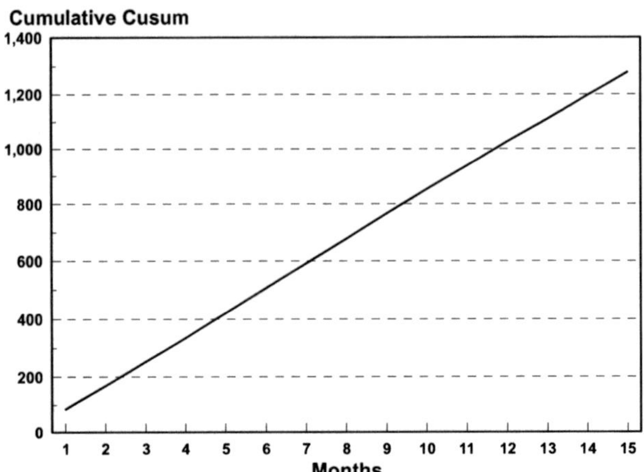

Figure 14.7 : Cumulative Cusum Chart - Example 5

trend? The only explanation for this difference is that the present data is without an inherent trend, but that the distribution of the present data (average and standard deviation) differs significantly from the historical data. By changing the standard (originally 84%) against which the cumulative difference cusum is calculated until the resulting chart shows no trend, this can be verified. By using 85,2% as the comparison standard the difference cusum displayed in figure 14.9 results. This chart shows no resultant trend, which agrees with our previous findings. By calculating the average and standard deviation for our present fifteen months' data we find that μ = 85,2% and σ = 2,178%. This confirms our suspicion that there was a significant improvement in availability as compared to the historical data, but that there is no trend in the present data indicating further improvement.

Forecasting

Forecasting is a technique where the past is used to predict the future. One method would be to use the last n-period moving average (or the exponentially smoothed value) as an estimator of the expected value one period into the future. A better way is to fit a suitable mathematical curve through the historical data points (which could be the raw data point or smoothed points) and then use this curve to predict the future. Any known curve can be fitted to the data, but the following array of curves should normally suffice:

Table 14.5 : Cumulative Difference - Example 5

Month	Availability %	Average %	Difference %	Cumulative Difference %
1	84	84	0	0
2	83	84	-1	-1
3	86	84	2	1
4	81	84	-3	-2
5	85	84	1	-1
6	86	84	2	1
7	85	84	1	2
8	86	84	2	4
9	89	84	5	9
10	87	84	3	12
11	85	84	1	13
12	88	84	4	17
13	84	84	0	17
14	87	84	3	20
15	82	84	-2	18

Linear curve: $y = ax + b$

Quadratic curve: $y = ax^2 + bx + c$

Hyperbolic curve: $y = \frac{a}{x} + b$

Exponential curve: $y = ab^x$

Geometric curve: $y = ax^b$

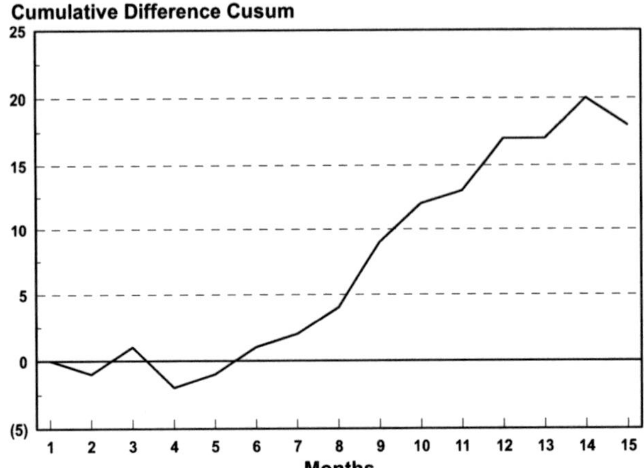

Figure 14.8 : Difference Cusum Chart - Example 5

Fitting procedures

Linear curve

The form of the equation for a linear curve is:

$$y = ax + b \tag{14.5}$$

The coefficients are calculated from:

$$a = \frac{(x_1 - \bar{x})(y_1 - \bar{y}) + (x_2 - \bar{x})(y_2 - \bar{y}) + \ldots\ldots + (x_n - \bar{x})(y_n - \bar{y})}{(x_1 - \bar{x})^2 + (x_2 - \bar{x})^2 + \ldots\ldots + (x_n - \bar{x})^2}$$

$$b = \bar{y} - a\bar{x} \tag{14.6}$$

$\bar{x}$ = Average of x – values in the data

$\bar{y}$ = Average of y – values in the data

x_1 to x_n = Individual x – values in the data

y_1 to y_n = Individual y – values in the data

Quadratic curve

To ascertain that a quadratic curve will fit through the data, it is advisable to start by plotting the points (x_i , y_{i+1}-y_i). If these points are in a straight line a quadratic relationship may be assumed. The equation is of the form:

$$y = ax^2 + bx + c \tag{14.7}$$

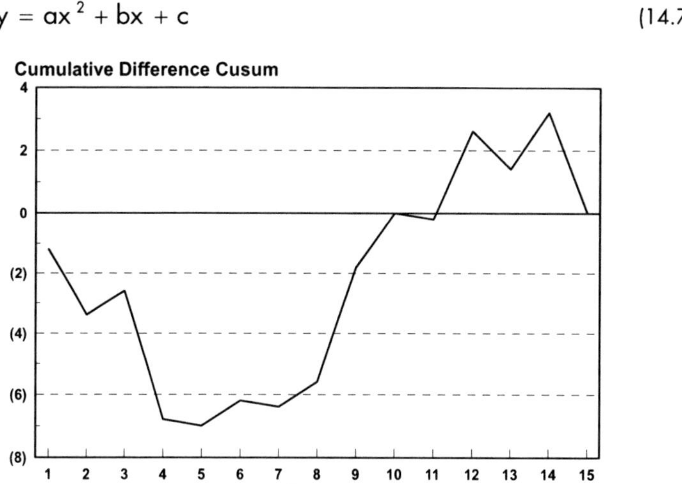

Figure 14.9 : Alternative Difference Cusum Chart - Example 5

The coefficients can be calculated by the simultaneous solution of the following three equations:

$$\begin{aligned}
\sum_{i=1}^{n} y_i &= a\sum_{i=1}^{n} x_i^2 + b\sum_{i=1}^{n} x_i + cn \\
\sum_{i=1}^{n} x_i y_i &= a\sum_{i=1}^{n} x_i^3 + b\sum_{i=1}^{n} x_i^2 + c\sum_{i=1}^{n} x_i \\
\sum_{i=1}^{n} x_i^2 y_i &= a\sum_{i=1}^{n} x_i^4 + b\sum_{i=1}^{n} x_i^3 + c\sum_{i=1}^{n} x_i^2
\end{aligned} \tag{14.8}$$

By replacing the x_i's and y_i's with the various data values, three equations in a, b and c results, which can be easily solved.

Hyperbolic curve

If the points $(1/x_i , y_i)$ form a straight line when plotted, a hyperbolic curve will fit on the data. The equation for a hyperbolic curve is:

$$y = \frac{a}{x} + b \tag{14.9}$$

The coefficients are calculated from:

$$\begin{aligned} \sum_{i=1}^{n} y_i &= a\sum_{i=1}^{n} \frac{1}{x_i} + bn \\ \sum_{i=1}^{n} \frac{y_i}{x_i} &= a\sum_{i=1}^{n} \frac{1}{x_i^2} + b\sum_{i=1}^{n} \frac{1}{x_i} \end{aligned} \tag{14.10}$$

By substituting the values of x_i and y_i from the data in the above equation, two simple equations with a and b as unknowns result. This can be easily solved.

Exponential curve

For the exponential curve to fit a specific data set, the points $(x_i , \log y_i)$ must lie in a straight line when plotted. The equation for the exponential curve is:

$$y = ab^x \tag{14.11}$$

The coefficients can be calculated in the usual way from the simultaneous solution of the equations:

$$\begin{aligned} \sum_{i=1}^{n} \log y_i &= n\log a + \log b\sum_{i=1}^{n} x_i \\ \sum_{i=1}^{n} x_i \log y_i &= \log a\sum_{i=1}^{n} x_i + \log b\sum_{i=1}^{n} x_i^2 \end{aligned} \tag{14.12}$$

Geometric curve

The geometric curve will fit a specific data set if the points (log x_i, log y_i) have a correlation coefficient that are within acceptable limits (see next paragraph for a discussion of the correlation coefficient). The geometric equation is of the form:

$$y = ax^b \tag{14.13}$$

and its coefficients can be calculated by the simultaneous solution of:

$$\begin{aligned} \sum_{i=1}^{n} \log y_i &= n\log a + \log b \sum_{i=1}^{n} \log x_i \\ \sum_{i=1}^{n} x_i \log y_i &= \log a \sum_{i=1}^{n} x_i + \log b \sum_{i=1}^{n} \log x_i^2 \end{aligned} \tag{14.14}$$

Correlation Coefficient

To establish whether a straight line fit is good or bad, the following coefficient can be calculated:

$$r = \frac{(x_1 - \bar{x})(y_1 - \bar{y}) + (x_2 - \bar{x})(y_2 - \bar{y}) + \ldots\ldots + (x_n - \bar{x})(y_n - \bar{y})}{\sqrt{\left[(x_1 - \bar{x})^2 + (x_2 - \bar{x})^2 + \ldots\ldots + (x_n - \bar{x})^2\right]\left[(y_1 - \bar{y})^2 + (y_2 - \bar{y})^2 + \ldots\ldots + (y_n - \bar{y})^2\right]}}$$

r = Correlation coefficient (14.15)

$\bar{x}$ = Average of x – values in the data

$\bar{y}$ = Average of y – values in the data

x_1 to x_n = Individual x – values in the data

y_1 to y_n = Individual y – values in the data

The above test is valid to determine whether a straight line is a good fit on a specific data set. It can be used on all five curves described above by first linearizing the data. This is summarized in table 14.6.

Table 14.6 : Values used in the r-test

Curve	*Values used in r-test*	
	x_i	y_i
Straight line	x_i	y_i
Quadratic	x_i	$y_{i+1}-y_i$
Hyperbolic	$1/x_i$	y_i
Exponential	x_i	$\log y_i$
Geometric	$\log x_i$	$\log y_i$

The limits within which the value of r must fall to present a good fit are as follows:

Table 14.7 : Acceptable values of the Correlation Coefficient

Number of data pairs (x_i, y_i)	*Acceptable Limits for the value of r*
5	$0,88<r<1,0$
10	$0,63<r<1,0$
25	$0,40<r<1,0$
50	$0,28<r<1,0$
100	$0,20<r<1,0$

The best way of establishing a good fit is by calculating the r- value for all five types of curves and then using the one with the highest r-value.

Forecasting

After fitting a known graph to the data, it is really a simple matter to calculate the next point on the graph. The next x-value is substituted into the equation for the curve and the y-value calculated.

It is important to note that the forecast value is based on the premise that the trend as evident in the data will continue into the future. This should be an acceptable assumption if the number of periods ahead for which the forecast is made is small compared to the number of data points in the original data.

Although the y-value calculated as described above gives the correct value if the trend continues exactly as found from the original data, there is always a certain amount of uncertainty involved. A better way of forecasting would thus be to calculate the range of values within which the specific y-value could possibly lie. This is done by firstly calculating an interval size:

$$\Delta y = t_{\alpha/2} S_e \left[1 + \frac{1}{n} + \frac{n\left(x_0 - \bar{x}\right)^2}{S_{xx}} \right]^{1/2} \tag{14.16}$$

where

$$S_e = \left[\frac{S_{xx} S_{yy} - S_{xy}{}^2}{n(n-2)S_{xx}} \right]^{1/2}$$

$$S_{xx} = n\sum_{i=1}^{n} x_i{}^2 - \left[\sum_{i=1}^{n} x_i \right]^2$$

$$S_{yy} = n\sum_{i=1}^{n} y_i{}^2 - \left[\sum_{i=1}^{n} y_i \right]^2$$

$$S_{xy} = n\sum_{i=1}^{n} x_i y_i - \left[\sum_{i=1}^{n} x_i \right]\left[\sum_{i=1}^{n} y_i \right]$$

x_0 = x – value for which forecast must be done

n = Number of data points in the original data

$\bar{x}$ = Average of the x – values in the data

x_i, y_i = Original data points

$t_{\alpha/2}$ can be read from the following table (top of next page) where (the number of degrees of freedom) can be calculated from:

$\nu = n - 2$

Table 14.8 : Values for r-test 95% confidence interval estimation

Table with values of $t_{\alpha/2}$ for α=0,05					
n	$t_{\alpha/2}$	*v*	$t_{\alpha/2}$	*v*	$t_{\alpha/2}$
1	12,706	11	2,201	21	2,080
2	4,303	12	2,179	22	2,074
3	3,182	13	2,160	23	2,069
4	2,776	14	2,145	24	2,064
5	2.571	15	2,131	25	2,060
6	2,447	16	2,120	26	2,056
7	2,365	17	2,110	27	2,052
8	2,306	18	2,101	28	2,048
9	2,262	19	2,093	29	2,045
10	2,228	20	2,086	30	1,960

After calculating the interval size Δy, it can be added to the y-value, calculated by substituting into the curve equation. This results in a 95 % confidence interval. It can thus be expected with 95 % confidence that the next point will have a value within:

$$y_0\text{-}\Delta y < y < y_0+\Delta y \tag{14.17}$$

Example 6

By using the availability data of examples 3 to 5, we can illustrate the forecasting technique. The coefficients for a linear curve are:

$$a = \frac{(1-8)(84-85{,}2)+(2-8)(83-85{,}2)+\ldots\ldots+(15-8)(82-85{,}2)}{(1-8)^2+(2-8)^2+\ldots\ldots+(15-8)^2}$$

$$= 0{,}121429$$

$$b = 85{,}2-(0{,}121429\times 8)$$

$$= 84{,}22857$$

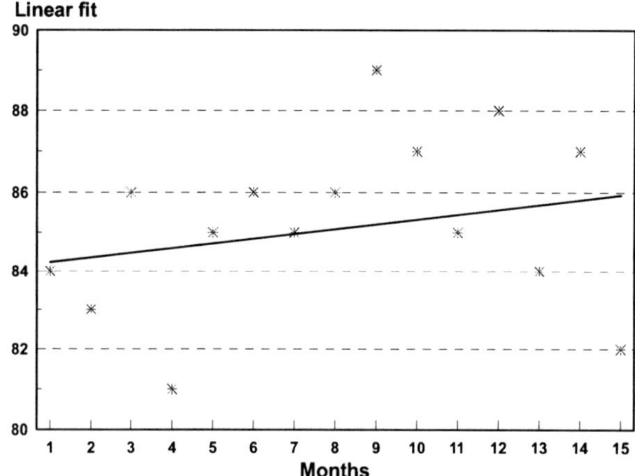

Figure 14.10 : Linear Curve fit - Example 6

The resulting curve is shown in figure 14.10. Using the formulas supplied above the data was also fitted with a quadratic curve, a hyperbolic curve, an exponential curve and a geometric curve. The resulting curves are shown in figure 14.11. The correlation coefficients for the various fits are shown in table 14.9.

The best fit is given by the geometric curve with an r-value of 0,93. The linear and exponential curves with r = 0,25 fall on the same line and present the second best fit (although its r-value is outside the

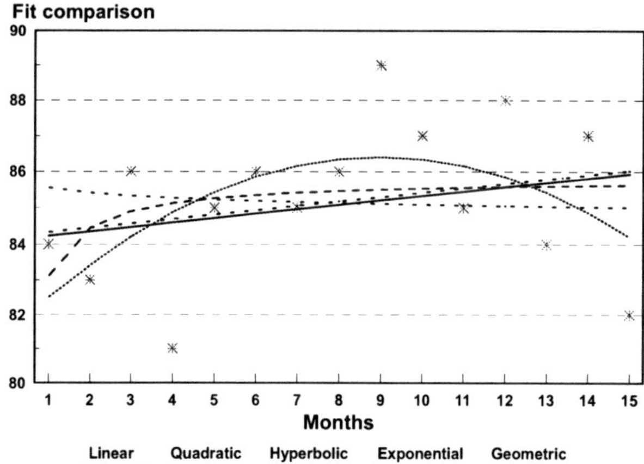

Figure 14.11 : Various regression fits - Example 6

bounds as set by table 14.7). The geometric curve has a downward slope, thus suggesting that the availability is busy decreasing. The function of this geometric curve is:

$$y = 85{,}5x^{-0{,}0024}$$

By substituting successive month numbers into this function as x-values the corresponding forecasts of the availabilities (as y-values) can be calculated. At the same time a 95% confidence interval for each of these values can be calculated. These results for the present example are shown in table 14.10 and are portrayed in figure 14.12 which shows the progressive widening cone of possible values as the forecasts are too far in the future.

Table 14.9 : Correlation coefficients - example 6

Curve	*r*
Linear	0,25
Quadratic	-0,06
Hyperbolic	-0,30
Exponential	0,25
Geometric	0,93

Uses of the forecasting technique

As was stated in the introduction to this section, forecasting are use extensively in the maintenance budgetary process. This is not where its usefulness stops, though. The following are examples of situations where the technique of forecasting could be used to one's advantage (some of which are of a budgetary nature):

⇒ Forecast of spare parts use

⇒ Forecast of manpower requirement

⇒ Forecast of number of breakdowns

⇒ Forecast of maintenance cost

⇒ Forecast of availability

⇒ Forecast of MTBF

⇒ Forecast of component life

Table 14.10 : Forecasting results

Month	Availability Forecast %	Δy %	Top boundary $(y+\Delta y)$ %	Lower boundary $(y-\Delta y)$ %
16	84,93	5,30	90,23	79,63
17	84,92	5,48	90,40	79,44
18	84,91	5,66	90,57	79,25
19	84,90	5,84	90,74	79,16
20	84,89	6,02	90,91	78,87

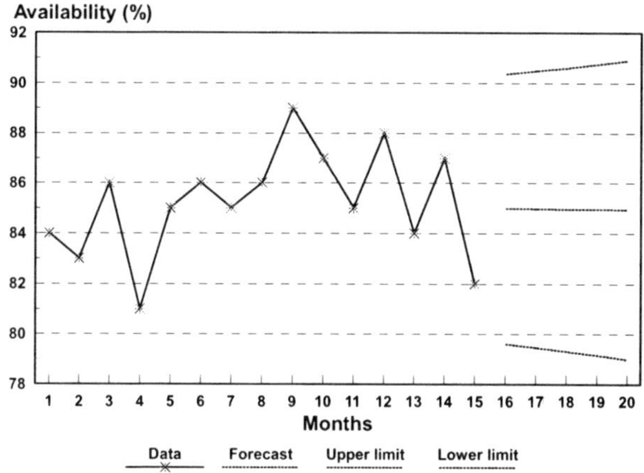

Figure 14.12 : Availability Forecast - Example 6

References

1. Coetzee, J.L., Quantitative Techniques in Maintenance Management. Annual short course, 1995.
2. Rao, C.R. (ed.), Handbook of Statistics, volume 9, North-Holland, Amsterdam. 1980.
3. Wild, Ray, Production and Operations Management, 4th edition. Cassell, 1989.

This page was left blank on purpose

Use it for notes

Chapter 15

Use of Queuing Theory in Maintenance Capacity Decision Making

Queuing theory is the theory of optimizing the flow of customers through a service facility. A good example is the optimization of the flow of people through a queue of customers waiting to be served by a bank teller. Queuing theory can help us, based on some knowledge of the situation and system requirements, to analyze the system with an objective to improve it. Thus different system combinations can be tested analytically using queuing theory to find the best option for the specific situation. Typical maintenance situations that can be optimized using queuing theory include:

⇒ The number of artisans needed to maintain a certain number of machines.

⇒ The work capacity (throughput or service rate) of a maintenance workshop or facility (e.g., milling machine).

⇒ The number of facilities needed of a certain kind (service bays, workbenches, lathes, etc.).

Theoretical background

A queuing system is specified by six characteristics. Some of these are shown in figure 15.1.

- The six characteristics are the following:
- *Arrival or inter-arrival distribution.* This is the statistical distribution that governs the arrivals of new customers.
- *Departure distribution.* This is the statistical distribution that governs the departure of customers from the system. This is also called the service distribution (the rate at which the servicing of customers take place, statistically distributed).

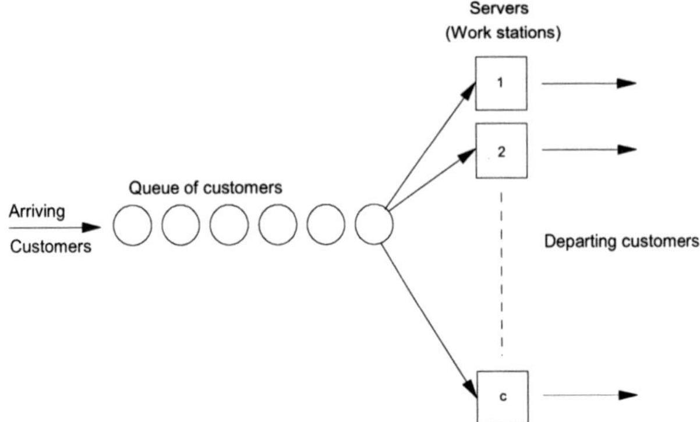

Figure 15.1 : Generalized Queuing System

- The *number of service channels* (or servers and their configuration - series, parallel or a combination of these).
- The *service discipline*. This is a rule for selecting the next customer to be served from the queue. The most common is the "first come, first served" discipline.
- The *maximum number of customers* allowed in the system.
- The *size of the potential customer pool* - whether it is finite or infinite.

The notation used in the queuing model is:

n = number of customers in the system

$p_n(t)$ = transient probability of exactly n customers in the system at time t

p_n = steady state probability of exactly n customers in the system

λ = mean arrival rate of customers

μ = mean service rate per busy server

$\rho = \lambda/\mu$ = traffic intensity

c = number of parallel servers

W_s = expected waiting time per customer in the system

W_q = expected waiting time per customer in the queue

L_s = expected number of customers in the system

L_q = expected number of customers in the queue

There are a number of basic relationships that hold. The expected number of customers in the system:

$$L_s = \lambda W_s \tag{15.1}$$

Likewise, the expected number of customers in the queue:

$$L_q = \lambda W_q \tag{15.2}$$

By definition the expected waiting time per customer in the queue is:

$$W_q = W_s - \frac{1}{\mu} \tag{15.3}$$

By multiplying both sides of this relationship by λ and substituting from the formulas for L_s and L_q:

$$L_q = L_s - \rho \tag{15.4}$$

In practice, if we have both λ and μ, as well as one of the expected values W_s, W_q, L_s or L_q, we can calculate the other three from these relationships. Normally one should, by measurement or specification, know the mean arrival rate of customers λ and the mean service rate per server μ. To get one of the expected values you could calculate L_s from:

$$L_s = \sum_{n=0}^{m} np_n \tag{15.5}$$

and L_q from:

$$L_q = \sum_{n=c+1}^{m} (n - c)p_n \tag{15.6}$$

The other values can then be calculated from the relationships defined above.

To be able to solve queuing models one need to be able to determine the various distributions that govern the queue. These are given without mathematical proof. They are derived by solving difference-differential equations derived from the principles underlying the queuing theory.

The distribution of arrivals has a Poisson distribution:

$$p_n(t) = \frac{(\lambda t)^n e^{-\lambda t}}{n!}, \qquad n = 0,1,2,\ldots\ldots\ldots\ \ldots.. \tag{15.7}$$

From this it follows that the distribution of inter-arrival times is exponential:

$$f(t) = \begin{cases} \lambda e^{-\lambda t}, & t > 0 \\ 0, & t \le 0 \end{cases} \tag{15.8}$$

The distribution of departure times, given that there are N customers in the system at time t=0, is a truncated Poisson distribution:

$$\begin{aligned} p_n(t) &= \frac{(\mu t)^{N-n} e^{-\mu t}}{(N-n)!}, n = 1,2,3,\ldots\ldots\ldots .N \\ p_0(t) &= 1 - \sum_{n=1}^{N} p_n(t) \end{aligned} \tag{15.9}$$

This yields the distribution of service times, which is exponential:

$$g(t) = \begin{cases} \mu e^{-\mu t}, & t > 0 \\ 0, & t \le 0 \end{cases} \tag{15.10}$$

Machine service modeling

If we have a total of K machines that have to be maintained by R artisans (each machine needs one artisan to repair it when broken), the following model results. In this case λ is known as the rate of breakdowns of a single machine. Likewise μ is the rate of repair of a single machine. The steady state solution is given by:

$$p_n = \begin{cases} \binom{K}{n} \rho^n p_0, & 0 \le n \le R \\ \binom{K}{n} \dfrac{n!\,\rho^n}{R!R^{n-R}} p_0, & R \le n \le K \end{cases} \tag{15.11}$$

with

$$p_0 = \left[\sum_{n=0}^{R} \binom{K}{n} \rho^n + \sum_{n=R+1}^{K} \binom{K}{n} \frac{n!\,\rho^n}{R!R^{n-R}} \right]^{-1} \tag{15.12}$$

where

$$\rho = \frac{\lambda}{\mu} = \frac{\frac{1}{MTTF}}{\frac{1}{MTTR}} = \frac{MTTR}{MTTF} \tag{15.13}$$

MTTF = Mean Time To Failure

MTTR = Mean Time To Repair

Using this, the expected number of customers in the queue can be calculated from:

$$L_q = \sum_{m=R+1}^{K} (n-R)p_n \tag{15.14}$$

and the expected number of customers in the system from:

$$L_s = \sum_{n=0}^{K} np_n \tag{15.15}$$

The expected number of idle artisans is given by:

$$\overline{R} = \sum_{n=0}^{R} (R-n)p_n \tag{15.16}$$

The effective arrival rate of new breakdowns (given that there are already n machines that are being repaired) is:

$$\lambda_{eff} = \lambda(K - L_s) \tag{15.17}$$

Example 1

A company has 20 identical machines. The machines have a MTBF (mean time between failures) of 12 hours and a MTTR (mean time to repair) of 2 hours. There is at present 3 artisans allocated to the maintenance of these machines. The company finds that they are unable to get availabilities of higher than 70%. One of the managers suggested that an increase in the number of artisans will solve the problem.

By applying the model above, using a computer spreadsheet model, the following results can be calculated.

$$\lambda = \frac{1}{MTTF} = \frac{1}{12-2} = 0{,}1 \quad \text{failures/hour}$$

$$\mu = \frac{1}{MTTR} = \frac{1}{2} = 0{,}5 \quad \text{repairs/hour}$$

$$\rho = \frac{\lambda}{\mu} = \frac{0{,}1}{0{,}5} = 0{,}2$$

Table 15.1 : Machine Service Model Results - Example 1

Number of Artisans	Average number of machines in repair	Average waiting time of machine in queue	Average turn-around time for machine repair	Estimated Availability	Average number of idle Artisans
2	10,0	80,3	100,3	49,9	0,0
3	6,0	32,0	60,0	70,0	0,2
4	4,2	10,1	41,8	79,1	0,8
5	3,6	3,0	35,8	82,1	1,7
6	3,4	0,8	34,0	83,0	2,7
7	3,4	0,2	33,5	83,2	3,7
8	3,3	0,0	33,4	83,3	4,7

These results show clearly that the number of artisans is the bottle neck in this situation. By increasing the number of artisans to 4 or 5 the availability can be increased to 79% or 82% respectively. With 4 artisans the artisan utilization will be

$$\frac{4-0{,}8}{4}\times 100\% = 80\%$$

which is fairly high measured against industry standards (65% seems to be a good figure). But, as these are dedicated posts 80% might be a good figure to aim for. With 5 artisans this figure decreases to 66%.

Optimum service rate

In maintenance we often have situation where we want to optimize the work throughput (service rate) of a single facility. Such a facility could for example be a maintenance workshop or a single workstation in such workshop. The problem is one where we expect a job arrival rate of λ and we wish to size our facility to optimize the total cost of the system.

The nature of this situation implies a single service channel. The total cost per unit time with a service rate μ is:

$$TC(\mu) = C_1\mu + C_2L_s \tag{15.18}$$

where

C_1 = Cost of service capacity per unit time

C_2 = Cost of waiting time per unit time per customer

For a single channel server:

$$L_s = \frac{\rho}{1-\rho} = \frac{\lambda}{\mu-\lambda} \tag{15.19}$$

Thus

$$TC(\mu) = C_1\mu + C_2\frac{\lambda}{\mu-\lambda} \tag{15.20}$$

To obtain the optimum service rate, differentiate TC(μ) with respect to μ and equate to zero:

$$\frac{d(TC(\mu))}{d\mu} = 0$$
$$\therefore C_1 - C_2 \frac{\lambda}{(\mu - \lambda)^2} = 0 \qquad (15.21)$$

From this it follows that the optimum service rate is given by:

$$\mu = \lambda + \left[\frac{C_2\lambda}{C_1}\right]^{\frac{1}{2}} \qquad (15.22)$$

Example 2

While designing a workshop, a company finds that it can invest at four different levels. The more expensive layouts are estimated to be able to deliver higher service rates, but at additional cost. On the basis of knowledge of the situation, we are asked to assist them in finding the optimal solution. The average arrival rate of jobs at each workstation is 0,3 jobs/hour. There are four possible levels of expenditure.

Table 15.2 : Capital expenditure vs. workstation performance - example 2

Design service rate (jobs/hour)	***Capital cost per work-station $***
0,35	100 000
0,5	170 000
0,7	250 000
0,95	360 000

The average cost per additional unit service rate can be calculated as follows:

$$C_1 = \frac{\frac{(170000-100000)}{(0{,}5-0{,}35)} + \frac{(250000-170000)}{(0{,}7-0{,}5)} + \frac{(360000-250000)}{(0{,}95-0{,}7)}}{3}$$

$$= \$\ 435556$$

The cost of waiting time per job is estimated at R250000 per hour.

$$C_2 = \$\ 250000$$

The optimal service rate can now be calculated:

$$\mu = \lambda + \left[\frac{C_2\lambda}{C_1}\right]^{1/2} = 0{,}3 + \left[\frac{250000 \times 0{,}3}{435556}\right]^{1/2} = 0{,}71 \quad \text{jobs per hour}$$

It is thus clear that the second most expensive option should be taken.

Optimum number of service facilities

When designing our maintenance infrastructure we often need to know the optimum number of service facilities. This could be the number of workstations or the number of mobile cranes needed of a certain kind. In this case we have an expected job arrival rate of λ and a service rate of μ per busy server. The objective is to find the number of servers c that will optimize the total cost of the system.

By the definition of the situation we have a multiple server system. The total cost per unit time with c servers in the system is:

$$TC(c) = C_1 c + C_2 L_s(c) \qquad (15.23)$$

where

C_1 = Cost of additional server per unit time

C_2 = Cost of waiting time per unit time per customer

The steady state solution for the multiple server case is given by:

$$p_n = \begin{cases} \left(\dfrac{\rho^n}{n!}\right)p_0, & 0 \le n \le c \\ \left(\dfrac{\rho^n}{c^{n-c}c!}\right)p_0, & n > c \end{cases} \tag{15.24}$$

with

$$p_0 = \left[\sum_{n=0}^{c-1}\frac{\rho^n}{n!} + \frac{\rho^n}{c!\left(1-\rho/c\right)}\right]^{-1}, \qquad \frac{\rho}{c} < 1 \tag{15.25}$$

where

$$\rho = \frac{\lambda}{\mu} = \frac{\text{MTTR}}{\text{MTTF}} \tag{15.26}$$

The number of jobs waiting in the queue is:

$$L_q(c) = \left(\frac{c\rho}{(c-\rho)^2}\right)p_c \tag{15.27}$$

Because c is discrete, the optimum cannot be obtained by differentiation as in the previous case. We thus make use of the fact that the total cost of the optimum number of servers must be lower than for one server more or one less. This gives the following two relationships which can be used to obtain the optimum:

$$\begin{aligned} TC(c-1) &\ge TC(c) \\ TC(c+1) &\ge TC(c) \end{aligned} \tag{15.28}$$

which can be used to derive the condition:

$$L_s(c) - L_s(c+1) \le \frac{C_1}{C_2} \le L_s(c-1) - L_s(c) \tag{15.29}$$

where $L_s(c)$ is calculated from the general relationship

$$L_s(c) = L_q(c) + \rho \tag{15.30}$$

Example 3

An open pit mining organization has a in pit lubrication facility for daily servicing of mobile equipment. The equipment is scheduled to arrive at the service facility through the day at an almost constant arrival rate. The average rate of arrivals is 0,4 machines per hour and the service rate per lubrication point is 0,55 machines per hour. The cost of providing an additional service point is $ 545/hour and the estimated cost of lost production is $ 40 000 per machine hour lost. We want to establish how many service points we should install, based on economic realities.

The problem is again solved using spreadsheet techniques. By calculating for different values of c, one can find the optimum from the following table.

Table 15.3 :
Lubrication service point calculation table - example 3

c	$L_s(c)$	$L_s(c)-L_s(c+1)$	$L_s(c-1)-L_s(c)$
1	2,666667	1,828572	
2	0,838095	0,097780	1,828572
3	0,740315	0,011513	0,097780
4	0,728802	0,001366	0,011513
5	0,727436		0,001366

Clearly the optimum is where $c = 3$:

$$L_s(3)-L_s(4)=0{,}011513<\frac{C_1}{C_2}=0{,}013625<L_s(2)-L_s(3)=0{,}097780$$

Thus three lubrication service points should be installed.

References

1. Coetzee, J.L., Quantitative Techniques in Maintenance Management. Annual short course, 1995.
2. Taha, Hamdy A., Operations Research - an introduction. Collier Macmillan, 1976.

This page was left blank on purpose

Use it for notes

Maintenance Systems

This page was left blank on purpose

Use it for notes

Chapter 16

The relevance of Maintenance Systems

The maintenance operational process

As we are interested in discussing maintenance systems and their success, we have to start by defining what constitutes a maintenance system. It is important to understand at the outset that a maintenance system does not only consist of a computerized maintenance management system (CMMS). The maintenance system is really the whole of the process as defined by the Maintenance Cycle (chapter 3). Each of the parts discussed there forms an important component of the total maintenance system. The Maintenance Cycle is thus in actual fact thé maintenance system that we are discussing in this section. This "system" is described in full detail in the maintenance policy document. The maintenance cycle is repeated here for convenience as figure 16.1.

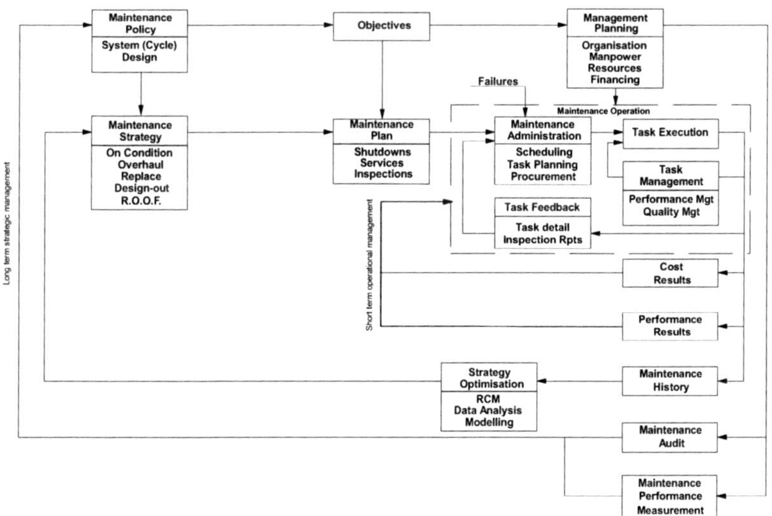

Figure 16.1 : The Maintenance Cycle

If any one of the constituent parts of the maintenance cycle does not function as it should, it will lead to the maintenance system not functioning successfully. Thus, the following must be true:

- A maintenance policy document must exist which defines the "maintenance system" in enough detail.
- The policy must be augmented by proper detailed procedures.
- Each part of the greater system must function as set forth in the policy document and procedures.
- There must be a high level of systems discipline in the organization. There must be an attitude of "we do it like this in our organization" - not because we are system freaks, but because we know that everything works well if we do it in this way.
- There should be a computerized maintenance operational and management system that supports the maintenance process (the system) adequately.
- Systems and operational personnel must be very disciplined in using the computerized system. Tasks should be performed as scheduled by the CMMS and correct and complete information should be fed back into the system.
- Management should be totally committed to using the information outputs of the CMMS to manage the maintenance organization. This implies that the management style of the organization have to be system driven as opposed to operating.

Control of maintenance actions

A generalized schematic diagram of a generic feedback control process is presented in figure 16.2. This process consists of five parts:

- Input - the input to a control process consists of the standards or expected performance of the process. If we use a car's speed control as example, this input will be the speed at which the driver wishes to drive.
- Process - the process that is being performed. In the case of our example this is the throttle opening which the speed control unit maintains in an attempt to provide the correct speed.
- Output - the output of a control process is the required (controlled) quantity. For our example this will be the actual speed of the vehicle.
- Measurement - in a feedback control process the output should be

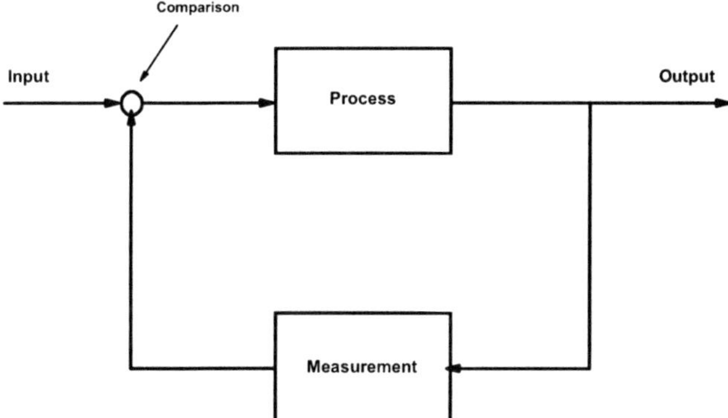

Figure 16.2 : Generic feedback control process

measured with a view to compare it against the standard that was set. In the case of our speed control the actual speed of the car (the output) will be measured by the speed control unit, using a sensor on the speedometer or drive shaft.

- Comparison - the last function is the comparison of the measurement results with the standard (input) and making small corrections so as to alter the output to the required value. The speed control will do this to increase or decrease the car's speed to the required value.

The Maintenance Cycle consists of a few superimposed control processes. *Firstly*, the management cycle uses as input the requirements set in the Maintenance Policy. The process is the managerial actions which lead to the annual results (output). This is compared to the requirements during the monthly Performance Measurements and the annual Maintenance Audit with a view to changing the process so as to achieve the required results. The *second* control process uses as its input the maintenance strategies set for the various machines. This is transformed into maintenance plans which are performed during the process of this control loop. The output consist of the various output parameters cost, machine performance and history. These are compared against the input and changes made to the strategies as needed. *Thirdly* the work requests from the Maintenance Administration (input) are being executed by the artisans (process). The results of the work being done is overviewed (measured) by the foremen and corrective action taken (comparison) where necessary.

It should be fairly obvious that, in order to control the maintenance actions, a good measurement system is required. This is one of the main functions of a CMMS. A good CMMS will thus provide the following measurements:

- *Maintenance performance measurement.* Refer to chapter 11 in this regard. This will facilitate a part of the measurement requirements of the Management Cycle. The other part, the annual Maintenance Audit (chapter 12) is a separate activity, which is of a more structural nature, and normally does not form part of the CMMS.
- *Equipment performance measurement.* This consists mainly of availability information, reliability information (MTTF), operability information (production results) and cost information. It is used as a basis for improving equipment maintenance strategies and plans.
- *Task execution measurement.* Task completion is compared against task plans - this is then used to improve planning and execution procedures. Backlog and worker utilization and efficiency are used to increase the level of productivity.

Maintenance history and maintenance policies

Maintenance policies or strategies for individual machines are developed using the technique of Reliability Centered Maintenance (RCM) or its equivalent. To be able to apply RCM properly, the existence of good equipment history is essential. This is then used as an input to the RCM-analysis technique, using Maintenance Data Analysis (MDA) and Failure Data Modeling (FDM) as supportive techniques. See our course "Introduction to Maintenance Engineering" in this regard.

Equipment history is accumulated through the proper use of the CMMS in the planning and execution of maintenance actions. The documentation of task results and equipment part exchanges lead to a wealth of data being accumulated, which collectively are known as history. As far as our policies are concerned, the most important elements of history are the equipment performance results (showing whether our policies have succeeded or not) and failure data. The failure data is used for Maintenance Data Analysis and Failure Data Modeling, leading to improved equipment maintenance policies.

Managing maintenance

A computerized maintenance management system is indispensable in the management of the maintenance function. Figure 16.3 shows a schematic representation of a CMMS. This shows that the typical CMMS consists of four "databases" and three main functional areas. The four databases are:

- *Equipment register* - all fixed equipment related data, including a unique identification of each machine.
- *Work Order database* - all work to be done is defined in this database, whether it is regularly scheduled, ad hoc work or breakdown work.
- *Responsibility structure* - the responsibility of various managers regarding the maintenance of specific plant areas and equipment is defined here. It also defines the hierarchical management structure to facilitate reporting at different management levels.
- *History database* - this is the database where history is collected through the use of the CMMS.

The three functional areas are:

- *Scheduling* - the scheduling of tasks for execution.
- *Work Management* - the functional area that assists maintenance supervision in successfully supervising maintenance work.
- *Machine Management* - this area assists maintenance managers in managing the results of maintenance. It also facilitates the continuous improvement of equipment maintenance policies.

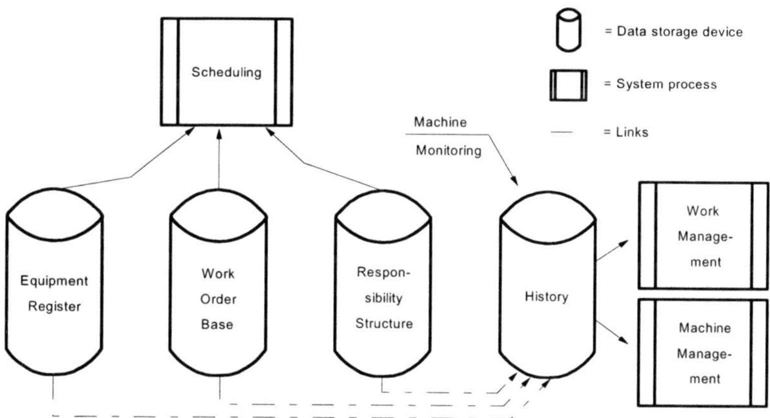

Figure 16.3 : Schematic representation of a CMMS

We named three of the four database areas the "pillars" of a CMMS. These are the *Equipment Register*, the *Work Order database* and the *Responsibility structure*. A CMMS can rather be lacking in the areas of its functionality - that can at least be remedied through programming. If a CMMS is not sufficiently sophisticated in the design of these three "pillars", though, it will always suffer the consequences of a bad design. The reason for this is, of course, that these three databases contains the structure of the total maintenance operation. This includes the physical plant structure (locations, equipment numbers), work structure, responsibilities, organization structure and all relationships between these various entities.

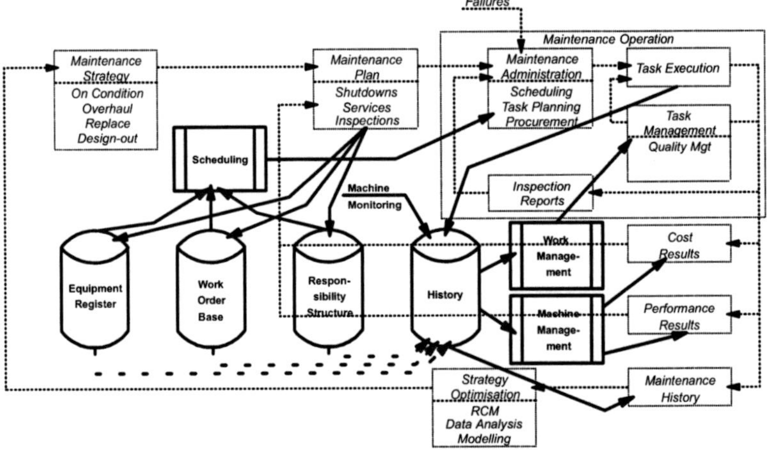

Figure 16.4 : Use of a CMMS in the Maintenance Cycle

Figure 16.4 shows the relationship between this schematic representation of a CMMS and the Maintenance Cycle. It is clear how the various functional areas support the corresponding functions in the Maintenance Cycle. It is also apparent how the maintenance plan forms the basis of all fixed system information and how operational data produces the history base.

System core values

No business achievement is possible without proper systems' support. Although our main accent in systems will be the CMMS, systems are much wider than one normally envisages, and include:

- The knowledge of all the people in the organization;
- The aggregated understanding of the modus operandi of the organization, both that written in procedures and that embedded in peo-

ple's heads;

- All the strategies, policies and procedures of the organization;
- The hardware organization (the physical design, layout of machinery and plant);
- The people organization, in terms of organization structure, communication structures, and informal structures;
- The software organization, the structures inherent in the deployment of business systems;
- The computerized management support for performing all of the above.

Such systems have to be properly documented and integrated into the organization to be effective. Specific values, which are of importance, are:

- People must be trained in their use.
- People must believe in them.
- People must use them.
- They must form the primary basis for all management decisions.
- They must be updated regularly as is necessary (they must reflect a living organization - the initiative for their upgrading must come from the people in the maintenance organization). Although system stability is very important, stagnant systems reflect a stagnant business.

Modes of systems use

Systems represent the nervous system of the organization. They are used in two major modes, i.e. they *firstly* form the spine of all action that takes place and *secondly* provide information for use in management control.

- The *first* mode (maintenance operations support) includes Work Order Management, Scheduling, and Procurement, which drives the total maintenance action.
- The *second* mode (maintenance management support) closes the management control loop and makes control possible through measurement tools. These tools include machine performance management, organizational performance management, cost management, and maintenance plan optimization.

This page was left blank on purpose

Use it for notes

Chapter 17

Maintenance System Design

The Components of a Maintenance System

Although all Maintenance Information Systems will not be organized in the same way, there are certain generic components that any such system should have. We begin this chapter on Maintenance System Design by first listing all these components, then describing them shortly before going into a fairly detailed design description of the various components.

For convenience the main system functional areas are grouped under the following three functional classifications:

- Maintenance Administration - all those facilities needed to keep the maintenance 'job' running.
- Maintenance Management - that part of the system which facilitates the management of maintenance.
- Maintenance Optimization - more advanced features to facilitate *Maintenance Performance Measurement* and *Maintenance Plan Development*.

Each of these main functional areas is in its turn divided into a number of maintenance system components, which we will subsequently use as system design areas for which more detailed design descriptions will be developed:

- Maintenance Administration
  - ⇒ Maintenance Data Base
  - ⇒ Work Order Management
  - ⇒ Scheduling
- Maintenance Management
  - ⇒ Responsibility Structure
  - ⇒ Equipment Performance Monitoring
  - ⇒ Cost Control

   - ⇒ Work Management
   - ⇒ Stock Control
- Maintenance Optimization
   - ⇒ Maintenance Performance Measurement
   - ⇒ Maintenance Plan Development

As was promised in the first paragraph, each of these functional areas will now be described shortly to provide an overview of what a Maintenance Information System should comprise, before going into more detailed design descriptions.

Systems overview

Maintenance Planning

Equipment Data Base

The equipment data base deals mainly with information such as the description, function, present location, supplier and capital value of equipment as well as its relationship with other pieces of equipment. Its main functionality and benefits lie in the areas of equipment identification, equipment registration and history retention.

The equipment data base forms the heart of any maintenance system and especially of the planning part of such a system. This can be pictured as shown in figure 17.1.

Work Order Management

All work performed by the maintenance department are initiated, performed and regulated against a unique work order number created during work order definition. Work order systems mostly allow for job cards to be issued and/or used as feedback documents to update the work order history.

Just as the equipment data base forms the heart of the total maintenance system, the work order management module forms the basis for all maintenance work performed. Work order management consists of the logic shown in figure 17.3.

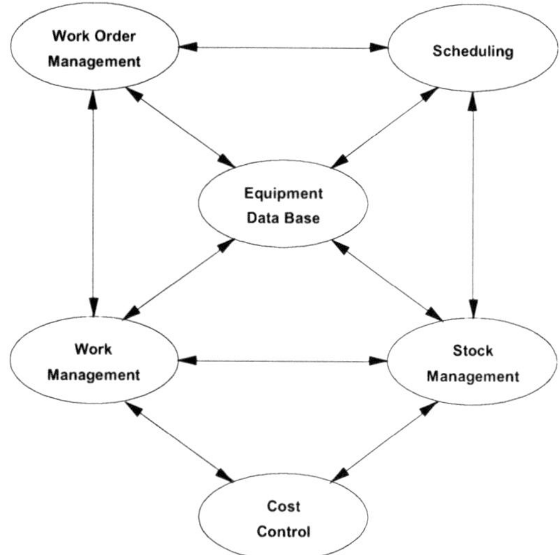

Figure 17.1 : Equipment Register relationship

Scheduling

In a maintenance department any one or more of the following types of schedules exist with the necessary level of integration between them:

- Long term schedule - a schedule to put dates against major maintenance activities.
- Task schedule - the detail schedule for a specific activity.
- Workshop schedule - a typical jobbing production schedule.
- Shutdown schedule - the schedule used during major plant shutdowns.

The relationship between these various types of schedules is as is shown in figure 17.4.

Maintenance Management

Responsibility Structure

In parallel with the equipment data base, which describes the plant and its structure, it is necessary to have a facility that describes the management structure of the organization. This includes a description of each post and its position in the management hierarchy. This is of paramount importance and forms the basis of management reporting. A responsibility structure for a typical small maintenance organization will look as follows:

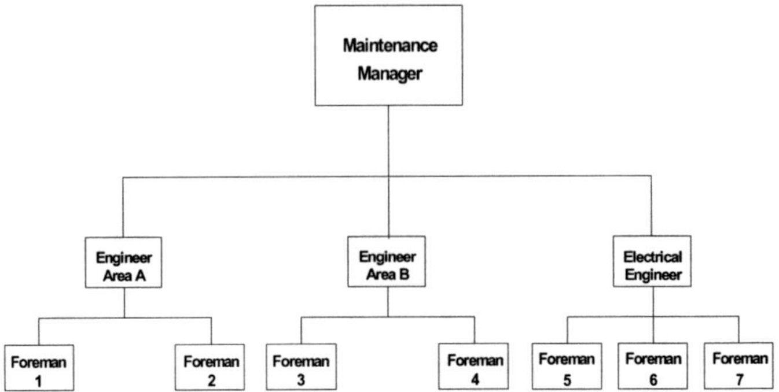

Figure 17.2 : Responsibility Structure

If this structure, which normally reflects the organization structure, is known, reporting can be differentiated in terms of design of reports and the level of detail included.

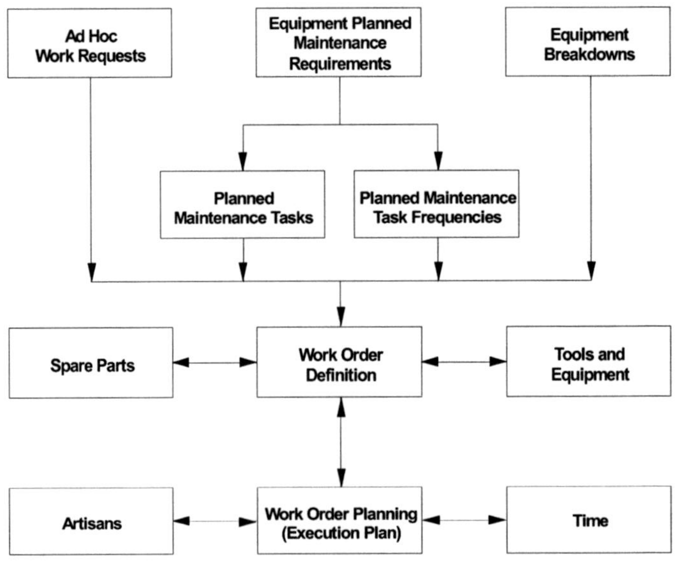

Figure 17.3 : Work Order Management

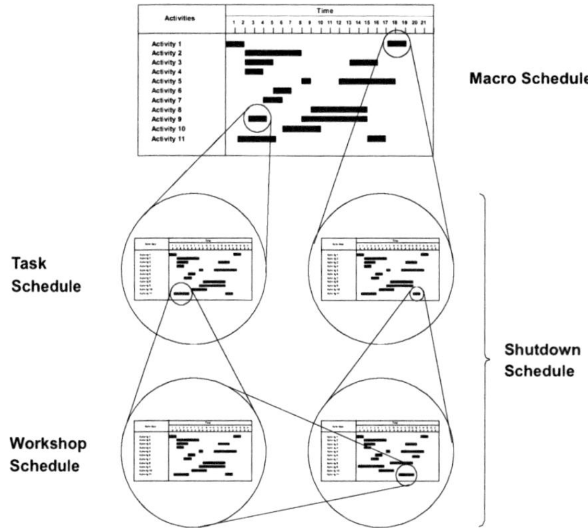

Figure 17.4 : Scheduling relationship

Equipment Performance Monitoring

The primary objective of the maintenance department lies in the "production" of *availability*, *reliability* and *operability* of machines (equipment). The maintenance system thus should have facilities for monitoring, and reporting on, these and many more quantities. Refer to chapter 11 for a more detailed description. The main quantities to be monitored are the following:

- equipment availability
- equipment utilization
- equipment production rate
- component failure rates
- equipment production loss
- equipment cost
- condition monitoring results
- performance monitoring results

These quantities are to be monitored against previously established standards and against accumulated history for the quantity involved. The results of this module should be portrayed graphically as far as is possible to assist the maintenance manager in optimizing his maintenance strategies. This optimizing stance can be defined in terms of figure 1.1.

Cost Control

Based largely on the long term schedule and on the expected resource impact of non-scheduled breakdowns and ad-hoc work, the cost control module assists the user in preparing and controlling expenditure against his maintenance budget. The budgeting process can be visualized as the compiling and summarization of detail work order budgets, thus facilitating cost control at all management levels.

- The main areas that should be addressed are the following:
- The preparation of quantity budgets, which are the starting process for the preparation of cost budgets. The availability of such quantity information will provide the system with a powerful tool for control at work execution level.
- The preparation of cost budgets, which forms the standard against which actual costs can be measured.
- The creation of cost accounts required for control over work order costs.
- Obtaining actual costs, including material costs, labor costs, maintenance equipment costs and outside work costs.
- Analyzing maintenance costs, so that the system user can be presented with meaningful information, which will ensure quick and to-the-point actions when required.
- Presenting cost and budget information to the system user in the required formats and at the appropriate level of detail.

Work Management

Work management includes:

- preparation of task documentation such as job cards, check lists and work permits
- the issue of such documents to the responsible personnel
- the feedback of actual job data
- the generation of management reports

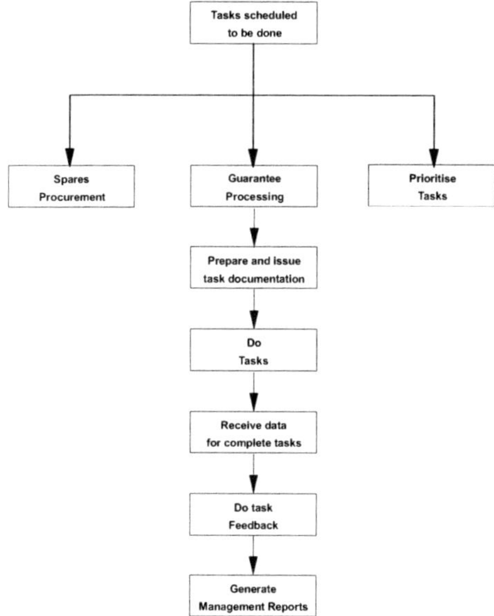

Figure 17.5 : Typical work flow diagram

Before the preparation of task documentation can commence, the various jobs are prioritized and checked for applicable vendor guarantees. At the same time the availability of spares for those jobs that are to be performed is verified. A typical work flow diagram is shown in figure 17.5.

Stock Control

Although stock is managed by a dedicated stores function in most organizations, it is so important to the maintenance function that maintenance stock control should form an integrated part of the maintenance system. Only in this way can proper integration of this critical area with the maintenance system be ensured.

- Stock control can be subdivided into three functional areas:
- Stock record keeping
- Inventory management
- Maintaining a stock catalogue

Each of these three main areas in turn consists of the following functions:

- Stock record keeping
  - ⇒ Stock balances
  - ⇒ Stock master records
  - ⇒ Stock taking
- Inventory management
  - ⇒ Stock replenishment
  - ⇒ Stock levels
  - ⇒ Economic order quantities
  - ⇒ Usage forecasting
  - ⇒ Monitor performance
    - * Commodity turnover
    - * Stock levels
    - * Order quantities
    - * Order lead times
- Maintaining a stock catalogue
  - ⇒ Stock catalogue user list
  - ⇒ Stock catalogue creation/maintenance
  - ⇒ Stock catalogues modification
  - ⇒ Catalogue distribution

Maintenance Optimization

To optimize maintenance, one should take two views, a macro view and a micro view. In the macro view maintenance should be optimized as was pictured in figure 1.1. The main tool for this optimization is an integrated *Maintenance Performance Measurement* instrument as was discussed in chapter 11. The system should have functionality to atomize this instrument, such that it provides maintenance management the facility to easily assess where the organization's maintenance is positioned on the road to maintenance excellence. The model that does optimization at this level must take into account the balance between the following:

- Level of prevention
- Availability of equipment
- Utilization of equipment

- Production loss due to downtime
- Production rate
- Total maintenance cost function
- Product selling price

The objective of such optimizing action should be to find a level of prevention that optimizes the maintenance department's contribution to the total profit of the organizations.

The micro view is that of optimizing the maintenance strategies that form part of the maintenance plan. This includes R.C.M. support functionality and maintenance optimization functionality to support the maintenance plan development processes as was discussed in chapters 6 to 9. Reliability Centered Maintenance (R.C.M.) is a macro optimizing technique in the sense that it optimizes the total mix of maintenance strategy choices. Although it operates at a fairly low level in the plant structure its result is an optimization of the total strategy mix.

Detailed Design

Equipment Data Base

The equipment data base forms the heart of any maintenance system, as was shown in figure 17.1. The equipment data base consists of three main parts:

⇒ Plant definition

⇒ Spare parts definition

⇒ Equipment usage

Plant definition

Equipment Classification

1. *Equipment Group* - normally it is very convenient to group equipment by production function such as all oxygen compressors, all 100 ton dump trucks, all conveyor drive heads. Such group can serve as reporting key and can thus facilitate between-group comparisons and plant functional breakdown analysis.
2. *Equipment Type* - whereas the previous classification (equipment

group) grouped all similar equipment together, the equipment type identifies a unique type of equipment within a group. Examples are the following:

Table 17.1 : Equipment Classification

Group	Type
Oxygen Compressors	Sulzer Compressor Asea Compressor
100 ton Dump Trucks	Wabco Trucks Unit Rig Trucks
Conveyor Drive	200 kW Drive Heads 400 kW Drive Heads 200 kW Modified Drive Heads

The purpose of the equipment type is thus to discern between equipment of various manufacturers, various sizes, standard vs. modified, etc. One of the advantages of the equipment type is that all equipment of a type is per se identical. Thus most of the information carried against a type is automatically applicable to each machine belonging to that type - such data includes its part number (if applicable), manufacturer, model number, description and so on.

Equipment Structure

Equipment structure is the hierarchical decomposition of a piece of equipment into functional sub-components that can each still be classified as a piece of equipment. A valid example of such structure is shown in figure 17.6.

Equipment Registration/Data

A single piece of equipment must be registered in the equipment data base against a unique equipment number. This equipment number must be unique for the total plant. Even if this piece of equipment is later scrapped, this number must remain intact against the history of the scrapped machine. The number may thus never be re-used. All the equipment specific data in the equipment data base is carried against this unique number. Such data includes equipment type, the serial number, date purchased, purchase price, equipment description, number of overhauls to date, etc.

Equipment Modifications

In practice it often happens that a specific machine is modified to enhance its reliability, operability or maintainability. If this change is of a major nature the modification can best be handled by defining a new equipment type and changing this machine's type. Mostly the change to a machine is such that the machine should remain within its previous equipment type. This can be handled in one of two ways:

- Give each modification on a certain piece of equipment an unique serial number against which the modification description, the reason for the modification and the expected result can be listed.
- Define a new modification level for the equipment type against which the modification description, the reason for the modification and the expected result can be listed. Each piece of equipment within the specific equipment type can then be assigned one of the modification levels for that type. This can even be enhanced further if the equipment type and the modification level together constitute an unique "equipment type" for which an unique equipment structure/spares structure is defined.

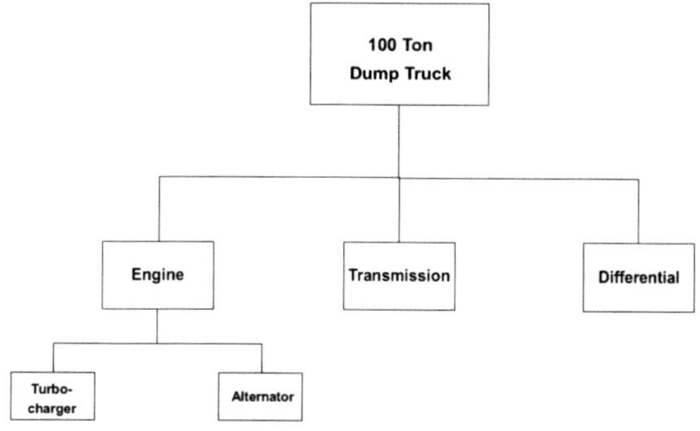

Figure 17.6 : Sample Equipment Structure

Another important feature of modification handling that should be incorporated into the maintenance information system concerns the control over modifications. There should exist a modification approval request form which should be completed and submitted to the maintenance engineer for approval. The approved form should then be handed over to maintenance planning, who will then arrange for drawing and documentation changes, order the necessary spares/materials and schedule the modification task. Following the successful completion of the task, the necessary changes must be made to the equipment data base and the results of the modification reported monthly to the appropriate management level.

Equipment Dependencies

In most production situations there exist production related dependencies between the various production machines. Examples of this are:

- Simple serial dependency - when one machine is down it completely stops the production of another machine.

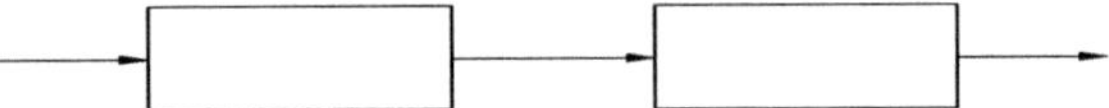

- Complex serial dependency - when one machine is down it only affects the production of the downstream serial machine by a certain percentage.

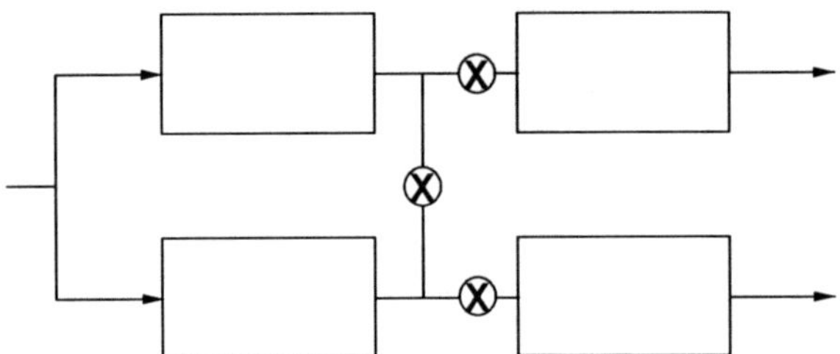

It is important to define these dependencies to the maintenance information system for the following reasons:

- In reporting equipment production results this is often a valuable parameter.
- When a machine breaks down one of the logical questions normally

is: "What other machines will be affected to such an extent that it can be maintained during this stoppage?"

- Maintenance scheduling is directly affected by this type of situation.

Another type of dependency is in the situation of parallel redundancy (standby). Again this should be registered in the system as it affects management reports as well as maintenance scheduling.

Equipment Guarantees

Guarantees play a significant role in most maintenance departments. Spares and contract maintenance are both subject to failure before the expected life after replacement/maintenance work is reached. To be able to manage guarantees effectively they must be registered in the maintenance information system. Each guarantee should be entered against a specific equipment number, should be allocated a serial number and should include the guarantee period, guarantee conditions and supplier details.

Spare Parts Definition

Parts Registration/Data

Just as a piece of equipment must be registered, each part that is important in the maintenance of such machine must be registered against a unique part number. Each part number should in turn have a part description in the equipment data base.

Parts Structure

In much the same way that an equipment structure is defined to the system, a part structure should also be maintained. This is especially necessary where more than one level of parts and parts/subassemblies are maintenance significant. Only levels that are significant need be registered.

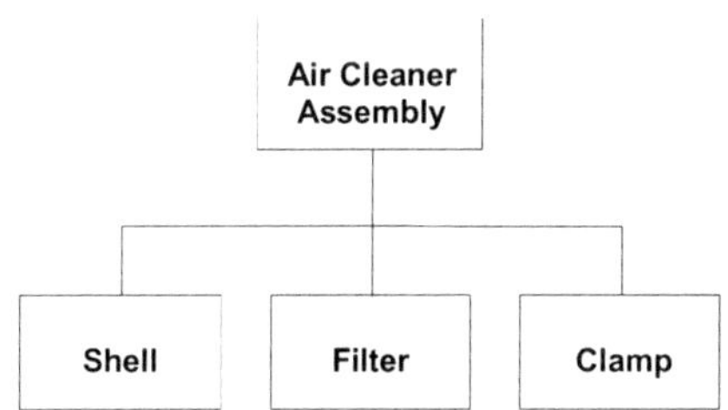

Figure 17.7 : Sample parts structure

Equipment/Parts Structure

This function forms the connecting link between the equipment structure and the parts' structure. This is necessary because the parts' structure can be used for more than one piece of equipment.

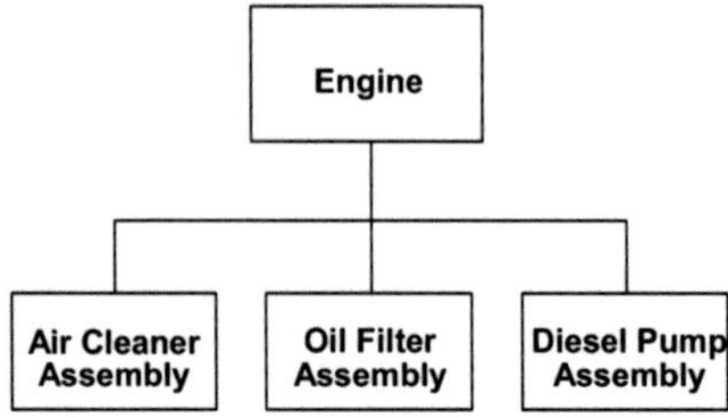

Figure 17.8 : Sample equipment/parts structure

Equipment usage

To be able to schedule maintenance work properly, it is necessary to keep record of the cumulative use of each machine. Normally this use is based on either a hour meter fitted to the machine or by logging the production activity of the machine (in terms of tonnage or cubic meters throughput or units produced). The cumulative use of each sub-assembly and/or spare part used in the machine can naturally be deducted from these figures for each sub-assembly/spare part that is registered as such and for which installation/removal records are kept.

Meter registration

Whether a certain machine usage is recorded from a physical hour meter or from a production log, it is important to register this "meter". Such registration should at least include an unique meter number, meter description, the reading frequency (for scheduling of reading occasions) and the reading unit of measure.

Meter/Equipment Structure

As the same meter readings can often be employed to determine the usage of more than one machine (especially in process type of plants), the system must have a means of knowing which machines' usage is given by which meters (figure 17.9).

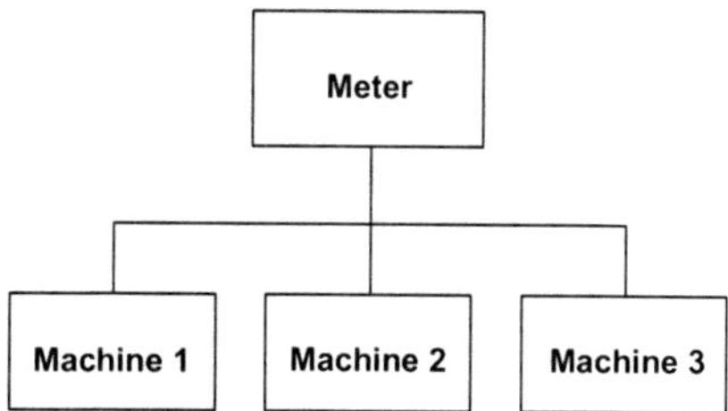

Figure 17.9 : Sample meter/equipment structure

Meter Readings

A facility must exist for the input of daily/weekly/monthly meter readings. The readings/activities must be logged against the specific meter and reading date.

Plant Codification

The specific codification scheme used to codify the plant is very much a matter of personal choice. With the advent of computerized maintenance systems, the plant code structure decreased in importance. The basic elements of such coding must of course still exist, but they need not be incorporated into one overall plant code, as was done previously. The important coding elements are the following:

- the equipment group
- the equipment type
- the equipment number
- the equipment location

Plant codes should be chosen to make the various machines and locations easily identifiable to the people working with them. Where-as the computer can handle any type of code, not all codes are as easily assimilated and used by human beings.

A good method of setting up a codification scheme is to start by using plant lay-out diagrams and following these steps:

⇒ Divide the total plant in logical functional blocks, each of which is assigned a locality code such as block A, block B, etc.

⇒ Divide each block into smaller functional logical blocks, each of which is assigned a sub-locality code such as A02, which is block 02 within the larger block A.

⇒ Make a list of all machines in the plant.

⇒ Group the machines into equipment groups.

⇒ Classify the machines in a specific group into machine types.

⇒ Number all the machines in a type with an unique serial number.

⇒ Do the same for all sub-assemblies of each machine (as well as sub-assemblies in stock).

Choose a method (or methods) of physically numbering the various locations (on fixed structures and/or floors) and machines (on their casings so that their numbers cannot be lost through the replacement of a part). Initiate a program of fixing all these numbers to the relevant members. Register all machines in the equipment data base and create the necessary connection to the location number (see later in the section on "Responsibility structure").

Maintenance Scheduling

Scheduling Techniques

There are four types of schedules that are important in maintenance. They are:

⇒ Long term schedules

⇒ Shut down schedules

⇒ Workshop schedules

⇒ Task schedules

These will be discussed in the following section. To effect these the following scheduling techniques are needed:

⇒ Allocation of time slots

⇒ Critical path method scheduling

⇒ Scheduling for workshop processing

⇒ Work Prioritization

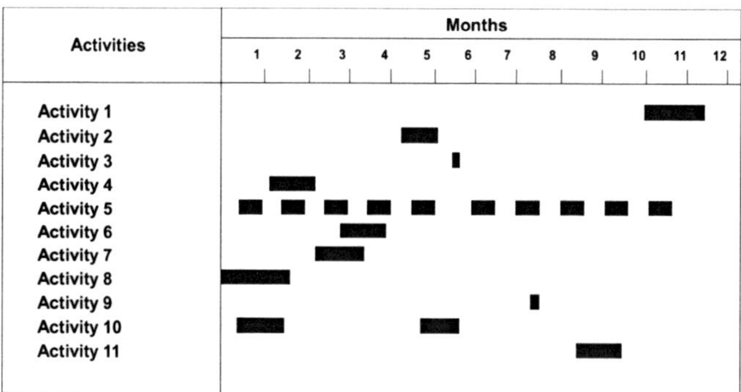

Figure 17.10 : Time slot Gantt chart

Allocation of time slots

This is the simplest of the three techniques. It comprises the calculation of the next occurrence of a specific event (i.e. a planned service) and recording the event and its associated event duration on a Gantt chart (or some other device). This can be illustrated by the example in figure 17.10.

Critical Path Method Scheduling

This method is well known and it is not within the scope of this document to fully document the method. In essence it consists of the scheduling of tasks, each having the following attributes:

⇒ Its duration.

⇒ The resources needed.

⇒ Other tasks that must of necessity be completed before this one can start (its immediate predecessors).

One of the most popular ways to present the results of such a critical path method schedule are by utilizing a Gantt chart as is shown in figure 17.11.

Scheduling for workshop processing

Maintenance often has scheduling situations that are of a batch nature. These are typically the situations that do not lend themselves to network scheduling as that would be an over complication of the problem, and/or may not handle the scheduling process ade-

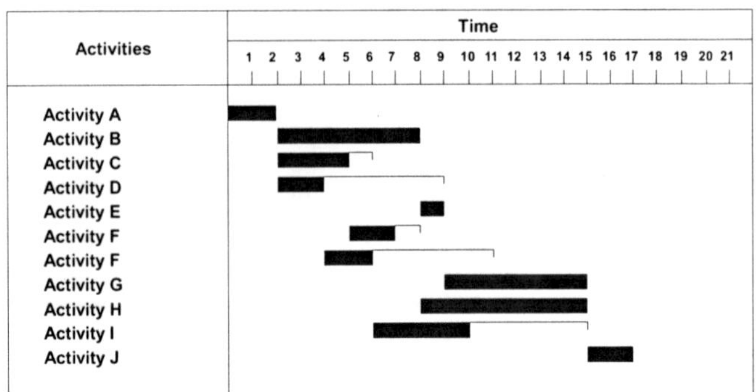

Figure 17.11 : CPM Gantt chart

quately. Furthermore, these situations are too complex to be handled by the simple time slot scheduling approach. Typically one or a few of a specific job have to be handled in an optimal way. This type of scheduling may be very simple if only a few jobs have to be handled by virtually unlimited resources. It can become very complex, though, when the typical machine workshop with multiple jobs, each with different requirements, has to be handled by many different machining centers.

The problem consists of the following elements:

- m different jobs.
- n different processing stations.
- An optimal sequence of processing each of the m jobs through the n processing stations: Thus a m x n matrix **A** can be prepared, where a_{ij} presents the order of processing of the i'th job through the n processing stations. Thus if 2 jobs are processed through 3 stations the matrix may be:

$$A = \begin{pmatrix} 2 & 1 & 3 \\ 3 & 1 & 0 \end{pmatrix} \qquad 17.1$$

  This will imply that job 1 will be processed through the three stations in the order station 2, station 1 and station 3, whereas job 2 will be processed in the order station 3 and station 1 (station 2 will not be used for this job).

- Each job has a certain processing time on each processing station. This can again be represented by a mxn matrix **B** where b_{ij} presents the processing time of the i'th job on the j'th processing station.

Thus for the above example this may be:

$$B = \begin{pmatrix} 65 & 35 & 40 \\ 10 & 0 & 15 \end{pmatrix} \qquad 17.2$$

This matrix shows that job 1 will take 65 minutes on station 1, 35 minutes on station 2 and 40 minutes on station 3, while job 2 will not be processed on station 2, but will use 10 minutes of station 1's time and 15 minutes of station 3's time.

- The priority of each job - this can be presented by a 1xm matrix **C** where c_{ij} is the priority of job i.

As can be seen this scheduling problem cannot be effectively handled by a human planner if more than say 10 jobs have to be optimally processed through 10 stations, as this already entails

$$\begin{aligned} & (m!)^n \times n \\ = & (10!) \times 10 \\ = & 3{,}96 \times 10^{66} \end{aligned}$$

possible scheduling options that could be selected (neglecting the fact that not all jobs will pass through all processing stations). The only way in which this scheduling problem can be effectively resolved is through computerized optimizing algorithms comprising simulation of the various options available. An alternative would be to use the jobbing algorithms developed for jobbing shops, but as they are of a more intuitive nature, the result will not be as good.

Work Prioritization

Although prioritization isn't a pure scheduling technique, it is important as a method of sequencing work in an optimal way, and is thus discussed as a scheduling technique. There are various ways available for the prioritization of work. The simplest method available is by allocating a priority to every job from the priority pool:

⇒ 1 Very urgent - must be handled immediately

⇒ 2 Urgent, but can wait if must

⇒ 3 Do as time comes available

The problem with such simple schemes is first that they can be easily manipulated to suit the requester and second that priority allocations depend very much on the frame of reference of the person doing the allocation.

Another way of prioritization is by using predefined priority allocation tables. Such tables can take a few parameters into account and produce a fair result.

Still another way is by combining a few risk factors to establish a relative level of risk, which in turn will determine the priority of the task at hand. Typical risk factors are:

- Production loss suffered while job is outstanding.
- Damage that could suffered to plant if the job is not completed soon.
- Condition of standby equipment currently running (while the machine on which the job must be done is out of commission).
- Chance of using a second component such as the one in for repair (in the case of using the priority scheme for sub-assembly repair) while none is available as spares.

These factors can be combined by addition and/or multiplication to give a compound risk factor, from which a valid priority can be derived using a priority assignment table. These priorities are now used to select which work should be done first from the waiting pool of work.

Scheduling Maintenance Work

As was stated previously, maintenance scheduling comprises four types of schedules:

⇒ Long term schedules

⇒ Shutdown schedules

⇒ Workshop schedules

⇒ Task schedules

Long term schedules

To perform long term scheduling use is made of the allocation of time slots. The various major maintenance activities such as shutdowns and major preventive work are fitted into time slots using this technique. As this is really only a scaled-down version of the Critical Path Method (no interrelationships exist between the chunks of work scheduled here), some of the techniques of C.P.M. (i.e. resource scheduling) could be used in the scheduling process.

Shutdown and Task Schedules

This comprises the detailed scheduling of tasks for single items from the long term schedule. A certain preventive task or shutdown is now taken and is broken down into activities, which is scheduled using the Critical Path Method. This methodology could be used for all tasks on the long term schedule but is normally used only for those tasks that can materially benefit from this scheduling action. Following the scheduling action this total task schedule is "frozen" so that it can be re-used during subsequent occurrences of this task. It can however be updated after each application from the experience that were gained during task execution.

Workshop schedules

There are three types of workshops active in the maintenance world:

- The maintenance *jobbing shop* (i.e. machine shop) where a variety of tasks are handled by differing combinations of a number of processing stations. Here the workshop processing scheduling technique of previously discussed should be used.
- The maintenance *project shop* (i.e. overhaul workshop where large machines are overhauled). This is a very apt application for the Critical Path Method. The total task is broken down into activities, which are then scheduled using C.P.M. techniques.
- The *area maintenance workshop* - this is the "first line of defense" workshop from which all smaller routine maintenance, preventive tasks and breakdowns are handled. Scheduling is done using the prioritizing technique. As was stated there, prioritization is not a pure scheduling technique, but is more of a work selection technique. It assists the workshop management to determine which jobs from a pool of waiting jobs should be handled first. These jobs are then assigned to artisans.

Scheduling Specifics

During the scheduling task certain current information is required (i.e. meter readings, availability of personnel and scheduling calendars). The scheduling process will also produce job cards, which are real time copies of tasks defined.

Scheduling Calendar

The system must include a facility to state for each day whether that day is regarded as a working day and what the normal start and finish times for that day are. This is necessary so that the scheduling routines can schedule tasks during those specific days and time.

Personnel Availability

This consists of a variety of registers that must be held in the system data base:

1. Skill - each skill that the company employs must be defined, together with the rate at which the skill is priced. See the "Responsibility Structure" section.
2. Position - for each responsibility code (see section on "Responsibility Structure") there must exist a list of specific positions, each with a specific skill. See the "Responsibility Structure" section.
3. Employee - for each employee that is appointed into a post, a specific record with his name and control number must exist. See the "Responsibility Structure" section.
4. Vacations - a list of the vacations scheduled for each artisan must exist (start and finish dates).

Job Card Definition

The output of the scheduling process consists mainly of defined job cards that are real time scheduled copies of standard tasks defined. Such job cards will by definition include the work order structure, the work order information and task information. It also includes the date of issue and information on the planned start and finish dates, planned duration, planned man hours and any guarantees that could apply.

Maintenance Work Order Systems

Work Order Management

In the introductory paragraph the concept of work order management was introduced. The parts of such a system were shown to be incorporated in the diagram shown in figure 17.3. As can be seen from that figure, the need for work to be done can emanate from ad hoc work requests, planned maintenance requirements and from equipment breakdowns. Any of these creates a need for a work order to be defined and utilized.

Work Order Definition

Before defining a work order a survey must be made to establish the following:

⇒ The best way of doing the job.

⇒ Which safety requirements should be borne in mind.

⇒ Tools to be used.

The work order is then defined with a unique work order number and a full description of the work to be done. This description should include the safety precautions and the tools to be used. If the system allows it, it is also handy to have a short description of the work to be done for inclusion on printed reports. Other fields that can be of benefit include a type of work order (breakdowns, preventive maintenance, routine maintenance), maintenance type (mechanical, electrical) and the budgeted amount for this work order.

Work Order Structure

We often find in maintenance work that, because of the fact that some jobs are quite large and involved, we have to break a work order down into smaller constituent parts. An example would be a plant shutdown, for which one overall work order will be defined to facilitate cost collection and global shutdown reporting. Such a global work order will then typically be broken down into several smaller work orders for individual parts of the shutdown (i.e. oxygen plant shutdown, gas purification shutdown, chlorine plant shutdown, etc.) This can again be further broken down into specific portions of a specific plant's shutdown (i.e. a specific machine's shutdown work). This work order breakdown is important for the following reasons:

- It facilitates cost collection at the lowest work order level and a cost 'roll-up' from there to the highest level.
- It facilitates Critical Path Method scheduling at the lowest work order level and a build-up of these smaller plans (which are easier to construct and optimize) to the full plant level.
- It facilitates reporting at every work order level.

The typical structure will then be as follows:

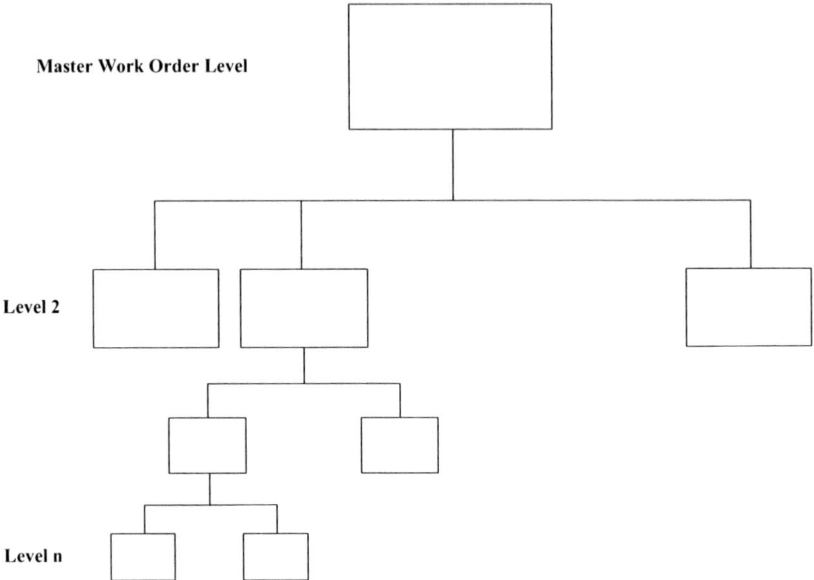

Figure 17.12 : Work Order structure

As can be seen from the above diagram any number of work order levels is possible. It will only in rare cases be beneficial, though, to include more than three to four levels in the work order structure.

Work order allocation by equipment

It is a fact that many work orders are not fully plant and equipment specific. This is especially so in the case of the installation of the same equipment type in different parts of the plant. It is then beneficial to "re-use" the same work order as defined repeatedly. This is done by allocating this work order to each of the equipment occurrences and adding a frequency at which this work should be done for scheduling purposes.

Task Definition

Each lowest level work order can be split further into various tasks that must be performed. This is especially necessary as each lowest level work order can consist of the work of many skills. Such a task definition (which will eventually be an individual job card) typically consists of the task number, work order number, a task description, the type and number required of the specific skill and the various task standards (standard maintenance equipment cost, standard parts cost, standard duration of task, predecessors)

Check Lists

In the case of routine and preventive maintenance tasks, the task description does not give enough information of the various checks that must be performed. Because of this, most maintenance systems include the definition of check lists that are issued with the specific job card(s) to the artisan performing the task. The artisan then does every check on the check list and indicates whether the specific check was successful or not. It is of benefit to include minimum and maximum values of a check that is measurable. In such cases the artisan should also be required to give feedback on the specific value of his measurement for history purposes.

Work Management

While the various tasks for which job cards have been issued are in the process of being executed, there are certain very specific system interfaces that must be kept in mind.

Time and Attendance

To facilitate task efficiency reporting, track must be kept of the time every artisan spends at the company. This consists of his clocking in and clocking out times per work day.

Job Card due date changes

While it is certainly the idea that tasks be completed as planned, unforeseen events and work priority changes can have the effect that the execution of a specific task must be delayed or the task must be stopped temporarily. The system should be able to register such job card due date changes together with the reason for the change. This will primarily be used in backlog reporting.

Job Card feedback

When a job card has been completed a wide selection of feedback information should exist. This includes the following:

⇒ Reason for failure (if a failure is involved)

⇒ Position at which failure occurred (i.e. left front)

⇒ Part which failed

⇒ Production loss (hours)

⇒ Actual start and finish dates

⇒ Actual duration

⇒ Actual man-hours spent

This job card feedback is extremely important as it forms the basis of work efficiency reporting and is also a crucial part of the history base.

Check List feedback

Check list feedback usually forms an extension of the job card feedback. This includes whether a check was done or not and specific measurements that were made.

Job efficiency reporting

A very important part of the work management process is the provision of adequate information on which the maintenance manager/ supervisor can act. This includes backlog reporting, utilization of workmen, efficiency of workmen and adherence to schedules reporting.

Maintenance History

One of the most important aspects of any maintenance system is the build up of a proper history base from which maintenance standards and strategies can be optimized. This is not a separate part of the system, but occurs automatically while operating the system. Typical actions that build the history base include:

⇒ Job card feedback.

⇒ Check list feedback.

⇒ The replacement of certain parts and/or sub-assemblies (by way of stores requisitioning).

The history base eventually consists of the following parts:

⇒ Actual task performance

* Task content (hours used)

* Task duration
* Task cost

⇒ Part failure history

⇒ Condition monitoring history (as per check list feedback)

⇒ Failure type frequency of occurrence

⇒ Cost history

* Maintenance materials
* Maintenance labor

While the system certainly carries maintenance history as an automatic by-product of the process of planning, scheduling and executing maintenance work, these history bits are distributed throughout the system data base. To make history retrieval more effective it might be necessary to consolidate history into a few history files through the regular running of a batch process.

Responsibility Structure

Introduction

In parallel with the equipment data base, which describes the plant and its structure, it is necessary to have a facility that describes the management structure of the organizations. This includes a description of each post and its position in the management hierarchy. This is of paramount importance and forms the basis of management reporting. A responsibility structure for a typical small maintenance organization is shown in the figure 17.2. If this structure, which normally reflects the organization structure, is known to the system, reporting can be differentiated in terms of design of reports and the level of detail included.

Position definition

A specific position can be defined by the following attributes:

⇒ Skill

⇒ Position

⇒ Employee

Skill

This function defines the different skills that are employed by the organization. Each skill must be defined by a skill code, a skill description and a rate at which the particular skill is priced. This includes skills such as "Fitter" and "Electrician" as well as "Divisional Manager", "Section Engineer", "Clerk" and "Planner".

Position

Each position that is approved by management must be registered in the system. This is done by defining the position by a unique position number, a position description and the skill code applicable for this specific position.

Employee

Every employee that is employed by the company is assigned a unique employee number or "control number". This can now be used by the system to uniquely identify the employee. The employee is catalogued by registering his or her employee number, name and the position number against which he or she was appointed.

Locality definition

Each locality in the plant or mine must be defined to the system before responsibilities can be allocated. In the "Equipment Data Base" section the equipment situated in the location were defined in some detail. Before telling the system who is responsible for what, it is essential that the geographical composition of the organization is made known to the system. Each locality is identified by its locality number and locality description.

Responsibility definition

To complete the responsibility structure part of the system, a few loose ends must be tied. This is done by specifying to the system which equipment are situated in which localities, who is responsible for which locality and which positions report to which manager or supervisor.

Equipment allocation by locality

The first step in defining the responsibility structure is to assign machines to the various locations. For every equipment number defined to the system a corresponding locality number is specified.

Locality allocation by supervisor

The next step is to assign the responsibility for the maintenance of equipment located in the various localities to specific supervisors. It is important to note that responsibilities for equipment maintenance need only to be allocated at the supervisor level as higher level responsibilities will be implied through inference by the reporting structure. Thus for each locality a specific supervisor's position number is specified as having primary responsibility for the equipment maintenance in that position. If more than one supervisor are responsible for the same equipment (for example if mechanical and electrical maintenance responsibilities are separated), both relationships must be specified. In such a case a responsibility type must also be specified to distinguish between the various responsibilities for the same location's equipment.

Reporting hierarchy

Lastly, the reporting structure is defined. This includes allocating artisans per foreman as well as allocating foremen per engineer, engineers per manager and so forth. Thus for each position the position overseeing that particular position is made known to the system.

Equipment performance monitoring

Introduction

The primary objective of the maintenance department lies in the "production" of availability and operability of machines (equipment). The actual levels of availability, operability and the parameters that affect them thus have to be monitored. The main quantities to be monitored are the following:

⇒ equipment availability

⇒ equipment utilization

⇒ equipment production rate

⇒ component failure rates

⇒ equipment production loss

⇒ equipment cost

⇒ condition monitoring results

⇒ performance monitoring results

These quantities are to be monitored against previously established standards and against accumulated history for the quantity involved. The results of this module should be portrayed graphically as far as is possible to assist the maintenance manager in optimizing his maintenance policies. This optimizing stance can be defined in terms of the maintenance cost optimality criterion and the classical business profitability criterion as shown in figure 1.1.

Data base design

The Equipment Performance Monitoring module largely makes use of data from the history base created by the work order management, cost management and work management components of the system. There are some very specific data items, which will only be addressed within this module though. They relate specifically to the production related performance of the machine, equipment condition monitoring and measurement standards.

Production plan

The production plan can either be obtained through an interface to the production system or by manual input from a paper production plan. It consists of a list of all equipment, each with its planned production hours per full production day and its planned production output per full production day. This is augmented by a production calendar stating the planned production hours per calendar day.

Production

The actual production of each production machine per production day is obtained from the production system through automated interface or manual input. The production is recorded per production machine per calendar day.

Downtime

To calculate equipment availability and utilization figures a record of all downtimes is needed. This can again be obtained from the production system through either automated or manual interfaces. Downtimes are listed against the specific machine for a specific calendar day together with its start and ending times and a reason code. The reason code is used to identify the nature of the downtime and to ascertain whether the specific downtime is production or maintenance related. The system should also have a separate facility for defining new reason codes. This should consist of the reason code, a reason description and whether it is production or maintenance related.

Equipment condition

Two basic quantities are necessary to monitor equipment condition with a view to preventing unplanned and destructive failures. These are the standard or acceptable performance levels and the present level of performance. Thus for each machine on which condition monitoring is to be done a specific condition is defined through a condition code and a condition description. It is of course possible to define an unlimited number of conditions being monitored on the machine, each with a unique condition code and description. Such conditions can include different types of monitoring on the machine or multiple occurrences of the same type of monitoring on different parts of the machine. For each defined condition maximum and minimum values that are regarded as normal are specified. The present level of performance is captured by stating for each condition measurement the condition code, the date of measurement and the actual value as measured.

Measurement standards

If meaningful deductions are to be made from the equipment performance data, it is important to have a standard against which comparisons could be made. Each standard that is defined consists of the equipment number for which it is valid, a standard type and minimum and maximum comparison standards. The standard type consists of a specific code associated with a specific monitoring quantity as defined by the system. These include:

⇒ equipment availability

⇒ equipment utilization

⇒ equipment production rate

⇒ equipment production loss

⇒ equipment cost

Functional design

The functional design should conform to the Integrated Maintenance Performance Measurement instrument developed using chapter 11 as basis.

Data presentation techniques

Refer to chapter 14 : Analysis of Maintenance Results, with special reference to the techniques of Control Boundaries and Data Smoothing.

Cost Management

Introduction

The cost management module assists the user in preparing his or her maintenance budget and controlling his or her expenditure against it. The budget is based largely on the long term schedule and on the expected resource impact of non-scheduled breakdowns and ad-hoc work. The budgeting process can be visualized as the compiling and summarization of detail work order budgets, thus facilitating cost control at all management levels. The main areas that should be addressed are the following:

- The preparation of quantity budgets, which are the starting process for the preparation of cost budgets. The availability of such quantity information will provide the system with a powerful tool for control at work execution level.
- The preparation of cost budgets, which forms the standard against which actual costs can be measured.
- The creation of cost accounts required for control over work order costs.
- Obtaining actual costs, including material costs, labor costs, main-

tenance equipment costs and outside work costs.

- Analyzing maintenance costs, so that the system user can be presented with meaningful information, which will ensure quick and to-the-point actions when required.
- Presenting cost and budget information to the system user in the required formats and at the appropriate level of detail.

Database design

The maintenance cost system data base needs only address two items, namely the budget and the accumulated cost for a specific task. This makes the design of a database for this aspect of the system a simple matter.

Budget

The budget for a specific machine (equipment) must always be broken down in terms of a budget per cost type. It must also be broken down in months. After the budget has been developed it is stored in this format for comparative purposes.

Task cost

All actual maintenance costs should be handled as task cost by the maintenance system. This is in fact a by-product of good data base design. The job card number (task number) is used as the primary means of cost accumulation. This number is used instead of a cost code number for cost allocation purposes. For each cost transaction the following is stored: the job card number, the date, a reference document number (purchase order number, stores issue number, etc.), the cost type and the amount involved.

Functional design

Quantity budgets

At budget time a long term schedule using time slots is prepared for all scheduled work. To this is added a scheduled forecast of the number of sub assemblies used (based on expected lives derived from maintenance history). This can then be broken down into a forecast quantity listing per calendar month.

Standard cost

For budgeting purposes it is important that standard costs be developed for every type of standard task on the quantity budgets. For cost control purposes it is also of benefit if any deviation from budget can be divided into a quantity deviation (at standard cost) and a price deviation (from standard cost). During the year, as new purchases are made, the actual prices are stored in the spares' data base. At budget time the latest prices are installed as the standard prices for the following year. These include reconditioning prices of sub assemblies and other reconditionable parts, which are installed as the standard cost of such units. For each planned task a standard cost is developed manually (but computer aided). It is based on the cost history for the task, the price of the different commodities used in completing the task and the inflation rate.

$$QD = (Q_b - Q_a) \times P_s \qquad 17.3$$
$$PD = (P_s - P_a) \times Q_a$$

$$QD = \text{Quantity Deviation}$$
$$PD = \text{Price Deviation}$$
$$Q_b = \text{Budgeted Quantity}$$
$$Q_a = \text{Actual Quantity}$$
$$P_s = \text{Standard Price}$$
$$P_a = \text{Actual Price}$$

These deviations have the property that:

$$TD = QD + PD \qquad 17.4$$

$$TD = \text{Total Deviation (from budget)}$$

Cost budgets

By multiplying the number of a particular component or service with its standard cost, a cost budget for the specific item is derived. By adding all these little "cost budgets" for a specific machine, a total cost budget for the machine is created. This is an automated process based on the quantity budget and the standard costs in the spares' data base. To this cost budget per machine is added the sundry cost per machine. This is based on the cost history of the previous year combined with the prevailing inflation rate. The same principle applies to cost budgets for sundry costs, which are not machine related.

Maintenance cost analysis

The same graphic techniques as described under the Equipment Performance Monitoring module apply here. The main differences here is that costs should also be analyzed cumulatively and that the standard against which is measured changes from month to month. Because of this it is deemed better to compare a cumulative actual cost graph with a cumulative budget line. The techniques of data smoothing can again be applied on the actual data to improve the quality of the comparisons that could be performed.

Work Management

Introduction

Work management includes:

⇒ Preparation of task documentation such as job cards, check lists and work permits.

⇒ The issue of such documents to the responsible personnel.

⇒ The feedback of actual job data.

⇒ The generation of management reports.

Before the preparation of task documentation can commence, the various jobs are prioritized and checked for applicable vendor guarantees. At the same time the availability of spares for those jobs that are to be performed is verified. refer to figure 17.5 for a typical work flow diagram.

Database considerations

There are no new database elements necessary for the work management module. All the elements that will be used already exist in the modules Equipment Data Base, Responsibility Structure, Work Order Management and Cost Management. The discussion here will thus be limited to the functional design and operation of such a work management module

Functional design

Prioritize tasks

As was stated earlier in this document, prioritization is not a pure scheduling technique, but is more of a method of sequencing work in an optimal way. It assists the workshop management to determine which jobs from a pool of waiting jobs should be handled first. These jobs are then assigned to artisans.

Guarantee processing

Guarantee processing consists of checking whether a valid guarantee exists which will cover the present work. If this is the case a guarantee claim must be lodged with the guarantor. This precludes the own maintenance team doing the work unless specifically arranged with the guarantor. If a valid guarantee did exist a new guarantee must be negotiated with the guarantor following the guarantee repair work.

Spares procurement

Before a task can be assigned to an artisan, all spares and materials must be procured. This will comprise requisitioning from stock for stock items and initiating purchase requests for all other items. If stock is not available, the materials must be put on back order. Periodic follow up of all outstanding stock back orders as well as outstanding purchases must be done until all materials have been received.

As the various spares and materials are received it is stored in the materials sub store in a separate shelf or bin until everything is ready for the task to be done. In some systems allowance is made for the reservation of stock, which will then preclude the storing of such stock items in the own sub store. Some stores' organizations will also allow batches of purchased materials to be stored in special bins. Generally speaking however it will be the responsibility of the maintenance organization to stock up for each task. This must be done in a very disciplined way as sub stores can lead to an unnecessary build up of dead capital.

Some tasks, such as workshop overhauls and breakdowns, have two phases of execution. The first phase consists of the artisan stripping the machine or part of the machine, cleaning all parts and then supplying a list of all spares and materials needed to the planning department. This then triggers the second phase during which the materials will be procured and the task completed. In this case it becomes even more important to store the old and new spares in a planned fashion until the task can be completed. A good way of accomplishing this, especially for sub assembly overhauls, is to have lockable containers, which are large enough to hold the sub assembly with its old and new spares. These containers can then be stored in a sub store area. The fact that some tasks require two phases complicates the design of the maintenance system. The best way of handling this type of task is to issue two distinctly different job cards. The first of these will include only for the strip down, cleaning and spares identification part of the task. This will later be followed by a task to assemble and test the unit. It is normally of benefit to use the same artisan for both tasks, as a second artisan cannot be made responsible for the spares' identification of another artisan.

Task documentation

For a task to be done properly the artisan must receive well prepared task documentation. This should at the maximum consist of a job card, a check list, a work permit and engineering drawings. The job card is a real time copy of a task defined in the Work Order Management module. It will thus have printed on it information such as the task number, work order number, a task description, the type and number required of the specific skill and the various task standards (standard maintenance equipment cost, standard parts cost, standard duration of task). It will also have reference to special tools to be used, safety precautions to be taken, drawings to be used and the specific pages in the maintenance manual that contain important task directions. The job card will have an own unique job card number printed on it, which can be used for cost collection purposes.

In the case of routine and preventive maintenance tasks, the task description does not give enough information of the various checks that must be performed. Because of this, most maintenance systems include check lists that are issued with the specific job cards to the artisan performing the task. The artisan then does every check on the check list and indicates whether the specific check was successful or not. It is of benefit to include minimum and maximum values of a check that is measurable. In such cases the artisan should also be required to give feedback on the specific value of his measurement for history purposes.

The task documentation is supplied by the planner to the specific foreman who distributes it to his personnel. He will typically put it on a work assignment board, which will at a glance show which tasks are outstanding for which artisans and the order in which they will be completed.

Task feedback

This is one of the most important facets of the work management cycle. If the task feedback is not done properly the whole maintenance system will lose at least half of its functionality. Because of the fact that the maintenance history will at best be incomplete all facilities in the system that makes use of history will be rendered useless. This includes the Cost Management module, most of the Equipment Performance Monitoring module and all facilities for maintenance optimization.

While it is certainly the idea that tasks be completed as planned, unforeseen events and work priority changes can have the effect that the execution of a specific task must be delayed or the task must be stopped temporarily. This could be handled in one of two ways. The first method comprises the registration of a job card due date change together with the reason for the change. The alternative is to close the present task and to initiate a rescheduled copy of it for later execution. This is important to render backlog reporting useful.

When a job card has been completed a wide selection of feedback information should exist. This includes the following:

⇒ Reason for failure (if a failure is involved).

⇒ Position at which failure occurred (i.e., left front).

⇒ Part which failed.

⇒ Production loss (hours).

⇒ Actual start and finish dates.

⇒ Actual duration.

⇒ Actual man-hours spent.

Further important bits of information are available from the completion of the check list. This includes whether a check was done or not and specific measurements that were made.

The task feedback information should be checked by the foreman for completeness and accuracy before feeding it back to the planning office. All that remains then is for the planning office to do immediate and accurate feedback of the information into the maintenance system.

Management reports

A very important part of the work management process is the provision of adequate information on which the maintenance manager or supervisor can act. This includes backlog reporting, utilization of workmen, efficiency of workmen and adherence to schedules reporting. Backlog reporting should list all outstanding tasks with their respective issue dates, planned completion dates and estimated job duration. This could be augmented by the work order turnover index and the utilization and efficiency of workmen indices as well as the adherence to schedule index as defined in chapter 11. This enables management to ascertain that enough importance is being attached to task efficiency, productivity and the completion of scheduled tasks.

Materials Management

Introduction

Although the material management function is often controlled by a separate organization, it forms a very important logical part of the maintenance function and should thus be included in a discussion of maintenance systems. Materials Management can be subdivided into six areas:

⇒ Stock record keeping

⇒ Stock issues and returns

⇒ Inventory management

⇒ Maintaining a stock catalogue

⇒ Purchasing

⇒ Reporting

Each of these six main areas in turn consists of the following functions:

- Stock record keeping
  - ⇒ Maintaining stock balances
  - ⇒ Maintaining stock master records
  - ⇒ Periodic stock taking action
- Stock Issues and returns
  - ⇒ Stock issues
  - ⇒ Stock returns
- Inventory management
  - ⇒ Stock replenishment model
  - ⇒ Minimum stock level
  - ⇒ Economic order quantity
  - ⇒ Usage forecasting
  - ⇒ Monitor actual performance
    - * Commodity turnover
    - * Stock levels
    - * Order quantities
    - * Order lead times
- Maintain stock catalogue
  - ⇒ Maintain stock catalogue user list
  - ⇒ Create stock catalogues
  - ⇒ Change stock catalogues when necessary
  - ⇒ Distribute catalogues
- Procurement
  - ⇒ Source selection
  - ⇒ Price determination
  - ⇒ Purchasing
  - ⇒ Administration and record keeping
  - ⇒ Quality control
- Reporting
  - ⇒ Stock levels
  - ⇒ Stock usage
  - ⇒ Financial reports

⇒ Reconciliation reports

⇒ Forecasting reports

Database considerations

The spares' database was discussed as a part of the equipment data base. The spares' database is very closely linked to the materials management database and the two should be seen as one logical unit. Thus no spares' detail will be kept in the materials management database as that has already been addressed in the spares' database.

Commodities

A record must be kept of all commodities (stock items) that have been created and are kept in stock. Such a record should at least consist of the commodity number, the spare number (if applicable), commodity description, bin number, present quantity on hand, maximum quantity, minimum quantity, economic order quantity, purchasing lead time, standard issue price, new year's (budget) standard issue price, last purchase price and the unit of issue. This listing will always contain the newest status information on all commodities. It may also be of benefit to keep another listing of all commodity record changes. This will provide commodity history, which can then be analyzed for a specific commodity to determine quantities such as the average price over a period, the last date issued, the consumption over the last year and the economic order quantity.

Issue

For each materials' issue a record must be kept of the relevant stock detail and the requisitioner's detail. This should at least consist of the issue number, requisition number, job card (or cost code) number, date, commodity number, equipment number (for sub assemblies carried in stock), number requested and number issued. This listing is important for audit purposes.

Return to stores

A return to stores (R.T.S.) action is the reverse of a stores' issue. Again a record must be kept for each such occurrence. The same type of information is captured and is important for audit purposes. The record should at least include the R.T.S. number, the issue number (against which this item was issued), date, commodity number, equipment number (for sub assemblies carried in stock) and the number returned.

Scrap advice

A second type of "stores' issue" that can take place occurs when a stock item is declared redundant. It must then be taken from stock, at which time the following listing should be kept: scrap advice number, date, commodity number, equipment number (for sub assemblies carried in stock) and the number scrapped.

Supplier

It is important to keep supplier records so that important supplier information is on record and supplier performance history can be kept. A listing that will suffice as supplier record is one with the following fields: supplier number, supplier name, supplier address, contact person, telephone number, fax number and supplier grading.

Spares link to supplier

This listing lists all the suppliers that can supply a specific spare. This listing must also include the purchasing lead time required for purchasing this spare at this supplier.

Order

The total purchasing activity revolves around the placing of purchasing orders. The maintenance organization will place buying requisitions for materials and spares not kept in stock, while the stores' organization will place buying requisitions for stock items that have to be replenished. From each of these will emanate a buying order. The listing that should be kept to control the buying action should at least include: purchase order number, buying requisition number, supplier number, job card number (or cost code), ordering date, spare number (if applicable), commodity number (if applicable), quantity ordered, quantity received, price, price per unit, promised delivery date and actual delivery date.

Functional design

Stock record keeping

1. Maintaining stock balances - each time that a stock movement (issues, returns and receiving orders) takes place, the stock balance figure in the commodity listing is changed to reflect the new balance.
2. Maintaining stock master records - for each commodity that are kept a stock master record is created and maintained. The stock master record will be kept in the commodity listing discussed above. A commodity number has to be created for each such instance. This commodity number can be a meaningless follow number or a number that has a type of classification built into itself. Examples of built in classifications are where a part of the number relates to a group of commodities or where the commodities are classified according to equipment or user group.

   In a larger store it is very important to make sure that the bin number quoted in the master record is correct as that can speed up the issue and replenishment process considerably. It is even more important that the spare number listed is correct as this is the link between the stores and maintenance databases. Thus no proper lookup function will exist in any direction if this field is not entered correctly.

   Another important facet of stock record keeping is to keep fresh price information at hand. This consists of the present standard price at which the commodity is priced to the user, the latest purchase price and the new standard price used to budget for the new year. This last price is calculated in one of the following ways. The first method is by using the latest price as is. Another method is by using the latest price and escalating it by some escalation factor representing the average price escalation expected for the next year. A third method is by using the actual average price experienced over the last year. This is done by analyzing the commodity record change listing for changes in the newest buying price over the period. Lastly the value found in the third method can be escalated by some escalation factor representing the average price escalation expected for the next year.

The purchasing lead time can be found by doing an analysis of the various lead times available at the different suppliers in the spares link to supplier listing. It can first be found by calculating the mean lead time of all suppliers of the spare. Alternatively, the median value or the lowest or highest lead time for the spare can be used.

3. Periodic stock taking - one of the most important safeguards against loss of control in a stores' organization is a one to one relationship between the actual stock and the stock as recorded in the stores' control system. Because of this the stores' master records' quantity information is updated periodically by performing a stock taking action.
4. Stock issues and returns - during each materials' issue an entry must be made in the Issue listing and a change in stock level effected in the Commodity listing. At the same time the change must also create a new entry in the Commodity Record Change listing. During a materials' return to stock action the reverse takes place. An entry is made in the R.T.S. listing and a change in stock level effected in the Commodity listing. A new entry representing the change is also created in the Commodity Record Change listing.

Inventory management

Refer to the model as defined in chapter 22 on Inventory Management in this regard.

Maintain stock catalogue

The creation, maintenance and distribution of stock catalogues are tasks that need no further explanation. A good exploded view drawing with reference numbers to a computer listing with the commodity numbers, the descriptions, spare numbers and unit of issue are really all that is needed. It is no more than a printout of the commodity listing with a picture reference added. Add to this a proper indexing scheme and a very usable stock catalogue result. To control the issue and maintenance of these units, it is important to maintain a stock catalogue users' list. This list should also have facilities to mark whether a specific catalogue or updates has been supplied to a particular user.

Procurement

Source selection

The purchasing function has as very important task, the task to visit vendors with a viewpoint to set up positive relations with them, evaluate them and select the best ones from the many possible candidates. During a specific purchasing action he or she can then make a selection based on price, conformance to specifications and service only.

Price determination

The buyer determines the price by asking for tenders and quotes from all the suppliers that he or she has on his or her supplier listing for the particular product. After comparing the different bids, he or she can choose a particular vendor based on past performance and price. If the lowest bid is not taken it might be worthwhile to negotiate with the successful bidder for a better price. Discounts may also be obtained, especially if quantity purchases are made. Other ways of reducing prices, which may sometimes work are by deciding to do own manufacturing or by doing a full scale value analysis on the item to ascertain whether its manufacturing cost can be lowered.

Purchasing

The purchasing action begins with placing an official order. This will be followed by follow up actions to keep lead times as short as possible. A part of this action is to arrange transport if necessary to get the material.

Administration and record keeping

As in all disciplines, the work is not done until the paperwork are done. In the procurement function this is may be even more so. It is of paramount importance to keep a good filing and records system. A very important part of the administration of the purchasing department is the establishment and use of a good vendor rating system. There are systems such as the Categorical Method, the Weighted-Point Method and the Cost-Ratio Method. All of these have benefits and drawbacks but are useful in determining a supplier rating. Factors affecting the rating are items such as quality, supplier location, supplier facilities and financial standing.

Other important factors in purchasing administration are the concepts of item price history, item purchasing history, commodity expenditure profiles and supplier expenditure profiles. All of these can be calculated from the data in the "order", "supplier" and "spares link to supplier" listings.

Quality control

The purchasing department is responsible, together with the company quality department or engineering department, to draw up a tailored quality specification for every item purchased on a regular basis and a general quality specification for all other items. They must also do site inspections of supplier quality systems and items in the process of being manufactured. Lastly they must negotiate warranties and oversee all warranty claims.

Maintenance Optimization

See the section on Maintenance Optimization in the introductory part of this chapter.

The bigger systems picture Where does the Maintenance System fit in?

Management through information

The maintenance manager has to plan, organize, lead and control the maintenance department in an efficient way. To do so effectively, he/she needs good information as the information that he/she receives provides the foundation to most of the decisions and actions that he will take.

There vast quantities of data available to the manager of today. To use such data effectively, it is necessary that the CMMS and other information systems translate the relevant data into information that is useful for decision-making.

The value and cost of information

Cost-effectiveness of information is difficult to quantify, because the value of the information is often fairly intangible. The value of information depends on the following four factors :

⇒ Information quality

⇒ Information timeliness

⇒ Information quantity

⇒ Information relevance

Components of the total Management Information System environment

The Management Information System may consist of various component or sub-systems that share data. The different elements are listed in the diagram below:

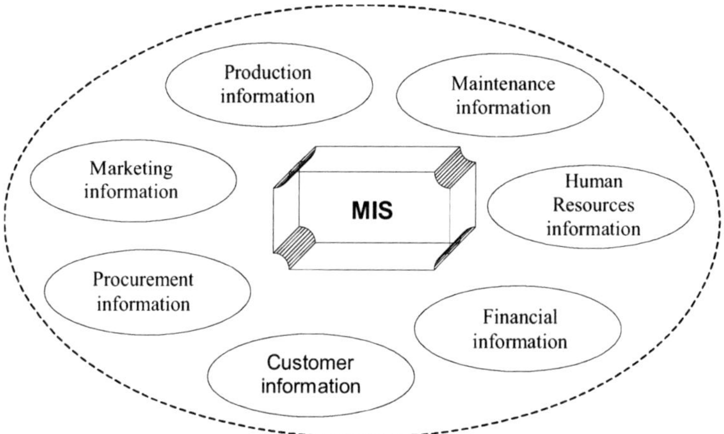

Figure 17.13 : Maintenance systems environment

Management with information at different levels

The different levels of the organization will need different levels of information. Senior management will need a wider scope and less detailed information than the lower level maintenance manager, directly in charge of area maintenance. Such lower level manager will need more detailed information regarding his/her area of responsibility and less business information from the larger organization. These differences in information needs are as follows:

⇒ For top managers the MIS must provide summarized information to build and formulate the strategy and business philosophy.

Their need information that is more sophisticated, taking more of the relationships between diverse pieces of data in account. Such information largely depends on the financial performance of the organization and the outside business environment.

⇒ Middle management needs more frequent and structured information. Such information typically include information regarding the current maintenance operational financial status, high level maintenance operational results (availability, reliability, operability, etc.), maintenance productivity and maintenance operational purposefulness (chapter 11).

⇒ Maintenance operational management needs detailed, highly accurate information on a day-to-day basis. These needs include task management reports, equipment maintenance results reports and maintenance schedules.

Chapter 18

The Systems Implementation Process

Project team

Certainly one of the most important aspects of the implementation process concerns the appointment of a project team. Firstly, a project leader should be appointed. This person should typically be one of the most knowledgeable engineers in the organization in the area of maintenance systems. The size of the project team will of course depend on the size of the project. In a typical situation this team should consist of the project leader, one system administrative officer (planner), one supervisor, a secretary/clerk and one or two systems analysts/programmers to effect the modifications.

The above mentioned personnel must of course be relieved of all their usual duties to be able to implement the CMMS. This task must not be underestimated, as the implementation of such a system is a major intervention in the maintenance organization.

The definition of requirements

When contemplating to buy or build a CMMS, one of the most important steps concerns the definition of the requirements. This is normally a part of the project on which too little time and effort is expended, leading to a bad system fit. As with any project, the most important part is the specification. When buying physical plant, most engineers and technical personnel know exactly what they want of such a physical system. But when specifying information systems, we are at a loss as to voice our specific needs. This is mainly due to information being intangible as opposed to our daily contact with physical assets.

A good way of handling the requirements specification phase is to make use of a consultant who has a good knowledge of Maintenance Information Systems to drive the specification process. Another way would be to make use of an in company information specialist. The problem with this last approach is that, while such a person knows the information side of things, he/she normally tends to underestimate the complexity of the maintenance problem.

Due to the importance of this phase the previous section went into more detail regarding the specification of maintenance information systems than is necessary for our present discussion. The reason is that you as system user should gain as much insight as possible into the detailed operation of such systems. Only by doing this, can you make a meaningful contribution to your own system future.

The user specification of a system should at least address the following areas:

- The required user reports - this is the most obvious part of the user specification and should thus be done first. One could start by getting the various user groups (engineers, superintendents, foremen, planners and artisans) together and list their information needs. This can then be combined into one list of reports. The next step is to prioritize these to determine the relative importance of each. This should be followed by detailed discussions on the more important reports (use the Pareto principle) to ascertain exactly which fields (data) would be needed to produce these reports. Make a full alphabetical listing of these data entities.
- Using the same approach as the one for reporting above, compile a listing of system functionality. This could be done by working through the detail of the previous section of this document in the various user groups. Again prioritize the functions and use the Pareto principle to compile a list of the more important functions.
- Draw logical flow diagrams for each of the important functions to define the way in which they should operate for your business.
- The three documents prepared above could now be used to draw up a requirements list. In essence this listing will be used for system selection. This requirements list should contain all the more important reports, functions and system features (from the flow diagrams), as well as computer technical features, again in prioritized order. Allocate a weight to each requirement according to the priority of the item.

Buy or build?

The building of an own system is, in the opinion of the author, again becoming more and more of an opinion. In the late 70's and early 80's no significant systems were available in the market. Users that required maintenance systems thus had to either make use of hand systems or build their own systems. During the second half of the 80's better systems became commercially available, while the own build option were only totally viable on main frame computers. Now, with the maturity of networked microcomputers, sophisticated system building technology is available at reasonable prices to users who want to build their own systems.

Buying a system

Advantages of buying a system

1. You buy into the experience of the system supplier. This could span the functional needs of many maintenance organizations. Whether this is true depends on the way in which the supplier keeps contact with, communicates with and takes heed of the needs of its users.
2. You can be up and running within a fairly short time, as the system is complete and just have to be "spliced" into the own operation.
3. Later releases of the system will bring the possibility of improving your own maintenance operation.
4. The software supplier is available to assist in doing modifications of the system and solving problems.

Disadvantages of buying a system

1. Most proprietary maintenance systems have a fairly fixed way in which they operate. This has the effect of forcing the user to change his preferred way of doing things to that of the software supplier.
2. System modifications typically range from fairly difficult to impossible. Most software suppliers use their system's adaptability and their own willingness to assist in these matters as selling points. In practice this often only holds until the contract is signed. Of course there are systems which have the ability to be changed by the user or a third party software house, using general software development tools, but they are the exception.
3. Mostly it is only viable to make use of later releases if the system is used as is. Any own modifications not supported by the supplier will typically be lost during the upgrade process.

4. Typically one does not find software packages that are a very good fit to your own situation. This leads to extensive modifications being necessary if you do not want to forfeit some of your needs.
5. Most of the commercially available packages are very expensive. The same goes for modifications, maintenance fees and regular upgrades.

Building an own system

Advantages of building an own system

1. You can build the system to exactly suit your needs. By building the system self, you have control over your own maintenance system destiny.
2. System changes can be effected fast, thus aiding in "selling" the system to the users.
3. The system can be built in stages. Normally, maintenance users are not ripe to utilize the full spectrum of maintenance system functionality within the first year or two. It is thus of benefit to build only a fairly basic system at first and then improve on that over time.
4. It should be possible to build a system at a fairly reasonable price if existing resources are utilized.

Disadvantages of building an own system

1. The team (or person) developing the own system has to build experience by way of trial and error. This can to a certain extent be remedied by studying existing systems and by attending courses such as the present one.
2. The time to get up and running may be longer than the buy-off-the-shelf option.
3. The company has to ensure that it retains the expertise necessary to maintain and update the system.
4. The correct design of the database is of paramount importance for the future success of the system. If only in company resources are used during this crucial phase of system development, it may lead to a system without real long term viability.
5. In company personnel that are capable of developing a maintenance system are not readily available in all organizations.

What should my strategy be?

Both strategies discussed have advantages and disadvantages, as listed above. Whether one uses the one or the other firstly depends on which circumstances exist in the company. The success of implementation will also depend on which additional steps are taken to manage the risk of the project.

Buying a system

Prerequisites for buying a system

1. A system must be available that conforms to most (i.e. 80%) of the requirements.
2. The system that is bought should be adaptable using own company resources. This must be the proven experience of other system users. The ease with which changes can be brought about and the limitations regarding modifications are very important factors.
3. There should be a choice as to whether future upgrades will be taken and whether a maintenance contract is signed with the vendor.
4. The system's source code should be available to your company in the event of the supplier not being able to support the product any longer.
5. The system should be written in a commercially "safe" development environment.
6. If later upgrades will be taken, a guarantee of compatibility with the present release and any own system modifications should be written into the contract.

Steps to reduce risk when buying a system

1. Make use of a knowledgeable maintenance consultant with extensive systems experience to assist you in compiling your systems requirements and selecting the software package.
2. Prepare your personnel beforehand regarding the areas of incompatibility of the system and the areas in which system modifications will be difficult. These are the areas that can sink a good system.

Building an own system

Prerequisites for building a system

1. The company should have in house systems expertise that are readily available to the project.
2. Steps should be taken to ensure that the database design is sound.

Steps to reduce risk when building an own system

1. Make use of a knowledgeable maintenance consultant with extensive systems experience to assist you in compiling your systems requirements and in designing the database.
2. Systems personnel should study the design of commercially available systems and attend courses such as the present one to shorten their learning curve.

System selection

The end product of the definition of requirements as discussed earlier in this chapter was a list of the more important system features (reports, functions, etc.). These were ordered in order of priority and weights were allocated to each of them corresponding to its relative priority. In the case where a system is bought, this list is now used to investigate and compare the various systems. This list should have three selection columns to the right of the listed requirements (the first for the weight, the second for the score of the system being investigated and the last for the weighted score).

Each system vendor is now visited in turn. At least one day should be set apart for this purpose. Following a general system presentation, conformance to each of the listed requirements are investigated in turn, using the prioritized order. The system being investigated is now scored (typically out of ten) regarding its conformance to the specific requirement. Important points to bear in mind during this process are:

a The person(s) doing the assessment should understand the requirements fully. He/she/they must also be able to discern real functionality from faked solutions presented by the system vendor.

b The functions should be investigated in detail and should be demonstrated using a live system.

c Rather take too long on a systems assessment, but be sure of the score that you give to the specific item.

The score is then multiplied by the weight to get the weighted score. All of these are then added to get an overall system score. The system with the highest score is the one that should be bought.

Additional aspects, that should be borne in mind during the selection process, are:

a. Systems that score higher on the higher weight requirements should be preferred even when they have a slightly lower overall score.

b. If you are not sure of some aspects of system design, rather arrange for more visits to make certain of you choice.

c. Concentrate your effort in ensuring that the chosen system has an adequate database design, taking into account any modifications to be done and the future development of the system.

d. Ensure that the chosen system's architecture is such that it can be readily modified by own systems personnel or the vendor.

e. One of the most important steps in the selection process is to investigate the chosen system for conformance to all the other requirements that were not listed. During the process of drawing up the requirements list, only the more important requirements were listed. Now is the time to work through all of these (important requirements that the chosen system do not meet) and the remaining list of requirements to establish what effort would be required for full conformance.

f. Draw up a fully fledged project data model and compare that with the database of the chosen system. This will show whether the database can be expanded/modified to accommodate the full functionality required. If this is not the case, the purchase of the chosen system must be seriously reconsidered.

Functional adaptation

The areas in which the chosen system lacks functionality should now be made the subject of a systems development project. This could be done using own personnel, the vendor or a specially bought in task group. In any of these options, the original group compiling the requirements and selecting the system should now compile a modification specification. This should consist of a document with a section for each modification area. Each of these sections should contain full functional descriptions (the way in which the function operates, including flow charts), sample documents and reports and suggested screen layouts/descriptions.

As modifications to the system are completed, the original task group should test them for functional suitability, data integrity and performance. Any non-conformances should be directed back to the modification team for rework. In the case of a system that is totally self developed, this procedure is followed for every part of the system's functionality.

User training

All users, including engineers, supervisors, system administrative personnel and artisans have to be trained in the use of the system prior to using the system. This could take place in parallel with the previous step (functional adaptation). The training is best performed in a phased way, system administrative personnel being trained first, then supervisors, then the engineers and last (just before final conversion) the artisans. The training should have the following formats:

- System administrative personnel are trained in the total use of the system, with an accent on the operations part of maintenance (scheduling, work management). Following their training they should start using the system (which is still being modified) to input the fixed information (see the paragraph on system testing and set-up below).
- Supervisors are trained in using the work documentation (work orders, job cards, task lists, etc.) and task management information supplied by the system. The accent in their training is in making them aware of the importance of using work documentation correctly, as well as in using the system for task management.
- Engineers are trained in the global structure of the system, the facilities that are available in the system and the use of the system outputs for management. At this point in time both the system administrative personnel and the supervisors have completed their training. The engineers are thus now put in a position where they can start managing the implementation. They must understand that they play a critical role in the future success of the system. They must motivate their personnel both by word of mouth and by using system outputs for management.
- Artisans are trained in the use of work documentation. The accent in their training is on motivating them to use the system documen-

tation properly. They must be made aware that proper system functioning will lead to a more planned and predictable work environment, which will be of benefit to them. In the case of online task documentation, they have to be trained in the use of that as well.

System testing and set-up

It has been mentioned above that the system should be tested by the original specification team as functionality/modifications become available. This should be done using real data where possible. Therefore, the set-up of the system for the own business proceeds in parallel to the system testing. The aspects which should be covered during system set-up includes the following:

⇒ Equipment registration

⇒ Equipment classification

⇒ Equipment structure

⇒ Spares registration

⇒ Spares structure

⇒ Work order definition

⇒ Work order structure

⇒ Task lists

⇒ Equipment usage initialization

⇒ Personnel registration

⇒ Area/equipment responsibilities

⇒ Organization structure

⇒ Calendars

⇒ Measurement standards

During this phase test transactions should be processed to test the compliance of the system with the specification. These transactions' data will later be removed by the development team prior to final conversion. All system errors and non-conformances are referred back to the development team for rework.

The best way of managing this phase is by drawing up a list of tasks to be done. Each of these tasks, after completion, is audited by the project leader and its status changed to complete after any corrections are completed satisfactorily.

Final conversion

After the system has been tested successfully and the set-up process completed, the scene is set for the final conversion. This should be phased as far as possible so as to detect any outstanding problems while still using the system in a limited way. Thus the conversion should take place section by section.

During the conversion phase the system should be used in parallel with the old system for a period of at least two to four weeks. The results of the two systems must be compared critically during this time. Any deviation should be reported and solved immediately. At the end of a predetermined period of successful parallel running, the section stops using the old system in favor of the new system. The conversion process then moves to the following section/group of sections. Another aspect of the conversion process concerns the fine tuning of the training of personnel. During this period the artisans now have to start using the new documentation, while the supervisors manage their work using the system's task management facilities.

A macro view of the systems installation process

Figure 18.1 shows the essence of the implementation of a Maintenance Information System and its associated systemization of the maintenance effort. The various steps are not in the exact order of execution or even in order of importance, but show the basic logic of the implementation. In addition, training is included in this diagram, while training was already covered earlier in this chapter.

The various constituents of the implementation of the Maintenance System and their application (apart from training) are described shortly:

- Maintenance audit – a Maintenance Systems implementation project typically begins with a baseline audit (see chapter 12) to establish the present level of maintenance practice. The audit output usually consists of a report highlighting the areas of concern regarding the total maintenance function, as well as the specific concerns. The results of such audit is used to finalize the detailed implementation plans.
- Maintenance policy – it is best practice to form a Maintenance Systems steering committee, consisting of at least of all maintenance managers, with the maintenance chief as chairperson. This steering

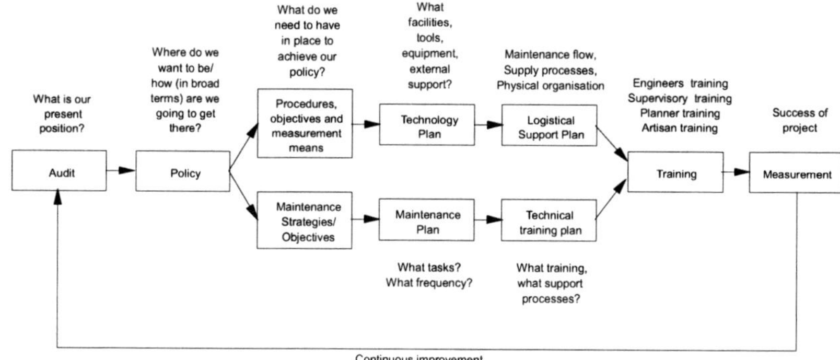

Figure 18.1: Typical macro implementation process

committee will oversee the successful implementation of the total Maintenance System. The first step in this process is the creation of a maintenance policy – see chapter 10.

- Maintenance procedures, objectives and measurement means - while the policy is being formulated as explained above, the process of identifying areas for the development of managerial and operational procedures to systemize the maintenance environment is started. This is a major project activity and will take place over a large part of the project duration. Procedures are developed for areas identified by the project team and agreed to by the steering committee. Draft copies of such procedures are circulated to steering committee members, who distribute them further if necessary for comments within a reasonable time. After such comments have been received, the specific procedure is finalized and presented for ratification and approval as final systems document by the steering committee. These procedures later form an important part of the training process. While this process is under way, the steering committee identifies and develops short and long term maintenance objectives in line with the policy and procedures. These set the agenda for coordinated managerial action to lead the maintenance function into the future. At the same time, attention is given to the development of measurement means - a Maintenance Performance Measurement instrument (chapter 11) and a Maintenance Audit instrument (chapter 12) - in line with the policy, procedures and objectives.
- Technology plan - a suitable technology plan is developed in conjunction with the steering committee to support the policy, proce-

dures and objectives. This is not a major project activity, but is very important to ensure the accomplishment underlying premises of the policy, procedures and objectives. The technology plan comprises an in-depth investigation into the business' maintenance facilities, tools, equipment and external support needed to ensure success. Recommendations in this regard are presented to the steering committee for action.

- Logistical Support plan - this activity takes place in conjunction with the technology plan. Whereas the latter concerns itself with the physical facilities, the former involves the logical workflow and organization that are necessary to support the maintenance function in the business. This and the previous activities are strongly interrelated to the creation of the maintenance plan as covered below. It comprises an in-depth investigation into the workflow and physical organization aspects of the business' maintenance facilities, as well as the relevant supply processes. Recommendations in this regard are presented to the steering committee for action.
- Maintenance plan development - this activity is the major activity of the second leg of the Maintenance Systems development as shown in figure 18.1. This activity is described in chapters 4 to 9 of this textbook.
- Technical training plan - a technical training plan is developed in parallel with and flowing from the process of designing the maintenance plan. This is again not a major project activity, but is very important to ensure that personnel have the required technical ability to support the maintenance plan. Recommendations in this regard are presented to the steering committee for action.

Chapter 19

Management Support

The importance of managerial support

Managerial support is one of the most important factors for the success of any system. A system, due to its structured nature, imposes a certain discipline on the organization. Because of mankind's inherent resistance to change and discipline, energy has to be expended in the process of change that goes with system implementation. This must come from upper management. Without this, the project is doomed to certain failure.

The best way of harnessing the support of upper management is by creating a Systems Steering Committee, consisting of representatives from upper management, all maintenance engineers and the project leader, with the engineering manager as chairman. The systems implementation should be driven from this committee. Thus all important project decisions should be submitted to the steering committee for decision/approval. In this way the project becomes management driven. This implies that management is committed to the system and its results.

If this is not done, management, together with the whole of the organization, will sink the system due to it being "worthless".

The management champion

As in any important intervention, the use of a management champion can bring success in a situation where otherwise doom would have reigned supreme. Systems implementation nearly always implies that people have to make changes to the way that they do their job. This creates a certain level of resistance that has to be overcome.

The role of the management champion, who could be any of the upper management (including the engineering manager) or one (or more) of the subsidiary engineers, is to "sell" the system to the people. This could be done in regular talk sessions, through regular letters, informal contact with people, through a "poster campaign" or any combination of these.

The personal qualities of the management champion(s) are important:

⇒ A man/woman of natural stature.

⇒ Influential.

⇒ Creative in his/her thinking.

⇒ Natural ability to drive.

⇒ A believer in system driven management.

Involvement of managers in the implementation process

One can be fairly certain that the implementation process will fail if all maintenance managers (including supervisors) are not actively involved. Although the management champion plays a very crucial role in selling the system, each manager has the final responsibility for the effective implementation in his/her area of responsibility.

The important point to remember when contemplating your own involvement in the implementation is that your own success in relation to that of your peers can depend on it. A difficulty that tend to interfere with this is the fact that during the early stages of the project, it is only the project members that are actively involved in the evolution of the system and the implementation plans. It is only during the Steering Committee meetings that some managers will gain insight into some aspects of the process. Each manager thus has to make it his/her business to stay informed, probably during visits to the project team. A secondary motive during these visits should be to maintain good relations with the project team (instead of the other way round) so as to ensure their commitment to your success. This "inverted" way of maintaining good relations between users and the project team is of paramount importance in the quest for system success.

In the own section the future system should be made a standard agenda item on the monthly/weekly staff meeting. In this time slot information can be passed on to subordinates, while answering their questions and addressing their concerns. Maintenance administration personnel (planners) should be involved in these meetings. The objective during these meetings (and whenever the opportunity arises between meetings) should be to develop a positive attitude towards and enthusiasm for the system. This effort must be continued through the user training, system testing, final conversion and at least the first year of full system operation. By this time the necessary discipline should have been established and the system should be a part of the way of life.

One of the most important failures in the implementation process occurs when the line managers are negative towards the project. This must be managed with particular ardor, as it can cause the whole implementation to fail. Use can be made of techniques such as group discussions, information sessions and motivation talks to solve this crucial problem.

This page was left blank on purpose

Use it for notes

Chapter 20

Factors influencing Systems Success

Maintenance Cycle definition

We previously stated in some detail (in chapters 3 and 10) how the maintenance policy document and maintenance procedures define the Maintenance Cycle for the particular concern. It was also shown that the CMMS supports the operational and information needs of the Maintenance Cycle in the company. Thus it cannot be logically conceived to have a successful CMMS installation if the Maintenance Cycle was not properly defined. In such a situation each employee will do as he/she pleases, having no structure to guide the way in which the organization functions.

Any successful maintenance systems installation thus starts by formulating a Maintenance Policy, Objectives and Maintenance Procedures, formalizing them and implementing them successfully. This will then ensure that the necessary structure is in place for successfully implementing the CMMS.

The maintenance plan

Referring to the inner cycle of the Maintenance Cycle (figure 3.3), equipment history is utilized through the application of RCM (Reliability Centered Maintenance) to develop maintenance policies (or strategies) for individual machines. These policies are combined into a maintenance plan for each machine, and the collection of all these machine maintenance plans can be called The Maintenance Plan for the organization. It thus contains all previously specified (preventive) tasks per equipment type, per craft and per maintenance frequency. This process of developing a maintenance plan was described in detail in chapters 6 to 9.

This maintenance plan thus defines all tasks that have to be loaded into the work database. And as this work base forms the basis for the success of the maintenance department (and the CMMS), it is important to construct it from a scientifically compiled maintenance plan.

The quality of the maintenance plan directly effects the success of the CMMS in assisting the organization in reaching high levels of availability, reliability and operability at a reasonable cost. Without a good maintenance plan the chances for success are fairly poor.

Set-up of the database

This aspect was covered in the previous chapter. We do not want to repeat the process here, but want to stress the importance of doing it properly. We have previously called the three primary data bases the three "pillars" of a good CMMS. While the design of these "pillars" is important, as was previously stated, the information in them are even more important. These data bases must thus properly reflect the actual equipment structure, the maintenance plan as discussed above and the various responsibilities and the relationships between them.

If the set-up process was not conducted properly, the users of the system will, within a short period, describe the CMMS as being unreliable and will stop using it.

Job card flow

One of the primary means of communication with the CMMS is the job card. If produced by the system, it communicates to the foreman/artisan what work should be done, any special arrangements to be made and the criticality of the task. It also communicates to the system what work was actually done, the time it took, resources used, cause(s) of defect(s), sub-assemblies (rotables) exchanged and any comments regarding the condition of the equipment. These elementary data fragments are taken into the history base.

The job card system will only function properly if the job card flow has been designed specifically for the organization, properly explained to all personnel, accepted by them and they having committed themselves. An example of such a job card flow is shown in figure 20.1.

Accuracy of feedback

In chapter 17 we divided a CMMS's functionality into the following three main areas for convenience:

⇒ Maintenance planning

⇒ Maintenance management

⇒ Maintenance optimization

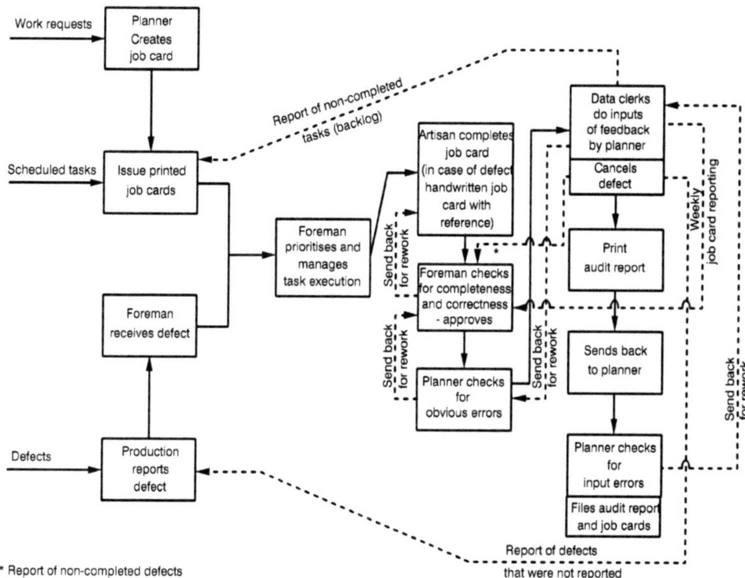

Figure 20.1 : Sample job card flow

Maintenance planning can, to a certain extent, function without proper task feedback. This is because it's function is to administer the maintenance plan. Without proper task feedback it can still go on administering the maintenance plan, but without the ability of enforcing the plan and of longer term improvement in the maintenance plan.

Maintenance management and Maintenance optimization, on the other hand, cannot function without proper task feedback. Task feedback supplies the data for the production of task management and, to a certain extent, equipment management reporting. It also provides failure history that can by analyzed through MDA (Maintenance Data Analysis) and RCM to improve the maintenance plan.

It is therefore very important to achieve a high level of accuracy of feedback. In actual fact, without accurate feedback, we can rather remain without the additional burden of a CMMS. Figure 20.2 shows the Systems Success Cycle, a figure devised to explain that the quality of feedback can make or break a CMMS installation.

The outer cycle starts at the top with a situation where the feedback is good, resulting in good input data. That leads to the data in the database being correct, which will lead to correct output infor-

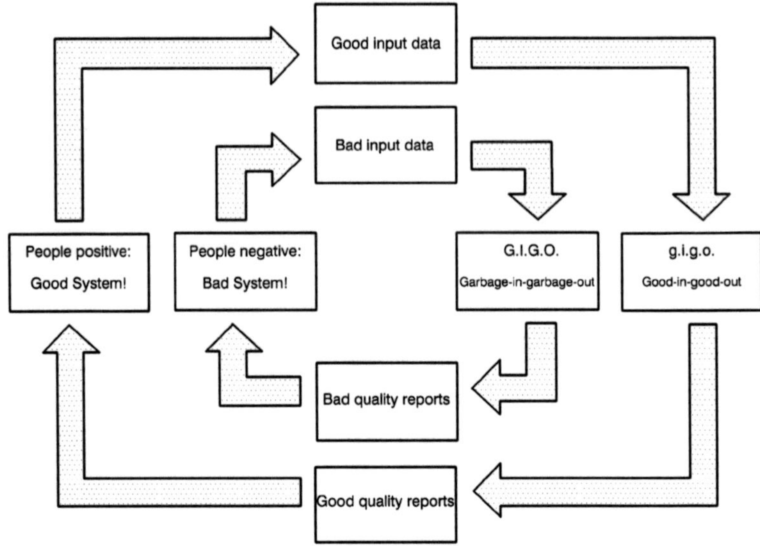

Figure 20.2 : The Systems Success Cycle

mation ("gigo or good-in-good-out"). The reports that are produced are thus correct, which causes people to be positive concerning the system. They will thus comment: "This is a good system!" It may be a good system, in that it does what is should do, but they are actually (at least partly) commenting on the quality of feedback.

If the cycle starts on a bad foot, though, the inner cycle will result. Bad feedback will eventually result in the comment: "This is a bad system", which does not necessarily reflect on the quality of the system's functionality.

When a system has been installed badly, the inner cycle results. To move from the inner to the outer cycle requires a major effort, which could take months or even years. It thus pays to ensure that one starts off in the outer cycle by tight management of feedback during the early stages of the project.

System audits

The Maintenance Information System often go unchallenged. It is important to challenge the system and its implementation from time to time to ensure that a benefit is gained from the implementation.

But, when investigating this possibility, one soon finds out that no standardized methodology regarding the application of the idea of auditing in the maintenance systems field exists. Maintenance Systems Auditing is a process for comparing the state of affairs in the maintenance system and its application with a set of pre-defined standards to establish whether improvement is necessary or not.

If the maintenance function in the organization achieves a high level of maintenance performance, it will help assure high levels of plant profitability. If, on the other hand, the performance of the maintenance function is poor, the effect on plant profitability can be devastating (due to high levels of downtime and high maintenance costs). Moreover, if one does not start by measuring (through a proper audit) the performance of the maintenance system, performance improvements cannot be realized.

One should thus from time to time use the requirement listing that was used to select the present system and apply that critically to the system (as adapted) to assess *firstly*, whether the system and its functional adaptations conforms sufficiently to the needs of the organization. *Secondly*, the audit should assess, using the same scale, what the present level of use of the system is and identify functional areas and plant areas where a project should be initiated to gain efficiency and profitability by improving system use. *Thirdly*, the audit should assess at what level managers are utilizing system outputs for real systems driven management, with a view of taking managerial action if necessary to improve the situation.

Goal achievement of the maintenance function in the organization leads to a high level of maintenance performance, resulting in a marked contribution to high levels of plant profitability. That largely depends on the effectiveness of systems in the organization as explicated above. It is thus of paramount importance that the systems function effectively.

Regular maintenance system audits ensure that flaws in present systems, system use and system thinking are brought to the fore, which if acted upon will lead to effective system performance and use. During such audits, the following should be determined:

⇒ Whether the systems conform sufficiently to the needs of the organization.

⇒ What the present level of use of the systems is.

⇒ The identification of functional areas and plant areas where projects should be initiated to gain efficiency and profitability by improving system use.

⇒ Assess at what level managers are utilizing system outputs for systems driven management, with a view of taking managerial action if necessary to improve the situation.

Maintenance Logistics

This page was left blank on purpose

Use it for notes

Chapter 21

Maintenance Scheduling

Scheduling Techniques

One of the primary activities of the Maintenance Administration function is that of scheduling. Good maintenance is dependent on the right maintenance strategies being applied on equipment at the right time. All the effort going into the creation of maintenance plans will be lost without good scheduling support. This includes simple time axis scheduling as well as detailed scheduling of the various activities in large maintenance shutdowns and projects. Properly executed scheduling is thus of crucial importance to the success of the maintenance function. The scheduling types that are used frequently in maintenance are:

⇒ Long term scheduling

⇒ Preventive work scheduling

⇒ Shutdown scheduling

⇒ Project workshops scheduling

⇒ Job shop scheduling

⇒ Area workshop scheduling

To effect this, a number of scheduling techniques has to be applied. These will be discussed in the subsequent paragraphs. They are the following:

⇒ Critical Path Method Scheduling

⇒ Time Slot scheduling

⇒ Intermittent scheduling

⇒ Work Prioritization

Critical Path Method scheduling

There are two major network scheduling techniques that can be used in maintenance work. They are PERT (Program Evaluation and Review Technique) and CPM (Critical Path Method). These techniques are largely applicable to the scheduling and control of large-scale, one off projects. The difference between PERT and CPM lies in their way of representing the logical task order in a network. A scheduling network is constructed using arrows and nodes (nodes form the beginning and end of each arrow). CPM uses arrows to represent tasks (activity on arrow), while PERT uses nodes to represent tasks (activity on node). In CPM nodes are the joints between tasks, while in PERT arrows perform this function. Such joints are called events. We will only develop the CPM technique further, although both techniques could be used with success.

Principles of CPM

- *Activities* (or tasks) are represented by arrows and denoted by capital letters following from left to right and from top to bottom through the network.
- *Nodes* are represented by circles numbered from left to right and from top to bottom.
- The first and last nodes of the network serve as the *start* and *end* of the project.
- Activities with zero duration sometimes need to be inserted in a network to facilitate network construction. Such activities are represented by dotted, unnumbered arrows called *dummy activities*.
- Each activity has a *time duration*, which is the time that such activity will take in the specific organization and circumstances. Such duration is written next to the arrow.
- The relationships between activities are governed by which activities must of necessity be complete before the present activity can start. Such activities are called *predecessors* of the present activity.
- Every activity needs certain quantities of *resources* (men, money, materials) for completion.

Rules of CPM network construction

- A CPM network may only have *one start* and *one end* node.
- Arrows may not be bent. Dummy activities are used to ensure that all activities are represented by straight arrows.
- Arrows may not cross each other.

- The start of any activity must be to the left of its end. This ensures a logical task flow from the left to the right of the network.

Statistics calculated during CPM scheduling

- *Early start* - (ES) - this is the earliest time at which the activity can start (taking the start time of the first activity as zero). It is calculated from the start of the network by totaling all preceding activity durations. At junctions the largest number calculated is used. This is calculated during the so called forward pass (progressing from the start node towards the end node).
- *Latest finish* (LF) - this is the latest time at which the activity can finish without affecting the project finish time adversely. It is calculated by successively subtracting activity durations from the project finish time. At junctions the smallest number calculated is used. This is calculated during the so called backward pass (progressing from the end node towards the start node).
- *Total float* (TF) - the maximum free time available for the activity. This is the time difference between the latest finish and the early start times minus the activity duration.

Representation

Networks are constructed by concatenating activities represented by arrows. The standard representation of such activities is shown in figure 21.1.

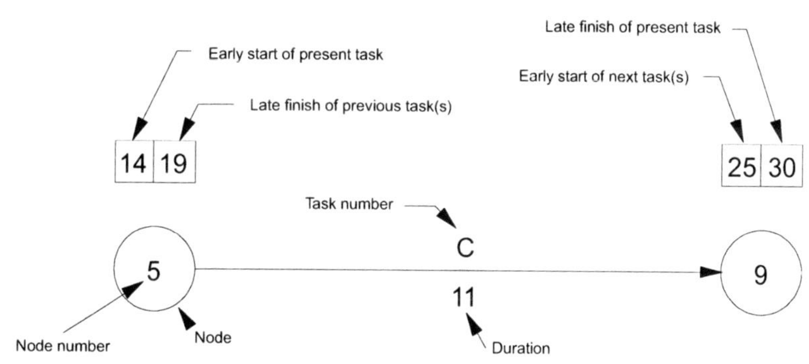

Figure 21.1 : Arrow structure

Network construction and scheduling

The method is best illustrated by a simple example. A project that consists of 11 tasks (activities) has the following predecessors and durations:

Table 21.1 : Example network activity data

Activity	*Predecessor*	*Duration*	*Men*
A		2	3
B	A	6	1
C	A	3	1
D	A	2	2
E	B	1	1
F	C	2	3
G	D	2	1
H	E	6	2
I	B,F	7	1
J	G	4	1
K	H,I,J	2	2

The first step in the scheduling process is to construct a network diagram representing the project. This is done by representing each activity by an arrow, while representing the activity start and finish events by circles (nodes). Nodes are then numbered from left to right. This is shown in figure 21.2.

The activity from node 3 to node 7 is an example of a dummy activity and is necessary to provide the correct diagram logic. Nodes 3 and 7 are in actual fact the same node, but in inserting the dummy activity, the network becomes much more presentable (and usable). The next step is then to calculate the network statistics shown in table 21.2.

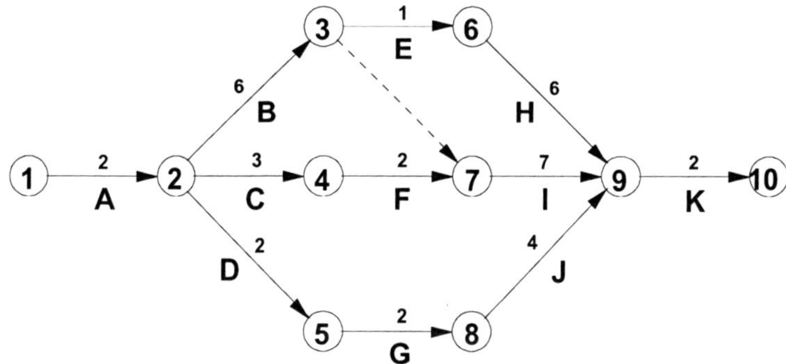

Figure 21.2 : Example network diagram

Activities C, D, F, G and H are said to have slack. All those activities with no slack are on the critical path (any time increases there will lead to an increase in the total project duration and thus to a later project completion time), The critical paths for the present project are ABEHK and ABIK. The full network, with its statistics included, is shown in figure 21.3.

Table 21.2 : Example network statistics

Activity	*Early Start*	*Late Finish*	*Total Float*
A	0	2	0
B	2	8	0
C	2	6	1
D	2	9	5
E	8	9	0
F	5	8	1
G	4	11	5
H	9	15	0
I	8	15	0
J	6	15	5
K	15	17	0

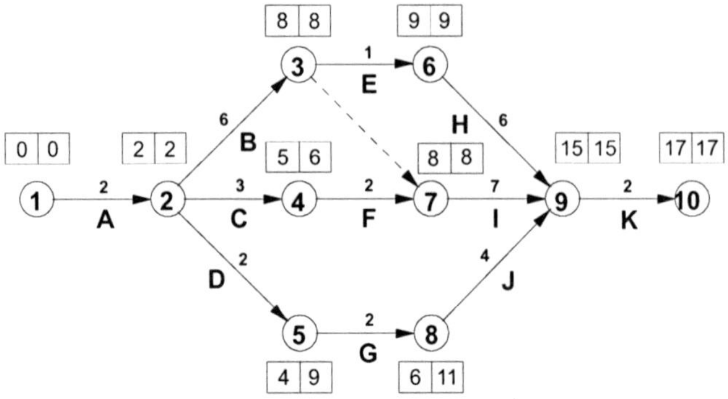

Figure 21.3 : Example network diagram

An additional aspect of network analysis is that the quantities of resources for the total project can be determined based on the resource requirements of the individual activities. This can form the basis for the balancing of resources (to ensure that the work load can be handled economically). The resource graph is best constructed from a project bar graph.

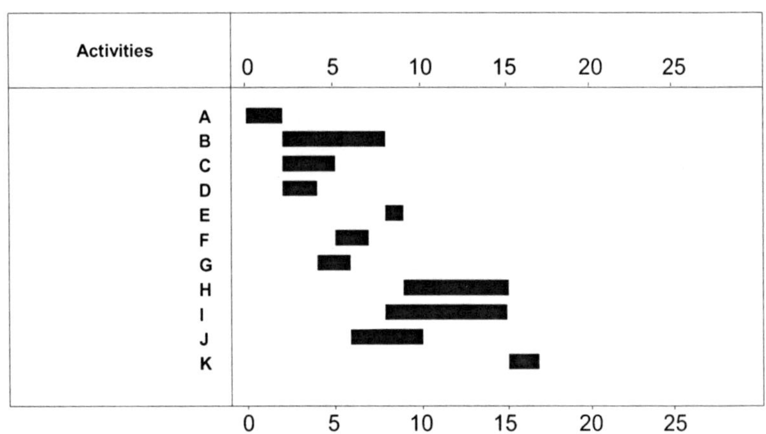

Figure 21.4 : Basic project bar graph

Critical Path Schedules are mostly presented using the Gantt chart. This is a modification of the basic bar chart, which was introduced in the figure above. The Gantt chart includes the following information:

- Task start, end and duration using a simple bar.
- Task float using a thin extension (whisker) to the bar. This shows to what extent the task completion can be delayed without affecting the project end time.

- A second, differentiated bar next to the original scheduling bar, showing actual progress being made.
- Triangles showing milestone dates/times, where progress should be monitored.

The Gantt chart for the present example (without progress bar and milestones) is shown in figure 21.5, while a manpower resource graph is shown in figure 21.6.

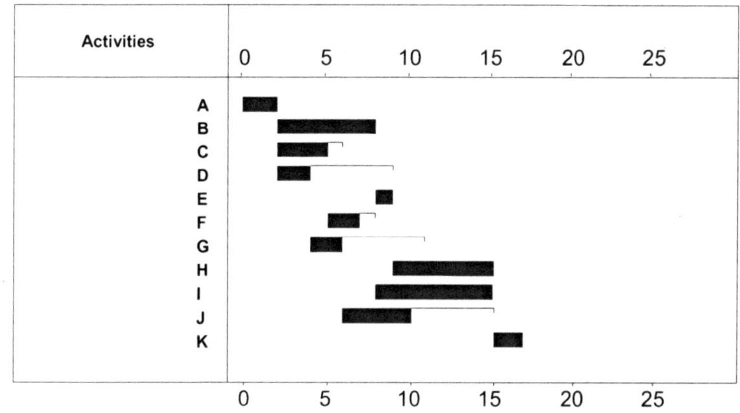

Figure 21.5 : Example Project Gantt Chart

In this example an overload occurs from 5 to hour 7 - consequently, unless we arrange either to subcontract this work or obtain additional resources, we cannot expect to meet our project completion time. Possible solutions to solving this overload are:

⇒ Subcontract one or more of the activities.

⇒ Obtain additional resources.

⇒ Reschedule, using the available resources.

In the present example it is possible to move the start of activities G and J two hours ahead. That will solve the overload problem from hour 5 to hour 7 and will add 1 man to the load from hour 10 to hour 12.

Example

A large open cast mine operates a fleet of 170 ton rear dump trucks. Every 15000 running hours such a unit requires a mini-overhaul. This consists mainly of exchanging some major components with overhauled units. The task relationships and durations are shown in table 21.3, in-

Table 21.3 : 170 ton dump truck mini-overhaul - task list

Activity	Description	Dura-	Prede-	Labor
A	Clean and prepare machine	2		2L
B	Remove load body	5	A	2F,1R
C	Remove wheels	10	B	2F,1L
D	Remove final drives	18	C	2F,2L
E	Remove engine	10	C	2F,1L,1E
F	Remove transmission	2	C	2F,1L,1E
G	Remove differential	3	F,E	2F,1L
H	Replace steering cylinders	40	G	2F,1L
I	Strip and repair front brakes	28	D	2F,2L
J	Remove suspension cylinders	22	H,I	2F,2L
K	Carry out frame repairs	48	G	2B,1L
L	Respray frame, let dry	34	J,K	1B,1L
M	Install reconditioned final drives	24	L	3F,2L
N	Install reconditioned engine	10	L	2F,1L,1E
O	Install reconditioned differential	6	L	2F,1L
P	Install reconditioned transmission	4	M,N,O	2F,1L,1E
Q	Install recon. suspension cylinders	24	L	2F,1L
R	Repair and spray load body	130	B	2B,1L
S	Replace load body	8	Q,P,R	2F,1R
T	Replace wheels	12	S	2F,1L
U	Commission all fluid lines	4	S	1F
V	Commission electrical system	3	S	1E
W	Commission - start up	1	V,T,U	1F
X	Test machine	6	W	1F
Y	Hand machine to production	1	X	1F

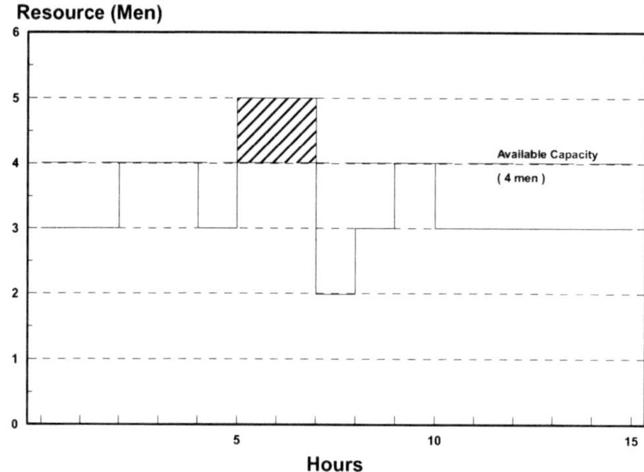

Figure 21.6 : Example Project Resource Requirements

cluding personnel resources. The basic network as constructed from the table is shown in figure 21.7. The network statistics are shown in table 21.4.

The completed network is shown in figure 21.8. Clearly there is only one critical path, ABCEGHJLMPSTWXY (total float 0). The project Gantt chart and resource chart for fitters are shown in figures 21.9 and 21.10. By evaluating these two figures one can immediately see that the schedule can be optimized regarding the use of fitters by the following actions:

Move task D ahead by 2 hours (the duration of task F, which will eliminate the peak from hour 17 to hour 19).

By moving task N ahead 6 hours or task O ahead 10 hours the peak of 9 fitters from hour 126 to hour 132 can be eliminated in favor of lengthening the peak of 7 fitters. Seven fitters will then be needed from hour 126 to hour 142.

In the same way the schedule can be optimized for other resources.

Time slot scheduling

Time Slot scheduling comprises the calculation of the start time (or date) of future occurrences of a specific activity (i.e., a planned service, shutdown or major overhaul). This (the start time/date) is then listed as being the scheduled time of occurrence, while the duration is listed as the length of the activity. Thus the future scheduled activity fills a time slot from a specified start time to the activity end time (start

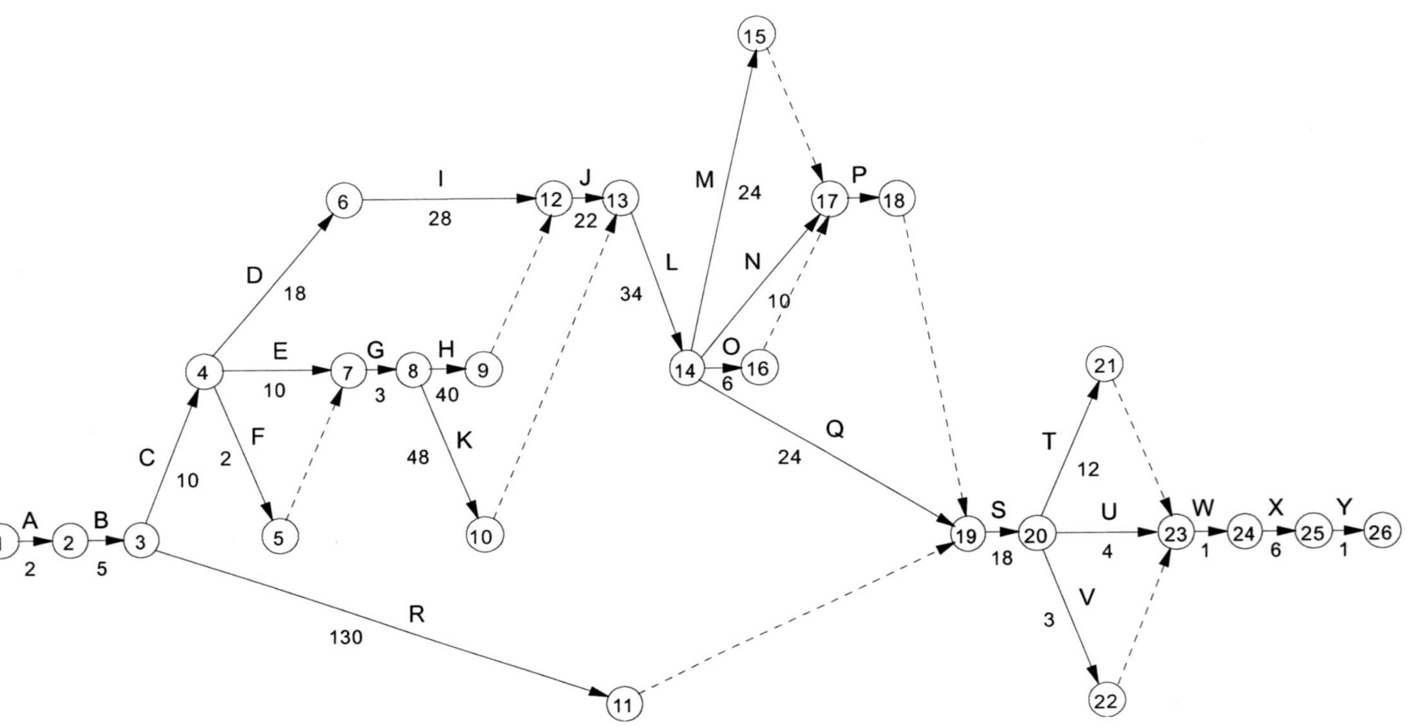

Figure 21.7 : 170 ton dump truck - basic network

Table 21.4 : 170 ton dump truck mini-overhaul - statistics

Activity	Description	Duration	Early Start	Late Finish	Total Float
A	Clean and prepare machine	2	0	2	0
B	Remove load body	5	2	7	0
C	Remove wheels	10	7	17	0
D	Remove final drives	18	17	42	7
E	Remove engine	10	17	27	0
F	Remove transmission	2	17	27	8
G	Remove differential	3	27	30	0
H	Replace steering cylinders	40	30	70	0
I	Strip and repair front brakes	28	35	70	7
J	Remove suspension cylinders	22	70	92	0
K	Carry out frame repairs	48	30	92	14
L	Respray frame, let dry	34	92	126	0
M	Install reconditioned final drives	24	126	150	0
N	Install reconditioned engine	10	126	150	14
O	Install reconditioned differential	6	126	150	18
P	Install reconditioned transmission	4	150	154	0
Q	Install recon. suspension cylinders	24	126	154	4
R	Repair and spray load body	130	7	154	17
S	Replace load body	8	154	162	0
T	Replace wheels	12	162	174	0
U	Commission all fluid lines	4	162	174	8
V	Commission electrical system	3	162	174	9
W	Commission - start up	1	174	175	0
X	Test machine	6	175	181	0
Y	Hand machine to production	1	181	182	0

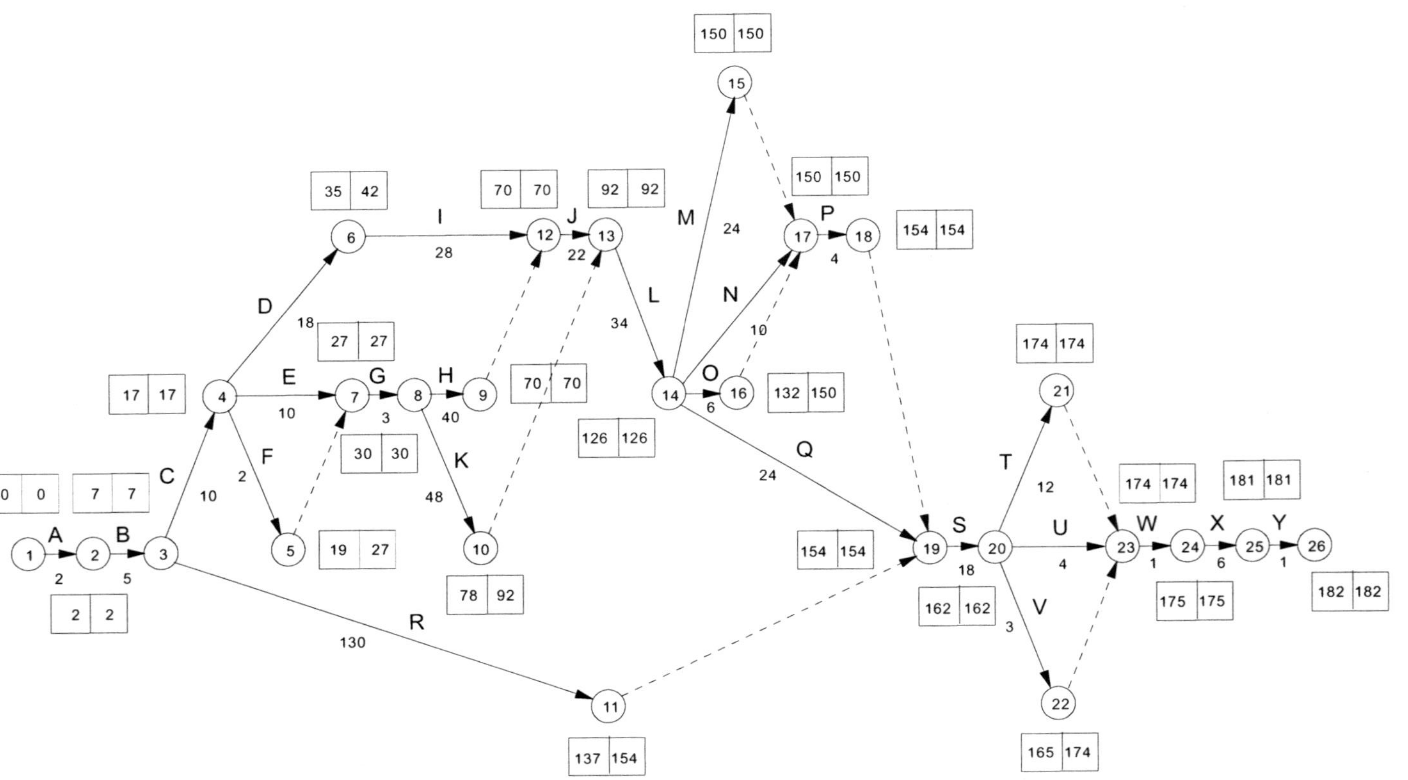

Figure 21.8 : 170 ton dump truck - complete network

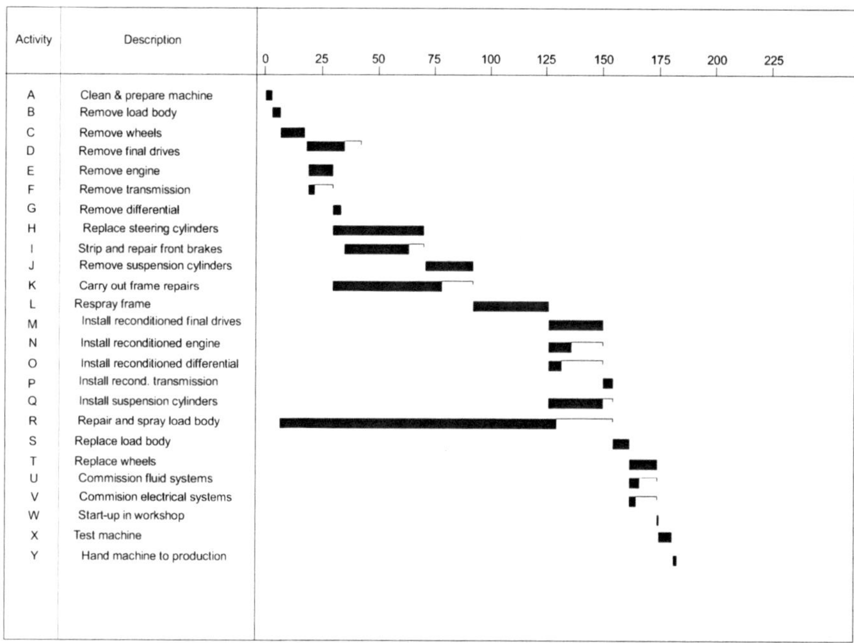

Figure 21.9 : 170 ton dump truck mini-overhaul Project Gantt chart

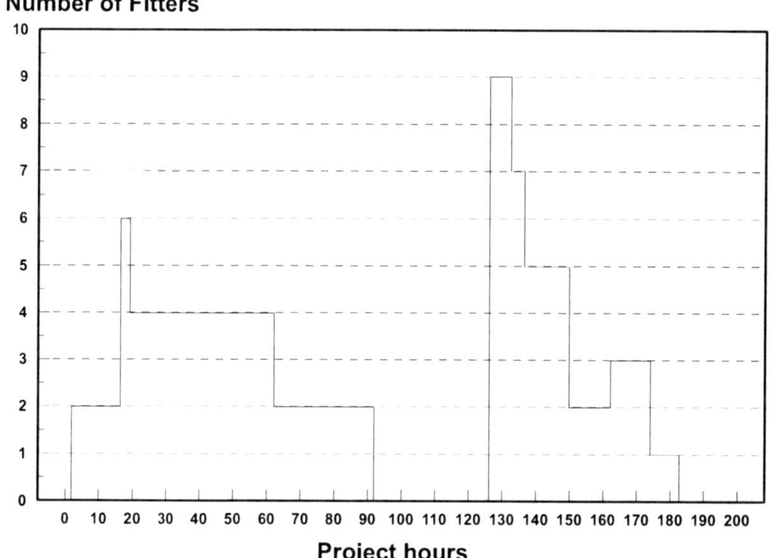

Figure 21.10 : 170 ton dump truck mini-overhaul Resource balancing

time plus duration). A typical way of presenting such a schedule is by recording the activity and its associated duration on a bar chart. This is illustrated in figure 21.11.

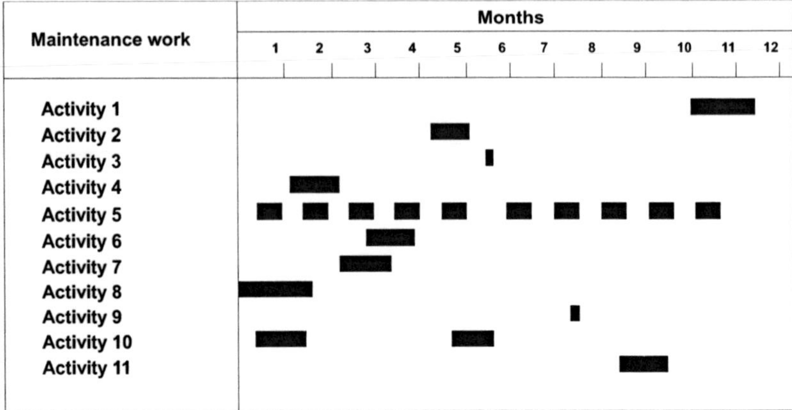

Figure 21.11 : Sample time slot schedule

Intermittent scheduling

Maintenance often has scheduling situations that are of a batch nature. These are typically the situations that do no lend themselves to network scheduling as that would be an over-complication of the problem, and/or may not handle the scheduling process adequately. Furthermore, these situations are too complex to be handled by the simple time slot scheduling approach. Typically one or a few of a specific job have to be handled in an optimal way. This type of scheduling may be very simple if only a few jobs have to be handled by virtually unlimited resources. It can become very complex, though, when the typical machine workshop with multiple jobs, each with different requirements, has to be handled by many different machining centers.

To illustrate the complexity of the intermittent production situation we can state that the problem consists of the following elements:

- **m** different jobs
- different processing stations
- an optimal sequence of processing each of the m jobs through the n processing stations: Thus an **m x n** matrix **A** can be prepared, where $\mathbf{a}_{ij}$ represents the order of processing of the job through the **n** processing stations. Thus if 2 jobs are processed through 3 stations the matrix may be:

$$A = \begin{pmatrix} 2 & 1 & 3 \\ 3 & 1 & 0 \end{pmatrix} \qquad 21.1$$

This will imply that job 1 will be processed through the three stations in the order station 2, station 1 and station 3, whereas job 2 will be processed in the order station 3 and station 1 (station 2 will not be used for this job).

- each job has a certain processing time on each processing station. This can again be represented by an **m x n** matrix **B** where $\mathbf{b}_{ij}$ represents the processing time of the job on the processing station. Thus for the above example this may be:

$$B = \begin{pmatrix} 65 & 35 & 40 \\ 10 & 0 & 15 \end{pmatrix} \qquad 21.2$$

This matrix shows that job 1 will take 65 minutes on station 1, 35 minutes on station 2 and 40 minutes on station 3, while job 2 will not be processed on station 2, but will use 10 minutes of station 1's time and 15 minutes of station 3's time.

- the priority of each job - this can be presented by a **1xm** matrix **C** where $\mathbf{c}_i$ is the priority of job i.

$$C = \begin{pmatrix} 2 & 1 \end{pmatrix} \qquad 21.3$$

Although the problem in intermittent production systems is a complex one, a proven heuristic scheduling approach exists. This approach was developed and refined over time during an age where computers with high computing power did not exist. The approach consists of four phases:

- *aggregate planning* - this is a fairly broad level of planning where no detail is involved.
- *loading* - the work in the aggregate plan is allocated to work centers.
- *Sequencing* - the order in which waiting jobs are to be processed is specified using a priority sequencing rule.
- *detailed scheduling* - having the task sequence available and using the due dates and estimates of task durations, the start and ending dates can be added to create the detailed schedule.

Aggregate planning

The aggregate planning task is the basic scheduling framework during which the tasks awaiting completion for the period are listed, together with their requested due dates and estimated duration. During this process the necessary resources (materials, people) are also procured and job routings through the various work centers are determined. Aggregate planning is of course not a static process and new jobs are being added daily. An example of an aggregate planning worksheet is shown in figure 21.12.

Loading

During the loading process the tasks for which all the steps in aggregate planning have been completed are allocated to specific work centers. The work centers are thus "loaded" with jobs. Such loading can of course only proceed until the capacity of the work center for the planning horizon has been fully reserved. When work centers are not permanently manned, personnel can also become a limitation. In such cases both the work centers and the workmen must be loaded (and of course synchronized). A good way of loading is by using a stacked horizontal bar chart - see figure 21.13. Tasks are stacked on each other from left to right. This chart shows when the load on a spe-

Tasks	Due Date	Duration	Requirements	

Figure 21.12 : Aggregate planning work sheet

Work Centre	Cumulative work centre load			
Work centre 1	Job A	Job C	Job E	Job G
Work centre 2	Job A	Job D	Job F	
Work centre 3	Job A	Job C		
Work centre 4	Job B	Job D	Job E	
Work centre 5	Job B			

Figure 21.13 : Loading bar chart

cific work center is becoming unrealistically high so that it signals the need for reassignment (if possible).

Loading is often decentralized to the first line supervisor. This gives him and his team an important measure of ownership and involvement.

Sequencing

Jobs awaiting processing at the various work centers (see figure 21.13) need to prioritized to determine which of them should be processed first, etc. This is done by applying a priority sequencing rule. Typical rules for this purpose are:

- First come first served (FCFS) - the tasks are processed in the order in which they arrive at the work center. Thus in figure 31, the most left hand job will be processed first.
- Last come first served (LCFS) - the last job that arrived is processed first.
- Job with the earliest due date is processed first.
- Shortest processing time (SPT) - the task with the shortest processing time is processed first.

Practical experience, as well as several computer simulation studies have proved beyond a doubt that the last rule (SPT) produces the best result. It performs the best in three areas:

⇒ Lowest average completion time of tasks

⇒ Lowest average number of tasks in the system

⇒ Lowest average job lateness

The drawback of this technique is that jobs with long processing times tend to have very long turnaround times. This can be countered by introducing a truncated SPT rule. This works exactly like the normal SPT rule unless a job ends up waiting longer than x time units to be processed - then give that job top priority. The value for x is set by management. This results in the standard deviation of completion time decreasing, while average completion time increases.

Detailed scheduling

Now that the order of the jobs have been established (see figure 32 for updated aggregate scheduling listing), the detailed scheduling can commence. This is typically done using the information in the updated aggregate scheduling listing (figure 21.14). The result can be pictorially shown on a horizontal bar chart such as that shown in figure 21.15. This chart shows the total work load for the work center in

Tasks	Due Date	Duration	Requirements	Work C'tre 1	Work C'tre 2	Work C'tre 3	Date	Time

Figure 21.14 : Complete aggregate schedule

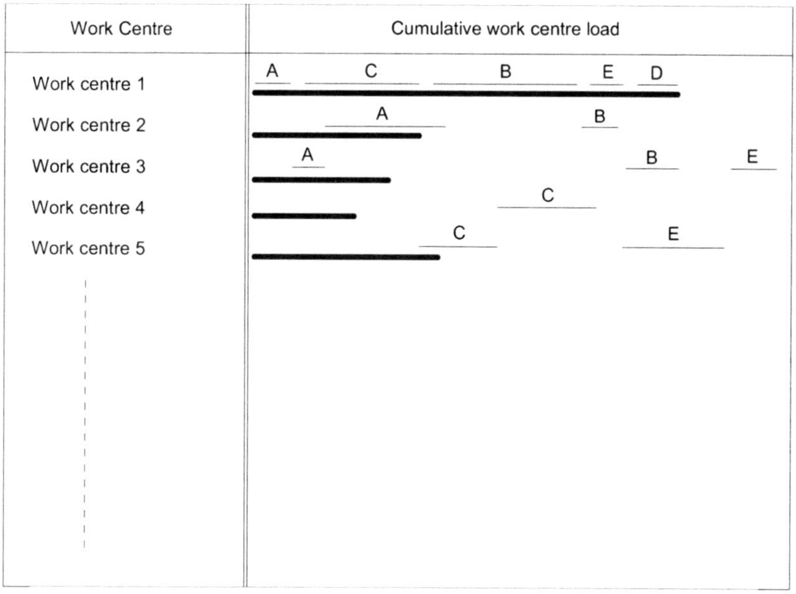

Work Centre	Cumulative work centre load
Work centre 1	A C B E D
Work centre 2	A B
Work centre 3	A B E
Work centre 4	C
Work centre 5	C E

Figure 21.15 : Detailed scheduling bar chart

thick solid lines, while the thinner lines represent the various tasks that must be processed. This schedule may be updated daily or weekly depending on the situation.

Computers can of course play an important role in this process to simplify the intermittent scheduling task and to make it more efficient. The aggregate schedule then consists of all tasks registered for completion at the specific workshop. The load of the various work centers/personnel/other facilities are maintained dynamically as tasks are assigned. The tasks per workstation can then be planned in detail following the sequencing action. This can be augmented by a simulator that could assist the planner by finding the best routing/sequencing combination.

Work prioritization

Although prioritization isn't a pure scheduling technique, it is important as a method of sequencing work in an optimal way, and is thus discussed as a scheduling technique. There are various ways available for the prioritization of work. The simplest method available is by allocating a priority to every job from the priority pool:

⇒ 1 Very urgent - must be handled immediately

⇒ 2 Urgent, but can wait

⇒ 3 Do as time comes available

The problem with such simple schemes is first that they can be easily manipulated to suit the requester and second that priority allocations depend very much on the frame of reference of the person doing the allocation.

Another way of prioritization is by using pre-defined priority allocation tables. Such tables can take a few parameters into account and produce a fair result.

Still another way is by combining a few risk factors to establish a relative level of risk, which in turn will determine the priority of the task at hand. Typical risk factors are:

- Production loss suffered while job is outstanding.
- Damage that could suffered to plant if the job is not completed soon.
- Condition of standby equipment currently running (while the machine on which the job must be done is out of commission).
- Chance of needing a component such as the one in for repair (in the case of using the priority scheme for sub-assembly repair) while none is available as a spare.

These factors can be combined by addition and/or multiplication to give a compound risk factor, from which a valid priority can be derived using a priority assignment table. These priorities are now used to select which work should be done first from the waiting pool of work.

An example of such a priority allocation mechanism is illustrated by the format shown in figure 21.16. In such a scheme priority A is the highest, with priority D the lowest. The values for such priority allocation can be determined jointly between plant production and maintenance management.

Maintenance Scheduling

As was stated in the opening paragraph, there are a variety of scheduling types used in maintenance. These are:

⇒ Long term scheduling

⇒ Preventive work scheduling

⇒ Shutdown scheduling

Priority Allocation Sheet

Production loss (a)		Compound risk = (a x b x c x d)	
Damage potential (b)			
Standby condition (c)			
Spares availability (d)		Priority	

Evaluation Scales

Production loss (%) 0 – 100: 1 | 2 | 3 | 4 | 5

Damage potential (%) 0 – 100: 1 | 2 | 3 | 4 | 5

Standby condition: Good 1, Fair 3, Poor 5

Spares availability: Available 1, Not available 5

Compound risk: 1 - 16 : D 17 - 81 : C 82 - 256 : B 257 - 625 : A

Figure 21.16 : Priority allocation sheet

⇒ Project workshop scheduling

⇒ Job shop scheduling

⇒ Area workshop scheduling

The Time Slot scheduling technique is used for long term scheduling and preventive work scheduling. The various maintenance activities are fitted into time slots, each with a specific start and finish time/date. Examples of work scheduled in this way are: shutdowns, statutory work and major preventive work (long term schedules) and routine services, condition monitoring, inspections, preventive replacements/overhaul (preventive work scheduling). Critical Path Method scheduling is used for those tasks that can materially benefit from this optimizing scheduling method. Examples of such tasks are shutdown schedules and project workshop schedules. Intermittent scheduling is ideal for use in maintenance service workshops that have to process jobs from various parts of the plant through limited resources. Lastly, Work Prioritization is typically used in the area maintenance workshop (the "first line of defense" from which all smaller routine maintenance, preventive tasks and breakdowns are handled). This allows workshop management to determine which jobs from a pool of waiting jobs should be processed first. These jobs are then assigned to artisans for completion.

References

1. Adam, E.E. and Ebert, R.J., Production and Operations Management - Concepts, Models and Behavior.
2. Coetzee, J.L., Quantitative Techniques in Maintenance Management. Annual short course, 1995.
3. Taha, Hamdy A., Operations Research - an introduction. Collier Macmillan, 1976.
4. Wild, Ray, Production and Operations Management, 4th edition. Cassell, 1989.

Chapter 22

Inventory Management

The maintenance department is extremely dependent on a properly managed stock of maintenance spares and materials. As such, the maintenance manager cannot afford not to have a proper knowledge base concerning inventory management. He/she is one of the main stock users and the one who will be negatively affected if the stock management is not up to standard. Moreover, as the only user of the maintenance spares and materials, he/she is ultimately responsible for the investment in stockholding and the availability of spares when needed.

The quantity and timing of purchase is one of the main issues in inventory management. It is important because, if too small a quantity is purchased, the unit cost will be higher, shortages will increase and the expediting work load will escalate. On the other hand, if too large a quantity is purchased, the result will be excess inventory and raised costs. A number of factors must be taken into account in establishing the correct quantity and timing of stock purchases.

The basic characteristics of an inventory system can be presented under four main groupings:

- *Economic parameters* - the inventory management problem is primarily a problem of economics. The following parameters are thus of cardinal importance.

  ⇒ *Acquisition cost K* - this involves the fixed charge associated with the placement of an order. Each time a purchase order is issued the purchasing, inspection, inventory control, receiving and financial department must service it. We need to know the additional or incremental cost incurred to handle one more order through the system.

  ⇒ *Holding cost h* per unit time this includes the interest on the invested capital, storage costs, handling cost and depreciation.

  ⇒ *Shortage cost p* per unit time - this is the penalty incurred as a result of running out of stock when the spare is needed.

- *Demand* - this is the rate at which the stock items are required for maintenance work. The demand can be described as being deterministic or probabilistic. The probabilistic view of demand is more realistic in real world circumstances.
- *Ordering cycle* - this is the time span between successive placement of orders. This may be initiated in two ways:
  - ⇒ *Continuous review* - the inventory level is updated continuously until a certain lower level is reached. A new order is then placed. This is also referred to as the two bin system.
  - ⇒ *Periodic review* - orders are placed at regular intervals.
- Lead time - the time between the placing of the order and delivery.

Economic order quantity

The principle of ordering in the 'best' quantity, called the economic order quantity is illustrated in figure 22.1. Although the minimum does not occur exactly at the point where the holding cost equal the acquisition cost, this is a good position for a rule of thumb. Without using any formulas one can expect the economic order quantity to be that quantity for which the acquisition cost roughly equals the holding cost. The objective is thus to minimize the total cost of materials' procurement.

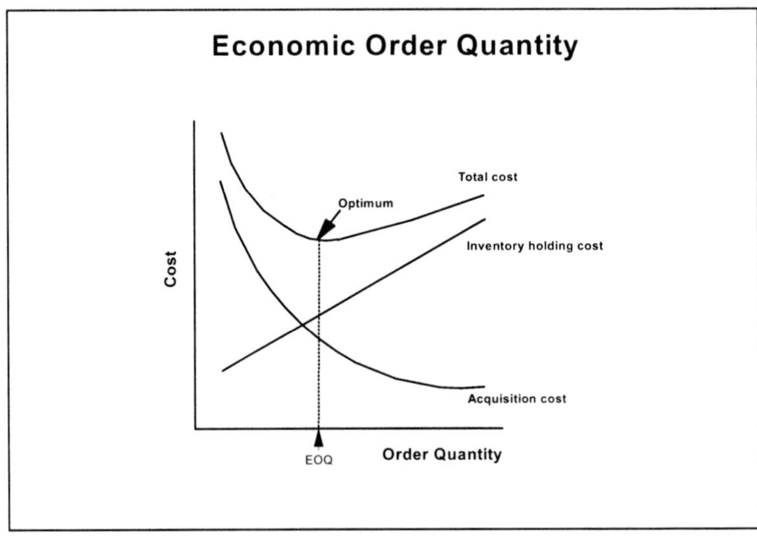

Figure 22.1 : Economic Order Quantity graph

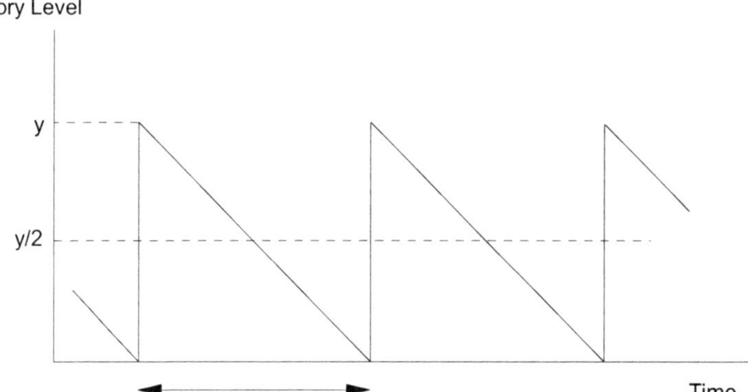

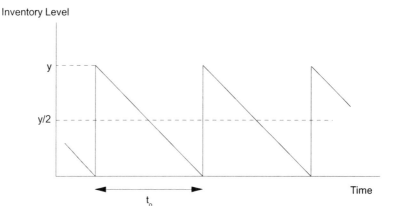

Figure 22.2 : Deterministic inventory model

A basic deterministic inventory model for determining the economic order quantity is shown in figure 22.2. The notation for this model's development is:

K = Acquisition cost per order

β = Rate of demand (units/unit time)

y = Order quantity

h = Holding cost per inventory unit per unit time.

The length of an inventory cycle:

$$t_0 = \frac{y}{\beta} \qquad 22.1$$

The average inventory level = y/2.

The total cost per unit time:

$C_t(y)$ = Acquisition cost/unit time + Holding cost per unit time

This can be written as:

$$C_t(y) = \frac{K}{y/\beta} + h\left(\frac{y}{2}\right) \qquad 22.2$$

The minimum cost occurs where

$$\frac{dC_t(y)}{dy} = 0$$

Thus

$$\frac{-K\beta}{y^2}+\frac{h}{2}=0$$

By solving for y the basic economic order quantity formula results:

$$EOQ = y^* = \left[\frac{2K\beta}{h}\right]^{1/2} \qquad 22.3$$

The optimum policy consists of ordering y* units every

$$t_0^* = \frac{y^*}{\beta} \qquad 22.4$$

time units. The optimum cost is:

$$C_t(y^*) = \frac{K}{y^*/\beta} + h\left(\frac{y^*}{2}\right) \qquad 22.5$$

Example 1

The maintenance department uses on average 15 units per month of a certain roller bearing. The cost of processing an order has been estimated at $ 40, while the unit holding cost of a smaller commodity is $ 1,80 per month. We are interested in calculating the size of the lots which should be used for the purchase of the bearings.

$$EOQ = y^* = \left[\frac{2K\beta}{h}\right]^{1/2} = \left[\frac{2\times 40\times 15}{1.8}\right]^{1/2} = 25.8$$

A lot size of 26 is thus prescribed by the EOQ model. In practice it will be better to use a lot size of 30 or 2 month's use of the bearing as the value of $C_t(y^*)$ does not differ significantly from that of $C_t(30)$.

$C_t(y^*)$ = $ 46.48 per month

$C_t(30)$ = $ 47.00 per month

In comparison to that, the cost differs significantly if 1 month's stock or 3 month's stock are purchased.

$C_t(15)$ = \$ 53.50 per month

$C_t(45)$ = \$ 53.83 per month

If these cost differences are multiplied over thousands of stock items the monthly premium of not using the correct ordering quantity can become a significant expenditure.

ABC analysis

Inventory management is very time consuming if you want to apply the best principles to all stock items. ABC analysis is a technique to decrease this workload substantially without materially affecting the cost of stockholding. The stock is classified into three groups based on value. These are:

- *A items* - those items with high stock value (price x quantity), but which constitutes only a small proportion of stock items. Typically the A item category includes only 10 to 15% of stock items, but which contributes 70 to 75% of purchased value. For these items tight control will be exercised with regular stock reviews. The objective of this will be to keep the investment in these items at an absolute minimum.
- *B items* - those items with medium stock purchase value and a moderately low number of commodities. Typically 25-35% of items fall in this category, at a cost of 15-20% of stockholding. Normal inventory control with good records and regular attention should suffice in this category.
- *C items* - the remaining items (those with low value and high volume) fall in this category. They typically constitute 50-65% of stock items with a value of 5% of total purchased value. For such items only simple controls are necessary. It is common practice to establish a simple reordering procedure for such items, which can be administered by clerical employees.

Figure 22.3 shows a graph that depicts the concept of ABC analysis.

Minimum-maximum control

Minimum - maximum control is one of the most widely used methods of inventory control. It involves the establishment of mini-

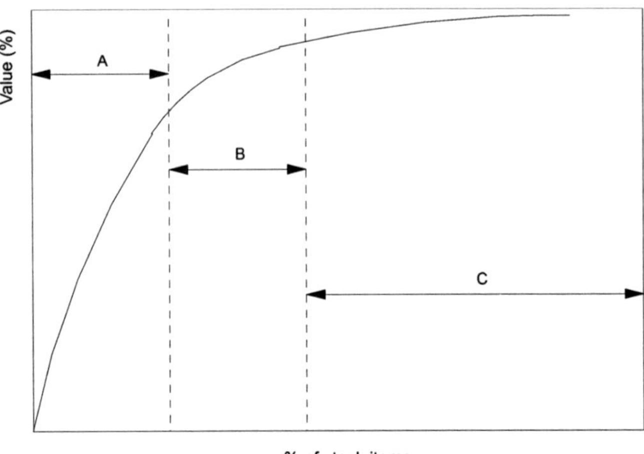

Figure 22.3 : ABC analysis

mum and maximum inventory levels with a view to controlling the actual stock level within these bounds.

In theory the minimum inventory level could be zero. The last stock item will then be used just before the new stock arrives. The maximum stock level will then be equal to the order quantity. In practice it would be unwise to follow such an extreme policy. This will, due to fluctuations in demand and delivery lead times lead to costly stock-outs.

The solution is thus to establish a minimum (or safety) level of stock, below which the inventory level should not drop under normal circumstances. The maximum inventory then consists of this minimum level plus the ordering quantity. The purpose of the "safety stock" is to ensure against contingencies such as sudden increases in demand, long lead times, defective deliveries and stock record errors. The size of the safety stock is established by taking into account the risk involved in having stock-outs of the particular item.

This system is illustrated in figure 22.4. It is important to note that the introduction of this minimum level will lead to an unnecessary high inventory value if this stock is never used to its full extent. It is thus of the utmost importance that this minimum level should be as low as possible. A further feature of figure 22.4 is that the order point is selected such that the demand during the expected lead time can just be satisfied without using the safety stock. Should demand be higher

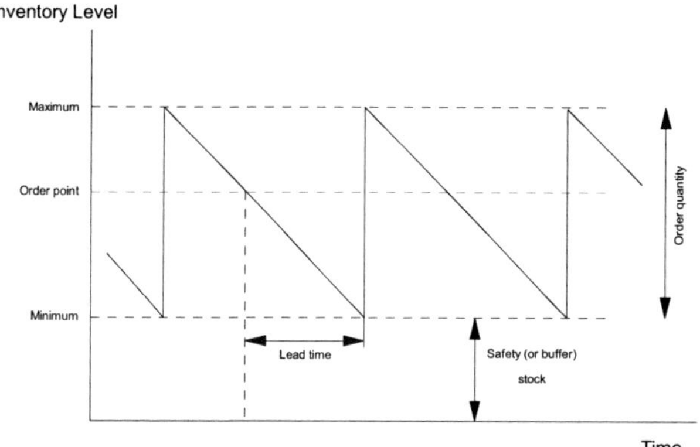

Figure 22.4 : Minimum Maximum Inventory Control

than expected or the lead time longer than expected the safety stock will be used until the new stock arrives.

Inventory control model

The inventory control model discussed in the previous paragraphs has one important problem: it does not take into account any variability in demand and lead time. This does not represent the real word situation adequately. We thus introduce a probabilistic model in which stock is reviewed continuously. This model is shown in figure 22.5. Note that we accept that there will sometimes occur stock-out situations (no buffer or safety stock is allowed for - this is added later to ensure that the level of service is adequate).

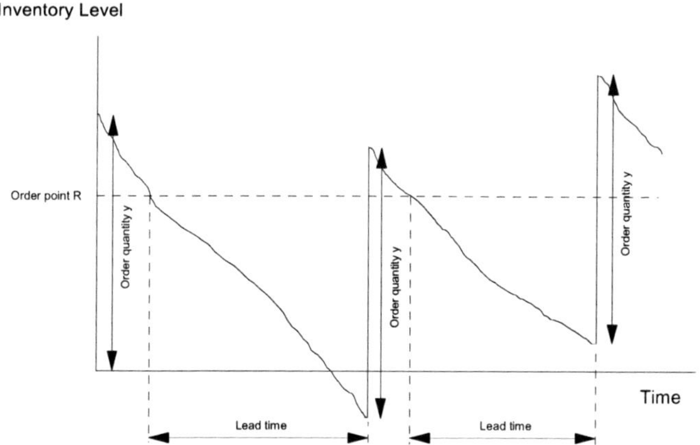

Figure 22.5 : Stochastic inventory model

The variables for this model are the following (some of them we have already encountered):

Set-up cost K - the marginal cost associated with an order (the extra cost that has to be incurred to place this order)

Purchase price c

Holding cost h - this includes the interest on invested capital, storage costs, handling costs, depreciation costs, etc. (cost per unit per year)

Shortage cost p - cost incurred if the item is out of stock when it is needed (cost per unit per year)

Number ordered per cycle y

Expected total demand per year D

Reordering point R

Demand - number of items needed during lead time based on history - it is presented by the average $\overline{x}_d$ and the standard deviation σ_d.

Ordering lead time based on history and represented by the average $\overline{x}_0$ and the standard deviation σ_o.

A generalized stock replenishment model will be discussed that should be able to handle virtually all industrial maintenance stock replenishment situations. This comprises a probabilistic model in which stock is reviewed continuously and an order of size y is placed every time the stock level reaches the reordering point R. The model gives the optimum values of y and R that will minimize the total expected inventory costs per annum.

Assumptions of the model are:

- Demand and lead time are stochastic
- Unfilled demand during lead time is backlogged
- The distribution of demand during lead time is independent of the time at which it occurs
- There is no more than one outstanding order at a time

Let

$$r(x \mid t) = \text{conditional probability density function of demand } x \text{ during lead time } t, x > 0$$

$$= \frac{1}{\sqrt{2\pi}\sigma_d} e^{-\frac{1}{2}\left[(x-\bar{x}_d)/\sigma_d\right]^2}$$

$s(x)$ = probability density function of lead time t, $t > 0$

$$= \frac{1}{\sqrt{2\pi}\sigma_o} e^{-\frac{1}{2}[(x-\bar{x}_o)/\sigma_o]^2}$$

$f(x)$ = absolute probability density function of demand x during lead time t

$$= \int_0^\infty r(x \mid t)s(t)dt$$

The solution for optimal y* and R* is obtained from

$$y^* = \left(\frac{2D(k + p\bar{S})}{h}\right)^{\frac{1}{2}} \qquad 22.6$$

$$\int_{R^*}^\infty f(x)dx = \frac{hy^*}{pD} \qquad 22.7$$

where

$$\bar{S} = \int_R^\infty (x - R)f(x)dx \qquad 22.8$$

These equations must be solved by iteration. If the value of equation 22.6 is calculated for R=0 it gives the value of y* = y'. Likewise for equation 22.7 the value y* = y" is obtained. If y" >= y' then optimal values of y* and R* exist and are unique. In such a case, these values can be calculated as follows. Calculate the first trial value of y* from

$$y_1 = \left[\frac{2DK}{h}\right]^{\frac{1}{2}} \qquad 22.9$$

Use this value as y* in equation 22.7 to calculate R_1, the first approximation of R*. This value can again be used in equation 22.6 to calculate y_2. The process is now repeated by using y_2 in equation 22.7 and so forth. The procedure is repeated until two successive values of R are approximately equal. The last calculated values for y and R will then yield y* and R*.

Minimum stock level

The minimum stock level in the stock replenishment model above is zero. This is the correct theoretical position but could be unwise in practice as it involves planning that is much too close for safety. A minimum stock level is thus established which serves as a factor of safety. This level must be determined by the users and will depend on the importance of the stock item, the value of the additional investment and the availability of substitutes on short notice. Any item, which could cause production delays should have a fairly high minimum stock level.

Economic ordering quantity

The economic ordering quantity for a stock item is the value of y* as calculated above while {minimum stock level+R*} represents the reordering point.

Usage forecasting

In the model presented above the values and $\overline{x_d}$ σ_d actually represent a usage forecast. It is assumed that the demand will be normally distributed with average $\overline{x_d}$ and standard deviation σ_d.

Example 2

The cost of a single acquisition for a certain company was found to be $ 100. The annual demand of a certain stock item is 1000 and the shortage cost per item is $ 10. The holding cost per unit per year is $ 2.00. The demand during lead time follows a negative exponential distribution with an average of 200 units.

To find out if the problem has a feasible solution:

$$\hat{y} = \left[\frac{2 \times 1000 \times (100 + (10 \times 100))}{2}\right]^{1/2} = 1449.14$$

$$\tilde{y} = \frac{10 \times 1000}{2} = 5000$$

Since y" >= y', a unique solution for y* and R* exists. We get by applying our values to the formulas above (formulas 22.6, 22.7 and 22.8 above) that:

$$\bar{S} = \frac{1}{\lambda} e^{-\lambda R}$$

$$y^* = \left[100{,}000 + 2{,}000{,}000 e^{-0{,}005R}\right]^{1/2}$$

$$R^* = -200 \ln\left(\frac{y^*}{5{,}000}\right)$$

We use the simple deterministic formula to calculate our value of y as first approximation. This value is y*=316 units. We now use this value to calculate a value for R* from the formulas above. This value is then again used to calculate a better value for y* and so forth, until the answers that we get stabilize. In our case the eventual answers are:

$y^* = 574$

$R^* = 432$

Thus the optimal solution is to order 575 units at the time when the stock level reaches 433 units. This differs considerably from the simple EOQ formula, which prescribed that we order 316 units when there are 200 units left (the demand during lead time).

Maintenance perspective

The question now remaining is: how do I know what technique to use, and when. The basis of a good maintenance inventory control system should be to classify all items by doing an ABC analysis. We can then control our inventory accordingly:

A items

⇒ Represents those items that are "75%" of the stock value, but 15% of the number of stock items.

⇒ Use the stock control model presented above or at least the economic order quantity formula to determine reorder points and order quantity.

⇒ Set a relatively low buffer (safety) stock if absolutely necessary.

B items

⇒ Represents "20%" of the stock value in "30%" of the number of stock items.

⇒ Use minimum - maximum control. Order economic order quantity when there are still enough items left to cover the time until the minimum is reached.

Set a buffer (minimum) stock that will prevent any unnecessary stock-outs from occurring.

C items

⇒ Represents the bulk of items ("55%") which makes up only 5% of stock value.

⇒ Use fixed interval reordering system.

⇒ Set a liberal safety stock level to prevent stock-outs.

Purchasing

Spare parts, materials, maintenance equipment, facilities, and tools are the lifeblood of a maintenance organization. The efficiency with which these supplies are procured at the right quality, at the proper quality, at the proper place and time, and at the proper price to a large extent determines the result of the maintenance organization.

We have in this chapter concentrated on the inventory control part of the maintenance supply chain. We now shortly look at the purchasing function. This is not meant as a complete discussion of this fairly extensive function, but rather a short overview of three important aspects of the purchasing and supply process. These are:

⇒ Supply line management

⇒ Supplier management

⇒ Purchase price management

Supply line Management

A modern concept in purchasing is that of the supply line. Whereas the purchasing function in the past concentrated only on procurement of supplies from one or more suppliers, there is now the realization that you need to manage the whole supply chain if you want to be able to consistently have the necessary supplies available when needed. This value chain concept realizes that there are much inherent value embedded in the simple truth that all the activities in the chain must add value to get customer satisfaction.

The integrated maintenance materials supply line should have the following characteristics:

⇒ The customer defines the required quality of the purchased product and/or service.

⇒ The pipeline chain links do not act independently; they are all part of one big team process that adds value to the product.

The maintenance supply chain can in essence be pictured as follows:

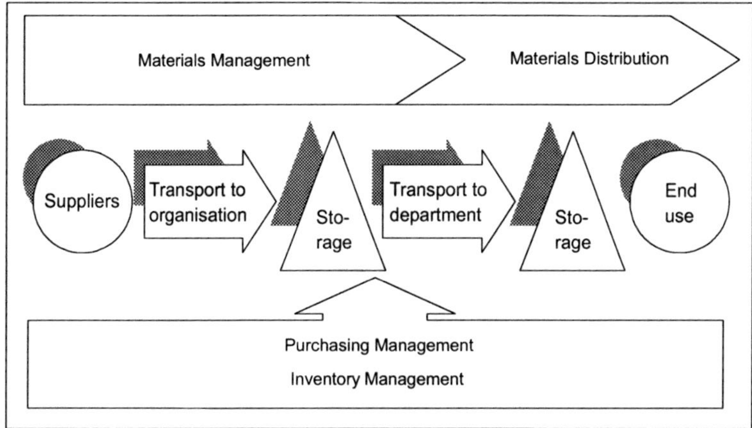

Figure 22.6: Maintenance Supply Chain

Supplier Management

Selecting the right supplier is one of the most important aspects effective of purchasing management. The supplier has a large effect on the price, quality and timeous procurement of the required materials. Selecting the right supplier can prevent out-of-stock situations, unnecessarily high prices and long lead times.

Aspects that should be considered in supplier management:

⇒ What do the maintenance organization regard as the characteristics of a good supplier?

⇒ Should the organization only buy locally, or also nationally or internationally?

⇒ Should the organization buy from distributors only or also directly from manufacturers?

⇒ How many suppliers should the organization have for a specific item?

⇒ If there is no adequate supplier, how does the organization develop acceptable suppliers?

⇒ What process is used to select, classify and certify suppliers?

Purchase Price Management

The price of the purchased material reflects at the same time both the value of product purchased and the cost of maintenance. As it is important to achieve an acceptable maintenance cost per production unit, the correct balance must be struck between the quality of material purchased and the purchase price.

There are different approaches to determine the right price to pay:

Value = Quality / Price

A fair price that ensures acceptable quality at the lowest competitive price.

The cost of manufacturing the piece of equipment has a large influence on the purchase price. Manufacturing cost consists of the following components:

⇒ Direct cost of materials

⇒ Direct labor cost

⇒ Manufacturing overheads

⇒ Profit mark-up

The relationship between the maintenance department and the suppliers of services and products should be mature and transparent. They both have to survive and to make a profit to ensure a long-term successful relationship. Any negotiations between these parties should be done from this viewpoint. The suppliers and maintenance department should understand each other's processes, the cost of manufacturing and the profit margin that both the companies need. They should have a mutual agreement to improve continuously and to share excess profit.

References

1. Coetzee, J.L., Quantitative Techniques in Maintenance Management. Annual short course, 1995.
2. Hugo, W.M.J., Van Rooyen, D.C., and Badenhorst, J.A., Purchasing and Materials Management. Van Schaik Academic, 3rd edition, 1997.
3. Taha, Hamdy A., Operations Research - an introduction. Collier Macmillan, 1976.
4. Westing, J.H., Fine, I.V. and Zenz, Gary J., Purchasing Management, 4th edition. Wiley, 1976.

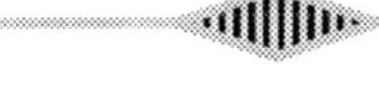

Appendices

This page was left blank on purpose

Use it for notes

Appendix A

Renewal Theory

Definitions

There are four functions that are of primary importance in renewal theory (the so-called reliability functions).

Probability Density Function

The probability density function (p.d.f.) is defined as:

$$f(t) = \frac{1}{N}\frac{\Delta n}{\Delta t} \qquad A.1$$

Δn = Number of failures in time interval $[t, t+\Delta t]$

Δt = Length of time interval

N = Original population

If $\Delta t \to 0$:

$$f(t) = \frac{1}{N}\frac{dn}{dt} \qquad A.2$$

The probability density function gives the probability of failure occurring at any specific time. Its units are failure/item-time. Thus, at any point it gives the probability of a failure occurring during the following time unit. Figure A.1 shows a typical probability density function.

Failure Distribution Function

The failure distribution function is defined as:

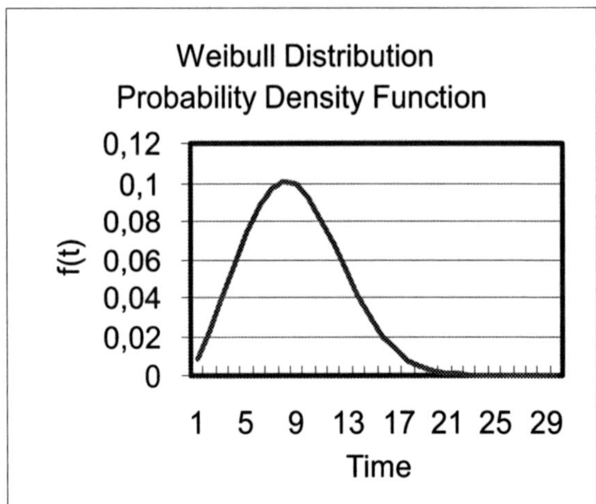

Figure A.1 : Failure Density Function

$$F(t) = \frac{\sum n_i}{N} \qquad \text{A.3}$$

$\sum n_i$ = Number of failures up to time t
N = Original population

If $\Delta t \rightarrow 0$:

$$F(t) = \int_0^t f(t)dt \qquad \text{A.4}$$

A typical failure distribution function is shown in figure A.2. This function gives the cumulative probability of failure. It thus represents the probability that failure has occurred on or before a certain time. It also states that all components will eventually $(F(\infty) = 1)$ fail.

Survival (or Reliability) Function

The survival function R(t) is defined as:

$$R(t) = 1 - F(t) \qquad \text{A.5}$$

The survival (reliability) function is thus the complement of the failure distribution function. It gives the probability of survival up to any specific time t. A typical survival function graph is shown in figure A.3.

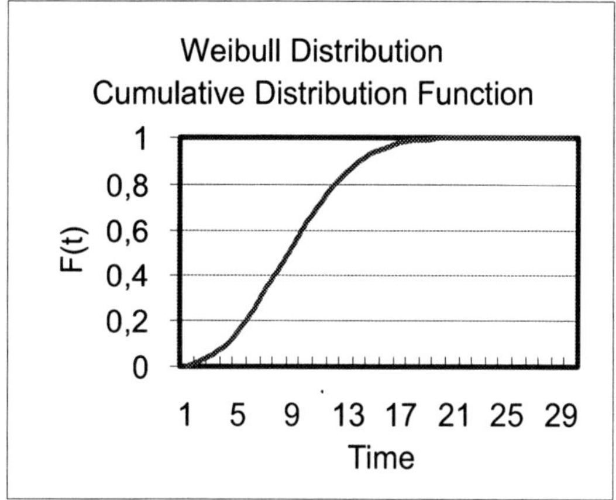

Figure A.2 : Failure Distribution Function

Hazard function

Certainly the most important function in the renewal theory is the hazard function. The shape of the hazard function to a large extent determines what maintenance strategy will be used to maintain a specific component. The hazard rate function is defined as:

$$z(t) = \frac{1}{n(t)} \frac{\Delta n}{\Delta t} \qquad \text{A.6}$$

Δn = Number of failures in time interval $[t, t + \Delta t]$

Δt = Width of time interval

$n(t)$ = Population surviving at time t

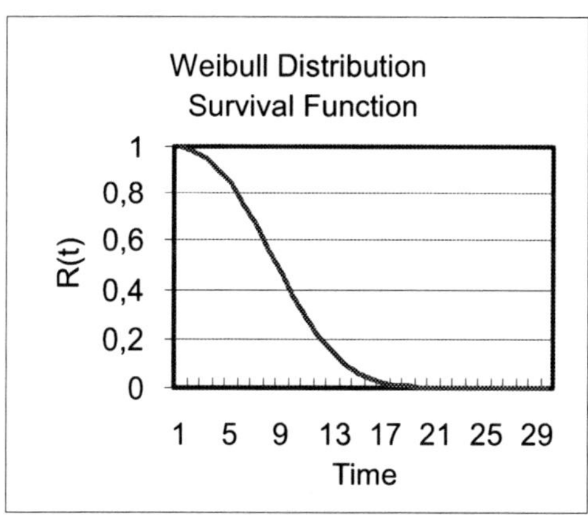

Figure A.3 : Survival Function

A typical example of a hazard function is shown in figure A.4. The following manipulation shows how the definition of z(t) can be translated into a relationship between the Density Function and the Survival Function.

$$z(t) = \frac{1}{n(t)}\frac{\Delta n}{\Delta t}$$

$$= \frac{1}{n(t)} N f(t)$$

$$= \frac{N}{N - \sum n_i} f(t)$$

$$= \frac{1}{\frac{N - \sum n_i}{N}} f(t)$$

$$= \frac{1}{1 - F(t)} f(t)$$

$$= \frac{f(t)}{R(t)} \qquad \text{A.7}$$

As was discussed earlier, the hazard rate gives the risk of failure at any specific time. It is the conditional probability of failure at that time, given that failure has not occurred before then. Figure A.5 shows the three possible shapes of the hazard rate function.

An increasing hazard rate lends itself to a policy of Use Based Preventive Replacement or Use Based Preventive Overhaul, as the hazard af-

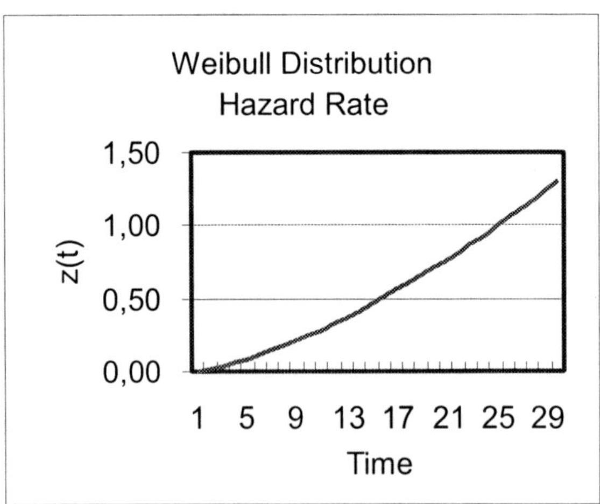

Figure A.4 : Hazard Function

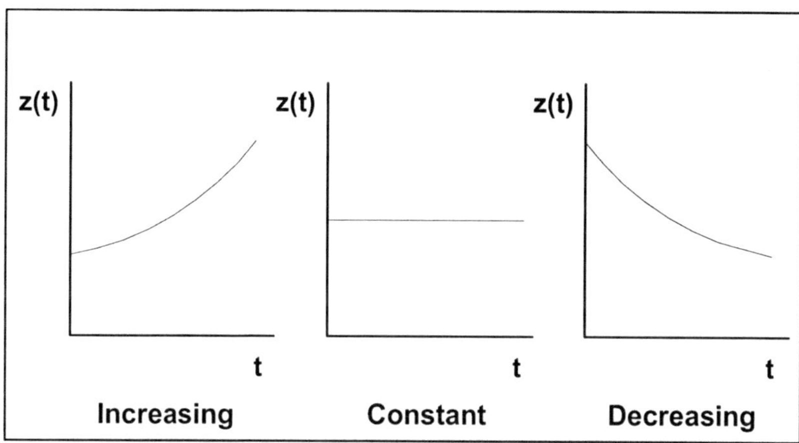

Figure A.5 : The three shapes of the Hazard Function

ter such action will be lower than before it. In the case of constant and decreasing hazards the only policy choices available are condition monitoring or inspection, corrective maintenance and redesign.

Expected life

The expected life of the component is given by:

$$E(t) = \int_{-\infty}^{+\infty} tf(t)dt \qquad \text{A.8}$$

for the case where no preventive replacements take place and:

$$E(t) = \frac{\int_{-\infty}^{t_p} tf(t)dt}{1 - R(t_p)} \qquad \text{A.9}$$

for the case where a preventive replacement (or complete restoration) takes place at time t_p.

Examples

Example 1

The following table gives the operating times at which 10 components failed in the same position (socket). The first failed at 8 hours and were then replaced by a new component. This (new) component lasted a further 12 hours, and so forth.

Table A.1 : Failure data of a typical electronic component

Failure number	*Operating time* h
1	8
2	20
3	34
4	46
5	63
6	86
7	111
8	141
9	186
10	266

Solution:

See table A.2 for the calculation results. The following are sample calculations for the row in table A.2 marked with the asterisk (*).

$$f(t) = \frac{1}{N}\frac{\Delta n}{\Delta t} = \frac{1}{10 \times 12} = 0{,}84 \times 10^{-2}$$

$$F(t) = \frac{\sum_{i=1}^{3} n_i}{N} = \frac{3}{10} = 0{,}3$$

$$R(t) = 1 - F(t) = 1 - 0{,}3 = 0{,}7$$

$$z(t) = \frac{1}{n(t)}\frac{\Delta n}{\Delta t} = \frac{1}{7 \times 12} = 1{,}19 \times 10^{-2}$$

Table A.2 : Results of calculations - example 1

Time interval *h*	*Failure Density* *f(t)* *(x10⁻²)*	*Distribution Function* *F(t)*	*Survival Function* *R(t)*	*Hazard Function* *z(t)* *(x10⁻²)*
0-8	1,25	0,0	1,0	1,25
9-20	0,84	0,1	0,9	0,93
21-34	0,72	0,2	0,8	0,89
35-46	0,84*	0,3*	0,7*	1,19*
47-63	0,59	0,4	0,6	0,98
64-86	0,44	0,5	0,5	0,87
87-111	0,40	0,6	0,4	1,00
112-141	0,33	0,7	0,3	1,11
142-186	0,22	0,8	0,2	1,11
187-266	0,13	0,9	0,1	1,25

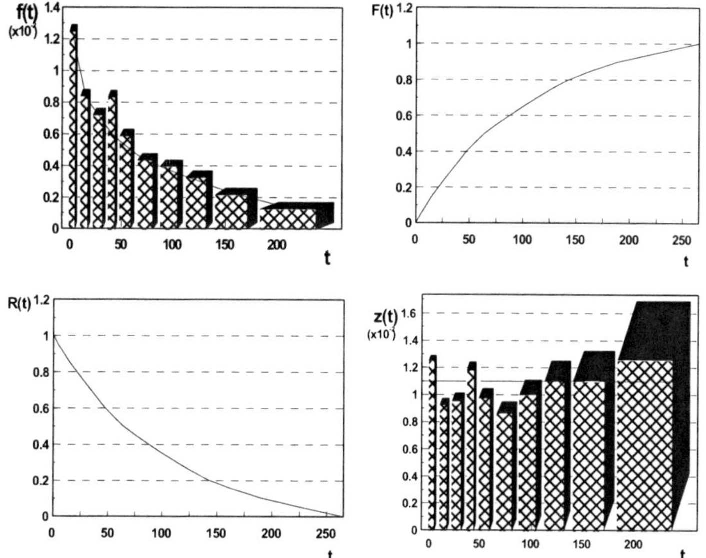

Figure A.6 : Reliability functions for example 1

Example 2

Table A.3 : Failure data for 172 components

Time interval h	*Number of failures*
0-1000	59
1001-2000	24
2001-3000	29
3001-4000	30
4001-5000	17
5001-6000	13

Solution:

Table A.4 : Results for example 2

Time interval h	*Number of failures*	*Failure Density f(t) (x10⁻⁴)*	*Failure Distribution F(t)*	*Survival Function R(t)*	*Hazard Function z(t) (x10⁻⁴)*
0-1000	59	3,43	0,00	1,00	3,43
1001-2000	24	1,40	0,34	0,66	2,12
2001-3000	29	1,69	0,48	0,52	3,26
3001-4000	30	1,74	0,65	0,35	5,00
4001-5000	17	0,99	0,83	0,17	5,69
5001-6000	13	0,76	0,92	0,08	10,00

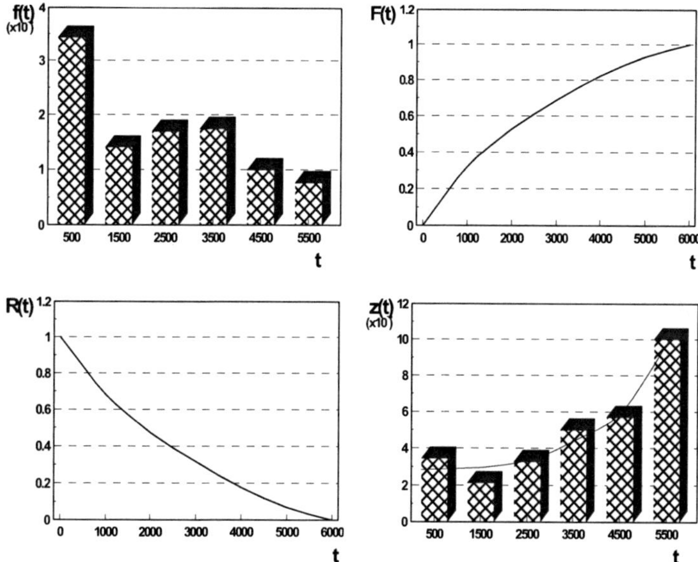

Figure A.7 : Reliability functions for example 2

Weibull Distribution

The Weibull distribution is a distribution that was developed specifically for use in component failure work. It is a very versatile distribution, which could be used for most maintenance renewal problems.

The Weibull density function is given by:

$$f(t) = \frac{\beta}{\eta}\left(\frac{t}{\eta}\right)^{\beta-1} e^{-\left(\frac{t}{\eta}\right)^{\beta}} \qquad \text{A.10}$$

β = Shape parameter

η= Scale parameter

The density function and the cumulative distribution function for the Weibull distribution is shown in figure A.8. As can be seen the special case of β=1 simulates the exponential distribution. For $\beta \approx 3{,}5$ the Weibull distribution simulates the Normal distribution. The (cumulative) distribution function for the Weibull case is given by:

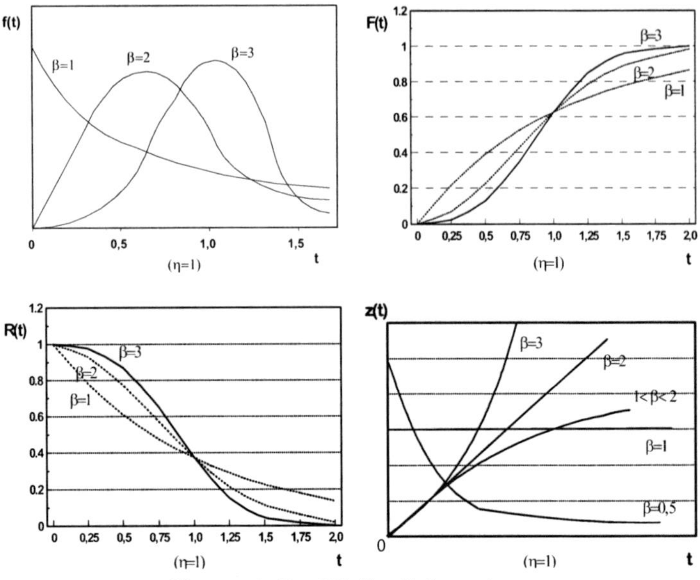

Figure A.8 : Weibull functions

$$F(t) = 1 - e^{-\left(\frac{t}{\eta}\right)^{\beta}} \qquad \text{A.11}$$

The survival function is given by:

$$\begin{aligned} R(t) &= 1 - F(t) \\ &= e^{-\left(\frac{t}{\eta}\right)^{\beta}} \end{aligned} \qquad \text{A.12}$$

The hazard rate function is:

$$\begin{aligned} z(t) &= \frac{f(t)}{R(t)} \\ &= \frac{\beta}{\eta}\left(\frac{t}{\eta}\right)^{\beta-1} \end{aligned} \qquad \text{A.13}$$

It can be seen from the graphs of F(t) and R(t) in figure A.8 that the probability of failure (survival) on or before the expected life ($\eta = 1$) is 63,2% (36,8%) in all cases.

As can be seen from the hazard graphs in figure A.8, a value of a) $\beta<1$ results in a decreasing hazard rate, a value b) $\beta=1$ in a constant hazard rate (exponential case), a value of c) $1<\beta<2$ in a convex increasing hazard, a value d) $\beta=2$ in a hazard that rises in proportion to use and a value e) $\beta>2$ in a concave increasing hazard rate. These values are extremely important as they directly affect, if not determine, the maintenance strategy for the component. In cases a) and b) use based prevention cannot be used (the hazard will not decrease using such maintenance), while use based maintenance is a very valid option in cases c), d) and e) - the use of use based prevention in such cases will depend on the economics involved. The sharper the increase in the hazard with age, the more viable an option use based prevention becomes. Condition based prevention is of course an option in all cases, its viability not depending so much on the hazard involved, but on the physical characteristics of the component's interaction with its environment.

The value of η on the other hand determines the x-axis scale of the various graphs. This parameter (η) is thus called the scale parameter. Another name for η is the characteristic life, which is the same as the expected life. One would thus expect that 63,2% of all components will fail before or at this life (36,8% will survive up to this life).

Parameter Estimation

The shape of the hazard rate curve now determines which continuous distribution can be fitted to the data. Most renewal failure data sets encountered in the maintenance environment can be fitted with one of the Weibull family of distributions. A case could also be made for the use of the Exponential, Gamma, Normal and Lognormal distributions in some cases, but normally the Weibull should suffice. The Normal and Exponential distributions can even be simulated by the Weibull distribution with $\beta\approx3{,}5$ and $\beta=1$ respectively. A special case occurs when the hazard first increases and then decreases over time. The only distribution that can adequately model this situation is the Lognormal distribution.

Following the choice of distribution from the shape of the actual hazard curve, the parameters of the distribution that is to be fitted to the data should be determined. These parameters (like β and η in the case of the Weibull distribution) determines the size and shape of the distribution. This then ensures a fit that can represent the actual data.

Weibull distribution

The estimation of parameters for the Weibull distribution is fairly involved. The Weibull distribution is a two parameter distribution and the procedures followed to estimate the parameters are thus more laborious. We know that for the Weibull distribution:

$$z(t) = \frac{\beta}{\eta}\left(\frac{t}{\eta}\right)^{\beta-1} \qquad \text{A.14}$$

Using the maximum likelihood method, the following two equations are derived:

$$\frac{1}{n}\sum_{i=1}^{n} \ln t_i = \frac{\sum_{i=1}^{n}\left(t_i^{\beta}\ln t_i\right)}{\sum_{i=1}^{n} t_i^{\beta}} - \frac{1}{\beta}$$

$$\eta = \left[\frac{\sum_{i=1}^{n} t_i^{\beta}}{n}\right]^{1/\beta} \qquad \text{A.15}$$

The first equation is used to find the value of β iteratively or by drawing graphs of the left side and right side of the equation for different values of β on the same graph paper. The intersection of the two graphs gives the required value of β. The second equation is then used to calculate η.

Mathematical Modeling

Optimal preventive replacement age of equipment subject to breakdown - optimization of profit/cost

Preventive replacements have been a major maintenance strategy for at least the major part of this century. It remains very important for those components and systems that have an increasing hazard rate and for which the cost of a failure replacement is higher than that of a preventive replacement.

The total replacement cost per cycle is:

$$C_t = C_p R(t_p) + C_f[1 - R(t_p)] \qquad \text{A.16}$$

C_t = Total cost per cycle
C_p = Cost of a preventive cycle
C_f = Cost of a failure cycle

The expected cycle length is: (average life expectancy per unit):

$$L_e = t_p R(t_p) + t_f[1 - R(t_p)] \qquad \text{A.17}$$

L_e = Expected cycle length
t_p = Length of a preventive cycle
t_f = Length of a failure cycle

From equation A.9 we know that:

$$E(t) = \frac{\int_{-\infty}^{t_p} tf(t)dt}{1 - R(t_p)} \qquad \text{A.9}$$

The replacement cost per unit time is:

$$C(t_p) = \frac{C_t}{L_e} = \frac{C_p R(t_p) + C_f[1 - R(t_p)]}{t_p R(t_p) + \int_{-\infty}^{t_p} tf(t)dt} \qquad \text{A.18}$$

The optimum replacement age is calculated by differentiating $C(t_p)$ and equating $\frac{dC(t_p)}{dt}$ to zero.

From this t_p is then calculated for the specific distribution. An alternative method would be to calculate $C(t_p)$ for various values of t_p and constructing a graph from which the optimal t_p value can be read at the point of lowest total replacement cost per unit time.

Optimal preventive replacement age of equipment taking replacement times into account - optimization of profit/cost

The previous model did not take into account the time used (and paid for) to effect preventive and failure replacements. This is not necessarily an oversimplification as in many cases the replacement time is negligible or the preventive and failure replacement times are of similar magnitude.

The total replacement cost per cycle is again given by:

$$C_t = C_p R(t_p) + C_f[1 - R(t_p)] \qquad \text{A.19}$$

C_t = Total cost per cycle

C_p = Cost of a preventive cycle

C_f = Cost of a failure cycle

In the case of the expected cycle length, the effect of the replacement times is evident:

$$L_e = (t_p + T_p)R(t_p) + (t_f + T_f)[1 - R(t_p)] \qquad \text{A.20}$$

T_p = Time needed to make a preventive replacement

T_f = Time needed to make a failure replacement

Again:

$$E(t) = \frac{\int_{-\infty}^{t_p} tf(t)dt}{1 - R(t_p)} \qquad \text{A.9}$$

The replacement cost per unit time in this case is:

$$C(t_p) = \frac{C_t}{L_e} = \frac{C_p R(t_p) + C_f[1 - R(t_p)]}{(t_p + T_p)R(t_p) + \int_{-\infty}^{t_p} tf(t)dt + T_f[1 - R(t_p)]} \qquad \text{A.21}$$

The optimal value of t_p is again determined by differentiation or graphical means.

Optimal preventive replacement age of equipment - optimization of availability

In the two previous models the objective was to minimize the cost of the replacement cycle. Now the objective is to maximize availability by minimizing the effect of downtime.

The total downtime per cycle is:

$$D_t = T_p R(t_p) + T_f[1 - R(t_p)] \qquad \text{A.22}$$

D_t = Total downtime per cycle

T_p = Downtime due to a preventive cycle

T_f = Downtime due to a failure cycle

The expected cycle length is again:

$$L_e = (t_p + T_p)R(t_p) + (t_f + T_f)[1 - R(t_p)] \qquad \text{A.23}$$

T_p = Time needed to make a preventive replacement

T_f = Time needed to make a failure replacement

with

$$E(t) = \frac{\int_{-\infty}^{t_p} tf(t)dt}{1 - R(t_p)} \qquad \text{A.9}$$

The downtime per unit time is:

$$D(t_p) = \frac{D_t}{L_e} = \frac{T_p R(t_p) + T_f[1 - R(t_p)]}{(t_p + T_p)R(t_p) + \int_{-\infty}^{t_p} tf(t)dt + T_f[1 - R(t_p)]} \qquad \text{A.24}$$

The optimal value of t_p is again determined by differentiation or by graphical analysis.

Block replacement

When a number of identical components, with a narrow failure density, work at the same work rate, block replacements may be worthwhile if the cost of a block replacement is lower than that of individual replacements.

The total replacement cost per cycle is:

$$C_t = nC_b + nC_f[1 - R(t_b)] \qquad \text{A.25}$$

C_t = Total cost per cycle
C_b = Cost of a block replacement (per unit)
C_f = Cost of a failure replacement (per unit)
t_b = Length of a block replacement cycle
n = Number of units in block

The replacement cost per unit time:

$$C(t_b) = \frac{nC_b + nC_f[1 - R(t_b)]}{t_b} \qquad \text{A.26}$$

The optimal value of t_b is obtained by differentiation or graphical analysis.

Optimum frequency of inspections (or Condition Monitoring) of components subject to breakdown - profit/cost model

While the previous models (use based prevention) are only valid when the hazard is increasing, condition based prevention can be used regardless of the shape of the hazard function. The present model is thus aimed at optimizing the inspection (or condition monitoring) frequency.

The average total replacement/reconditioning cost per cycle:

$$C_t = C_p\eta_c(t_i) + C_f[1 - \eta_c(t_i)] \qquad \text{A.27}$$

C_t = Total cost per cycle (average)
C_p = Cost of a preventive cycle
C_f = Cost of a failure cycle
$\eta_c(t_i)$ = Inspection efficiency to predict failure
t_i = Time between inspections

The expected average cycle length:

$$L_e = \int_0^{\infty} tf(t)dt + T_p\eta_c(t_i) + T_f\left[1-\eta_c(t_i)\right] \qquad \text{A.28}$$

T_p = Time needed to make a preventive replacement

T_f = Time needed to make a failure replacement

The replacement/reconditioning cost per unit time is:

$$C(t_i) = \frac{C_t}{L_e} = \frac{C_p\eta_c(t_i) + C_f\left[1-\eta_c(t_i)\right]}{\int_0^{\infty} tf(t)dt + T_p\eta_c(t_i) + T_f\left[1-\eta_c(t_i)\right]} \qquad \text{A.29}$$

The optimal value of t_i is determined by differentiation or graphical analysis.

Optimum frequency of inspections (condition monitoring) of components (and equipment) subject to breakdown - availability model

The average total downtime per cycle:

$$D_t = T_p\eta_c(t_i) + T_f[1-\eta_c(t_i)] \qquad \text{A.30}$$

D_t = Total downtime per cycle (average)

T_p = Downtime due to a preventive cycle

T_f = Downtime due to a failure cycle

$\eta_c(t_i)$ = Inspection efficiency to predict failure

t_i = Time between inspections

The expected average cycle length is again:

$$L_e = \int_0^{\infty} tf(t)dt + T_p\eta_c(t_i) + T_f\left[1-\eta_c(t_i)\right] \qquad \text{A.31}$$

T_p = Time needed to make a preventive replacement

T_f = Time needed to make a failure replacement

The downtime per unit time is:

$$D(t_i) = \frac{D_t}{L_e} = \frac{T_p\eta_c(t_i) + T_f[1 - \eta_c(t_i)]}{\int_0^{\infty} tf(t)dt + T_p\eta_c(t_i) + T_f[1 - \eta_c(t_i)]} \qquad \text{A.32}$$

The optimal value of t_i is again determined by differentiation or graphical analysis.

References

1. Coetzee, J.L., Introduction to Maintenance Engineering. Annual short course, 1994.
2. Coetzee, J.L., Maintenance Strategy Setting - a dangerous affair. Maintenance in Mining Conference, Johannesburg, 1996.
3. Jardine, A.K.S., Maintenance, Replacement and Reliability. Pitman, 1979.

This page was left blank on purpose

Use it for notes

This page was left blank on purpose

Use it for notes

Appendix B

Repairable Systems

In the renewal theory we have assumed that repair will always result in the as good as new condition. This is not always true. In such cases we have to resort to alternative analysis techniques. Repairable systems are typically systems (or components) where reliability degradation takes place over time. In such cases we must revert to some type of regression modeling to describe the state of the failure rate over long term time T. This can then be used in mathematical models to optimize maintenance strategy. The regression models that are used for this purpose include Non-homogeneous Poisson Process models and general mathematical functions.

Non-homogeneous Poisson Process models

Two formats of the NHPP model has gained general acceptance. The **first** of these is:

$$\rho_1(T) = e^{\alpha_0 + \alpha_1 T} \qquad \text{B.1}$$

This model models repairable systems when α1>0.

From the definition of a Non-homogeneous Poisson Process it follows that the expected number of failures in the interval (T_1, T_2):

$$E\{N(T_2) - N(T_1)\} = \frac{e^{\alpha_0}}{\alpha_1}\left(e^{\alpha_1 T_2} - e^{\alpha_1 T_1}\right) \qquad \text{B.2}$$

The survival function in the interval (T_1, T_2):

$$R(T_1, T_2) = e^{-\frac{e^{\alpha_0}}{\alpha_1}\left(e^{\alpha_1 T_2} - e^{\alpha_1 T_1}\right)} \qquad \text{B.3}$$

The mean time to failure in the interval (T_1, T_2):

$$MTTF(T_1, T_2) = \frac{\alpha_1 (T_2 - T_1)}{e^{\alpha_0}\left(e^{\alpha_1 T_2} - e^{\alpha_1 T_1}\right)} \quad \text{B.4}$$

The **second** generally accepted NHPP model is the so called "Power law process." This is written as:

$$\rho_2(T) = \lambda \beta T^{\beta - 1} \quad \text{B.5}$$

This model can model repairable system for $\beta>1$. $\beta=2$ gives a linearly increasing failure rate.

The expected number of failures in the interval (T_1, T_2) for this model:

$$E\{N(T_2) - N(T_1)\} = \lambda\left(T_2^{\beta} - T_1^{\beta}\right) \quad \text{B.6}$$

The survival function in the interval (T_1, T_2) is:

$$R(T_1, T_2) = e^{-\lambda\left(T_2^{\beta} - T_1^{\beta}\right)} \quad \text{B.7}$$

and the mean time to failure:

$$MTTF(T_1, T_2) = \frac{(T_2 - T_1)}{\lambda\left(T_2^{\beta} - T_1^{\beta}\right)} \quad \text{B.8}$$

Parameter estimation for the NHPP models

Using maximum likelihood theory, the parameters for the model

$$\rho_1(T) = e^{\alpha_0 + \alpha_1 T} \quad \text{B.1}$$

can be estimated from

$$\sum_{i=1}^{n} T_i + n\alpha_1^{-1} - nT_n\left\{1 - e^{-\alpha_1 T_n}\right\}^{-1} = 0$$

$$\alpha_0 = \ln\left\{\frac{n\alpha_1}{e^{\alpha_1 T_n} - 1}\right\} \quad \text{B.9}$$

T_i = Arrival time to i_{th} failure

n = Number of failures

The parameter α_1 is estimated iteratively from the first equation. This value of α_1 is then substituted into the second equation, which will yield the value of α_0. A simple interactive search or repeated halving can be used to find α_1.

In a similar way the parameters for the NHPP function

$$\rho_2(T) = \lambda\beta T^{\beta-1} \qquad \text{B.5}$$

can be found from

$$\beta = \frac{n}{\sum_{i=1}^{n} \ln \frac{T_n}{T_i}} \qquad \text{B.10}$$

$$\lambda = \frac{n}{T_n^{\beta}}$$

Cost modeling for the NHPP models

Similarly to the renewal cost models, replacement frequency for a repairable system can be calculated from the following equations. For the NHPP model

$$\rho_1(T) = e^{\alpha_0 + \alpha_1 T} \qquad \text{B.1}$$

the optimal replacement interval is calculated interactively from

$$e^{\alpha_1 T^*}\left(T^* - \frac{1}{\alpha_1}\right) = \frac{C_p}{C_f e^{\alpha_0}} - \frac{1}{\alpha_1} \qquad \text{B.11}$$

C_f = Cost of minimal repair of the system at failure

(Minimal repair is repair where renewal does not take place)

C_p = Cost of system replacement

Alternatively the optimal number of failures n* that should be allowed between system replacements can be calculated from:

$$n^* = \frac{(m-1)e^{\alpha_0}}{\alpha_1} \qquad \text{B.12}$$

where m is calculated iteratively from

$$\frac{m}{\alpha_1}\left(\ln m - 1\right) = \frac{C_p}{C_f e^{\alpha_0}} - \frac{1}{\alpha_1} \qquad \text{B.13}$$

For the NHPP model

$$\rho_2(T) = \lambda \beta T^{\beta-1} \qquad \text{B.5}$$

the optimal replacement interval can be calculated from

$$T^* = \left[\frac{C_p}{\lambda(\beta - 1)C_f}\right]^{1/\beta} \qquad \text{B.14}$$

and the optimal number of failures between system replacements from

$$n^* = \frac{C_p}{C_f(\beta - 1)} \qquad \text{B.15}$$

General mathematical models

The successive failure data can also be used to fit a general mathematical model. This can be used to visually inspect the trend in the data and to forecast the future behavior of the system. This is done by fitting a known curve to the data and assuming that any established trend(s) will continue up to the next failure to occur. Any known curve can be fitted to the data, but the array of curves and the fitting and forecasting techniques discussed in chapter 14 should normally suffice.

References

1. Ascher, H. and Feingold, H., Repairable Systems Reliability. Marcel Dekker, 1984.
2. Coetzee, J.L., Introduction to Maintenance Engineering. Annual short course, 1994.
3. Coetzee, J.L., The analysis of failure data with a long term trend. Masters Thesis, University of Pretoria. 1995.
4. Coetzee, J.L., Reliability Degradation and the Equipment Replacement Problem. ICOMS-96, Melbourne, Australia, 1996.

5. Coetzee, J.L., Maintenance Strategy Setting - a dangerous affair. Maintenance in Mining Conference, Johannesburg, 1996.
6. Coetzee, J.L., The role of NHPP models in the practical analysis of maintenance failure data. Reliability Engineering and System Safety **56**, 1997.

This page was left blank on purpose

Use it for notes

Appendix C

Integrated Failure Data Analysis

We have studied two techniques for failure data analysis (appendix A and B). In *renewal theory* we studied the case where the assumption was made that repair (or overhaul) resulted in the *as good as new* situation. In *repairable systems theory*, on the other hand, we studied the case where *reliability degradation* takes place over time and repair is not to the as good as new situation. This is called the *as bad as old* or *minimal repair* situation. In the *first* case (renewal) the component (or system) was repaired (or overhauled) to the as good as new condition. In the *second* case the system (or component) is minimally repaired (or overhauled) at failure to the as bad as old condition. In this last case repair (or overhaul) results in bringing the system (or component) back to the condition it was in just before failure. This does not imply that it will immediately fail again, but that it was not restored to the original (new) condition.

Each of these theories, on its own, presents a viable alternative for maintenance failure data analysis. The problem now is to decide which one of these theories to use when. Of course, one could decide (assume) that one or the other theory is the most viable one, but this will not necessarily lead to the best solution. The better way is to use the data itself to lead one in the analysis process. This approach will be discussed in some detail in the following paragraphs.

Data Trends

The following three data sets have the same set of lives of a component (or system) under scrutiny, but are distinctly different due to a difference in data trend.

14, 34, 42, 72, 244

34, 14, 244, 72, 42

244, 72, 42, 34, 14

The first data set exhibits a situation of reliability growth (lives are getting longer) and is called a "happy" data set. The second set displays no specific trend and is called a "noncommittal" data set. In the last case a deterioration in the consecutive lives of the component is evident. This data set is called a "sad" data set. Figure C.1 depicts this difference pictorially.

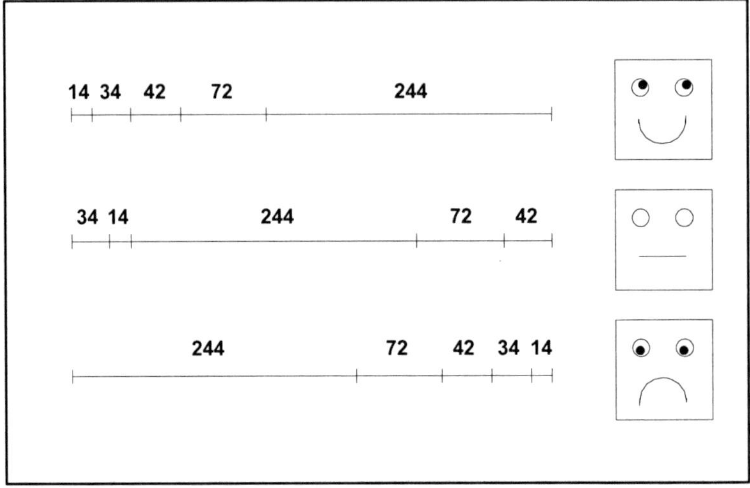

Figure C.1 : Three data sets: "Happy", "Noncommittal" and "Sad"

Only the noncommittal data set is independent and identically distributed (iid). The subsequent failures in the data set thus:

⇒ Can be assumed to come from the same statistical distribution.

⇒ Are independent of one another. The one failure thus has no influence on the next.

This (the data being iid) implies that the various failure times of the failure data set can be re-ordered into intervals as we did in *renewal theory*. This is not the case for "sad" data, where we have reliability degradation. In this case we must make use of *repairable systems theory* to analyze the data. The same is true for "happy" data, where we have a situation of reliability growth. We again have to make use of repairable systems theory, although we did not discuss the cost models involved in the analysis of "happy" data. In short, when we have a data trend ("happy" or "sad"), the data is not iid and renewal theory is not applicable. In such cases repairable systems theory must be applied for the analysis. If we do not have a trend, we can assume that subsequent data points come from the same distribution, but they are not necessarily independent. We thus need two tests, a trend test and dependence test to ensure that a data set is iid before applying renewal theory. In practice, data independence is normally assumed. Figure C.2 depicts the analysis process.

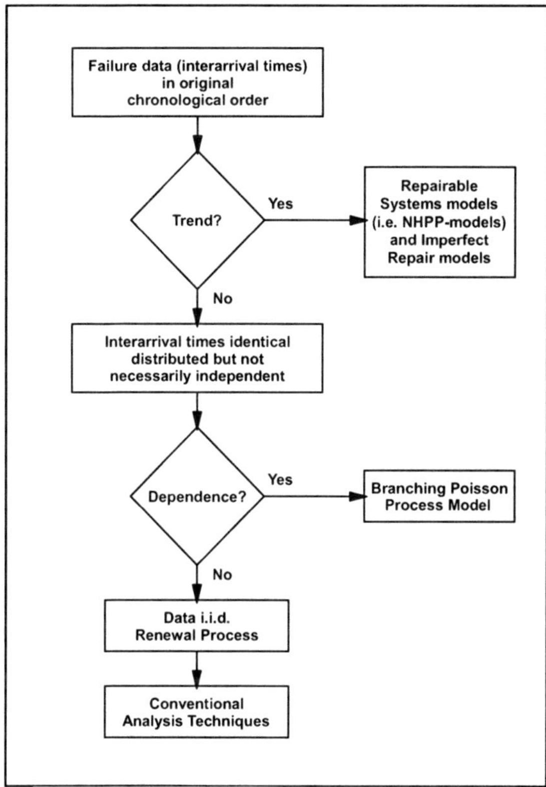

Figure C.2 : Data Analysis Framework

As can be seen for data without a trend but where independence is not proven, a branching Poisson process is the correct one for analysis. We will assume, for the purpose of this book, that data independence always exists. This is not an unreasonable assumption in most practical situations.

A Word of Caution

It is important not to confuse the concepts of "happy", "noncommittal" and "sad" data sets (terms to describe data trend) with the shape of the hazard rate curve. The hazard rate curve spells out the change in hazard over the life of a specific component. Data trend however, shows the change in the actual lives of successive installations of different components of the same type. Figure C.3 intends to illustrate this difference.

In this figure, the noncommittal data set can at any point in time have an increasing, constant or decreasing hazard rate. For data with a trend no hazard rate curve can be drawn, as the data is not iid.

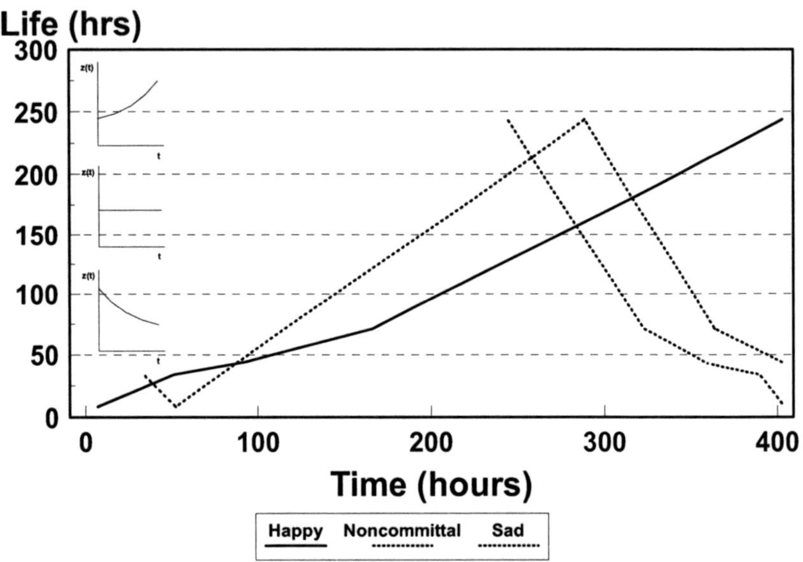

Figure C.3 : Data trend curves versus Hazard curves

Laplace Trend Test

A simple test for trend was developed in 1773 by Laplace. This remains the best test for trend in many failure analysis situations. If the n successive lives in a certain application are depicted by

$$t_1, t_2, t_3, \ldots\ldots\ldots \quad \ldots\ldots\ldots \quad \ldots\ldots t_n$$

and the arrival times to failure by

$$T_1, T_2, T_3, \ldots\ldots\ldots \quad \ldots\ldots\ldots \quad \ldots\ldots T_n$$

$$\text{with } T_k = \sum_{i=1}^{k} t_i \qquad \text{C.1}$$

then the standardized variate

$$L = \frac{\frac{1}{n-1}\sum_{i=1}^{n-1} T_i - \frac{T_n}{2}}{T_n\left[\frac{1}{12(n-1)}\right]^{\frac{1}{2}}} \qquad \text{C.2}$$

has a normal distribution with mean 0 and variance 1 (at the 5 % level of significance) under the null hypothesis of the data being iid. This variate is now calculated for the specific data set. If the result of the calculation is small (negative) it shows that the sample mean of the first n-1 lives is small compared with the midpoint of the observation interval $t_n/2$. This indicates an improvement in reliability or a "happy" data set. Likewise, a large (positive) result implies a "sad" data set and a result near to zero a noncommittal data set. For our three demonstration data sets these values are:

-2,1 "Happy" data set

-0,3 "Noncommittal" data set

+2,1 "Sad" data set

A value of the Laplace variate between -1 and +1 implies a noncommittal data set, while values smaller than -2 and larger than +2 implies "happy" and "sad" data sets respectively. The region between -2 and -1 and the region between +1 and +2 are gray areas where a case could be made for the application of either renewal theory or repairable systems theory. As one progresses from +1 to +2 (or from -1 to -2), the case for the application of renewal theory becomes weaker and weaker. The repairable systems theory can of course be applied in all cases, but will not provide meaningful information in the case of i.i.d. data (no trend).

References

1. Ascher, H. and Feingold, H., Repairable Systems Reliability. Marcel Dekker, 1984.
2. Coetzee, J.L., Introduction to Maintenance Engineering. Annual short course, 1994.
3. Coetzee, J.L., The analysis of failure data with a long term trend. Masters Thesis, University of Pretoria. 1995.
4. Coetzee, J.L., Reliability Degradation and the Equipment Replacement Problem. ICOMS-96, Melbourne, Australia, 1996.

5. Coetzee, J.L., Maintenance Strategy Setting - a dangerous affair. Maintenance in Mining Conference, Johannesburg, 1996.
6. Coetzee, J.L., The role of NHPP models in the practical analysis of maintenance failure data. Reliability Engineering and System Safety **56**, 1997.

Appendix D

Selected Failure Data Analysis examples

The examples are split into two categories, those where the *renewal theory* applies and those where the *repairable systems* theory applies. The answers to these examples have all been calculated using standard spreadsheet software. The tables and graphs that are shown, are copies of parts of these spreadsheets. It is recommended that the reader redo these examples on an own spreadsheet model and compare it with the answers supplied here.

The examples are done such that, in each category, the first example is done in full detail, and each subsequent one in less detail. The idea is to, in the first example, show how such an analysis should be done. In following examples the accent is then more on putting the problem to the reader, providing the correct answers and pointing to any notable results.

The objective in each of these calculations is to find the correct maintenance strategy for that specific situation.

Renewal theory

Example 1

The lives (in days) of the line switches used on a loco over a period of one year is as follows:

5, 19, 14, 7, 16, 4, 20, 16, 7, 24, 11, 8, 6, 7, 21,
26, 12, 3, 11, 5, 6, 4, 5, 4, 16, 5, 13, 18, 20, 4, 6

The cost of a new line switch is \$ 830, labor cost to replace the switch after failure is \$ 360 while the labor cost to replace it preventively is \$ 65, traveling cost of breakdown crew to failed locomotive is \$ 160 and loss of revenue due to the locomotive being out of service is \$ 800. The time to effect a failure replacement is 3 hours, while the preventive task takes 0.6 hours.

The cost and time data is translated into the parameters C_p, C_f, T_p and T_f as follows:

$$C_p = \$830 + \$65 = \$895$$

$$C_f = \$830 + \$360 + \$160 + \$800 = \$2150$$

$$T_p = \frac{0{,}6}{24} = 0.025 \text{days}$$

$$T_f = \frac{3}{24} = 0.125 \text{days}$$

Doing a Laplace trend test on the failure data yields 0.5771 (see table on next page) - thus the data is without a trend and Renewal Techniques can be used. Fitting a two parameter Weibull distribution yields $\beta = 1.754$ and $\eta = 12.505$ (see table on next page).

The value of β (the shape parameter) that lies between 1 and 2 tells us that *firstly* the hazard rate is increasing, *secondly* that its rate of increase is higher when the switch is fairly new, than when its older (the hazard rate increases in a convex way) and *thirdly* that, if the cost of failure is not much higher than the cost of prevention (because of the convex shape of z(t)), use based maintenance will probably not be an option.

The value of η (the scale parameter) of 12.5 days *firstly* informs us that the life of the component can be measured on a scale probably not exceeding $2\eta = 25$ days. *Secondly* η is also the characteristic life, which gives us an indication of the expected life. That is, this is the life that we would expect of a typical line switch (the actual expected life when using equation A.8 in a numerical integration is 11.13 days). *Thirdly*, we know that 63.2 % of all line switches will fail before or at this life. Alternatively, one could say that 36.8 % of line switches will survive up to this life (that is, will have lives higher than 12.5 days). Does this life (12.5 days) have some significance in terms of the replacement of the component? Should we replace the component before this age, or at this age, or how long after this age? None of these. We cannot decide upon the proper life of the component without an economic study. That is exactly what we will do now.

Doing a cost analysis gives a minimum cost level of \$ 177.98 / day at a replacement interval of 13 days (see table and graph over the page). The sensitivity of the answer is fairly low. If the time between replacements is increased by 20% to 16 days, the cost increases by only 1%. If the switch is just left to fail, the cost increases to \$ 190.93 per day, which is a 7.3% increase. Thus, the strategy should be to replace the line switch only on failure (because the difference between the opti-

Laplace Trend Test

Laplace
0.577138722

t	T
5	5
19	24
14	38
7	45
16	61
4	65
20	85
16	101
7	108
24	132
11	143
8	151
6	157
7	164
21	185
26	211
12	223
3	226
11	237
5	242
6	248
4	252
5	257
4	261
16	277
5	282
13	295
18	313
20	333
4	337
6	343

Parameter estimation

Beta	1.754254621	LH	2.209142255
Eta	12.50504279	RH	2.209142254

ti	ti^Beta	ln ti	ti^Beta ln ti
5	16.83338126	1.609437912	27.09228199
19	175.0892221	2.944438979	515.5395305
14	102.4708651	2.63905733	270.4264875
7	30.37505981	1.945910149	59.10713716
16	129.5188691	2.772588722	359.1025557
4	11.38063571	1.386294361	15.7769111
20	191.5745798	2.995732274	573.9061515
16	129.5188691	2.772588722	359.1025557
7	30.37505981	1.945910149	59.10713716
24	263.7800513	3.17805383	838.3072025
11	67.12247008	2.397895273	160.9526537
8	38.39279966	2.079441542	79.83558251
6	23.17797161	1.791759469	41.52935012
7	30.37505981	1.945910149	59.10713716
21	208.6936849	3.044522438	635.3726063
26	303.5453148	3.258096538	988.9799393
12	78.1913457	2.48490665	194.2981949
3	6.870560461	1.098612289	7.548082153
11	67.12247008	2.397895273	160.9526537
5	16.83338126	1.609437912	27.09228199
6	23.17797161	1.791759469	41.52935012
4	11.38063571	1.386294361	15.7769111
5	16.83338126	1.609437912	27.09228199
4	11.38063571	1.386294361	15.7769111
16	129.5188691	2.772588722	359.1025557
5	16.83338126	1.609437912	27.09228199
13	89.97881578	2.564949357	230.7911057
18	159.2456553	2.890371758	460.2791448
20	191.5745798	2.995732274	573.9061515
4	11.38063571	1.386294361	15.7769111
6	23.17797161	1.791759469	41.52935012
SUM	2605.724184	68.48340992	7241.789388

Example 1

Cost Model - replacement taken into account

Cp	895	Tp	0.025	Interval	1
Cf	2150	Tf	0.125		
Beta	1.754255	Eta	12.50504		

t	f(t)	tf(t)dt	integral (tf(t)dt)	R(tp)	C(tp)
0	0.000000	0.000000	0.000000	1.000000	35800.000000
1	0.020623	0.020623	0.020623	0.988174	879.091849
2	0.033818	0.067636	0.088260	0.960660	463.264504
3	0.044045	0.132136	0.220395	0.921513	329.215515
4	0.051860	0.207440	0.427835	0.873372	266.209358
5	0.057511	0.287557	0.715391	0.818514	231.444971
6	0.061192	0.367153	1.082544	0.759006	210.607666
7	0.063096	0.441675	1.524219	0.696722	197.567370
8	0.063434	0.507469	2.031688	0.633336	189.267647
9	0.062427	0.561844	2.593532	0.570303	184.016960
10	0.060308	0.603077	3.196609	0.508852	180.804608
11	0.057305	0.630360	3.826969	0.449982	178.990004
12	0.053642	0.643709	4.470678	0.394461	178.147671
13	0.049525	0.643825	5.114503	0.342848	177.984116
14	0.045140	0.631953	5.746456	0.295501	178.290624
15	0.040648	0.609719	6.356176	0.252604	178.915194
16	0.036187	0.578985	6.935161	0.214194	179.745192
17	0.031865	0.541705	7.476866	0.180184	180.696279

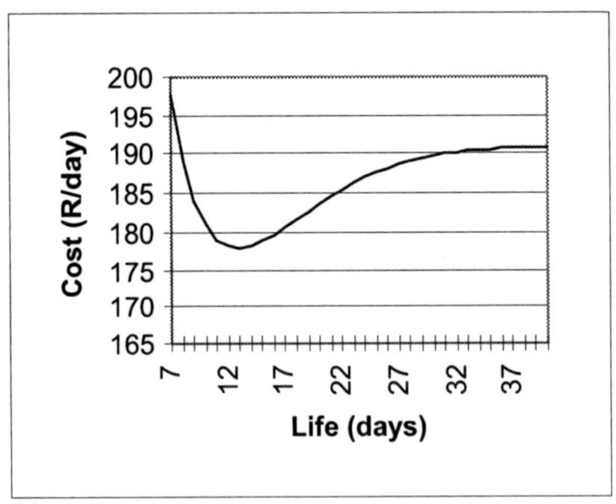

Example 1

mum and the run to failure cost is too low. However, one may opt to still practice preventive replacement based on the availability model (page 415) because the failure of a locomotive while in service is not acceptable from a service perspective. Otherwise, redesign may be the only option left.

Example 2

A bearing in a plant causes a high level of production loss. The following lives (in days) comes from failure data of the bearing:

74, 84, 62, 21, 49, 52, 59, 92, 44, 110, 76, 92, 60, 71, 43, 104, 84, 94, 79, 123, 95, 45, 76

The cost of failure repair is $ 28 808 and that for prevention $ 4 808.

The Laplace Trend Test yields -0.561. Thus we can use renewal techniques. The fit yields $\beta = 3.386$ and $\eta = 81.808$ days. Doing a cost exercise, yielding an optimum of 40 days @ $ 173.58 per day. The sensitivity in this case is very high, so that it is of paramount importance that the component be replaced on or near to the optimum of 40 days. The cost of running to failure is $ 391.61 per day. See the supporting tables and graphs on the next two pages. The strategy should thus be to replace the bearing every 40 days.

Example 3

The following failure data comes from a large mining shovel's dipper arm:

918, 759, 619, 1140, 1474, 137, 275, 1037, 1087 (hours)

The result of the Laplace test is -0,1166 and the values of β and η are 2.108 and 928.32 respectively. The cost of a failure (corrective) replacement is $ 350 000 and that of a preventive replacement $ 46 000. The large difference in cost between a corrective and a preventive strategy is that when the arm fails it has to be replaced with a new one, whereas it can be reconditioned under preventive circumstances.

The optimum time based prevention frequency is calculated to be 365 hours at a average cost of $ 245.31 per hour. Leaving it to run to failure will produce an average cost of $ 377.03 per hour. The sensitivity is again so high that it is important to recondition the arm at 40 days. No supporting tables and graphs are shown for this example.

Laplace Trend Test

Laplace
-0.561017346

t	T
74	74
84	158
62	220
21	241
49	290
52	342
59	401
92	493
44	537
110	647
76	723
92	815
60	875
71	946
43	989
104	1093
84	1177
94	1271
79	1350
123	1473
95	1568
45	1613
76	1689

Parameter estimation

Beta	3.386	LH	4.230250115
Eta	81.80859334	RH	4.230282427

ti	ti^Beta	ln ti	ti^Beta*lnti
74	2134118.856	4.304065093	9185386.472
84	3278005.384	4.430816799	14524241.32
62	1172298.639	4.127134385	4838234.021
21	29994.01	3.044522438	91317.43645
49	528450.0301	3.891820298	2056632.554
52	646230.3067	3.951243719	2553413.44
59	991071.3266	4.077537444	4041130.444
92	4460520.949	4.521788577	20169532.67
44	367054.6773	3.784189634	1389004.505
110	8168750.508	4.700480366	38397051.38
76	2335795.533	4.33073334	10115707.59
92	4460520.949	4.521788577	20169532.67
60	1049107.843	4.094344562	4295408.992
71	1855071.993	4.262679877	7907578.056
43	339565.9936	3.761200116	1277175.654
104	6755770.486	4.644390899	31376438.96
84	3278005.384	4.430816799	14524241.32
94	4797455.028	4.543294782	21796252.4
79	2662964.219	4.369447852	11635683.29
123	11923910.49	4.812184355	57380055.53
95	4972469.495	4.553876892	22644013.93
45	396075.1284	3.80666249	1507724.334
76	2335795.533	4.33073334	10115707.59
SUM	68939002.77	97.29575263	311991464.6

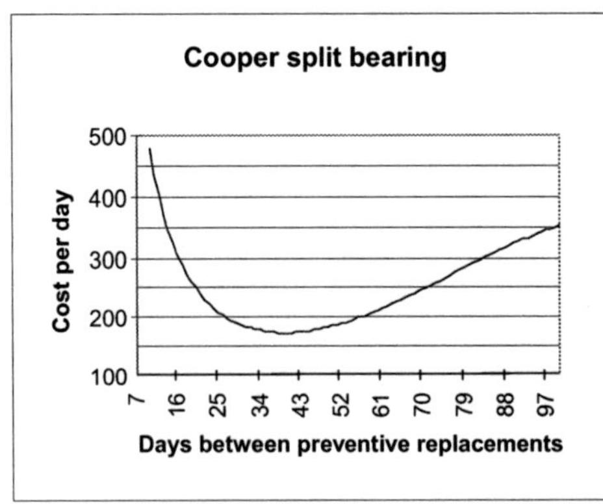

Example 2

Cp	4808	Tp	0.083333333	Interval	1
Cf	28808	Tf	0.083333333		
Beta	3.386	Eta	81.808		

t	f(t)	tf(t)dt	integral (tf(t)dt)	R(tp)	C(tp)
0	0.00000	0.00000	0.00000	1.00000	57696
1	0.00000	0.00000	0.00000	1.00000	4438.157976
2	0.00001	0.00001	0.00001	1.00000	2307.873574
3	0.00002	0.00005	0.00006	0.99999	1559.44927
4	0.00003	0.00012	0.00018	0.99996	1177.672978
5	0.00005	0.00026	0.00045	0.99992	946.191786
6	0.00008	0.00049	0.00093	0.99986	790.9148292
7	0.00012	0.00082	0.00175	0.99976	679.5927167
8	0.00016	0.00129	0.00304	0.99962	595.9360173
9	0.00021	0.00192	0.00497	0.99943	530.8298311
10	0.00027	0.00275	0.00771	0.99919	478.776076
11	0.00034	0.00379	0.01150	0.99888	436.2617687
12	0.00042	0.00509	0.01659	0.99850	400.9375472
13	0.00051	0.00667	0.02325	0.99803	371.1729278
14	0.00061	0.00856	0.03182	0.99747	345.8010423
15	0.00072	0.01081	0.04263	0.99680	323.9649184
16	0.00084	0.01344	0.05607	0.99602	305.0211084
17	0.00097	0.01649	0.07255	0.99512	288.4771662
18	0.00111	0.01999	0.09254	0.99408	273.9498697
19	0.00126	0.02397	0.11651	0.99289	261.136579
20	0.00142	0.02848	0.14500	0.99155	249.7951517
21	0.00160	0.03355	0.17854	0.99004	239.7295732
22	0.00178	0.03920	0.21774	0.98835	230.7794917
23	0.00198	0.04548	0.26323	0.98648	222.8124724
24	0.00218	0.05242	0.31565	0.98440	215.7181812
25	0.00240	0.06005	0.37571	0.98210	209.4039592
26	0.00263	0.06841	0.44411	0.97959	203.7914147
27	0.00287	0.07751	0.52163	0.97684	198.8137693
28	0.00312	0.08740	0.60903	0.97384	194.4137707
29	0.00338	0.09810	0.70713	0.97059	190.5420358
30	0.00365	0.10964	0.81677	0.96707	187.1557228
31	0.00394	0.12203	0.93880	0.96328	184.2174597
32	0.00423	0.13530	1.07410	0.95920	181.6944729
33	0.00453	0.14948	1.22357	0.95482	179.5578723
34	0.00484	0.16456	1.38814	0.95013	177.7820625
35	0.00516	0.18058	1.56872	0.94514	176.3442542
36	0.00549	0.19753	1.76625	0.93981	175.2240557
37	0.00582	0.21543	1.98168	0.93416	174.4031309
38	0.00617	0.23428	2.21596	0.92817	173.8649102
39	0.00651	0.25407	2.47003	0.92183	173.5943459
40	0.00687	0.27480	2.74484	0.91513	173.577703
41	0.00723	0.29646	3.04130	0.90808	173.8023814
42	0.00760	0.31904	3.36034	0.90067	174.2567627
43	0.00797	0.34252	3.70286	0.89289	174.9300778
44	0.00834	0.36687	4.06973	0.88474	175.8122928
45	0.00871	0.39206	4.46178	0.87621	176.8940102
46	0.00909	0.41806	4.87984	0.86731	178.1663822
47	0.00946	0.44483	5.32466	0.85804	179.6210361
48	0.00984	0.47232	5.79698	0.84839	181.2500077
49	0.01021	0.50049	6.29747	0.83836	183.0456845
50	0.01059	0.52927	6.82675	0.82796	185.0007547

Example 2

Example 4

A load-haul-dump machine has had tram motor lives of:

26, 26, 13, 9, 9, 13, 22, 22, 13, 9, 18, 31, 36 (weeks)

The cost of prevention is \$ 7 500 and that of failure \$ 20 500. Analysis of the data leads to a Laplace trend value of -0,489. The values of the parameters are $\beta = 2.405$ and $\eta = 21.537$ days. The optimum time for preventive replacement/overhaul is every 15 days at a cost of \$ 894.84 per day. Run to failure will cost \$ 951.85 per day.

The relative insensitivity of the cost will conceivably lead to a corrective strategy being chosen in this case.

Repairable Systems

Example 5

The following data represents the chronological failures of a power station feed pump in days:

40, 27, 51, 4, 16, 11, 6, 7, 1, 1, 14, 14, 4, 6, 9, 5, 4, 1, 11, 8, 13, 11, 3, 1, 12, 13, 17, 24, 9, 1, 12, 13, 2, 1, 13

A Laplace trend test on this failure data yields a value of 1.952. This is a fairly good indication of reliability degradation. The data are thus not i.i.d. and renewal techniques cannot be used. We thus decide to use NHPP-models. In this specific case the model $\rho_1(T)$ was decided upon. The resultant fit is shown on the next page. The values of the parameters for the fitted function is α_0=-3.14 and α_1=0.0035.

Additional information that is available is that it costs \$ 2500.00 on average to repair the pump each time it fails. Replacement of the total pump will cost \$ 45 000.00. The resultant optimal age for replacement of the pump is 328 days or at the 27_{th} failure. In both cases the resultant optimal cost is \$ 334,50 per day.

A set of graphs for this example is shown over the page. The *failure rate* in number of failures per day is concave upwards as is always the case with $\rho_1(T)$. Likewise the *expected cumulative number of failures* concave upwards. As can be expected, the optimal age (328 days) coincide with the optimal number of failures (27). The *cumulative mean time to failure* is a decreasing function, with CMTTF(328)≈12 days. The probability of survival over the next 50 days is a decreasing func-

Input Values		Results		Cost results per cycle				Iteration results			
n	35	alpha0	-3.139247108	Failure	Replacement	Total	Cost/day		m	LH	RH
Tn	385	alpha1	0.003470373	R	R	R	R	Fit		-3.96903E-09	0
Cf	2500	T*	328.8492884	65000	45000	110000	334.50	T*		127.4031328	127.40
Cp	45000	n*	27	65000	45000	110000	334.50	n*	3.1306163	127.4031703	127.40

Failure	ti	Ti
1	40	40
2	27	67
3	51	118
4	4	122
5	16	138
6	11	149
7	6	155
8	7	162
9	1	163
10	1	164
11	14	178
12	14	192
13	4	196
14	6	202
15	9	211
16	5	216
17	4	220
18	1	221
19	11	232
20	8	240
21	13	253
22	11	264
23	3	267
24	1	268
25	12	280
26	13	293
27	17	310
28	24	334
29	9	343
30	1	344
31	12	356
32	13	369
33	2	371
34	1	372
35	13	385

Ti	ρ	N(T)	E(N(T))	CMTBF	R(0,T)	R(ΔTi)	Cost/day if replaced at Ti R/day
0	0.0433	0	0.0		1.00E+00	0.0939	
50	0.0515	1	2.4	21.1414	9.39E-02	0.0600	
100	0.0613	2	5.2	19.3118	5.64E-03	0.0352	
150	0.0729	6	8.5	17.5966	1.99E-04	0.0187	433.33
200	0.0867	13	12.5	15.9941	3.71E-06	0.0088	375.00
250	0.1031	20	17.2	14.5019	3.26E-08	0.0036	350.00
300	0.1227	26	22.9	13.1173	1.17E-10	0.0012	333.33
350	0.1459	30	29.6	11.8366	1.44E-13	0.0003	335.71
400	0.1736	35	37.5	10.6561	4.99E-17	0.0001	343.75
450	0.2065		47.0	9.5715	3.82E-21	0.0000	361.11
500	0.2456		58.3	8.5780	4.85E-26	0.0000	380.00
550	0.2921		71.7	7.6711	7.28E-32	0.0000	404.55
600	0.3475		87.6	6.8455	8.60E-39	0.0000	437.50
650	0.4133		106.6	6.0963	4.95E-47	0.0000	476.92
700	0.4917		129.2	5.4184	7.83E-57	0.0000	525.00
750	0.5848		156.0	4.8067	1.72E-68	0.0000	580.00
800	0.6956		188.0	4.2561	2.33E-82	0.0000	640.63
850	0.8274		225.9	3.7620	7.47E-99	0.0000	714.71
900	0.9842		271.1	3.3195	1.8E-118	0.0000	802.78
950	1.1707		324.9	2.9243	8.2E-142	0.0000	900.00
1000	1.3925		388.8	2.5721	1.4E-169	0.0000	1015.00
1050	1.6564		464.8	2.2590	1.4E-202	0.0000	1147.62
1100	1.9703		555.3	1.9811	7.2E-242	0.0000	1302.27
1150	2.3436		662.8	1.7350	1.4E-288	0.0000	1478.26
1200	2.7877		790.8	1.5175	0.00E+00	0.0000	1683.33
1250	3.3159		943.0	1.3256	0.00E+00	0.0000	1920.00
1300	3.9442		1124.0	1.1565	0.00E+00	0.0000	2196.15
1350	4.6915		1339.4	1.0079	0.00E+00	0.0000	2512.96
1400	5.5805		1595.6	0.8774	0.00E+00	0.0000	2880.36
1450	6.6379		1900.2	0.7631	0.00E+00	0.0000	3306.90
1500	7.8957		2262.7	0.6629	0.00E+00	0.0000	3800.00
1550	9.3918		2693.8	0.5754	0.00E+00	0.0000	4372.58
1600	11.1713		3206.6	0.4990	0.00E+00	0.0000	5037.50
1650	13.2881		3816.5	0.4323	0.00E+00	0.0000	5809.09
1700	15.8060		4542.1	0.3743	0.00E+00	0.0000	6705.88
1750	18.8009		5405.1	0.3238	0.00E+00	0.0000	7747.14
1800	22.3634		6431.6	0.2799	0.00E+00	0.0000	8956.94
1850	26.6009		7652.6	0.2417	0.00E+00	0.0000	10364.86
1900	31.6413		9105.1	0.2087	0.00E+00	0.0000	12003.95
1950	37.6368		10832.7	0.1800	0.00E+00	0.0000	13910.26
2000	44.7683		12887.7	0.1552	0.00E+00		

Example 5

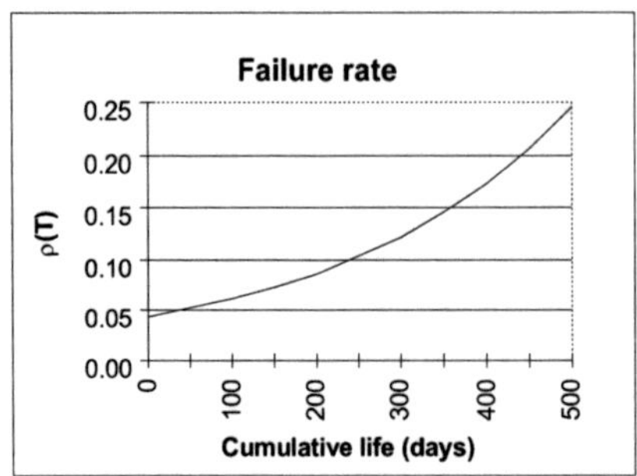
Failure rate
ρ(T)
0.25
0.20
0.15
0.10
0.05
0.00
0
100
200
300
400
500
Cumulative life (days)

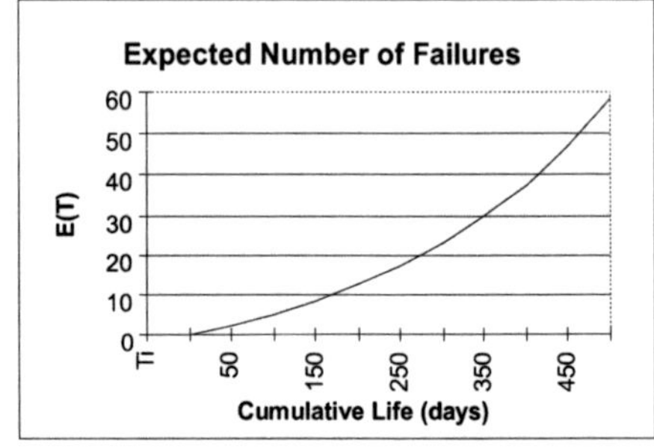
Expected Number of Failures
E(T)
60
50
40
30
20
10
0
Ti
50
150
250
350
450
Cumulative Life (days)

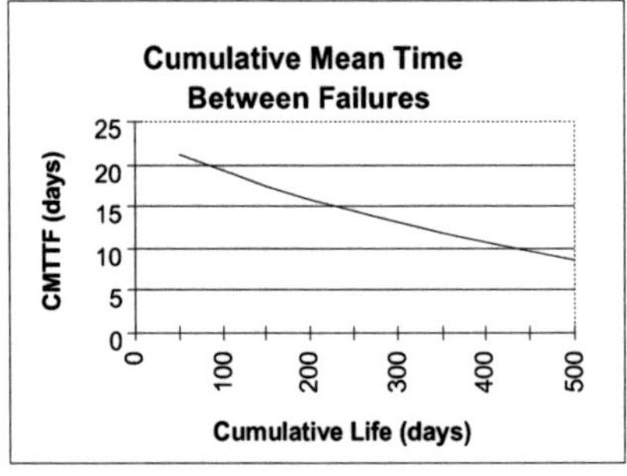
Cumulative Mean Time Between Failures
CMTTF (days)
25
20
15
10
5
0
0
100
200
300
400
500
Cumulative Life (days)

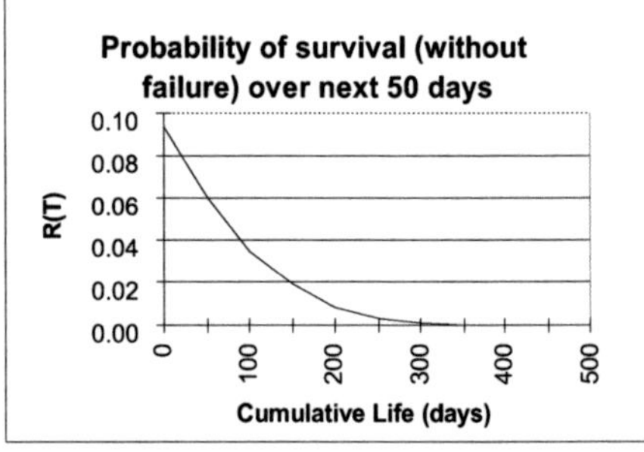
Probability of survival (without failure) over next 50 days
R(T)
0.10
0.08
0.06
0.04
0.02
0.00
0
100
200
300
400
500
Cumulative Life (days)

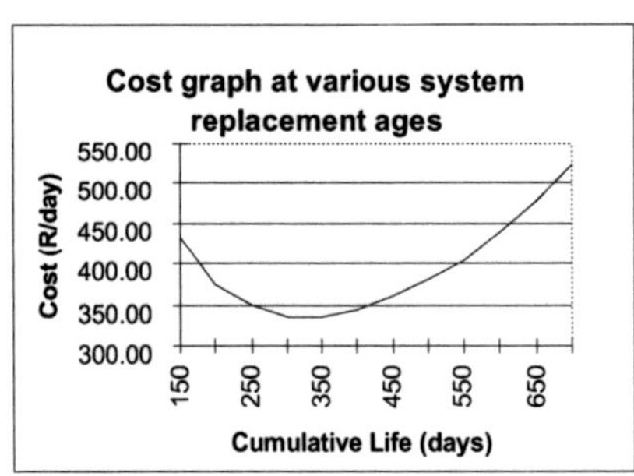
Cost graph at various system replacement ages
Cost (R/day)
550.00
500.00
450.00
400.00
350.00
300.00
150
250
350
450
550
650
Cumulative Life (days)

Example 5

tion as well and reaches a zero probability at around the optimal system replacement age. This is accidental and will not always be the case, as this point depends on both the failure characteristics and the cost characteristics of the particular case. The cost graph shows that it is fairly important that the system should be replaced at an age around the optimal age. As long as replacement is done at an age ranging from 250 days to 450 days, the cost is within 10% of the optimal, but outside these bounds it increases sharply.

This page was left blank on purpose

Use it for notes

Appendix E - Example Maintenance Policy document

Maintenance Policy - XYZ Company

Introduction

The effective use and maintenance of a company's assets has a significant effect on the general level of productivity. The cost of maintenance at XYZ constitutes a large portion of the total operational cost. It is thus necessary to formulate a purposeful maintenance policy to direct the Maintenance Department towards optimal results. In this venture the XYZ Mission, and the quality principles are thoroughly taken into account.

Vision

XYZ company maintenance vision written here

Mission

The mission of the maintenance team is to ensure optimum levels of availability, reliability and operability of equipment through effective maintenance practices, continuous improvement and a safe working environment, so as to meet the demands of our clients.

It is our aim:

a. To support our production and other colleagues in an efficient and professional manner in the achievement of their objectives.

b. To ensure that all assets operate at the required performance and availability levels for their planned economic lives.

c. To act to increase the reliability and performance of assets through a program of continuous improvement.

d. To manage human resources in such a way that it maximizes added value to both the individual and XYZ.

e. To create and maintain safe work practices and a safe work environment and to preserve our environment.

Management cycle

The management process has an annual repetitive cycle that is synchronized with the financial cycle. Although a case could be made to align the start of this cycle with that of the financial year, a better way is to start the cycle when the planning process for the next financial year should commence. This date has been set at 1 October of each year. The following figure shows the salient points of the management planning cycle.

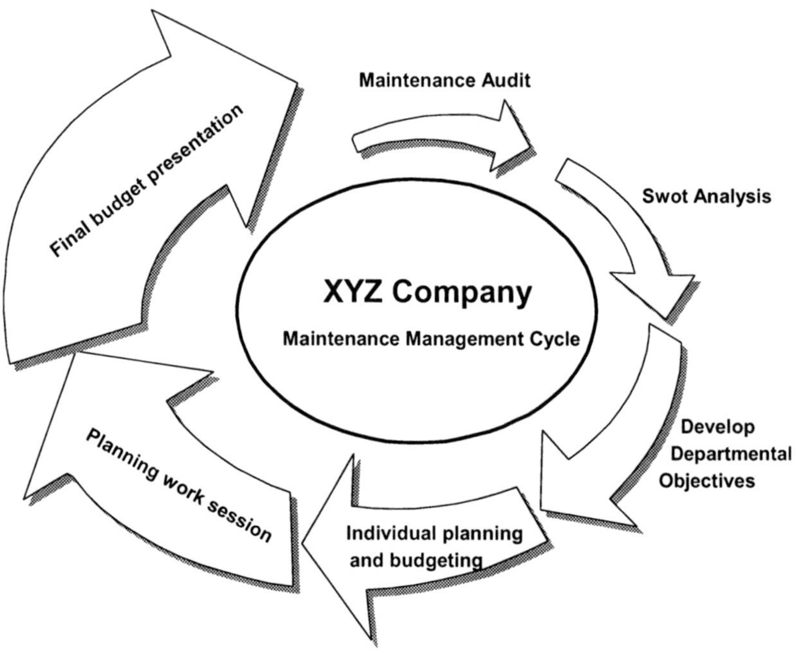

Table 1 details the various phases of the above cycle.

Maintenance Audit

The maintenance audit will be used annually as the start to the management planning cycle. The audit will consist of a computerized survey of the present status in the maintenance department, using the perception of a variety of maintenance personnel. This survey will audit a combination of hardware and systems issues. The instrument used for this purpose will conform to the requirements of XYZ.

Table 1: Management Cycle Definition

Step	*Date*	*Responsibility*	*Format*	*Actions Taken*
1	Oct	Engineering Manager	Group session(s)	Maintenance Audit
2	1 Nov	Engineering Manager/ Section Engineers	One day forum	SWOT Analysis Departmental Objectives
3	Nov/Jan	Section Engineers	Individual planning	Lower level objectives Budget Consolidate budget
4	Mid January	Engineering Manager	One day forum	Production presents their plan Maintenance presents their plan Consolidate plans
5	End February	Engineering Manager	Budget conference	Present final budget to MD
6	Apr/May	All Managers	Individual discussions	Personnel performance evaluation
7	June	Engineering Manager	Group session	Revise measurement standards

The audit will typically be performed using 3 groups of 10 people each . The people involved in the survey will typically be:

⇒ Engineering Manager

⇒ Section Engineers (4)

⇒ Chief Foremen (4)

⇒ Foremen (6)

⇒ Production foremen (6)

⇒ Planners (3)

⇒ Artisans (3)

⇒ Operators (3)

Management Planning

The management planning process can be subdivided into a number of sub-processes as defined in the table above. These are discussed in turn:

1. Maintenance Forum

   Following the maintenance audit, the management planning process is started during the first week of November, using a one day forum under the leadership of the Engineering Manager. All Engineers, Chief Foremen, Foremen and Planners take part in this official start to the budgetary process. This forum takes the results of the maintenance audit and the maintenance performance measurement process and use these to:

   - Do a SWOT (Strengths, Weaknesses, Opportunities and Threats) analysis.
   - Use the results of the audit, performance measurement and SWOT analysis to work through the maintenance policy (this document), revising and updating it.
   - Draw up Departmental Objectives that will ensure that:

     ⇒ The year's results conform to the Maintenance Policy.

     ⇒ Strengths and Opportunities are utilized optimally.

     ⇒ Weaknesses and Threats are being addressed to eliminate or reduce their effects. The accent here will be to turn them into opportunities or eliminate them completely. If this is not possible, the approach will be to minimize their negative effects.

2. Individual Planning

   The next step in the management planning process is to develop detailed plans and budgets within the constraints set by the Maintenance Forum.

   This is done using the following steps:

   - Each lower management level (down to lowest supervisor level) develops their own objectives and CPA's that fully supports those of the immediate superior level. Those of the top level maintenance managers (Section Engineers) supports the objectives set by the Maintenance Forum. Thus the various levels' objectives and CPA's cascade downward from top to bottom, thus ensuring attainment of the objectives set by the maintenance forum. Each level's objectives and CPA's are approved by the immediate superior level to make certain that the superior's objectives and CPA's are fully supported.

- Section Engineers are responsible for their own mini-planning processes that will result in budgets for their own division. This is done as follows:
  - ⇒ Obtain long term projections of all scheduled work to the end of the next financial year from the MMIS.
  - ⇒ Obtain condition monitoring reports for all equipment for which he/she is responsible.
  - ⇒ Obtain inspection reports of the physical condition of equipment from chief foremen / foremen.
  - ⇒ Consolidate the above information (taking his/her own objectives and CPA's into account) into a maintenance plan and budget for the following year. This plan includes the following:
    - * All maintenance work to be done on equipment in his/her responsibility area.
    - * Any necessary changes to his/her organization structure.
    - * Changes in personnel strength requested with a proper motivation.
    - * Facilities/resources needed (other than personnel).
    - * Training of personnel.
    - * Finances needed (operational budget).
    - * Capital budget.
  - ⇒ Update capital plan (equipment replacement and development projects) based on own objectives and CPA's.
- The Manager, Engineering Services approves and combines the individual engineers' plans and budget into one plan and budget for the Engineering Department.

3. Production Planning Forum

After both the Production and Maintenance Departments each developed their initial year plans in relative isolation, a process is needed for consolidating and integrating these into a viable plan for

XYZ. This is done using a one day forum under the leadership of the Engineering Manager. The Production Manager, Section Engineers, Chief Foremen (Production and Maintenance), Foremen (Production and Maintenance) and Planners take part in this process. The MD is also invited as guest to ensure that the result of this forum will lead to final plans and budgets for the two departments. This forum follows the following procedure:

- Production present their short and medium range plans, with emphasis on the following:
  - ⇒ The production hours needed from all primary production equipment.
  - ⇒ Production limitations:

    A listing of production limitations that will effect the maintenance plan significantly
  - ⇒ The production schedule.
  - ⇒ Problem areas.
- Maintenance present the outline of their total maintenance plan for the next financial year. This includes:
  - ⇒ Major scheduled shutdowns and services.
  - ⇒ Capital plan (equipment replacement and development projects).
- The two departments negotiate on any important issues where their respective plans influence each other's budgets substantially. The objective is to find solutions that will facilitate the integration of the two plans, while best serving XYZ's interests.

4. Budget Conference

   Following the Production Planning Forum the section and subordinate objectives, CPA's, maintenance plans, budgets and capital plans are adjusted where necessary based on the decisions taken at the Forum. The plans, budgets and capital plans are then finally combined in one assembled plan, budget and capital plan. These are then presented to the MD for approval.

5. Personnel Performance Evaluation

   The final personnel performance evaluation takes place during April/May, when each manager/supervisor evaluates the individual performance of each of his/her subordinates for the preceding 9/10 months based on the objectives and CPA's set during the previous year's management planning cycle. These evaluations form the basis for the size of the salary adjustment that the individual will receive in July.

These annual evaluations are supported by monthly, or at the very least bi-monthly, discussions with each individual subordinate of his/her progress towards attaining the objectives set during the previous planning cycle. At the same time feedback regarding the individual's performance in his/her CPA's is also communicated to him/her. The purpose of these sessions is to ensure steady progress towards the achievement of the objectives that were set.

6. Integrated Maintenance Performance Measurement

   Maintenance overall performance is measured using the XYZ Integrated Maintenance Performance measurement instrument (XIMP). This instrument measures 12 performance areas, the results of which are combined in four primary measurement areas:

   ⇒ Maintenance Results

   ⇒ Maintenance Productivity

   ⇒ Operational Purposefulness

   ⇒ Cost Justification

   The results of the above four main measurement areas are in turn combined into one overall Integrated Maintenance Performance figure, which is, as with the individual and combined indicators, compared against a predefined standard. This instrument is updated monthly with the previous month's results and is included in the monthly report. It is used as a primary management instrument - all levels of maintenance management strives towards the achievement of the goal(s) set at the start of the financial year. Action plans to reach these objectives are discussed monthly in the Engineering Management Meeting.

   The standards (goals) for the coming financial year, as well as the weights of the individual measurement indicators, are set in a special meeting during June. The Engineering Manager leads this meeting at which all the engineers are present.

The Maintenance Planning Process

Formal maintenance plans should be developed for all primary production equipment. The responsible engineer is the driver of the development process. Each such responsible engineer must compile an action plan for all his/her primary production equipment with goal dates for completing the maintenance plans. Following approval of this plan at the monthly Engineering Management Meeting, the responsible engineer will report back on a monthly basis regarding the status of the development of maintenance plans.

The basis for the development of maintenance plans is the Reliability Centered Maintenance (RCM) technique. The plans are developed by a team consisting of a facilitator (the Planning Engineer can typically be used for this by arrangement), chief foreman or foreman, production chief foreman or foreman, an artisan and an operator. The main requirement for the people used in this team is that they should be the most knowledgeable and experienced people regarding the operation and maintenance of the specific machine. Where possible the strategies developed will be the result of a proper failure data analysis using the available failure history. The resulting RCM study and maintenance plans must be audited and approved by the responsible engineer.

The resultant maintenance plan for a specific equipment type will consist of the following documents, neatly bound into a book that are available for reference purposes:

- A copy of the complete RCM analysis.
- Maintenance tasks that should be scheduled for performance at predefined intervals. These should list all action steps that should be performed, together with proper guidelines, lists of probable materials needed, any special equipment/tools needed and precautionary measures that should be taken.
- A forecast of the manpower needed in the different trades for the execution of the plan.

Maintenance Administration

The maintenance administration function supports the line organization in an effective way in the following areas:

⇒ Scheduling of tasks defined in maintenance plans.

⇒ Support of task execution through effective reports.

⇒ Development of task plans to optimize large and recurring tasks.

⇒ Procurement of critical materials/spares.

⇒ Recondition management.

⇒ Warranty Claim management.

⇒ Direct purchase process management.

⇒ Stock planning (how many of which items should be available when).

⇒ Operation of the MMIS.

This function is defined in detail in a number of work procedures that forms an integral part of this document.

Task Management

Each maintenance task is reported in full on a job card. Job card management, task supervision and task feedback are defined in detail in a number of work procedures that forms an integral part of this document.

Cost Monitoring

Due to the fact that XYZ's present cost systems do not give up to date cost information, cost cannot be monitored effectively. At present all possible avenues are utilized to manage cost as best as possible within these constraints. Each section engineer must present a monthly cost report for his/her section to the Engineering Manager. Although the cost information is not the best available, these reports should reflect the section's cost situation as well as is possible. In principle, the state of the cost systems will not be accepted as an excuse for incomplete/unsatisfactory cost reporting to the Engineering Manager.

Performance Monitoring

Maintenance performance must be monitored by all levels of maintenance management for all primary production equipment, using the following indicators:

⇒ Availability.

⇒ Reliability through Mean Time To Failure (MTTF).

When any item, for which a provision account exists, fails, a full failure investigation is launched by the responsible engineer. The purpose of this investigation is to determine the failure cause with the objective of total cause removal.

This page was left blank on purpose

Use it for notes

Index

This page was left blank on purpose

Use it for notes

A

ABC Analysis 389, 394
Acquisition Cost 385-387
Activities 364, 366
Administration (of maintenance) 42, 130, 132, 136, 142, 155, 183, 188, 189, 285, 291, 352, 363, 452
Annual Plan 129, 140
Annual Planning Process 129
As-Good-As-New 427
Auditing (of maintenance) 21, 38-40, 129, 131, 133, 134, 136, 139, 185-187, 189, 201, 215, 217, 225-227, 229-233, 236-238, 285, 331, 446, 448
Availability 21, 23-26, 32, 33, 81, 84, 101, 119, 120, 132, 133, 135, 138, 159-160, 165, 172, 175, 187, 188, 192, 194, 199, 200-203, 205, 206, 211-212, 222-223, 227, 231, 235, 241, 247, 248, 250, 251, 254, 264, 275, 286, 296, 297, 311, 312, 321, 322, 325, 356, 385, 394, 415

B

Backlog 392
Backlog : size of 167, 183
Backlog Management 220
Backlog Reporting 315, 316, 329
Bad-As-Old 427
Basic Repairable Systems Theory 121
Bath Tub Curve 62, 68-70
Block Replacement 50, 119, 416
Breakdown Frequency 141, 133, 140, 142, 159-160
Breakdown Intensity 164-165
Breakdown Severity 164, 166, 172, 176, 183
Breakdowns 26, 47,121, 149-150, 155-156, 165, 198, 267, 272, 273, 296, 313, 32, 383
Budget 39, 166, 207, 221, 266, 296, 322-324, 331, 333, 449
    quantity budget 296, 322, 324

C

Capacity (of maintenance) 34
Career Growth Path 195
Centralization 141, 142, 191
Check List 39, 218, 227, 296, 315, 316, 325, 327-329
Clerical Support 190, 203
Clocked Time 152-154
Company Profit 21, 24, 26, 40, 84, 92, 147, 186, 211
Computerized Maintenance Management System (CMMS) (see also MMIS) 21, 283, 284, 286-288, 339-344, 355, 356, 357
Condition Based Maintenance 50, 55, 62, 67, 112, 119, 190, 321
Condition Monitoring 22, 51, 105, 150-151, 158, 197, 202, 221-223, 241, 295, 319-321, 383, 416, 417, 449
  acoustic emissions 50
  analysis equipment 22
  oil analysis 22
  oil condition 50, 105
  shock pulse 50
  thermography 22, 50
  vibration 22, 50, 73, 105, 241
  Wear Debris 55, 72
Condition Monitoring Expert 105
Condition Monitoring History 317
Condition Monitoring Results 222, 295, 319
Condition Monitoring Techniques 197
Conditional Probability Of Failure 61, 112, 404
Continuous Improvement 132, 133, 287, 445
Control (of maintenance) 1 98
Control Boundaries 247, 248, 252
Control Charts 241, 245, 250
Core Values 207
Corrective Maintenance 51, 53, 67, 96-97, 101, 118, 164, 165, 167
Corrosion 53
Cost 23, 24, 26, 40, 47, 50, 55, 84, 95-97, 107-108, 116-119, 122, 131, 132, 147-148, 152, 155, 157-159, 162, 163, 165, 166, 168-172, 176, 182, 186-187, 191, 208, 209, 211, 217, 221, 231, 237, 241, 243, 251, 275-278, 285, 286, 296, 313, 315, 317, 320, 322-325, 328, 335, 356, 385-389, 412-415, 423, 428, 433, 434, 437, 440, 445, 451, 453

Cost
- acceptable 132, 138, 159, 168
- actual 296, 322
- allocation 221
- equipment 223, 295, 296, 315, 322,327
- high 23
- labor 296
- low 221
- machine 325
- operational 131, 445
- optimal 26
- optimization 24

Cost Accounts 296, 322
Cost Analysis 325
Cost Center 24, 26
Cost Component 162, 163
Cost Control 221, 296, 328
Cost Effectiveness 170, 171, 176
Cost efficiency 148, 157
Cost Graphs 26, 118-119, 122, 440
Cost History 317
Cost Intensity 172, 176, 183
Cost Justification 159, 168, 175, 176, 451
Cost Monitoring 453
Cost of Failure 116, 155
Cost of Lost Production 158
Cost Of Materials 158
Cost of Prevention 116
Creep 70
Curve Smoothing 241, 253
Cusum Charts 60, 110, 241, 253, 254

D

Data Selection Techniques 241
Data base Design 320, 323
Decentralization 141, 142, 191, 223
Decision Analysis 196
Defect 22
Density Function 108-112, 401-402, 404

Dependence Test 428
Design 23, 31, 33, 38, 41, 48, 53, 54, 58, 79-80, 83-84, 95, 101, 131, 138, 140, 185, 202, 211, 225, 227, 288, 291, 294, 317, 320, 322, 323, 325, 327 ,333, 342, 344, 356
Designer/Manufacturer 31
Deterioration 105, 222, 250, 428
Diagnose Faults 22
Distribution Function 60, 61, 108-112, 401
Downtime 149, 150, 321
Drenick's Limit Theorem 66
Du Pont Methods 177

Economic Feasibility 95-97, 102-104, 107, 108
Economic Ordering Quantity 394
Efficiency (of maintenance) 148
Embrittlement 53
Engineering Drawings 206, 218, 327
Environment 22, 47, 53, 75, 97-98, 103-104, 107-108, 116, 119, 132, 133, 139, 177, 186, 207, 245, 343, 346, 411, 445-446
Equipment
- allocation by locality 299, 319
- ergonomics 31
- increased sophistication 21, 23
- properties 31
- sophistication of 23
- technical complexity 23

Equipment Data Base 299, 318, 325
Equipment Dependencies 216, 217, 302
Equipment Group 215, 299, 300, 305, 306
Equipment Guarantees 303
Equipment History 223
Equipment Location 216
Equipment Modifications 301
Equipment Number 215, 288, 301, 303, 319, 321, 332
Equipment Numbering 215
Equipment Performance 50, 222, 286, 295, 319, 320, 325, 328
Equipment Production Loss 322
Equipment Production Rate 222, 322

Equipment Register 215, 287, 288, 301
Equipment Registration 347
Equipment Replacement 212, 449, 450
Equipment Structure 216, 300, 305, 347
Equipment Type 41, 215, 300, 301, 314, 355
Equipment Usage 216, 299, 304, 347
Equipment Utilization 321
Equipment/Parts Structure 304
Erosion 53, 73
Estimated Job Duration 329
EUT-Model 33, 34, 37, 38, 43
Expert Systems 22
Expertise And Competence Of Personnel 22, 31, 32, 188, 191, 195, 196, 342, 344
Exponential Curve 123, 258
Exponential Distribution 113, 411
Exponential Smoothing 251

F

Facilities 32, 142, 143, 188, 192, 194, 199, 201, 203, 205, 219, 231, 269, 277, 291, 328, 334, 335, 346, 380
Facilities
  cleaning equipment 22
  computer 203
  Equipment Servicing 202
  equipment washing 200
  filing 203
  improvement 39, 140
  machining 21, 201
  maintenance equipment 192
  material handling 201
  number of 269
  office 203
  personnel 203, 204
  service workshop 199
  standards 136
  testing 202
  tool store 200, 205
  tools 200, 202

Facilities
  typing 203
  welding 202
  work benches 202
  work dispatch (output) area 199
  workshop 22, 142, 194, 199-202, 204-206, 218, 231, 275, 276, 307, 308, 311, 327, 363, 376, 380, 383
  workshop flow 194, 218
Facilities Plan 142, 143
Failure
  cause 22, 69, 74-75, 89
  cause isolation 241
  definition of 54
  functional 54, 55, 83, 85, 88-89, 105
  multiple 47, 97, 104
  potential 54, 55, 75, 87-89, 105
Failure Analysis 22, 41, 124, 134, 197, 211, 223, 286, 427
Failure Condition 75, 105
Failure Consequence 96, 95-98, 104, 107, 104
Failure Density 59-61, 108, 110, 112
Failure Mechanism 58, 95
Failure Mode 41, 47-48, 50, 59, 74-75, 80-81, 83, 85, 89, 92, 95-98, 101, 102, 104, 108, 116, 117, 119, 134
Failure Originator 75
Failure Process 56
Failure Rate 59, 65, 95, 103, 121, 222, 421, 422, 440
Failure Situation 75, 80, 108, 112
Failure Theory 80
Failure Type 317
Failure Width 75
Fatigue 53, 71, 73
Fault Elimination 198, 223
Fault Tracing 198, 202
Fault Trees 22, 199
Feedback Of Job Data 195, 218
Financial Management 197
Fishbone diagram 241, 244
Flow Charts 190, 345
Flow Diagrams 340
Forecast of Component Life 267

Forecast of Maintenance Cost 267
Forecast of Manpower Requirement 267
Forecast of MTBF 267
Forecast of Number Of Breakdowns 267
Forecast of Spare Parts Use 266
Forecasting 256, 263, 331
Forecasting Techniques 241
Fracture 70

G

Gantt Chart 194, 307, 366, 368-369, 371
Gaussian Distribution (see Normal Distribution) 246
Geometric Curve 123, 261
Green Areas 205
Group Replacement 50
Guarantee Processing 326
Guarantees 297, 303, 312, 325

H

Happy Data Set 428-431
Hazard Function 49, 50, 59, 61-62, 65-66, 69, 106-108, 112-114, 403-404, 410-412, 416, 430, 434
History (of maintenance) 221, 316, 317, 323, 328
History Database 287
Hyperbolic Curve 123, 260

J

Improvement Justification 171, 172, 176
Indices 147, 159, 162, 173, 179-181, 186
Industrial Revolution 23
Infant Mortality 63, 68
Information : flow 22
Information Systems 291
Inspection 105, 120, 222
Inventory Control Model 391
Inventory Management 298, 330, 334, 385, 389, 391, 394
Investment
high return on 23

J

Job Card 217, 218, 292, 296, 311-316, 323, 325, 327, 328, 332, 346, 356, 452
Job Card Definition 312
Job Card Due Date Changes 315
Job Card Feedback 195, 316
Job Card Management 452
Job Efficiency Reporting 316
Jobbing Shop 309, 311

K

Key Objective 132

L

Labor 39, 50, 117, 140, 162, 163, 183, 192, 214, 296, 296, 317, 322
Laplace 430, 433, 434, 437, 440
Laplace Trend Test 430, 437
Level Of Prevention 25, 26, 27, 193
Linear Curve 123, 258
Load (of maintenance) 31
Locality Allocation by Supervisor 319
Locality Definition 318
Logistical Planning 192
Logistics (of maintenance) 22
Lognormal Distribution 411

M

Machine Efficiency 148
Machine Management 287
Machine Service Modeling 272
Maintenance
theory of 31, 33, 55, 198, 211
Maintenance Analyst 211
Maintenance Cost Intensity 169

Maintenance Cycle 37-38, 43, 129, 131, 133, 135, 148, 151, 154, 157, 164, 182, 188, 189, 210, 235, 237, 283-285, 351, 446
Maintenance Data Analysis 155, 197.210, 211, 286, 357
Maintenance Data Base 291
Maintenance Engineering 33, 99, 129, 211, 224, 286
Maintenance Expert 197, 211
Maintenance Forum 448, 449
Maintenance Function 21-24, 31-33, 40, 43, 53-54, 131, 132, 138, 140, 142, 147, 159, 167, 169-170, 173, 186, 187, 203, 231, 329, 363
Maintenance Performance Measurement 40, 129, 134, 147, 173, 182, 235, 291, 298, 322, 451
Maintenance Plan 21, 32, 41, 42, 47-48, 79-81, 83, 84, 89, 92, 95, 101, 130, 134, 135, 155, 164, 168, 183, 190, 191, 236, 291, 302, 355-357, 363, 449-452
Maintenance Planning 41, 357
Maintenance Planning Process 451
Maintenance Policy 39, 43, 129, 131, 138, 148, 157, 176, 182, 186, 191, 210, 229, 232, 235, 355, 448
Maintenance Procedures 210, 355
Maintenance Productivity 159, 162, 175, 183, 451
Maintenance Program 103, 197
Maintenance Results 84, 159, 172, 175, 179, 180, 241, 322, 451
Maintenance Significant Items 41, 83, 85, 86, 87, 216, 304
Maintenance System 134, 136, 190, 195, 198, 216, 218-219, 221, 223, 224, 291, 292, 305, 315, 323, 327-329, 339-342, 357
Maintenance System Design 291, 316
Maintenance Systems Technology 190, 224
Maintenance Technology
training in 224
Management (of maintenance) 21, 24-25, 32, 34, 37-38, 40, 131, 133, 136, 138, 140, 142, 147-148, 167, 170, 172, 177, 179, 181, 185, 207, 211, 223, 224, 230, 231, 233, 235-238, 291, 293, 352, 382, 449, 451, 453
Management : annual plan 129, 140
Management : theory 196
Management Information Systems 136

Management Planning 21, 43, 129, 133, 142, 151, 157, 182, 187, 235-2 38, 446, 448, 450
Management Processes 189, 195-198, 207-209, 213, 238, 449
Management Style 33
Management Team (of maintenance) 38, 131
Managerial Processes 37, 43, 136
Managerial Training 196
Material flow 22-23, 192
Materials 317
Materials Management 105, 223, 297, 298, 319, 329, 330, 333-335, 389
Materials Planning 192, 227, 231
Mean Time Between Failure (MTBF) 59, 117, 122, 123, 162, 241, 274, 422, 440
Mean Time To Failure (MTTF) 159-160, 178, 179
Mean Time To Repair (MTTR) 159, 161, 178, 179
Measurement (of maintenance) 21, 39-40, 55, 134, 147, 149, 151, 156-157, 159, 173, 174, 177, 179, 183, 185-186, 188, 220, 225, 231, 235-238, 245, 247, 251, 271, 320, 328, 448, 451
Measurement Standards 347
Measuring Performance 208
Medium And Long Term Plans 207
Meter Readings 305
Meter Registration 304
Meter/Equipment Structure 305
Micro View 298
Mini-Annual Plan 143
Minimal Repair 121, 122, 124, 427
Minimum-Maximum Control 389
Minimum Stock Level 394
Mission Statement 132
MMIS (see also CMMS) 452
Modification Of Plant 137
Momentary Probability Of Failure 61, 112
Moving Average Technique 251

N

Nippon Denso Method 177
Non-Homogeneous Poisson Process (N.H.P.P.) 121, 422, 423
Noncommittal Data Set 428-431
Normal Distribution 113, 245, 409, 431

O

O.E.M. Product Support 34
Objective Setting 38, 129
Objectives (of maintenance) 23, 129
On-Condition Task 101-102, 105
Operability 21-22, 24-26, 31, 32, 84, 132, 138, 148, 159, 161, 162, 175, 187, 231, 319, 445
Operational Consequences 95-96, 98, 104, 107, 108, 116-117
Operational Purposefulness 159, 164, 168, 175, 176, 181-183, 451
Operational Stress 56
Operations Modus Operandi 135
Optimal Preventive Replacement Age 412, 414-415
Optimization (of maintenance) 211, 291, 294, 298, 317, 326, 332, 336, 357
Optimization Of Availability 415
Optimizing Condition Based Maintenance 119
Optimizing Cost 120
Optimum Efficiency 153, 204
Optimum Frequency Of Inspections 416, 417
Optimum Number Of Service Facilities 277
Optimum Preventive Frequency 117-119
Optimum Service Rate 275
Ordering Cycle 386
Organization (of maintenance) 21, 33, 34, 37-40, 43, 131, 136, 137, 139-143, 151-152, 163, 167, 168, 173, 175, 177, 185, 195, 227, 339-341
Organizational Climate and Culture 135, 141, 162, 189, 193, 195-198, 208, 212-214, 224, 238, 330, 336, 449, 451
Organizational Culture 32
Organizational Efficiency 154
Organizational Structure 32, 39, 140, 191, 347
Overhaul Policy 212

P

Pareto Principle 84, 85, 87, 218, 241-243, 245, 340
Part Failure History 317
Pareto Charts 84, 241
Parts Registration/Data 303
Parts Structure 303, 304
Peak Workload 143
Performance (of maintenance) 21, 32, 40, 42, 53, 54, 75, 87-88, 132-135, 147, 153, 159, 162, 172, 173, 179, 186-188, 199, 202, 205, 208-209, 220-223, 225, 227, 231, 236-237, 295, 320, 321, 325, 328, 330, 332, 335, 346, 445, 448, 450-453
Performance Improvements 40
Performance Indices (see also indices) 147, 159, 162, 172, 179-181, 186
Performance Monitoring Results 295, 320
Performance Standards 227
Personnel 22, 23, 31, 53, 80, 98, 133, 135-137, 140-141, 143, 156, 163, 167, 179, 183, 188-190, 192-194, 197-198, 200, 203-205, 208, 210, 213, 220, 223, 229, 236-238, 296, 311, 312, 316-319, 339, 342-346, 352, 378-380, 445, 448-450, 452
Personnel
- artisan 53, 80, 135, 150, 153, 192, 194-196, 198, 200, 202, 217, 220, 272, 275, 312, 315, 326-328, 346, 356, 447, 452
- artisan helpers 196
- coaching and mentor system 195
- development of 22
- efficiency 316, 329
- engineering education 195
- experience 196
- expertise and competence 188
- flow 22
- goals and objectives 207
- people skills 196
- planning 163, 183, 192
- Problem Solving And Decision Making Skills 196
- responsibilities 347
- supervision 136, 155, 197
- technical skills 197

Personnel
  technicians 195, 196
  time and attendance 315
  time management skills 196
  training 195, 198, 214
  utilization 316, 329
Personnel Availability 312
Personnel negotiation skills 198
Personnel Performance Evaluation 450
Personnel Registration 347
Philosophy (of maintenance) 131
Planning (of maintenance) 193
Planning Coverage 193
Planning Effectiveness 193
Planning Lead Time 193
Plant Codification 305
Plant item breakdown 83, 305
Plastic Deformation 73
Policy (of maintenance) 38, 129-131, 189, 210, 212, 355, 445, 448
Policy Update 211
Potential Failure 55
Preventive Maintenance 49, 53, 61, 67, 97, 105-108, 112-114, 116-117, 119-120, 150, 151, 158, 190, 197, 212, 222, 313, 315, 327
Preventive Planning 192
Preventive Replacements 118, 120, 383, 404
Preventive Task 80, 95-97, 101, 102, 104, 107, 141, 176, 311, 383, 433
Pro-active Maintenance 51
Procurement 23, 201, 221, 326, 330-336, 385, 452
Production 149, 151, 159, 161, 183, 310, 316, 320, 382, 447, 449-450
Production
  function of 31, 32, 216, 229
  capacity 21, 26, 40, 175, 193
  rate 159, 161, 183
  support of production process 24, 132, 138
Production Plan 320
Production Planning Forum 449-450
Profit Impact (of maintenance) 21, 211

Q

Quadratic Curve 123, 259
Quality Control 23, 42
Quality Requirements 193
Quantitative Measures 61, 112
Queuing Theory 269

R

RCM Facilitator 80
Reliability functions 109, 111-112
Reliability 21, 24-26, 31, 32, 41-42, 47, 60, 66, 69, 79, 81, 84, 103, 109, 112, 113, 121-123, 129-130, 132-135, 138, 148, 155, 159, 160, 175, 183, 187, 190, 197, 210, 211, 222, 231, 286, 355, 356, 401, 402, 421, 427, 428, 430, 440, 445, 452
Reliability Centered Maintenance (RCM) 41-42, 47, 48, 54, 55, 59, 66, 79-81, 84, 85, 88, 101-102, 130, 135, 155, 190, 197, 210, 222, 223, 286, 355, 357, 452
Reliability Centered Maintenance implementation 222
Reliability Degradation 60, 121, 123, 421, 427, 428, 440
Reliability Policy 211
Renewal Theory 69, 121, 123, 211, 401, 403, 421, 427, 428, 431, 433-434
Repair 51
Repairable Systems 69, 121-123, 211, 427, 428, 433
Replacement 49-51, 66, 101-103, 107-108, 116, 118-119, 121, 122, 158, 212, 303, 306, 405, 412-417, 423-424, 433, 434, 437, 440, 449, 450
Replacement Frequency 423
Replacement Policy 212
Reporting Hierarchy 319
Resistance To Failure 57-58
Resource Planning 192
Resources 39, 79, 133, 142, 143, 175, 192, 307, 342-344, 364, 367, 369, 378, 383, 445, 449
Responsibility Structure 220, 287-288, 291, 293, 294, 306, 312, 317-319, 325
Risk Of Failure 50, 61-63, 97, 112, 404
Root Causes 22, 89, 209, 214

S

S-N Curves 72,
Sad Data Set 428, 431
Safe Working Environment 132, 445
Safety 47, 74, 95, 97-98, 104, 107, 108, 119, 136, 138, 189, 192, 193, 231, 313, 327, 389-390, 394, 396
Safety and Housekeeping 189
Safety Device 47, 97
Safety Of Equipment 132, 138
Scheduled Failure Finding Task 104
Scheduled Maintenance Enforcement Ratio 167, 176, 183
Scheduling 164, 172, 183, 194, 218, 229, 287, 291, 292, 306, 307, 310, 311, 315, 363, 382, 452,
Scheduling
  allocation of time slots 307
  bar chart 242, 366, 376, 378, 380
  batch processing 311, 377, 378, 380
  calendars 347
  CPM 194, 310, 311, 313, 363, 364, 368, 383
  detailed 377, 380
  effectiveness 216
  intermittent 363, 376, 383
  long term 293, 306, 310
  shutdowns 293,306,311,
  time slots 194, 196, 307, 310, 323, 383
Scheduling Calendar 312
Scheduling Facilities 218
Scheduling Intensity 164, 172, 183
Scheduling Maintenance Work 364, 383
Scheduling Output 194
Scheduling Specifics 311
Scheduling System Adequacy 218
Scheduling Techniques 194, 218, 306, 307, 309, 363, 383
Scheduling Utilities 194
Scrap Advice 332
Service Adequacy 202
Spare Parts 216
Spare Parts Definition 299, 303
Spares Procurement 326

Spares Registration 347
Spares Structure 347
Statutory Requirements 137
Stock
  continuous review 386
Stock Catalogue 206, 297, 298, 330, 334
Stock Control 219
Stock Management 385, 386
Stock Record Keeping 297-298, 329, 333
Stock Turnover 170, 176, 183
Strategies (of maintenance) 41, 47-48, 51, 53, 59, 64, 67, 69, 79, 83, 85, 86, 87, 89, 98, 113, 118, 121, 129-130, 135, 186, 210, 211, 243, 285, 286, 296, 299, 363, 403, 411-412, 421, 433
Strategy
  optimization of 157, 176, 182, 193
  age based 49
  calendar based 49
  design-out 41, 48, 54, 67, 95-97, 107
  opportunistic 50
  optimization of 41, 42
  routine services 49
  scheduled 101-103
  scheduled reconditioning 49, 101, 103, 106, 108, 324, 417
  scheduled replacement 101-103, 106, 108
  use based 41
Strategy Development 134
Strategy Tree 95, 211
Sub Store Space 200
Sundry Cost Component 169
Supplier Information 332
Survival Function 59, 61, 108, 111, 112, 120, 402, 404, 410, 422
SWOT Analysis 139, 448
System 53
System Operation 224
System Security 224
System Selection 344
System Testing And Set-up 346, 347

T

Task Content 317
Task Cost 317, 323
Task Definition 217, 314
Task Documentation 194, 327
Task Duration 317
Task Efficiency 151
Task Execution 42, 151, 183, 286, 311, 452
Task Feedback 195, 237, 328, 329, 357, 453
Task Lists 347
Task Management 42, 151, 155, 183, 346, 357, 453
Task Planning 42, 190, 191
Task Priorities 194, 218
Task Schedule 293, 306, 310
Task Supervision 453
Task Support 194,
Tasks
  time allowed 152, 154
  time planned for overdue scheduled 155, 156
  time planned for scheduled Tasks 155, 156
Tasks and Job Cards 217
Technical Feasibility (of a task) 50, 95-96, 102, 104-108, 116
Technological Improvement 137
Technology (of maintenance) 21-23, 32, 37, 43
Terotechnology 33
Time spent On Breakdowns 155, 156
Time Spent On Scheduled Tasks 155, 156
Time Spent On Tasks 152, 154
Tools And Equipment 200, 201
Total Direct Maintenance Cost 155
Total Maintenance Cost 158
Total Production Time 149
Trend
  underlying 241, 251, 253
Trend Graphs 177
Trend Test 434, 440

U

Use Based Maintenance 49, 50
Use Based Optimization 117
Use Based Prevention 116-117
Use Based Preventive Maintenance 49-50, 62, 106, 112-117, 119-120
Use Based Preventive Overhaul 404
Use Based Preventive Replacement 404

V

Value Of Stock At End Of Period 158
Vision And Mission (of maintenance) 207

W

Warranty Claim Management 452
Wear 53-54, 64-65
Wear
abrasive 72-73
fretting 73
oxidative 73
plasticity dominated 72
Wear out 65
Weibull Distribution 60, 108-110, 113-116, 409, 411, 412, 434
Work Environment 204, 205
Work Flow 192, 297, 325
Work In Process Storage 200
Work Load (of maintenance) 32
Work Management 219, 220, 287, 296
Work Order Allocation By Equipment 314
Work Order And Task Definition 191, 217
Work Order Database 287, 288
Work Order Definition 347
Work Order Structure 313, 347
Work Order Systems 292
Work Order Management 194, 217, 218, 291, 292, 312, 325, 327
Work Order Turnover 166, 183
Work Order Turnover Index 329
Work Permit 218, 296, 325, 327

Work Planning 191
Work Prioritization 307, 309, 310, 363, 383
Work Reception (Input) Area 199
Work Scheduling 194, 293, 306, 310, 311
Work Support 205, 206
Workshop Schedule 293, 306, 310, 311
Workshop Specialization 199

Printed in the United States
216682BV00003B/18/A

9 781412 200561